W9-AAV-885

SHOW TRIAL

FILM AND CULTURE SERIES

FILM AND CULTURE

A series of Columbia University Press

Edited by John Belton

For the list of titles in this series, see pages 407–408.

SHOW TRIAL

HOLLYWOOD, HUAC, AND THE BIRTH OF THE BLACKLIST

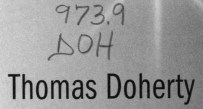

Thomas Doherty

Columbia University Press   New York

Columbia University Press
Publishers Since 1893
New York   Chichester, West Sussex
cup.columbia.edu

Cataloging-in-Publication Data available from the Library of Congress.

ISBN 978-0-231-18778-7 (cloth : alk. paper)
ISBN 978-0-231-54746-8 (e-book)

∞

Columbia University Press books are printed on permanent
and durable acid-free paper.

Printed in the United States of America

Cover design: Lisa Hamm
Cover image: (*front*) The Committee for the First Amendment arrives on Capitol
Hill to protest the tactics of the House Committee on Un-American Activities,
October 27, 1947. (*Left to right*) Richard Conte, Philip Dunne, June Havoc,
John Huston, Humphrey Bogart, Paul Henreid, Lauren Bacall, Joe Sistrom,
and Evelyn Keyes. © Bettemann/Getty Images. (*back*) An anti-Communist
pamphlet by friendly witness Oliver Carlson, published by the Catholic
Information Society, 1947.

CONTENTS

Contents

Part III. BACKFIRE

PROGRAM NOTES

n 1947 the Cold War came to, or rather was declared on, Hollywood. The year would see a parade of stoic motion picture personalities trudging up Capitol Hill, testifying before hostile committees, and entering into the pages of the *Congressional Record*. When the power center that was Washington discovered the publicity magnet that was Hollywood, the resulting headlines could only cement the relationship.

Long anticipated and extravagantly hyped, the main event lived up to advance billing. Over nine days in October 1947, the House Committee on Un-American Activities (HUAC), chaired by a dapper martinet named J. Parnell Thomas (R-NJ), held its soon-to-be notorious hearings into alleged Communist subversion in Hollywood.* Officially dubbed "Hearings Regarding the Communist Infiltration of the Motion Picture Industry," it was the first full-on media-political spectacle of the postwar era. Like the kickoff for a successful franchise, it spawned like-minded sequels, but the first episode attracted the widest publicity and left the harshest legacy. Subsequent versions were low-energy imitations; the original was the high-intensity template.

The initial entry was cinema-centric and, from the get-go, the lingo of showbiz ballyhoo (a three-ring circus, a Barnum show, a vaudeville burlesque)

---

* The House Committee on Un-American Activities (1938–1966) is abbreviated as HUAC for purposes of pronunciation—*hue-ak*. Although the acronym did not become common until 1970 or so, I am using it throughout.

clung to the proceedings.[1] Playwright-screenwriter Lillian Hellman, who herself would be hauled before HUAC in 1952, called it "a honkey tonk show."[2] Upping the budget, *Washington News* columnist Fred Othman beheld "a Grade A production in glorious Technicolor."[3] The theater critic and HUAC historian Eric Bentley, with a nod to a friend who had appeared as a featured witness, referred to the hearings as "a Brechtian tragi-comedy."[4] Chairman Thomas himself shilled for the production like a studio ad-pub man, promising the Hollywood investigation would be "the best show the committee has yet had."[5]

The compulsion to render the politics as performance was understandable: the hearings boasted all the trappings of a gala Hollywood premiere—glamourous stars, colorful moguls, emotional outbursts, and wide-eyed looky-loos, all recorded under the hot lights of the newsreel cameras and broadcast over radio. "The capital's biggest show of the year opens this morning when the House Committee on Un-American Activities, probing Communist influences in Hollywood, calls the first of 50 gilt-edge names as witnesses," ran the front-page notice in the *Hollywood Reporter*. "Despite the stage being Washington's largest hearing room, space for the public will be SRO, and then only for the first few able to squeeze in."[6] The competition at *Variety* found the motion picture backdrop equally irresistible. "The big show atmosphere of the opening day of the hearings on Capitol Hill today fulfilled all expectations," wrote Florence S. Lowe, the resident "gal reporter" at the trade weekly. "Even before the gavel of committee chairman Parnell Thomas gave the signal for 'lights, camera, action,' the big caucus room of the House of Representatives building took on all the drama and tenseness of a studio lot just before shooting."[7]

In all, forty-one witnesses were called—studio executives, official representatives of the motion picture industry, producers, directors, screenwriters, actors, critics, investigators, and lawyers. The first week was given over to witnesses mainly sympathetic to the committee, or at least not openly hostile, and were called "friendly" witnesses, collectively "Friendlies." The recalcitrants—nineteen in all—were dubbed "unfriendly" and embraced the tag as a badge of honor. The Unfriendly Nineteen were whittled down during the hearings to the Unfriendly Ten, or the Hollywood Ten, although at the time Hollywood wanted no part of them.

The immediate blowback from the hearings was profound and long-lived. On November 25, 1947, Eric A. Johnston, president of the Motion Picture

Association of America (MPAA), representing the executives of the major Hollywood studios, announced the peremptory firing of the Unfriendly Ten. The studios pledged never again to employ a known Communist or unrepentant fellow traveler.[8] The declaration marked the formal onset of the black-list era, a two-decade long purgatory during which political allegiances, real or suspected, determined employment opportunities in the entertainment industry. At the studios and the networks, hundreds of artists were shown the door—or had it shut in their faces.

But if the investigation destroyed careers, it also made them: three of the friendly witnesses ascended to pinnacles of power in the city they had come to under subpoena: the actors Robert Montgomery, who went on to serve as chief media advisor to president Dwight D. Eisenhower; George Murphy, who served as senator from California (1966–1971); and Ronald Reagan, who served two terms as governor of California (1967–1975) and president of the United States (1981–1989). Among the professionals on the dais, ironically, only one made serious political capital out of his HUAC service: Richard M. Nixon, then a freshman congressman from California, who leapfrogged from the House of Representatives to the U.S. Senate (1950–1953) and thence to the vice presidency (1953–1961) and presidency (1969–1975). Though not as upwardly mobile as Nixon, one of the ex-FBI men working for the committee, investigator and occasional interrogator H. A. Smith, also used his congressional sheen to move into a bigger chair, in Congress in fact, as a representative from California (1957–1972).

Convinced that Hollywood was a breeding ground for a pestilent ideology, HUAC set aside labor unions, government agencies, and the U.S. military to allocate enormous investigatory resources to a site devoted to the construction of dream castles. Were the congressmen cynical pols dragging Hollywood through the mud to grab headlines or noble sentinels flushing out a clear and present danger? Even W. R. "Billy" Wilkerson, the fervently anti-Communist editor-publisher of the *Hollywood Reporter*, suspected motives that were less than civic minded. "How better can the committee grab front page space, how easier can the personnel of that committee get their names in print, than by an attempted shakedown of motion pictures and their personalities?" he asked, knowing the answer.[9]

Rivaling the metaphors of showbiz razzamatazz, a more haunting parallel, dredged up from the dark recesses of American history, made the rounds: the witch hunt. To the men brought before the tribunal, the hearings were courts of Oyer and Terminer convened to condemn them as malefactors. Having prejudged the case, the presiding magistrates were not seeking justice but staging a show trail to accuse, indict, and punish. In truth, in the next decade, the HUAC hearings evolved into a quasi-religious ritual of confession, contrition, and self-flagellation in which the accused were to acknowledge their sins, seek forgiveness, and perform penance. In 1947, however, the cried-out-upon were proud heretics willing to go to the stake rather than deny the true faith. For the judges and the accused alike, the Hollywood hearings were truly a show—a stage-managed production with a script already written.

Of course, no one was actually burnt, or hanged, or pressed to death with stones for practicing the black arts of Soviet subversion. No matter how hysterical the rhetoric on both sides, what happened in America in 1947 was not the Salem Witch Trials, still less a Stalinist purge or Nazi blood bath. All the accused retained legal representation, exercised freedom of speech, and received due process in the courts. The Unfriendlies may not have been allowed to read their defiant statements before the committee, but they were hardly muzzled: the group handed out copies of their statements, published ads in newspapers, exhorted supporters at rallies, and produced fund-raising films. Most were wordsmiths by trade and incapable of shutting up.

Indeed, contrary to popular memory, the original round of HUAC hearings was—initially at least—fiercely criticized and staunchly opposed, not just by the Unfriendlies, but by a broad swath of the Hollywood community and the motion picture trade press. Hundreds of Hollywood artists filled the ranks of a hastily organized political action group, the Committee for the First Amendment. *Variety* and *Motion Picture Daily* were withering in their denunciations of HUAC and even the *Hollywood Reporter* heaped scorn on an outfit so ignorant about how Hollywood actually operated. Before and during the hearings, MPAA president Johnston, the official representative of the moneyed Hollywood establishment, talked tough and showed backbone: never, said he, would the motion picture industry preside over anything as un-American as a blacklist.

Yet no sooner had HUAC closed the show than Hollywood's posture changed from stiff-backed resistance to supine capitulation. Something happened over those nine days that rearranged the molecules in the postwar atmosphere.

"Postwar" was in fact the red-letter label. After 1945, Moscow, Washington, and Hollywood all agreed on the centrality of the movies as a transmission belt for culture and ideology. Terry Ramsaye, the editor of *Motion Picture Herald*, well understood how recent experience had forever transformed the role of the movies in American life. As a former newsreel editor and documentary filmmaker, Ramsaye was uniquely qualified to pass judgment on a medium he had been covering nearly since its inception. That part of the industry whose growth he had not witnessed firsthand he had researched for the first comprehensive history of American cinema, *A Million and One Nights*, published in 1926, a volume whose manuscript was fact-checked by a sharp-eyed editor with impressive motion picture credentials of his own, Thomas Edison.

Ramsaye first noted the obvious, that the HUAC hearings "drew from the press and radio an unparalleled order of attention," before explaining the reason for the hullabaloo. It wasn't so much the insidious threat from Communism or the dazzling glamour of Hollywood, but the fact that "the screen had become, in its maturity, integrated with the whole fabric of the national, and international, affairs, in this difficult, complex period, with social, political, and economic involvements."[10] Having seized so much of the spotlight during World War II, Hollywood was now, rightly, at center stage.

The cynical adage about the union of Hollywood and Washington—that when the capitals of entertainment and politics converge the result is mutually corrosive—is worth heeding, but the hearings of October 1947 were an apt merging of the two realms, a recognition by Washington of Hollywood's power over hearts and minds. In this, if in little else, the House Committee on Un-American Activities was dead on the mark.

THANKS AND ACKNOWLEDGMENTS

The gratitude one feels at having completed a book is surpassed only by the gratitude one feels toward friends and colleagues for the aid and comfort they offered during its composition.

I owe Jon Lewis and Steve Ross a special debt for their scrupulous, critical, and tremendously helpful review of the book during its manuscript phase, scrubbings that saved me from lapses of judgments, boneheaded mistakes, and infelicitous prose decisions. John Belton also offered sage suggestions and gentle corrections.

I have always depended upon the kindness of archivists: Rachel Bernstein, Louise Hilton, and Jenny Romero at the Margaret Herrick Library of the Academy of Motion Picture Arts and Sciences; Xochitl Oliva and Terri Garst at the Los Angeles Public Library; Rosemary M. Hanes at the Motion Picture Division of the Library of Congress; William H. Davis and Kate Millan at the Center for Legislative Archives at the National Archives and Records Administration; Mary K. Helsabeck at the Wisconsin Center for Film and Theater Research at the University of Wisconsin-Madison; Orissa Martinez at the Richard Nixon Presidential Library; Jennifer Mandel at the Ronald Reagan Presidential Library; Benjamin Singleton of the Moving Image Research Collections at the University of South Carolina; Hilary Sweet at the Writers Guild Foundation of the Writers Guild of America; and Eve Neiger and Anne Marie Menta at Yale University.

My editor at Columbia University Press, Jennifer Crewe, has been unfailingly supportive and patient. I was lucky to have Miriam Grossman and Kathryn Jorge shepherding the manuscript through production and project manager Ben Kolstad applying his eagle eye to the prose. For suggestions, information, and encouragement, my sincere thanks to Joyce Antler, Stan Brooks, Laura Browder, Greg Burk, Larry Ceplair, Jerry Cohen, Leslie Epstein, Jim Deutsch, Maura Farrelly, Scott Feinberg, Chris Horak, Andrew Hudgins, Marsha Hunt, Dolores Janieski, Lou Lumenick, Chuck Maland, Alicia Mayer, Ross Melnick, Ed Monsour, Dane Morrison, Paula Musegades, Farran Smith Nehme, Arnie Reisman, Lisa Rivo, Sharon Rivo, Abe Shragge, Michael Socolow, Neil Verma, Steve Whitfield, and Chris Yogerst.

Finally, and as always, there is the most important acknowledgment. In *Out of the Past*, one of the best Hollywood legacies of 1947, Robert Mitchum tells Jane Greer that the scenery means nothing unless you have someone to turn to and say, "Nice view, huh?" I am blessed beyond words to have such a person to share the view, and a life, with, my wife Sandra.

ABBREVIATIONS

AFL	American Federation of Labor
AMPP	Association of Motion Picture Producers
BMP	Bureau of Motion Pictures
CFA	Committee for the First Amendment
COMPIC	Communist Infiltration Motion Picture Industry
CPUSA	Communist Party of the United States of America
CSU	Conference of Studio Unions
HANL	Hollywood Anti-Nazi League
HUAC	House Committee on Un-American Activities
IATSE	International Alliance of Theatrical Stage Employees
MPAA	Motion Picture Association of America (1945–present)
MPA-PAI	Motion Picture Alliance for the Preservation of American Ideals
MPPDA	Motion Picture Producers and Distributors of America (1922–1945)
MPIC	Motion Picture Industry Council
NLRB	National Labor Relations Board
OWI	Office of War Information
PCA	Production Code Administration
SAG	Screen Actors Guild
SCG	Screen Cartoonists Guild
SDG	Screen Directors Guild
SP	Screen Playwrights, Inc.
SWG	Screen Writers' Guild

(*right*): The front page of *Hollywood Now*, the journal of the Hollywood Anti-Nazi League for the Defense of American Democracy and a forum to celebrate the Popular Front activism of above-the-line talent in the motion picture industry, December 16, 1938. The subscriber is journalist Ella Winter, wife of the league's co-founder, screenwriter Donald Ogden Stewart. (Beinecke Rare Book and Manuscript Library, Yale University)

Part I
BACKSTORIES

Chapter 1

HOW THE POPULAR FRONT BECAME UNPOPULAR

Given the climate of the times—the shadow of the Great Depression, the backfire from World War II, and the atmospherics of the emergent Cold War—the face-off between Washington and Hollywood staged in October 1947 seems preordained, a perfect storm converging with the predictability of an end-reel clinch—or, to borrow another dialectic, clashing with the kind of "historical inevitability" that the unfriendly witnesses were so fond of. A major confrontation had been brewing for at least a decade and, after the hiatus born of mutual advantage during the late war, an ugly showdown arrived right on schedule.

The immediate pressure system was the Cold War, the long twilight struggle declared with the slamming down, not the raising of, a curtain. On March 5, 1946, at Westminster College, in Fulton, MO, former British prime minister Winston Churchill conjured the image that crystallized American fears of Soviet expansionism and shaped the geopolitics of the postwar world. "From Stettin in the Baltic to Trieste in the Adriatic, an iron curtain has descended across the Continent," intoned the oracle with a proven track record. Reprinted, rebroadcast, and replayed in the newsreels (Churchill's left hand sweeps down for emphasis when he utters the magic words), the mental picture so vividly evoked the iron fist of tyranny and the final curtain of death, that the phrase quickly entered the vocabulary. Soon enough, it would also serve as the high-concept title for a Hollywood thriller.

Yet no less than the recently declared Cold War, the movie-minded hearings of the House Committee on Un-American Activities grew out of the tensions and traumas of the Great Depression and World War II. Whether on the dais or at the witness table, the contestants shared the felt experience of economic chaos and mortal danger—a deep-in-the-bones dread that catastrophe was lurking just around the corner. To the Depression-born, war-tempered generations, the world was always just a turn away from spinning off its axis. Early warning signs had to be heeded and alarms sounded.

A lot of the history—both backdrop and ongoing—was bound up with the great art-business-technology that had come to vital maturity by the mid-twentieth century. The long purgatory of the Great Depression and the horrors of World War II were boom times for the motion picture industry. Even as first hardship and then war convulsed the nation, Hollywood ripened into a sinuous, streamlined oligopoly commanding center stage in American culture—and acquiring enormous power to mold opinion, embed values, and transform thinking.

Philip Dunne: "They liked Roosevelt and they hated Hitler."

Hiding its transformative impact behind a soothing cover story, prewar Hollywood posed as a factory town cranking out frothy diversions to a careworn public. In 1941, in a statement prepared for the U.S. Senate, Will H. Hays, president of the Motion Picture Producers and Distributors of America (MPPDA), declared that motion pictures belonged to the realm of fine art, as distinct from the art of persuasion. Hollywood's sole purpose in American life was to entertain and give pleasure.[1] It was not entangled by political alliances; it was beyond them, above the fray.

Off screen, however, the salaried employees were undercutting Hollywood's official stance as a neutral port. In 1932, for the first time, a cast of A-list motion picture artists sailed into the tempest of election year politics—most rallying around Franklin Delano Roosevelt, a few siding with the Republican alternative. Over the course of four election cycles, Hollywood would remain a safe precinct for FDR, but the ferment of the Great Depression was not to be calmed by a single outlet for activism. Thousands of workers in the motion picture industry, both big-name stars and toilers in the trenches, aligned themselves with a more radical and emotionally satisfying movement for political and cultural reform, the Popular Front.

Neither a letterhead organization nor a doctrinaire belief system, the Popular Front was the open-ended rubric for a loose confederation of progressive peoples of all stripes: mainstream FDR Democrats, liberals, socialists, and Communists, all united in a shared commitment to civil rights and economic justice at home and the defeat of Fascism—Spanish, Italian, and especially German—abroad. For the disparate factions in the ranks, the ties that bound—a fidelity to the principles of the New Deal and an antipathy to the rising tide of Fascism in Europe—were stronger than the internecine conflicts. Screenwriter Philip Dunne, a member in good standing, summed up the sentiments: "They liked Roosevelt and they hated Hitler."[2]

Of all the Popular Fronters, the cadre with the deepest commitment and most tireless work ethic were the Communists. Lit with a religious devotion to the Marxist-Leninist gospel, brooking no deviance from the official doctrine—"the party line"—of the Communist Party of the United States of America (CPUSA), the Communists served as the shock troops of the movement, logging the longest hours on picket lines and doing the grunt work of on-the-shop-floor organizing. They wrote pamphlets, pinned up broadsheets, handed out leaflets, fired off letters to newspaper editors, hand-cranked mimeograph machines, and took on every mundane, thankless task essential to the efficient operation of a political action group. The Communists may have liked FDR and the New Deal, but they loved Joseph Stalin and the people's paradise aborning in the USSR.

Communism had never had much purchase in America—a nation too individualistic, too religious, and too prosperous for a communal, atheistic, and class-based ideology to take root. Even in the nadir of the Great Depression, when conditions seemed ripe for a revolutionary groundswell, the CPUSA attracted fewer dues-paying members (peak membership in 1939 never surpassed one hundred thousand) than did conservative Irish-Catholic societies in New York City alone.[3]

Nonetheless, while the broad spectrum of Americans remained deaf to the siren call of dialectical materialism, intellectuals and artists harkened to the sound with alacrity. The Leninist notion of a vanguard elite—of a self-selected band of creators and thinkers leading the benighted masses out of their false consciousness into the revolutionary dawn—proved irresistible to a class of workers who were more likely to be punch lines than heroes in their native land. The Communists put artists and intellectuals front and center in the battle for a new American Revolution.

A momentous shift in CPUSA orthodoxy facilitated the flow of Communism into the main currents of American cultural life. In 1935, the Comintern, the Moscow-based command center for international revolution, sent out a directive to Communists worldwide to forge alliances with heretofore counterrevolutionary pariahs—socialists, liberals, and New Deal Democrats. With Fascism ascendant in Italy and Germany, the ultimate defeat of capitalism would have to be postponed to drive off the wolves at the door. Making the best of the marriage of convenience, American Communists cloaked Soviet policy in native garb. "Communism," proclaimed Earl Browder, general secretary of the CPUSA, was but "twentieth century Americanism."[4]

In Hollywood, as elsewhere, the Communists got with the program. In foreign policy, the prime objective was to end American neutrality and intervene on the side of the Soviet-backed Republicans in the Spanish Civil War (1936–1939), the fraternal bloodbath seen as the preliminary bout in a future conflagration. In domestic policy, the Popular Front showed an unstinting support for civil rights, especially for African Americans, and the cause of labor over management.

That last cause—broader rights and rewards for the ranks of American labor—had immediate application on the soundstages and backlots of Hollywood.

Willie Bioff: "You got to be tough in this den of hyenas."

The history of labor relations in Hollywood is as tangled as the wiring on a studio soundstage, a story of broken circuits, crossed currents, and major blowouts. Greed and altruism, gangsters and idealists, pedantic argument and explosive violence—the off-screen action by the workers who built the scaffolding and the writers who sketched the blueprints generated enough pulse-pounding action and backbiting melodrama to fill out a season's worth of programming produced at the site of the job actions.

Like any industrial machine shop, the dream factory demanded highly organized and compartmentalized teams of skilled workers; it was a shop floor where any malfunctioning cog could cause the whole operation to grind

Chicago-bred mobster Willie Bioff, head of the International Alliance of Theatrical Stage Employees, leaves federal court in New York after pleading not guilty to charges of violating federal anti-racketeering law, June 12, 1941.

to a halt. The transition to sound technology launched with *The Jazz Singer* (1927) exponentially increased the need for precision teamwork and expert wranglers.[5] For every gauzy close-up on screen, dozens of grimy hands toiled outside the frame to get the shot.

Of course, in a city obsessed with billing, all Hollywood workers were not equal. The major status division was between the "above the line" royalty and the "below the line" vassals, a boundary that separated the high-priced creative talent (directors, screenwriters, and actors) from the working stiffs whose names were not in the credits much less up in lights. Reflecting a hierarchy of prestige and salary, the artists at the top of the ladder formed guilds not unions, with higher standards for admission as befit the fatter paychecks, while the blue-collar workers who set up the lights, the cameras, and the rest of the action gravitated into craft unions dedicated to their unique skill sets.

In 1925, after nearly a decade of failed attempts, the International Alliance of Theatrical Stage Employees and Moving Picture Machine Operators of the United States and Canada (IATSE) managed to organize the independent craft unions (working on shop floors that were not yet called soundstages) into a united front. Born as a theatrical union in the mid-nineteenth century, IATSE looked upon the motion picture business as a logical extension of its backstage hammerlock on the theater. It became—and has remained ever since—the preeminent omnibus union in the American motion picture industry. In 1926, it used its clout to negotiate the first union agreement in Hollywood history, the Studio Basic Agreement, a simple two-page document that served as the cornerstone for labor-management relations throughout the classical studio era.[6]

In March 1933, FDR's New Deal and the labor-friendly outlook of the National Industrial Recovery Act, and, in 1935, the creation of the National Labor Relations Board (NLRB) under the Wagner Act, encouraged workers throughout American industry to lock arms. Unionization was now a federally guaranteed right—if not a studio-sanctioned activity. Accustomed to ruling their domains with the iron fist of the Asian overlords they were named for, the moguls fought tooth and nail to undermine worker solidarity, whether on the soundstage or at the typewriter.

Under the Roosevelt administration, however, not even the moguls could halt the forward momentum of organized labor. In 1935, pursuant to the Wagner Act, the studios negotiated a closed shop with IATSE, ceding hiring power to the union. Other major trade unions such as the American Federation of Musicians, the International Brotherhood of Carpenters and Joiners, the Transportation Drivers, and the International Brotherhood of Electric Workers cut similar deals. Henceforth, whether on the soundstage or on location, to work in the motion picture industry required a union card—a golden ticket granting admission to a secure berth.

IATSE emerged from the negotiations with serious clout: it basically controlled the levers to the industrial infrastructure of motion picture production and exhibition.[7] In any dispute with the studios, IATSE held an unbeatable trump card—control over the exhibition end of the business. The leadership could order every projectionist in the union to walk out of every projection booth in the nation, shutting off the flow of revenue back to Hollywood. IATSE cardholders were the players who really lit up the screen.

In the context of the Great Depression, working in the studios was a prized gig: steady, well-paid employment within walking distance of authentic glamour. Still, the hours could be irregular and grueling. Hollywood historian Charles Higham may have exaggerated, slightly, when he quipped that "the industry's leaders drove their workers like Paraguayan miners to make movies on 18-to-20 or even 24-hour shifts," but unpaid overtime, nighttime work, and risky labor under duress were job requirements for the non-nine-to-five work week.[8]

Rather than use its leverage to press for concessions, however, IATSE sat on its gains. It was a company or "sweetheart" union—cozy with management and lax in looking out for the welfare of the dues-paying rank and file.

It was also mobbed up. Two classically, that is Chicago, trained hoods— Willie Bioff, an obese no-neck pimp, murderer, and extortionist, and George E. Browne, IATSE president, his partner in crime—ran IATSE like a protection racket, squeezing the moguls for kickbacks and raiding the union coffers. In 1934, Bioff had muscled into Hollywood and appointed himself the spokesman for IATSE's twenty-three thousand members. Validating the fait accompli, the moguls were happy to deal with a bribable union boss who could grease the machine works and keep the production line humming. Bioff got bags of cash, the moguls got peace on the shop floor, and the workers accepted a corrupt company union or lost their union cards or the use of their legs.[9]

In 1937, out of a sense that IATSE was the tool of the bosses—corporate and mob—a rival and more radical alternative emerged, led by a firebrand named Herbert K. Sorrell. A brawny street fighter—in fact, a former boxer— Sorrell was an old-school, rough-and-tumble brawler, not afraid to mix it up on the picket line or anywhere else for that matter. He was hard to deal with and impossible to intimidate. He was also assumed to be a secret member of the Communist party, an association more disreputable than the mob.

Sorrell's official title was business representative for the Motion Picture Painters Local 644, but he was an all-purpose, across-the-ranks agitator. From his base in the painters local, he brought together dissident unions and recruited fed-up IATSE members. Affecting the rugged proletarianism fashionable in Marxist labor circles, he referred to himself "as just a dumb painter," which fooled no one.[10] Street smart and incorruptible, he was banned from studio lots, threatened by Bioff's thugs, and considered a greater threat to studio profits than the competition from radio.

In November 1937, unable to ignore the gangsterism under its nose, the California assembly held hearings into IATSE racketeering and the "rumors" that goons from Chicago had been imported to provide muscle for the "dictatorship" of IATSE president Browne. Subpoenaed to testify, Willie Bioff claimed to earn a mere one hundred dollars a week, plus twelve dollars a day for expenses. He railed against the Communists in the union ranks in "unprintable" language. He cast himself as a simple servant—and protector— of the stagehands.[11] As for his brass-knuckled negotiating tactics? "You got to be tough in this den of hyenas," he explained. "You can't be a sissy and get anywhere."[12]

Despite the public airing of corruption charges before the California assembly, Bioff and Browne's criminal enterprise remained a local story until 1939 when, spurred by crusading reporting in the trade press, the open secret that was mob-run labor in Hollywood entered the national conversation. *Daily Variety* editor Arthur Ungar had been blowing the whistle on IATSE racketeering for years, labeling Bioff a parasite and urging the industry to "ignore him, scorn him, and laugh him out of town."[13] Getting nowhere, Ungar and Screen Actors Guild president Robert Montgomery fed incriminating material on the two thugs to syndicated columnist Westbrook Pegler, who came to town to do his own legwork.[14]

Pegler's columns broke the story wide open. For months, in his trademark poison-pen prose, Pegler pursued the "rodent types who muscled into the [IATSE] union, or racket."[15] "Hollywood makes an effort to keep pictures clean," followed up Ungar, still on the case locally and under police protection for his intrepid reporting. "So it should keep its labor relations clean by doing business with people who are morally and socially qualified to bargain, instead of being compelled to accede to the threats of a fugitive panderer."[16]

Pegler's columns brought Bioff and Browne to the attention of the Department of the Treasury. To nudge the prosecution along, Ungar and Montgomery hand-delivered their thick files on the pair to Secretary of the Treasury Henry Morgenthau Jr.

The indictment of Bioff and Browne and the exposure of IATSE as a tentacle of gangland Chicago was a moral and tactical victory for union reformers. "Willie Bioff, pudgy labor hoodlum who ruled the International Alliance of Theatrical Stage Employees in cooperation with other Chicago gang lieutenants, and George E. Browne, IATSE prexy, were indicted on charges of extorting $500,000 from four major companies," reported *Daily Variety* in 1941, not needing to wait for the trial to pronounce a verdict. Later that year, a federal judge in New York made it official, sentencing Bioff and Browne to prison for ten years and eight years, respectively. The fall of Bioff and Browne made Herbert Sorrell—clean legally if not ideologically— "an even bigger factor in union ranks."[17]

Sorrell did not squander his opportunity. On November 3, 1941, he parlayed his moral capital into the creation of a rival omnibus union, the Conference of Studio Unions (CSU). "With the International Alliance of Theatrical Stage Employees in some public duress because of the court ordeals of its leaders," as *Motion Picture Herald* delicately put it, motion picture workers welcomed the prospect of a new union federation.[18] Sorrell was elected CSU president and determined to make good on his mandate for progressive reform.

S. J. Perelman: "It's no worse than playing the piano in a call-house."

Meanwhile, (slightly) above the line, Hollywood's screenwriters were mirroring the divisions between IATSE and CSU: over the policy of a closed shop, over which of two unions would have jurisdiction, and over the role of Communist activists in union governance. Being writers, they left behind a voluminous paper trail.

Screenwriters were low men—and women—on the studio totem pole. Demeaned by their overlords, relegated to cubbyholes, and pressed into tag team collaboration, they sketched out story treatments, rewrote each other's prose, punched up dialogue, cooked up meet-cutes, and plotted second-act twists for producers whose literary tastes tended toward the racing pages. For the great novelists and esteemed playwrights who swallowed their pride and took the Hollywood money, self-deprecation served as a therapeutic defense mechanism. F. Scott Fitzgerald, the Jazz Age avatar turned payroll employee, referred to his new vocation as "scenario hack." Humorist S. J. Perelman was philosophical: "It's no worse than playing the piano in a call-house."[19]

Forcing writers to work in close quarters had an unexpected consequence. Even loners by nature recognized the wisdom in banding together to fight the exploitation of producers who stole screen credit, reneged on commitments, and treated the gifted artists as "schmucks with Underwoods," in Jack Warner's immortal put-down.

On February 3, 1933, in a confab in the back room of Stanley Rose's Bookshop in Hollywood, ten screenwriters met "for the purpose of discussing the betterment under which writers work in Hollywood." They hammered out a policy statement and formed the nucleus for what became the Screen Writers' Guild (SWG).[20] John Howard Lawson, a New York playwright who had followed the money to Hollywood in the early sound era, was elected president as "the middle ground candidate."[21] Lawson wore his Communist sympathies on his sleeve and put them in his scripts.

Fearing that a coalition of temperamental artists would be harder to deal with than a union of shop workers kept in line by the mob, producers were more resistant to granting collective bargaining rights to screenwriters than to stagehands. "If any Screen Writers' Guild members working on this lot are not satisfied with conditions here, I shall be only too pleased to tear up their contracts," snarled MGM head Louis B. Mayer, who insisted on undivided fealty.[22] In a perverse reversal of status claims, the moguls argued that the screenwriters were not workers but artists—hence independent contractors instead of salaried employees. As such, they had no standing to organize under NLRB guidelines. The screenwriters claimed they were not artists but common laborers, a scrivener proletariat—else why would they have to punch a time clock like an electrician when they came to work?[23]

Joining the battle, Irving Thalberg, executive in charge of production at MGM and the original genius behind the genius of the studio system, was determined to crush the SWG. Along with a like-minded group of well-paid, conservative screenwriters fronted by Rupert Hughes, James K. McGuinness, and William Slavens McNutt, Thalberg sponsored the creation of the Screen Playwrights, Inc. (SP) to undermine the SWG. On May 21, 1936, at the Beverly Wilshire Hotel, the opposition was formally constituted to "develop amicable relations for the arbitration of any dispute arising between producers and screenwriters" and "to protect themselves from the activities of radically-minded writers and organizations which are seen as imperiling the jobs of screenwriters."[24] For the next decade, the twin specters of job loss and radical subversion were conjured whenever a Hollywood union dared defy the company store.

In December 1936, with telling expediency, the Association of Motion Picture Producers (AMPP), the West Coast branch of the MPPDA, signed an agreement with the SP to make it the sole bargaining agent for Hollywood's screenwriters. The deal shut out members of the SWG from work at the major studios. Playing hardball, the producers put the screws to—and blacklisted—the rebel screenwriters.

What film historian Nancy Lynn Schwartz dubbed "the Hollywood writers' wars" commenced in earnest—a fierce decade-long battle between screenwriters and producers and between the SWG and the SP. To pore over the pages of depositions, affidavits, and testimony left in the wake of the rival groups is to suspect that union activism and legal briefs consumed more screenwriting time than studio assignments during the labor-intensive 1930s.

For a time, the studios held the upper hand. Desperate for work, SWG members bolted the guild and joined the SP. "Suddenly, the SWG with 900 members had 000 members and dissolved with the *pfft* of a pinpricked penny balloon," gloated Rupert Hughes.[25] He was not exaggerating: on March 1, 1937, the SWG declared itself officially dead, filing a "certificate of dissolution" with the office of the country clerk in Los Angeles.[26]

In good screenwriterly fashion, however, a second act twist was in the script. On April 12, 1937, the Supreme Court ruled the Wagner Act constitutional: the motion picture industry, being manifestly a form of interstate commerce, fell under its purview. The ruling revived the dead letterers of the SWG. On June 1, 1937, the guild formally reconstituted with five hundred re-energized screenwriters. The reborn guild immediately petitioned the NLRB for formal designation as the exclusive bargaining agent for Hollywood screenwriters.[27]

In September and October of 1937, flanked by high-priced attorneys, the combatants made their case before the NLRB. Charles Brackett, acting president of the SWG, testified that writers had been forced to resign from the SWG or wind up on a studio blacklist. SP president Grover Jones, Howard Emmett Rogers, and Virginia Van Upp all claimed to have left the SWG because of its radical and Communist leanings.[28]

To resolve the dispute, the NLRB ordered an election. In August 1938, the SWG scored a decisive victory, crushing the SP by a margin of 267–57 to become the exclusive collective bargaining agent for Hollywood screen-writers. At first, the studios brushed aside the results, but the writing, as it were, was on the wall.[29] No less than prop men, screenwriters were studio employees with a union seal of their own.

The bitter jurisdictional battles of the 1930s were the deep backstory to the congressional drama that unfolded in 1947. All the screenwriters who appeared before the House Committee on Un-American Activities in 1947—on either side—first bonded together or went for each other's throats during the Hollywood writers' wars of the 1930s. Reopening old wounds that never really healed, and exacting payback for grievances long nursed, the dueling testimony was about the political past as much as the political present.

Gale Sondergaard: "An actress used to be an isolated individual who had no contact with the outside world."

For the Communists of the Popular Front, Hollywood's soundstages and screenwriter stables were natural settings for radical agitation, but the logical place to take the revolution national was the end product of the labor, the motion pictures. Yet no mogul would jeopardize his empire by elevating Marxist-Leninist critique over boy-girl stuff. Blocked from making a visible mark on the canvas of the big screen, the artists turned to off-screen space to project their vision.

Low-caste scribblers and top-billed stars alike devoted thousands of off-the-books man hours to a dizzying array of political action committees with names like the Motion Picture Artists Committee, the Hollywood Citizens Committee for the Federal Theater, and the Motion Picture Democratic Committee. No organization, however, was more influential than the flagship Popular Front group in Hollywood, the Hollywood Anti-Nazi League for the Defense of American Democracy (HANL).

Formed in 1936, the brainchild of screenwriter Donald Ogden Stewart, a high-living patrician, MGM golden boy, and secret member of the CPUSA; critic-screenwriter Dorothy Parker, the renowned "quiptress" and reliable left-winger; and Otto Katz, a genuine Soviet agent who boasted of being the first Communist fundraiser to dig into Hollywood wallets to fill party coffers, the league sought to awaken the nation to the threat from the war machine gearing up in Germany.[30] At the peak of its cachet, HANL claimed some five thousand adherents from the celluloid community.[31] The league may have fit the textbook definition of a Communist front group—founded by Communists and faithful to the party line—but the vast bulk of its membership was composed of mainstream liberals. The anti-Nazi thrust also attracted a sizable subset of conservative Jews and Irish Catholics.

Under the league's banner, Hollywood's Popular Fronters mounted numerous consciousness-raising events—seminars, rallies, radio shows, and screenings of anti-Fascist documentaries. All of the outreach efforts exploited a unique local resource to draw crowds and attract publicity. Dozens of stars (Melvyn Douglas, John Garfield, Edward G. Robinson, and Karen Morley were particularly accommodating) lent their names and energies to anti-Nazi and pro-civil rights causes. Whether electioneering, signing manifestos, or speaking at rallies, the marquee names guaranteed a level of media coverage a Marxist study group could not match. Few of the stars were scrupulous about what petition they signed or under whose sponsorship they appeared.

"An actress used to be an isolated individual who had no contact with the outside world," observed Gale Sondergaard, explaining why so many of her peers were no longer content to prance around as glamorous clotheshorses. "Now, because she is a worker in a large industry, she has become a member of a trade union and interested in her fellow workers. I would feel as unhappy if a beautiful gown I wore were made under bad labor conditions as if it were the means of sending a bullet to Japan to kill some poor Chinese."[32]

Rallies, radio addresses, and full-page manifestos published in the trade press kept Hollywood activism highlighted in the public eye. "Here in Hollywood, the actors have taken their place on behalf of the American ideals which the Hollywood Anti-Nazi League has incorporated into its platform," boasted Melvyn Douglas.[33] On January 30, 1938, at the Shrine Auditorium, director John Ford and Dorothy Parker led a crowd of seven thousand cheering Hollywoodites at an anti-Nazi rally that condemned Hitler's fifth anniversary as chancellor of Germany. "Here I stand in my lisle stockings," joked Parker, who could well afford silk but was boycotting hosiery made in Japan. She then turned serious. "I was in on the birth of the Hollywood League Against Nazism when it started with seven members in 1936," she said. "Now, the Hollywood Anti-Nazi League has more than 5,000 members. That must prove that it is a real necessity."[34]

The celebrity bait lured the photographers, but the odd departure from the usual line readings spoken by screen stars—product endorsements and items in gossip columns—alienated the press, trade and mainstream alike. Commentators derided the "swimming pool reds" and "cocktail and tie" Bolsheviks, who took time off from the greens at the Beverly Hills Golf Course to lecture the hoi polloi on foreign policy. Merely because actors could speak into a microphone was no reason for them to use it to broadcast private opinions.

In another city, however, the entry of big-name stars and high-priced screenwriters into the political arena was nothing to snicker about. The earnest speechifying and boisterous rallies, the protests against the Fascist emissaries Vittorio Mussolini and Leni Riefenstahl (who came to Hollywood in 1937 and 1938, respectively, only to be run out of town by HANL), and the incessant fundraising galas for Republican Spain brought the motion picture industry to the attention of a newly formed committee on Capitol Hill, where politics was not a side job.

Martin Dies: "The only thing that counts in these investigations is what gets into the papers."

Martin Dies (D-TX) was a disgruntled former New Dealer who became an ardent opponent of progressive reform. He looked every inch the Texas lawman: blond, six foot three, powerfully built. Sized up by the *New Republic* in 1938 as "physically a giant, very young, ambitious, and cocksure," he was a publicity hound with a messiah complex that ripened into a persecution complex.[35]

First elected to Congress in 1930, Dies had been angling for a committee chair almost since his freshman year, putting forward resolution after resolution for Congress to investigate "the diffusion within the United States of subversive and un-American propaganda that is instigated from foreign countries or of a domestic origin and attacks the principle of the form of government as guaranteed by the Constitution."[36] Hollywood, Dies felt certain, was a central means of diffusion.

Dies had a short-lived legislative model to draw upon for inspiration. In 1934, at the urging of Samuel Dickstein (D-NY), whose main worry was Nazism not Communism, the House of Representatives authorized the creation of the first iteration of the committee that would make the slur "un-American" a permanent part of the lexicon of American politics. Chaired by John McCormack (D-MA), the special committee investigated Communism and Nazism in a mainly temperate and unsensational manner, hearing most of its testimony in executive session. In February 1935, before closing up shop, the committee recommended the compulsory registration of foreign agents. In September 1938, the Foreign Agents Registration Act become law.[37] It was to be the sole legislative legacy of any House committee on un-American activities.

On June 6, 1938, the Seventy-fifth Congress gave Dies authorization to revive and remake the McCormack Committee in his own image. The version he chaired and became forever identified with proved to be instantly notorious and perennially controversial.

The Dies version of the House Committee on Un-American Activities was officially called the Special Committee to Investigate Un-American Activities and Propaganda in the United States. Like the McCormack Committee, it was a special, not a standing committee, requiring reauthorization with each new Congress. Underfunded and understaffed, fueled by the fire in the belly of its single-minded chairman, the committee never attracted the congressional A-list but it always attracted headlines. "The only thing that counts in these investigations is what gets into the papers," Dies freely admitted. "Who in the world is going to bother about the official record?"[38]

Dies struck at an opportune moment. Current events had given a dire urgency to the notion of a "fifth column"—a nest of conspirators undermining the nation from within, working for an enemy who lurked outside the perimeter, ready to spring into action at the appointed hour. The language of infestation—rodents and rats, tarantulas and termites, all manner of insects and vermin "boring from within" to erode the health of the American body politic—pervaded any discussion of national security. In March 1938, when Germany annexed Austria, the phrase gained added currency. Had not the Nazis softened up their prey with seditious propaganda and agents provocateurs?

The original charter of the Dies Committee was to investigate two different flanks of the fifth columns operating in America: Nazism, spearheaded by the German American Bund, a twenty-five thousand-member strong paramilitary group headed by a burley former machine gunner for the German army named "Fuhrer" Fritz Kuhn and guided by command centers in Berlin;

and Communism, overseen by the CPUSA and controlled from Moscow. However, interest in the latter soon surpassed the former and a preoccupation with Communist penetration into Hollywood became a central focus.

The alliance between Communism and Hollywood—a Spartan ideology in the citadel of epicurean excess—may have been counterintuitive, but the vocal support for the Spanish Republicans by famed screen stars and the stance of the Hollywood Anti-Nazi League on civil rights and labor issues were note-for-note echoes of the Communist party line. The content of Hollywood pictures being too strictly censored to make the charges of on-screen propaganda credible, the Dies Committee focused its attention on personalities—how Communist agents were cashing in on the famous faces and bulging wallets of highly paid Hollywood stars. The term of choice for the well-meaning but harebrained artists was "unwitting dupes."

On August 12, 1938, in the spacious caucus room of the Old House Office Building, the Dies Committee launched its first set of hearings. The investigation probed labor unions, the German American Bund, the Federal Theater Project, and Hollywood. Each of the targets earned headlines but the largest type size—a lesson not lost on subsequent versions of HUAC—was reserved for the Hollywood-themed sessions.

Trade press reporters did not have to wait long for a local angle. Two days into the hearings, HUAC investigator Edward E. Sullivan submitted a report detailing his findings in Hollywood. "Evidence tends to show that all phases of radical and Communistic activities are rampant among the studios of Hollywood, and although well known, it is a matter which the film moguls desire to keep from the public," Sullivan revealed. "A number of film celebrities are using their large salaries to finance Communistic activities, including groups which were conducting campaigns in agricultural regions in California."[39]

J. B. Matthews created a bigger uproar when he named six motion picture stars as unwitting dupes of Moscow. A former preacher of the social gospel, pacifist, socialist, and fellow traveler, Matthews had been a major player in Communist front groups since the 1920s. In 1935, Matthews broke with the party to morph into a fierce—and soon professional—anti-Communist.[40] He was credited with coining the term "fellow traveler," to refer to a person who followed the party line without the obligations of regular attendance at meetings and the payment of monthly dues.[41]

Matthews warned that "the Communist Party relies heavily upon the carelessness or indifference of thousands of prominent citizens in lending their names for its propagandistic purposes." The bigger the name, the bigger the prize for the Communists, and the bigger the risk for guileless Americans lulled by the celebrity endorsement.

"Almost everybody in Hollywood except Mickey Mouse and Snow White has been signed up by the Communists at one time or another," declared Matthews, grinning.

"How about Charlie McCarthy?" teased Rep. Joe Starnes (D-AL), referring to the dummy sidekick of radio ventriloquist Edgar Bergen.

"The Communists have enough Charlie McCarthys of their own," replied Matthews.

In exposing six non-wooden stars whose personae had been exploited, Matthews said, he was settling on a mere sampling from the Hollywood registry, culling from a list that "could be expanded indefinitely."[42] Perhaps so, but he might better have stopped at five—Clark Gable, Robert Taylor, James Cagney, Miriam Hopkins, and Bette Davis—and not spoken the name of the sixth—Shirley Temple.

The biggest box office star in America and the most important asset held by Twentieth Century-Fox, Shirley Temple was nine years old. Tarring the child with a red brush was an accusation too risible for all but the most credulous Communist hunters. Editorialists, columnists, cartoonists, and members of FDR's cabinet rushed to guffaw at the notion of a nine-year-old fifth columnist. Secretary of Interior Harold Ickes chortled:

> [The Committee has] gone to Hollywood and there discovered a great Red plot. They have found dangerous radicals there, led by little Shirley Temple. Imagine the great Committee raiding her nursery and seizing her dolls as evidence![43]

That single instance of name-dropping did more than any constitutional impropriety to discredit the investigation. As a topper to the burlesque, stripper Gypsy Rose Lee got into the act by offering to bare all before the Dies Committee.[44]

Whiplashed by derision and stalled by lack of funds, Dies turned to media outlets to make his case. In 1940, in a pair of articles for *Liberty* magazine, he distilled many of the charges that would cling to Hollywood in the years ahead. "I was amazed to learn the extent of subversive activities there," Dies wrote, reporting on a fact-finding mission to the crime scene. "It was apparent to me that un-Americanism had made more progress in California and on the West Coast than in any other part of the country." HUAC investigators had confirmed that "Hollywood was becoming the powerhouse of Communist activities and propaganda" in America.

Though eager to paint Hollywood with a red stripe, Dies was careful not to infuse his rhetoric with a toxic element often tossed into the mix. Sometimes unspoken, sometimes snarled with crude candor, antisemitism found a wellspring of inspiration in Hollywood. In the 1930s, the American strain was abetted by Nazi propaganda, smuggled off German cruise liners and distributed by the German American Bund.[45] Antisemitic slurs were also circulated by Father Charles E. Coughlin, the popular radio priest, who was wont to stray from the Gospels to warn about the dark machinations of the Jews in America's midst. In 1939, scanning a sampling of issues of *Social Justice*, Coughlin's newspaper, screenwriter Ring Lardner Jr. was amazed at the "pure unadulterated Jew baiting" in the house organ of "Fritz Kuhn's clerical colleague." Lardner detected an "increasing attention of late to the menace of Hollywood," a city that unified a trinity of nativist hatreds. "From its actions, from its actors, and from its producers, Hollywood must be set down as America's Red nest," ran a typical editorial.[46] Melded together, Communism, Hollywood, and Judaism formed a single satanic trident.

Dies tried to keep the elements separated, though it was hard to deny the obvious connection. "Most of the producers are Jews who have made a remarkable success in building the film industry from an insignificant beginning to one of the greatest industries in the world," he observed open-mindedly, but an unfortunate consequence of the tribal solidarity was that the Jewish moguls feared Nazism more than Communism. Sitting beside Harry Warner at a screening of Warner Bros.'s *Confessions of a Nazi Spy* (1939), Dies could only shake his head at how the studio kingpin was transfixed by a film that "ignored or soft-pedaled Communism and portrayed Nazism as the greater menace." Sadly, Judeo-Hollywood "had been completely duped by the Communists."[47]

In August 1940, the perceived Communist-Hollywood symbiosis—without the antisemitism—was highlighted by grand jury testimony from John L. Leech, the former general secretary of the CPUSA in Los Angeles. Leech had been called to testify by Buron Fitts, district attorney for Los Angeles County, who was investigating fifth column activity in Southern California, including alleged Communist hit squads. Leech had named eighteen Hollywood stars as active members of Communist study groups

At a closed session with HUAC Chairman Martin Dies (*right*) at the Biltmore Hotel in Los Angeles, actor Fredric March (*center*) denies the accusations of former Communist John L. Leech that he ever contributed to the Communist party or "any other un-American cause." Actress Florence Eldridge, March's wife, looks on, August 17, 1940.

and financial supporters of front causes. The names were big, including James Cagney, Fredric March, Humphrey Bogart, Franchot Tone, Melvyn Douglas, Francis Lederer, and Luise Rainer.

The stars rushed to deny the allegations. The Dies Committee had been a congressional inquiry of dubious credibility; the Fitts grand jury was part of a criminal prosecution airing information from a witness in a position to know, in Hollywood's backyard. The accusation could not be laughed off or ignored; it had to be denied and refuted.

Martin Dies, of all people, came to the rescue of the accused. Playing disinterested arbiter, sitting as a "subcommittee of one," he agreed to listen to the stars explain and deny. No sooner had Dies moved into his hotel suite at the Biltmore Hotel in downtown Los Angeles than Humphrey Bogart appeared and demanded a chance to refute Leech under oath. Calling Leech a "plain liar" and "a screwball," he told newsmen that "I was getting this battery of lawyers to sue him, when I realized Mr. Dies was in town so I asked him for a hearing before him and he granted it." The actor brought along his business manager, Morgan Maree. "He knows where every penny has gone and he knows that I have not contributed a cent to any organization except the Red Cross and the Community Chest."

Bogart's conversation with Dies lasted twenty minutes. The session was conducted in secret, but the chairman permitted photographers into the suite afterward so he could pose for pictures with Bogart.[48]

Fredric March followed Bogart into Dies's chamber and called Leech an "unmitigated liar." James Cagney flew back to the coast from New York to defend his good name before Dies, who had by then moved on to San Francisco. "When a person is sick and in need, you don't ask his religion, his nationality, or his politics," said Cagney about the donations he had made to the Salinas lettuce strike in 1934.[49] Tone, Lederer, and Rainer met with Dies in New York to put their innocence on record.

Dies issued a clean bill of health to the nervous stars—an exoneration from an unimpeachable source. Feeling that "a prompt statement should be made in justice to" the stars named by Leech, Dies confirmed that all the actors were patriotic Americans who had donated to seemingly worthwhile causes with the best of intentions, but whose donations, on occasion, may have been channeled into less worthwhile causes by people with less worthwhile motives. "The yarn was a natural, containing some topflight names, mixed with a Hollywood tie-in of fifth column activities," observed *Variety* wearily. "It was a chance to kick around some of the folks right here at home, and the dailies didn't pass up the opportunity."[50]

As for Dies, sensing the diminishing returns in hunting down celebrity Communists when the Nazis were introducing the word *blitzkrieg* into the English language, he seemed to have softened on the threat posed by Communism in Hollywood. In 1940, he published a book on his findings entitled *The Trojan Horse in America*. The report contained twice as much coverage of Communists as Nazis or Fascists, but nary a mention of Hollywood.[51]

By then, though, the Communist stain on Hollywood was impossible to wash away. Despite official exonerations and editorial pushback, the residual suspicion left behind by the Dies Committee, the Fitts grand jury, and the Screen Playwrights never quite dissipated. Hollywood was the kind of place, so it appeared, that nurtured Communists, fellow travelers, and unwitting dupes.

The accusations also left behind a flesh-and-blood piece of collateral damage. The gravel-voiced character actor Lionel Stander, an authentic Communist, who had been named by Leech and who himself testified before the Fitts grand jury, was dismissed from the cast of Republic's musical *Hit Parade of 1941*. Stander was paid his salary, but the head-snapping swiftness of the decision to cut him loose showed how lethal the mere insinuation of Communist sympathies could be to a Hollywood career.[52]

Lillian Hellman: "I would like to make sure that our charity aid does not mask a pre-war movement in the United States."

Ultimately, whatever forward progress Communism might have made in Hollywood was halted not by Martin Dies but by Joseph Stalin. On August 23, 1939, a lightning bolt hit the ranks of the Popular Front: the Hitler-Stalin Pact, the agreement between Nazi Germany and Soviet Russia that carved up Poland, gave Stalin the Baltics, and flashed the green light for the Second World War. The sworn enemies had signed an oath to be blood brothers.

For the CPUSA, the exercise in realpolitik demanded an abrupt realignment of the party line: henceforth, the ardently anti-Nazi, pro-defense interventionists would be the adamantly neutral, anti-defense isolationists. Better to focus on domestic issues than get entangled in foreign alliances that might draw the nation into a senseless European bloodbath.

In Hollywood, the Communist artists who had campaigned for an aggressive anti-Nazi stance in Popular Front groups like the Theater Arts Committee, the Motion Picture Democratic Committee, and the Hollywood Anti-Nazi League were now joining the Hollywood Peace Forum and mobilizing under the slogan "The Yanks Are Not Coming." Unlike the corporate bosses at the studios, doing the bidding of FDR's merchants of war, the fresh converts to pacifism and isolationism showed "that Hollywood's rank and file is for peace," proclaimed the Communist cultural weekly the *New Masses*, always a reliable barometer of party orthodoxy.[53]

Screenwriters Donald Ogden Stewart, John Howard Lawson, Dalton Trumbo, Albert Maltz, Alvah Bessie, and Hebert Biberman—all core members of HANL—obediently put their typewriters to the anti-interventionist cause. "It has been said the writers have in their custody the consciences of the world," proclaimed Stewart in a statement signed by three hundred members of the League of American Writers, a Communist front group. "We cry out that our participation in this war could be such an evil. We call upon all writers to act with maximum effort and courage to the end that America shall not again engage in foreign adventure."[54]

However, not all members of the Popular Front were as ideologically elastic as its Communist wing. When HANL reversed course and adopted the party line (that December, the group changed its name to the Hollywood League for Democratic Action), the liberals fled. The great bulk of the membership— anti-Fascist progressives and FDR supporters—could not stomach so cynical a reversal, a literally overnight conversion of conscience.

Former allies who had once marched arm in arm exchanged bitter words and went separate ways. In January 1940, as "brave little Finland" was opposing the Soviet invasion let loose by the Hitler-Stalin Pact, liberals set up the Finnish Relief Fund and rallied to the cause of the besieged nation. Producer Herman Shumlin and playwright Lillian Hellman, both obedient Stalinists, opposed a benefit performance of Hellman's hit Broadway play *The Little Foxes* to raise money for the Finns. Following the new directives, Hellman scoffed at the bleeding hearts who got all weepy over "a pro-Nazi little Republic." She believed that such benefits hid a darker, militarist agenda: "I want to make sure that our charity aid does not mask a pre-war movement in the United States."

Tallulah Bankhead, the star of *The Little Foxes*, called out her producer and playwright. "Why should Mr. Shumlin and Miss Hellman suddenly become so insular?" she wondered. "If Spanish refugees, the Chinese dispossessed, and German refugees are deserving of aid, why not the Finnish women and children who are suffering the privations caused by wanton invasion?"[55] The question answered itself. "The Communists were the strongest *for* collective security until the Pact and then they abandoned it," recalled Philip Dunne in 1991, still seething over the betrayal. "It was a real split, it wasn't an argument over *details*, it was a real split."[56]

On June 21, 1941, when the Nazis barreled east to invade the Soviet Union, the Communist party line reversed again and so did the editorial policies of the stateside organs of Communist opinion. "The armed forces of German imperialism representing all that is twisted, and brutal, medieval and obscurantist, sinister and reactionary and evil in the world system which is writhing on the eve of its doom—has attacked the villages and homes, the fertile fields and ingenious workshops of the new civilization," sputtered the *New Masses*, demanding that America commit all its energies to *"assisting the most progressive government the world has known, on whose fate the whole future of mankind depends."* Italics in original.[57]

With Mother Russia under the tank treads of the Wehrmacht, American Communists re-enlisted in the war against Nazism. Yet neither the conservatives nor the liberals in Hollywood would forget where, in the end, the loyalties of their on-again, off-again comrades stood: that the North Star they looked to shone atop the Kremlin in Moscow. "An American Red is a punko who called World War II 'an imperialist struggle' on June 20, 1941, the day before Mr. Schickelgruber invaded Russia. And then called it 'a holy crusade' after the German Panzers hit the Russian border," sneered Walter Winchell in 1947. The preeminent gossip-cum-political columnist of his day had been a fervent anti-Nazi since 1933. He was not sidetracked by the Hitler-Stalin Pact, but he remembered the names of the people who were, and he was not alone.[58]

Chapter 2

HOLLYWOOD'S WAR RECORD

B etween the Hitler-Stalin Pact in August 1939 and the Nazi invasion of the Soviet Union in June 1941, even as the Communist wing of what was no longer a Popular Front urged an isolationist stance on stage and screen, the motion picture industry, so long quiescent to the rise of Nazism, sprang into decisive action. From 1939 to 1941, Hollywood signed up ahead of the formal call to arms with its own line of over-there propaganda designed to enlist the nation into the war raging in Europe.

The first entry, released in April 1939, was Warner Bros.' *Confessions of a Nazi Spy*, the film Martin Dies was so disappointed in. Based on a sensationalistic espionage trial held in New York in 1938 and billed as "the film that has the guts to call a swastika a swastika!", the farsighted docudrama warned of a division-sized fifth column of American Nazis, a renascent German war machine, and the inevitable confrontation between the forces of democracy and totalitarianism.

Though not the breakthrough hit Warner Bros. had hoped for, *Confessions of a Nazi Spy* opened the floodgates for anti-Nazi cinema. Beginning in September 1939, low-budget independent outfits and major studios alike geared up to indict Nazism and urge America to take defensive action. B-caliber quickies, women's melodramas, tense thrillers, and dark satires— the anti-Nazi thread connected films as diverse as *The Beast of Berlin* (1939), *Escape* (1940), *Foreign Correspondent* (1940), *The Mortal Storm* (1940), *Manhunt* (1940), *The Man I Married* (1940), and *The Great Dictator* (1940).

Patriotic renewal and national defense were the common themes of *Mr. Smith Goes to Washington* (1939), *I Wanted Wings* (1940), *Flight Command* (1940), *The Fighting 69th* (1940), and *Sergeant York* (1941).

Watching Hollywood's aggressive foray into geopolitics, the Communists stood on—or heckled from—the sidelines. After August 23, 1939, the *New Masses* lambasted the anti-Nazi pro-defense cycle as errant warmongering. Warner Bros.'s egalitarian Great War combat film *The Fighting 69th* was "an unbelievable mess of bilge and militarism." Twentieth Century-Fox's conjugal melodrama *The Man I Married*—originally titled *I Married a Nazi*—taught that "America must get ready to go to war and go to war soon, which is what our homegrown fascists want us to believe." The air power friendly *I Wanted Wings* was "propaganda of unbelievable vulgarity . . . all the words which describe it adequately are unprintable."[1] When the party apparatchiks sent out the word, the writers in the ranks took verbatim dictation.

Nicholas M. Schenck: "Whatever anti-Nazi films we made don't show one hundredth part of what we all know is going on in Germany."

American Communists found common cause with an unlikely group of kindred spirits in the U.S. Senate. Isolationist Republicans had long been infuriated at FDR's metastasizing federal agencies and his blatant orchestration of same for New Deal causes. Now, the Republicans believed, FDR's foreign policy was leading the nation headlong into war—with his Hollywood minions aiding and abetting at every corner Bijou.

The fresh attack on Hollywood's politics differed in a crucial way from the allegations of the Dies Committee. The reek of antisemitism swirled around the charges of war propaganda emanating from the U.S. Senate. No one denied that Hollywood's Jews had a personal stake in defeating Nazism, but a few senators implied that ethno-religious solidarity outweighed their patriotic duty to America.[2] On August 1, 1941, in a speech broadcast to a national audience over CBS, Sen. Gerald P. Nye (R-ND) addressed the America First Committee, an eight hundred thousand–strong band of ardent isolationists, to vent his suspicions about the Jewish moguls. Nye scanned Hollywood's marquees and spotted "at least 20 pictures . . . designed to rouse us to a state of war hysteria."[3] He demanded a senatorial probe into the saber-rattling films distributed by a cabal of foreign-born merchants of death.

Nye got his wish. From September 9 to 26, 1941, a subcommittee of the Committee on Interstate Commerce chaired by Sen. D. Worth Clark held hearings into "Propaganda in Motion Pictures." *Variety*—which, despite the lineage shared by most of its masthead and readership, almost never broached the Jewish angle—detected the impulse behind the investigation and smoked it out, attributing the hearings "to the hatred of big business and the strongly anti-Semitic feeling of many members of Congress from small, hinterland districts. [The] Clark committee is made up of a number of men from these territories and they consider Hollywood the combined epitome of both their pet hatreds."[4]

To represent the industry as counsel, the MPPDA chose Wendell L. Willkie, the Republican candidate for president in 1940 and a statesman held in universal esteem. An astute reader of the national zeitgeist, Willkie sensed that Hollywood had the wind at its back. Though wary of involvement in Europe, the vast majority of Americans had no love for the Nazis and supported FDR's push for military preparedness. They were also flocking to Hollywood's patriotic fare, especially *The Fighting 69th* and *Sergeant York*.

Making no apologies for Hollywood's anti-Nazi slate, Willkie labeled the hearings a waste of time. "We abhor everything which Hitler represents" and "are proud to admit that we have done everything possible to inform the public of the progress of the national defense program," he declared in a twenty-five hundred–word letter to the Clark Committee. Willkie also upbraided Senators Nye and his nativist ally Burton K. Wheeler (D-MT) for their not-so-veiled antisemitic slurs. The fact that the studios employed men "in positions both prominent and inconspicuous, both Nordics and non-Nordics, Jews and Gentiles, Protestant and Catholics, native and foreign born" only proved that Hollywood, like America, was a land of equal opportunity.[5]

With Willkie protecting their flanks, the moguls walked into the hearing room spoiling for a fight. Unapologetic and unbowed, Nicholas M. Schenck, president of Loew's, Inc., MGM's parent company; Harry M. Warner, president of Warner Bros. Pictures; Barney Balaban, president of Paramount Pictures; and Darryl F. Zanuck, vice president of production at Twentieth Century-Fox, offered full-throated defenses of the industry and its programming. The moguls not only flaunted their anti-Nazism and pro-Americanism, they argued that the two were synonymous.

Schenck spent two days on the stand parrying hostile questions. A street-wise, up-from-the-ghetto hustler who turned a handful of carny concessions and rickety nickelodeons into an entertainment empire, the Russian-born mogul held his ground. Condemning "the bestiality which is Hitlerism," he stood squarely behind the targeted slate of MGM films, *The Mortal Storm*, *Escape*, and *Flight Command*. At every turn, the cagey old businessman outfoxed his interrogators.

"You don't want unity with Hitler, do you?" Schenck snapped at Senator Clark. "Whatever anti-Nazi films we made don't show one hundredth part of what we all know is going on in Germany."[6]

Harry M. Warner followed with a ninety-minute statement denouncing the Nazis, praising the American military, and lauding his studio's role in alerting the American people to the dangers so alarmingly close to home. "In truth, the only sin of which Warner Bros. is guilty is that of accurately recording on the screen the world as it is or has been," said Warner. He closed with a declaration

Harry M. Warner, president of Warner Bros. Pictures, defends his studio before the U.S. Senate subcommittee investigating war propaganda in motion pictures, September 25, 1941.

that he had, in fact, made good on. "I am ready to give myself and all my personal resources to aid in the defeat of the Nazi menace."[7]

Zanuck opened with a sardonic recitation of his Midwest Protestant credentials ("Senator Nye, I am sure, will find no cause for suspicion or alarm in that background"), and then lacerated the committee for trying to "subject the industry to an impossible censorship." Like Warner, he did not deny but boasted of his patriotic record. "In this time of acute national peril, I feel that it is the duty of every American to give his complete cooperation and support to our President and our Congress, to do everything to defeat Hitler and to preserve America." He reminded the senators that Hollywood didn't create Hitler and the Nazis, "we have merely portrayed them as they are."[8]

A packed, partisan gallery greeted the perorations to democracy with rapturous applause. On September 26, 1941, the hearings hastily adjourned, never to resume. The Hollywood moguls had routed the Washington senators on their home turf.

The Government Information Manual for the Motion Picture Industry: "Yes, we Americans reject communism. But we do not reject our Russian ally."

With the outbreak of war on December 7, 1941, all was forgiven, or forgotten, "for the duration." No longer facing off across tables in congressional hearing rooms, Washington and Hollywood locked arms and initiated the greatest collaboration between motion picture artistry and government policy in American history. Name-above-the-title directors enlisted in the armed forces to revolutionize the practice of documentary cinema. Disney animators decorated the fuselages of B-17s with buxom morale-boosters. Leading men went into uniform, some into combat, most into home front work that was not all that dissimilar from their civilian jobs. The screenwriters tended to be assigned to propaganda and educational work with the Office of War Information (OWI) or, along with the hands-on filmmakers, into the motion picture units of the various branches of the armed service. The writers who remained in civilian clothes continued their labors at the studios, often on war-minded feature films that embedded OWI values. The complete menu of programming—newsreels, cartoons, documentaries, and feature films—was marshalled to telegraph wartime messages of tolerance, teamwork, and sacrifice.

The transformation was not by happenstance. Under the OWI's Bureau of Motion Pictures (BMP), the U.S. government issued detailed instructions on how best to adapt screen entertainment for wartime purposes. From June 1942 until June 1943, the agency was headed by Lowell Mellett, an intrusive bureaucrat who browbeat Hollywood into inserting ham-handed lectures into Hollywood feature films.

The advice from Washington was codified in a 167-page guidebook, *The Government Information Manual for the Motion Picture Industry.* The manual taught that an essential part of Hollywood's wartime mission was to buck up America's allies by celebrating the contribution of soldiers whose homelands were combat zones and signaling that Hollywood—and therefore America—knew that the great crusade against the Axis Powers was not a one-man show.

In valorizing "the might and heroism of our Allies," no comrade in arms stood taller than the Union of Soviet Socialist Republics, which to avoid the troubling call-sign "socialist" was better referred to as Russia:

> Yes, we Americans reject communism. *But we do not reject our Russian ally.* Where would we be today if the Russians had not withstood heroically the savage Nazi invasion of their land? Would we have the same confidence in eventual victory if we were not sure that the Russians would continue their stubborn struggle?[9]

Hollywood gave an emphatic answer to the questions. In obedience to the style book—and in accord with the temper of the times—three different studios produced three heartfelt A-picture salutes to the Russian war effort: *Mission to Moscow* (Warners, 1943), *The North Star* (RKO, 1943), and *Song of Russia* (MGM, 1944). All were ardently pro-Soviet, all were shamelessly dishonest in their depiction of the Communist system, and all seemed like a good idea at the time.

The North Star was first out of the gate: a big-budget extravaganza with an impeccable pedigree—produced by Samuel Goldwyn; directed by Lewis Milestone from a screenplay by Lillian Hellman; and set to a score by Aaron Copland, the composer laureate of musical Americana, and lyrics by Ira Gershwin, trying his hand at New Pioneer rhymes ("We're the younger generation/And the future of the nation!"). Goldwyn poured enormous resources into his most expensive project to date, a pageant featuring over a thousand performers, with more than one hundred speaking parts.[10]

At first sight, *The North Star* looks like a pastoral musical. Russia is a peaceful and industrious land where villagers work each according his ability, each according to his needs. They labor, they sing, they dance, they recite party slogans ("Everybody must work!").

The serenity of the steppes is shattered when waves of Luftwaffe strafe women and children and the Wehrmacht mops up with close-quarter slaughter. The vampirish perfidy of the invaders is quite literal: a medical unit drains the blood from Russian children for transfusions to wounded Nazis. Taking to the woods, the gallant Russians launch a guerilla insurgency, liberate their village, and summarily execute the Nazi doctors. "Killing Nazis was now a matter of national policy," a gratified Lillian Hellman reminded the faint of heart.[11]

Though traversing the same territory and timeline as *The North Star*, *Song of Russia* is more romantically buoyant. "A Yank in Moscow," blurbed the taglines, concealing the war-torn land angle. "Dashing Robert Taylor woos Susan Peters and it's a wow!" Helming the project was Russian-born director Gregory Ratoff, a former character actor who spoke English with a thick-as-Borscht accent. An alumnus of the Moscow Art Theater, Ratoff had fled to America in 1922 after witnessing the bloodshed of the Bolshevik Revolution, an expertise in Soviet history that in no way informed his film.

As promised, dashing Robert Taylor plays Robert Meredith, a famous symphony conductor on a tour of Russia, who falls hard for Nadja (Susan Peters), a beautiful concert pianist, tractor driver, machine gunner, and cook from the collective farm village of Tschaikowskoya, a wheat-rich eden populated by harmonic singers and acrobatic line dancers. Soon the lovestruck Meredith and the multitasking Nadja are bridging the barriers of language and culture with a whirlwind courtship conducted in swank Russian nightclubs followed by a marriage in a traditional Russian Orthodox church. A blowout wedding party is choreographed with the verve of a Freed unit musical.

When the Nazis blast apart the festive bacchanal, Nadja organizes guerilla resistance and Meredith braves the dangers of a land on fire to reunite with his beloved. Nadja wants to stay and fight with her people, but she is persuaded

Top: A troupe of folk dancers performs in MGM's *Song of Russia* (1944). *Bottom*: Walter Huston, as ambassador Joseph E. Davies, Manart Kippen as Joseph Stalin, and Gene Lockhart as Soviet Foreign Minister Maxim Litvinov in Warner Bros.'s *Mission to Moscow* (1943), the most duplicitous of Hollywood's pro-Soviet troika.

by her fellow partisans that the best way she can contribute to the war effort is to go with her husband to America, don evening wear, and perform concerts for Russian War Relief.

If the portrait of a munificent and pacific Soviet Union in *The North Star* and *Song of Russia* was merely fanciful, of a piece with Hollywood's sound-stage versions of Paris, Vienna, and Budapest, the picture of the USSR in *Mission to Moscow* was a willful act of historical revisionism. Based on the purblind memoir by Joseph E. Davies, who served as U.S. Ambassador to the USSR from 1937–1938, at the height of the Stalinist purges and show trials; directed by Warner Bros.'s jack-of-all-genres Michael Curtiz; and written by Howard Koch, future member of the Unfriendly Nineteen, the film has a mission of its own: to whitewash the Soviet past and erase Stalin's crimes in the interest of Allied unity.

Airbrushing the pages of history, the counterfactual hallucination opens with a rare double-barreled prologue: first, from the real-life Joseph E. Davies, an avuncular presence who wants to dispel American xenophobia and tell "the truth about the Soviet Union," a nation "sincerely devoted to world peace"; and second, from the actor Walter Huston, as Davies, who praises Russia's "gallant struggle to preserve the peace until ruthless aggression made war inevitable."

Davies is a down-to-earth lawyer who reluctantly accepts his diplomatic mission from FDR as a patriotic duty. The ambassador initially shares his countryman's wrongheaded notions about the USSR, but his eyes are opened by the rock-solid integrity and core decency of the Russian people, especially their warmhearted and idealistic leaders, Premier Vyacheslav Molotov, Foreign Minister Maxim Litvinov, and, above all, the wise and kindly Joseph Stalin. All are played by huggable character actors: Oskar Homolka, Gene Lockhart, and Manart Kippen, respectively.

Newsreel footage of Soviet tanks, planes, and synchronized humans parading through Red Square on May Day (May 1, 1938) precedes the Nazi invasion of Austria (March 12, 1938), but chronology is the least of the departures from reality. The Moscow Show Trials have actually left the Soviet government "strengthened by the purge of its traitors," while the Hitler-Stalin Pact was forced upon Stalin because of the anti-Soviet policies of the West.

After witnessing the nobility of the real Russia, Davies returns home to defend the socialist experiment against the calumnies of stateside Nazi sympathizers. In a pro-Soviet rally in Madison Square Garden, he explains the logic behind the Moscow trials, the Hitler-Stalin Pact, and the invasion of Finland, debunking the false narratives that have been foisted upon the American people.

Warner Bros. gave *Mission to Moscow* a roll out befitting a prestige production doing double duty as tribute to FDR and a gift to the USSR. On April 28, 1943, the studio took over the Earle Theater in Washington, D.C. for a preview hosted by the National Press Club. A contingent of four thousand media representatives attended. Speaking at a luncheon held before the preview, Ambassador Davies predicted: "Ten, twenty, and thirty years from now, the negative of *Mission to Moscow* will be taken out of the vault for reference in light of historical developments."[12] He had that right.

John E. Rankin: "Hollywood is the greatest hotbed of subversive activities in the United States."

While World War II raged, HUAC hibernated. In a global conflagration, the interest in fifth columnists was subordinated to combating the clear and present danger from the other four columns.

The founder and guiding light of the committee sensed his glory days were over. In 1944, an ailing Martin Dies—"sick, disgusted, and exhausted"—announced his retirement from Congress. "I felt that the country had been given all the facts it needed to defeat Communism, and I asked myself, 'What more can I accomplish under a hostile administration?'"[13]

With Dies putting himself on the sidelines, the committee that bore his name faced an uncertain future. Always controversial, HUAC was despised by FDR liberals who felt that the investigatory agenda sought more to discredit the Roosevelt administration than expose Nazi or Communist subversion. With each new session of Congress, liberal Democrats tried to block funding for a renewal of authorization.

Yet the efforts to abolish HUAC never quite succeeded: few congressmen wanted to be accused of being un-American by defunding the Un-American committee. In fact, what had once been a mere special committee of the House got not just a reprieve but a promotion.

HUAC's savior was John E. Rankin (D-MS), a slick parliamentary infighter who finessed his colleagues into voting to make HUAC a permanent standing committee of the House.[14] The war had schooled a generation of Americans in the lethal threat posed by subversive cells ready to spring into action at a signal from the Fatherland. Best to have antennae out and oversight ready.

Born in 1882 in the Jim Crow hamlet of Bolanda, Mississippi, Rankin was a lean, hungry-looking, rattlesnake-eyed, un-Reconstructed son of the Confederacy, virulently racist, nakedly antisemitic, and vulgarly nativist. First elected to Congress in 1920, he reaped the rewards of the seniority system and refined his skills as a back-channel fixer, assuring the continued subjugation of a tenth of the nation by blocking Democratic proposals to eliminate poll taxes and enact federal anti-lynching laws. In February 1944, after Walter Winchell denounced Rankin for ridiculing foreign-sounding names, the congressman took to the floor of the House to rail against "that little Communistic kike." In 1946, again on the floor or the House, Rankin took after Winchell as a "slime mongering kike."[15] No more hissible incarnation of rank bigotry walked the national stage, at least not one sent to Washington by the voters. On that score, Rankin's only real competition was his fellow Mississippian, Sen. Theodore Bilbo (D-MS).

Though a hater, Rankin was a cunning pol and HUAC was dear to his heart.[16] On January 3, 1945, in the opening minutes of the inaugural House session of the Seventy-Ninth Congress, before the progressives could rally their forces, he galvanized a coalition of Southern Democrats and Republicans into rescuing HUAC from liquidation.[17] Having secured HUAC a permanent slot in the congressional budget line, Rankin then stepped aside to let Rep. Edward J. Hart (D-NJ) chair the committee. Hart, however, had no appetite for the pursuit of un-Americans and soon resigned, leaving the interim chairmanship to Rankin.

Temporarily at the helm, Rankin set his sights on the most prominent outpost of Jewish influence in American life. On June 30, 1945, he announced an investigation into "the greatest hotbed of subversive activities in the United States," the command center for "one of the most dangerous plots ever instigated for the overthrow of this Government."[18] He vowed that "Hollywood individuals and organizations are to be investigated" and that "some big name Hollywood stars and executives will enter into it before we are through." Rankin stirred a combustible brew: Communism, Hollywood, and Jews.

Rankin dispatched three investigators to Los Angeles to expose the machinations of Hollywood Jewry, but solid opposition from the California delegation in Congress prevented him from staging a series of public hearings.

With an eye to the midterm elections of November 1946, the Truman administration and Helen Gahagan Douglas (D-CA), head of the California delegation and wife of actor Melvyn Douglas, intervened to block the Rankin hearings. A furious Rankin vowed that no man—"or woman"—would stop his exposure of the "gigantic plot to overthrow the government" being hatched in Hollywood's cafeterias.[19] Still, for the moment, he was stymied.

Rankin could have pursued his vendetta by assuming the chairmanship of HUAC, but he was unwilling to relinquish his position as chairman of the powerful Committee on World War Veterans Legislation. The decision was a lucky break for HUAC. Understanding how repellent Rankin would be as the public face of the controversial committee, the Democratic leadership preferred a saner temperament for the permanent chairmanship and replaced him with the milder-mannered Rep. John S. Wood (D-GA). Wood pledged to proceed carefully and avoid "any witch hunt."[20]

Yet Wood lacked the dogged determination to run down either witches or screenwriters; the hearings he presided over were lackluster, short on revelations, and shorter on headlines. HUAC languished until a new chairman took the gavel, a man whose blood was up for the hunt.

Eric A. Johnston: "I learned from personal experience that in many countries, the only America the people know is the America of the motion pictures."

By V-J Day, Hollywood's war work had not only contributed to the defeat of the Axis powers, it had pulverized the myth of pure entertainment. The last four years had proven Hollywood mattered—artistically, politically, culturally—and no one pretended otherwise, not even Hollywood.

A changing of the guard underscored the change in the role of movies in American culture. Since 1922, the official face of the motion picture industry had belonged to Will H. Hays, first president of the MPDDA, the cartel set up by the moguls in the wake of a wave of scandalous headlines (drug overdoses, rape allegations, and murder) that threated to derail the forward motion of a booming business. In the 1920s, moral degeneracy not Communist subversion was the menace thought to be emanating from Hollywood.

At ease on both Wall Street and Capitol Hill, Hays placed the industry on solid financial footing and secure political ground, cementing its ties to the high finance of the New York banks while keeping Washington regulators out of the picture. However, Hays's most ingenious contribution to the stability of Hollywood cinema was in the realm of moral policing. In 1934, he established the Production Code Administration (PCA), a branch of the MPPDA tasked with censoring (or "self-regulating") films during the process of production. To enforce the Production Code, the document that laid down the moral law, Hays appointed Joseph I. Breen, a no-nonsense, Jesuit-educated Irish Catholic. Breen took his assignment to clean up the movies as a solemn vocation. For the next twenty years, no Hollywood film was released without a thorough vetting from the Breen office.

Hays's service had been amply rewarded—he was the highest paid lobbyist in Washington, D.C.—but by 1945 he was a relic from the age of flivvers and flappers. With peace at hand, the industry anticipated a new world order with daunting economic challenges. It also confronted an audience, both at home and abroad, whose attitudes had been transformed by the war, who already seemed impatient with the old pieties and end-reel uplift.

Two very dark clouds also blackened the horizon. First, television, the medium dreaded since the 1930s, was ready to begin its broadcasting day. Hollywood's monopoly on screen entertainment was coming to an end.

Second, a final judgment was imminent in a government attack on Hollywood that was to prove far more lethal to the studio system than any body blow delivered by HUAC: the breakup of the vertically integrated monopoly forged by the major studios. Since the 1920s, the Big Five (MGM, Paramount, RKO, Warner Bros., and, after 1935, Twentieth Century-Fox) and the Little Three (Columbia, Universal, and United Artists) had held a vise-like grip on the means of motion picture production, distribution, and exhibition—a racket that assured a smooth pipeline of profit for the major studios while locking out independent producers from the cash flow.

The system was too crooked to remain forever unexamined by antitrust lawyers in FDR's Department of Justice. Beginning in July 1938, the federal government initiated a series of legal actions under the Sherman Anti-Trust Act to curtail the monopolistic practices. A decade-long pitched battle commenced, with the prosecutors attacking in fits and starts and the defendants maneuvering to delay the inevitable. Though Hollywood's legal experts fought tenaciously, they knew that so egregious a combination in restraint of trade would not long survive an impartial judicial review.

To navigate the treacherous postwar waters, the industry needed a new helmsman, skilled in public relations, modern business practices, and international trade.

The search for a successor to Hays settled on Eric Allen Johnston, president of the U.S. Chamber of Commerce, member of the War Mobilization and Reconversion Board, and failed contender for vice president on the 1944 Republican ticket. He was also, which didn't hurt, an Episcopalian with American roots stretching back to the Revolutionary War.

Born in 1895, reared in Spokane, WA, Johnston lived a classic Horatio Alger rags-to-respectability tale, right down to the early hardscrabble days as a newsboy hawking papers on the street. The literary motif continued into his higher education: while studying law at the University of Washington, he worked on weekends as a longshoreman on the Seattle docks. In 1917, upon American entry into the Great War, Johnston enlisted in the U.S. Marines. He missed combat on the killing fields of Europe, but served and traveled throughout China, Siberia, and Japan.

In 1922, mustered out and back stateside, Johnston sold and repaired vacuum cleaners, which led him into the electronics business, a high-return profit center in the Roaring Twenties. The role of a glad-handing front man suited him. When the stock market crashed in 1929, he not only survived but thrived in the bleakest of economic climates. By 1931, he was president of the Spokane Chamber of Commerce. An articulate and congenial public speaker, he presented a friendly face for the businessman in a decade with good reason to despise the type.

Beginning in 1942, upon his election as president of the U.S. Chamber of Commerce, Johnston traveled around the globe on behalf of American business—including a trip to Russia to praise our Soviet ally and inspect the industrial might developed under the latest five-year plan.[21] On the evening of June 26, 1944, accompanied by U.S. Ambassador Averell Harriman, he spent two and a half hours chatting with a jovial Joseph Stalin, who was decked out for the occasion in full military regalia. During the face-to-face, the official representative of American capitalism and the godhead of international Communism lauded each other's economic systems. So congenial was the mutual admiration that Stalin jokingly told Johnston, "*I'm* the capitalist; *you're* the Communist!"[22]

Johnston expanded on his meditations on a soon-to-be bipolar world in *America Unlimited*, published in 1944, a perfect title for an optimist who looked forward to the best years of the American century. Though the book did not mention the American motion picture industry once, the moguls knew star power when they saw it. Johnston was offered a sweet deal: a five-year contract at $150,000 a year plus $50,000 per annum in expenses.[23] A quick study, he readily adapted his Kiwanis-speak to the new assignment. "No means of communication carries as much influence as motion pictures," Johnston declared. "The industry is just now coming of age. It can exercise an even greater force and power in the postwar world."[24] The very model of the cordial, eloquent, enlightened American businessman, Hollywood's new representative seemed minted for the role.

On September 19, 1945, at 1:00 P.M., at a meeting of the MPPDA in New York, the baton was formally passed from Hays to Johnston. "I learned from personal experience that in many countries, the only America the people know is the America of the motion pictures," he said in a formal statement screened

In New York, outgoing MPPDA president Will H. Hays (*right*) poses with incoming MPAA president Eric A. Johnston (*left*), September 19, 1945.

in the newsreels. "We intend always to keep that in mind."[25] Concurrent with Johnston's appointment, the MPPDA changed its official designation to the Motion Picture Association of America (MPAA). The original name only gave more ammunition to the Department of Justice,

In confronting the challenges of the postwar world, the prospect of a congressional inquiry into Hollywood's earnestly patriotic films and profit-minded personnel might have seemed far down on the list of Hollywood's headaches. Who could seriously believe that a citadel of unbridled capitalism projecting a Roman Catholic catechism was, at heart, an outpost for Communist agents bent on destroying the system that had made its citizens rich?

Chapter 3

THE PRESERVATION OF AMERICAN IDEALS

D espite the "Americans All" ethos during World War II, not quite all ideological conflicts in Hollywood were put on hold for the duration. The high profile of the Hollywood Anti-Nazi League during the 1930s and the liberal outreach of the OWI, an agency packed with activists from the Screen Writers' Guild, might have made it seem as if only artists pledged to FDR—or to leaders further left—worked in the motion picture industry. Yet Hollywood was also home to a substantial hive of conservatives who dissented from the dominant left-of-centerism around town. Devout Catholics, conservative Jews, and frugal artists who resented the IRS siphoning off upward of 94 percent of their base salary beat against the progressive tide. The dissenters found the wide-eyed deification of Joseph Stalin in leftist circles particularly noxious. Backed by an influential scrum of gossip columnists, trade press reporters, and editors for the Hearst media syndicate, they formed a phalanx of right-wing reaction to left-wing activism that made any political point-counterpoint a battle of equals.

However, unlike the liberals, leftists, and Communists, who bonded around a bewildering array of political action committees, Hollywood conservatives had no league of their own—until the evening of February 4, 1944, when about two hundred writers, producers, directors, and industry personnel gathered at the Beverly Wilshire Hotel to oppose the prevailing liberalism, even unabashed pro-Sovietism, fostered by the OWI and underwritten by the SWG. The opposition force was called the Motion Picture Alliance for the Preservation of American Ideals, which made for a mouthful of an abbreviation: the MPA-PAI.

Producer-director Sam Wood was named president, with no fewer than three vice presidents at his side: animation king Walt Disney, costume designer Cedric Gibbons, and director Norman Taurog. Director Clarence Brown served as treasurer, Fox producer Louis D. Lighton as secretary, and MGM producer George Bruce as executive secretary. James K. McGuinness, veteran of the Screen Playwrights, Inc. and now story editor at MGM, assumed the role of chairman of an executive board packed with heavy hitters.[1]

The nation still being in the midst of World War II, the language of militarism came naturally to Wood in his inaugural address. "Highly indoctrinated shock units of the totalitarian wrecking crew have shrewdly led the people of the United States to believe that Hollywood is a hotbed of sedition and subversion, and that our industry is a battleground over which Communism is locked in death grips with Fascism," he declared. "In our special field of motion pictures, we resent the growing impression that this industry is made up of, and dominated by, Communists, radicals, and crack pots." Hollywood, Wood insisted, "is a reservoir of Americanism."[2]

The MPA-PAI became the chief opposition to Hollywood's left wing, whether liberal or Communist. The Communists called it the Motion Picture Alliance for the *Prevention* of American Ideals.[3]

Hedda Hopper: "Things I'd like to see: all our fellow travelers, who have such a passion for Russia, on a boat headin' in that direction."

Like the CPUSA, the MPA-PAI had its own cohort of fellow travelers, men and women whose fervent anti-Communism long predated the formation of an initialized organization. Two influential trade columnists and one powerful newspaper syndicate echoed and amplified Hollywood's anti-Communist chorus.

Among the opinion makers in Hollywood—the journalists, critics, and trade press reporters who covered the industry but were not, at least officially, on the studio payroll, who maintained a modicum of independence, and who were therefore listened to by the moguls as reliable gauges of the temperature of American moviegoers—none was more heeded than W. R. Wilkerson, the founding editor-publisher of the *Hollywood Reporter*, the six-days-a-week newspaper that provided gossip, reviews, analysis, and the inside-dopester lowdown for a film-minded demographic. Wilkerson—known universally if not always affectionately as Billy—presided from his front page "Tradeviews" perch, a must-read column where he advised and lectured the industry, sometimes like an amiable colleague, sometimes like a stern coach.

Launched in the inauspicious year of 1930, the *Hollywood Reporter* quickly established itself as a flagship trade paper in the company town. If *Variety* was the industry's bible, the *Hollywood Reporter* was the prayer book, close at hand, in the vest pocket. Unlike *Variety*, however, whose vaguely progressive outlook was subordinated to an obsession with box office tabulations, the *Hollywood Reporter* was infused with a deep-dyed political animus. Wilkerson was an early, vociferous, and relentless critic of Communist influence in Hollywood. Though he held HUAC in contempt for its willful ignorance of the workings of the studio system, he believed that both as a matter of patriotic vigilance and sound business practice the industry needed to purge its ranks of known Communists and lockstep fellow travelers. Otherwise, the poisonous fallout from the linkage between Hollywood and Communism would kill all the goodwill the industry had accrued from its admirable war record.

For Wilkerson, the SWG was the point of the Communist spear, an outfit always ready to cast "another vote for Stalin" and "take its orders from Moscow."[4] In August 1946, in a blistering barrage of front-page exposés, Wilkerson got specific, naming names and attaching them to Communist party cards. How Wilkerson obtained the cards remains a matter of conjecture: perhaps directly from the man with whom he was on intimate terms, FBI chief J. Edgar Hoover.

Screenwriter Lester Cole was the first Hollywood artist to see his name in print with a direct accusation disguised as a question. "Are you a Communist? Do you hold card number 46805 in what is known as the Northwest Section of the Communist party, a division of the party made up mostly of West Coast Commies?" demanded Wilkerson.[5] In the days that followed, Wilkerson accused ten other screenwriters of doubling as "Hollywood's Red Commissars": John Howard Lawson, Emmet Lavery, Oliver H. P. Garrett, Harold Buchman, Maurice Rapf, William Pomerance, Dalton Trumbo, Gordon Kahn, Ring Lardner Jr., and Richard Collins.[6] He provided the CPUSA card numbers for Buchman, Rapf, Trumbo, Kahn, Lardner, and Collins. An exasperated SWG spokesman could only respond that the *Hollywood Reporter* saw a "commie behind every typewriter in Hollywood."[7]

Wilkerson's main competition as an anti-Communist working the Hollywood beat was Hedda Hopper–née Elda Furry, a butcher's daughter from Hollidaysburg, PA.[8] In 1936, the former chorus girl and subaltern actress parlayed her fading screen career into a job in journalism as a top-billed gossip columnist. She proved more adept at writing her own copy than reciting the lines of others. Her only rival as a dirt-dishing diva was Louella Parsons, the Hearst syndicate's conduit to the stars, who tended not to dilute her gossip with political commentary.

Syndicated from her home base at the *Los Angeles Times*, Hopper's column was read—or scanned—by an estimated audience of 35 million. Radio shows like *The Hedda Hopper Show* and *This Is Hollywood*, augmented by frequent hosting gigs and guest appearances, solidified her eminence. As famous as the stars she yammered about, she cultivated an elegant and busybody-ish persona, not too far off the mark from her real self. Modeling the outlandish millinery that was her visual signature, she flaunted her proximity to celebrity with nonstop name-dropping ("David Niven, dining at my house the other night, told me . . .").[9] By 1947, Hopper had accumulated a decade of IOUs and a spider's web of you-scratch-my-back-and-I'll-scratch-yours tipsters.

Hopper waited for V-J Day to fire off her heavy artillery on Hollywood Reds and fellow travelers. "Things I'd like to see," she mused in 1946, "all our fellow travelers, who have such a passion for Russia, on a boat headin' in that direction."[10] Or: "Why are our top studios still hiring writers, directors, and actors whom they know to be definitely on the red side? Well, this would be a good time to take on some fresh faces as well as minds who still have American ideals and think our way of life superior to that under a dictator like Stalin."[11]

Wilkerson and Hopper were known bylines, one with a local, the other a national readership, but their influence paled beside the high circulation impact of the press syndicate and newspaper chain presided over by media mogul William Randolph Hearst. Though much shrunken since the 1930s, the reach of the Hearst empire in 1947 stretched out to seventeen newspapers, four radio stations, and nine magazines.[12] Year in, year out, the Hearst press scorched and burned the red backside of Hollywood with screaming headlines, editorial opprobrium, scarifying cartooning, and multi-part exposés. The International News Service, the Hearst-owned wire service, transmitted the coverage to dailies from coast to coast with billboard-sized headlines tracing the connect-the-dots links between Hollywood big shots and Communist lowlifes. Louder and more incessantly than even HUAC— as the *Screen Writer* complained in 1946—"the Hearst press have cried 'Red! Red! Red!'"[13]

Herbert K. Sorrell: "Willie Bioff tried that, and Willie isn't with us any more."

Cries of "Red! Red! Red!" also greeted the strikers who began to gather outside the studio gates as the war wound down. Now under the dynamic leadership of the two-fisted Herbert K. Sorrell, the Conference of Studio Unions did not wait for a formal end of hostilities in Europe to reignite its campaign against the major studios and the labor unions that served the moguls more than the rank and file.

No sooner was peace glimpsed on the horizon than, as *Motion Picture Daily* phrased it, "labor rumblings" began to add "a fuzzy tone to the otherwise euphonious film industry sound track."[14] What had always been, at least compared to other industrial workplaces, a relatively placid shop floor (the mob had seen to that) was roiled by dissension. After a decade of scarcity followed by wartime sacrifice, below-the-line workers demanded a bigger slice of the pie from an industry flush with profits.

On March 12, 1945, some six months prior to V-J Day, CSU went on strike. In what would be the persistent and corrosive point of contention, the catalyst was a jurisdictional dispute over which union should represent the stagehands, in this case the set decorators: CSU, which had been recognized as the bargaining agent by the War Labor Relations Board pending a final decision by the NLRB, or IATSE, which staked out a proprietary claim to motion picture workers on the basis of its 1937 agreement with the major studios. The clash was not only between labor and management but between two wings of the American labor movement, the accommodationist and the activist.

Sorrell faced a worthy opponent. The same month the strike erupted, Roy M. Brewer was appointed international representative for IATSE. Nebraska born and prairie tempered, Brewer had started in the motion picture business at age twelve as a rewind boy in the projection booth of his small-town theater. Moving up the ranks to projectionist, he organized his fellow booth men and learned to apply the leverage gained from hands-on control of the exhibition end of the business. By 1933, at age twenty-three, he was president of the Nebraska State Federation of Labor, making him the youngest head of a major union in the nation. Campaigning for Sen. George W. Norris, Nebraska's legendary progressive Republican, he got an education in the trench warfare of electoral politics. He earned $125 a week from his position with IATSE and, compared to Willie Bioff and George Browne, he was squeaky clean.[15]

Unlike his predecessors, and indeed IATSE president Richard F. Walsh, an electrician by trade who was first elected in 1941 and served in the position until 1974 without getting indicted, Brewer was dedicated to the removal of what he saw as a cancer eating into the sinews of American labor. If unchecked, "the nefarious efforts to subvert our labor organizations to a political program that is inconsistent with the fundamental principles on which the American labor movement was founded" would destroy "the real liberal movement in America."[16]

With two wings of the American labor movement—the conservative IATSE, with some twenty-three thousand workers, and the radical CSU, with some seven thousand workers—competing for the same turf, the result was predictable. From 1945 to 1947, the two unions engaged in an ugly series of jurisdictional battles over control of the Hollywood working class, all the nastier because it was intramural. When IATSE tried to undercut CSU by issuing union cards for additional painters, machinists, and electricians, Sorrell snarled, "Willie Bioff tried that, and Willie isn't with us any more."[17]

Months of picketing and work stoppages threw the studios into turmoil. Still, production crept along on the strength of non-striking IATSE members and what the studios called "replacement workers" and CSU called "scabs."

On October 5, 1945, at 5:30 in the morning, in an all-out effort to shut down production, Sorrell's foot soldiers concentrated their forces on Warner Bros., whose Burbank lot looked most vulnerable to a blockade. In the 1930s, the socially conscious programming and stalwart anti-Nazism of Warner Bros. had earned the studio the reputation of being the lone progressive island in a reactionary archipelago. When besieged literally at the gates, however, Jack Warner treated the strikers pretty much the way a nineteenth-century robber baron would have: he unleashed the private guards and called in the cops.[18]

With the melee outside spiraling out of control—fifty injured, forty arrested, including Sorrell—the studio was forced to shut down production for half a day.[19] Both sides cried foul, both claimed self-defense, and both gave as good as they got. For management and labor alike, the blood-spattered date would be remembered as Black Friday.

Despite restraining orders limiting the number of pickets, disruptions and violence continued for months. Brewer accused Sorrell of inciting "a labor civil war," something that was "typical Communist tactics."[20] CSU accused IATSE workers of charging the CSU picket lines. Goon squads from both sides roamed the streets. Sorrell got death threats; Brewer sent his daughter to school with a bodyguard.[21]

For newly elected MPAA president Eric Johnston the strike was a cold-water immersion into an industry whose glamorous front concealed a bare-knuckled underside. He stepped up to play peacemaker and

MPAA president Eric Johnston (*center*) tries to bring together the warring labor factions represented by Herbert K. Sorrell (*left*), leader of the Conference of Studio Unions, and Roy M. Brewer (*right*), international representative of the International Association of Theatrical Stage Employees, October 16, 1945.

honest broker. Representing the producers and the Good of the Industry, Johnston jawboned both union factions *and* the American Federation of Labor (AFL), to which IATSE and CSU were both signatories. By autumn, he had helped hammer out the outlines of a settlement.

On October 24, 1945, after eight months of picketing and hundreds of injuries and arrests, the AFL ordered both unions back to work. CSU could claim a measure of victory: it was recognized as the exclusive bargaining agent for the set decorators while IATSE's substitute workers/scabs were cashiered with severance pay. The AFL directive was a "complete vindication and victory," crowed Sorrell, who lorded his aggressive trade unionism over IATSE's cozy "non-striking alliance which is more on the line of a company-dominated union."[22]

How close the strike had come to lethal violence was underscored the week after the AFL directive. As Sorrell was exiting the driveway of his home in Glendale, a black Packard raced by and fired three shots into his car. The bullets missed his head by inches.[23]

Though—unlike Sorrell—never at personal risk, Johnston had survived his first trial by fire. Whether Johnston's efforts were "instrumental or incidental, the outcome has added greatly to his prestige in the industry," judged *Motion Picture Daily*. Upon news of the settlement, Johnston issued a public statement that was equal measure sigh of relief and wishful thinking. The AFL agreement "provides the basis for labor peace in the industry," he declared. "We hope to make the labor relations in the industry the best of any in the world."[24] With good reason to be optimistic, Johnston looked forward to "an era of labor peace."[25]

Pat Casey: "Your unions are engaging in coercive mass picketing in direct violation of law and court orders."

Eric Johnston's hoped-for era of labor peace was short lived. On September 26, 1946, a second CSU-orchestrated strike, this time started by the painters and carpenters, rocked the industry. In solidarity, electricians, set decorators, and cartoonists also struck and set up picket lines. True to its roots, IATSE aligned itself with management.[26] In time, the long-running strike would be deemed the "bitterest labor fight in Hollywood annals" by *Daily Variety*.[27]

To bring the studios to their knees, CSU targeted Warner Bros. and MGM.[28] Sorrell ignored court orders, took arrests and jail time in stride, and rallied his troops with incendiary speeches and manifestos published in the trade press.

Having thought the jurisdictional battles settled, Johnston and the studio executives were livid at the return of their labor woes. "[The] strike is being conducted in such flagrant violation of the laws of our land that it borders on anarchy," declared Pat Casey, chairman of the Producers Labor Committee. An ex-vaudeville showman and legendary behind-the-scenes fixer, Casey had handled labor negotiations for the moguls since 1926, but he had seen nothing like the present state of siege.[29] "Our employees are being beaten, their homes are being bombed, and your unions are engaging in coercive mass picketing in direct violation of law and court orders," he wailed at Sorrell.[30]

No longer pretending to be an honest broker, Johnston now stood squarely on IATSE's side of the picket line. "The jurisdictional strike has done more to hurt the cause of labor than any other single thing," he told the IATSE membership at the height of the conflict. "It cannot be defended on any grounds at all. It is without justification."[31] CSU faced three united opponents: the MPAA, the Producers Labor Committee, and IATSE.

As usual, Sorrell was not giving an inch. "Johnston wants federal laws passed to make slaves out of members of our free, democratic and autonomous unions," he said. "At the same time he wants to provide protection for his company maintained unions." The federal law Sorrell had in mind was the Taft-Hartley Act, then winding its way through Congress despite fierce opposition from President Truman and the Democrats. The legislation was crafted to limit radical labor tactics by neutering radical labor leaders like Herbert Sorrell.

An incident straight out of a Warner Bros. gangster film showed how high the stakes had become. On Sunday evening, March 2, 1947, while on route to the weekly CSU meeting, Sorrell was abducted by three assailants, one of whom was dressed as a police officer. He was handcuffed, pistol whipped, knocked unconscious, and bundled into a sedan that screeched off into the night. The thugs dumped Sorrell in a remote spot in the Mojave Desert, fired three shots at him as they sped away, and left him by the side of the road—battered, bloody, and bound head to foot. A spokesman for CSU laid the violence done Sorrell "directly at the door of the conspiracy between the producers and the racketeer labor leaders in Hollywood."[32]

By the next Sunday night, the resilient Sorrell was back in action, exhorting his troops at a comeback rally, beaten but unbroken.

On March 4, 1947, two days after the near-hit on Sorrell, Eric Johnston appeared before the House Labor and Education Committee in Washington, D.C. The MPAA president's first appearance before a congressional committee that year was to explain un-American activities in the industrial infrastructure—not the ideological superstructure—of Hollywood cinema.

For three hours, Johnston was grilled about the CSU strike, then in its seventh acrimonious month. He blamed Communist agitation for preventing a resolution. "Their tactics seem to aim at slowing down production," he said, making certain to assure Congress that however disruptive the Communists might be on the shop floor, they had never infiltrated the motion picture screen. "None of their influence or ideals get into pictures and only a few of them are in minor positions and not connected with the preparation of film scripts."[33]

The leftward tilt of American labor would soon be righted by congressional action. On June 23, 1947, over the veto of President Truman, Congress passed the Taft-Hartley Act, the most significant change in the federal oversight of organized labor since the New Deal. But where the New Deal had expanded the rights of American labor, Taft-Hartley restricted them. The act prohibited just the kind of jurisdictional strikes that had bedeviled the studios since 1945 and empowered the NLRB to order the strikers back to work. The most coercive provision of the law denied bargaining authority to unions whose leaders might "reasonably be regarded" as Communist or Communist sympathizers.[34] To avoid being so regarded, union leaders had to sign affidavits or loyalty oaths denying Communist sympathies or associations.

The Taft-Hartley Act struck at the heart of the IATSE-CSU dispute: it was a jurisdictional strike and it was spearheaded by a union leader who might "reasonably be regarded" as a Communist. The act gave a steel-tipped bludgeon to the federal government to force a settlement to the advantage of IATSE.

Armed with Taft-Hartley, and not averse to a junket out of Washington, a delegation from Congress decided to look into the situation on the ground. On August 4, 1947, a subcommittee of the House Labor Committee chaired by Carroll D. Kearns (R-PA) convened in Hollywood to hear testimony into the IATSE-CSU confrontation. A freshman in the newly elected Republican majority in Congress, Kearns had a propriety interest in the performing arts: he was a trained singer, former soloist with the Chicago Opera Company, and paid-up union member in the American Federation of Musicians. Kearns's on-location hearings promised to deliver "intrigue, argument, and violence," blurbed *Motion Picture Herald*, as if promoting a thriller. "The subcommittee is investigating labor practices and in Hollywood it is striking gold."[35] By "gold" it meant "red."

On August 21, 1947, Chairman Kearns got an up-close look at the level of visceral hatred between the two unions during a tour of the MGM lot with Sorrell and IATSE business agent B. C. "Cappy" Duval. While walking through the soundstages, his companions cursed at each other and nearly came to blows. On two occasions, the congressman had to physically pull the men apart.[36] *Daily Variety* passed on an expurgated blow-by-blow:

> "You're a lying so-and-so!" roared Sorrell, his fists clenched.
> "We'll have none of that!" ordered Kearns, stepping between [Duval and Sorrell].

The situation simmered down briefly until Sorrell, addressing Kearns, spotted three IATSE carpenters working on a flight of stairs and referred to them as "scabs." Duval moved menacingly into Sorrel's personal space.

> "I'll knock you on your *** if you interfere with me!" shouted Sorrell, cocking his fist.
> "You'll knock nobody on their ***!" snarled Duval.

Again playing referee, Kearns came between the men before any punches were thrown.

The rest of the tour was a tense standoff with each man claiming that *his* union represented whatever workers the entourage encountered. The mood lightened only when the group walked on to the set of MGM's aquatic musical *On an Island with You* (1948), featuring amphibian star Esther Williams and a bevy of scantily clad water ballerinas, who gave a special performance for the visitors. "Nobody yelled 'This job is ours!' during the show," grinned *Daily Variety*.[37]

Bathing beauties notwithstanding, to say the jurisdictional battles between IATSE and CSU left bad blood doesn't quite capture the level of acrimony: members of the rival unions wanted to strangle each other with their bare hands.

Chapter 4

THE MAGIC OF A HOLLYWOOD DATELINE

T he elections of 1946 brought about a political sea change: for the first time in fourteen years, the Republicans had control of Congress and a fresh roster of committee chairmen, ready to take the reins after a long stretch in the wilderness, stepped forward to undo the legacy of FDR. For the newly empowered Republicans, under Speaker of the House John W. Martin (R-MA), the decision to re-animate HUAC was as obvious as the choice of chairman: its longest serving and most media-minded member, Rep. J. Parnell Thomas.

Born in 1895 in Jersey City, New Jersey, the first son of an old-school Irish-Catholic pol, Thomas was a Wall Street bond salesman and investor who in 1925 transitioned to the no less lucrative field of public service as practiced across the Hudson. In 1926, he was elected mayor of Allendale; in 1930, he circled back to Wall Street; and in 1935 he returned to Jersey-style politics as a member of the New Jersey General Assembly. The next year, having earned a reputation as a Republican Party regular, the businessman-politician was elected to the House of Representatives from the seventh district of New Jersey.

Once sworn in, Thomas angled to get on the Dies Committee, cozied up to the chairman, and made uprooting Communism in the arts his bailiwick. In 1939, Dies rewarded Thomas with a plum assignment, appointing him chair of a series of New York-based hearings into the pro-New Deal and often pro-Communist productions of the Federal Theater Project. The revelations led to the elimination of the subsidy for FDR's theatrical agit-prop from the federal budget that year.[1]

For critics, the fact that Thomas had changed his name (from Feeney to Thomas) and religion (from Irish Catholic to Episcopalian) was evidence aplenty of his naked careerism and low character: they referred to him as "J. Parnell Thomas nee Feeney" to remind voters of the upwardly mobile apostasy of the formerly right-handed Irishman. Fifty-three years old at the time of the 1947 hearings, Thomas was a natty dresser, well-groomed and well-scented, though his appearance was not imposing. "He is a stubby, balding man with a round florid face," read the unvarnished portrait in *Motion Picture Herald*.[2] Ironically, shades of red would define the color scheme of his chairmanship: flush-faced fury, a ruddy complexion, and veins bulging in anger, as if he were on the verge of bursting a blood vessel from beating against the currents of the red tide. His enemies assumed the anti-Communist lather he worked himself into was cynical playacting. "I'm going places now that I'm chairman of the House Committee on Un-American Activities," an unflattering profile in *PM* quoted him confiding to a friend. "Going after Reds is going to make me."[3]

Thomas's right-hand man and attack dog was another veteran of the Dies Committee, Robert E. Stripling. In 1932, Dies had offered Stripling, a student at the University of Texas, a patronage job at $120 a month in the cloak room of the old House Office Building, not bad terms for the times. While attending night school, he made himself indispensable to Dies, an old friend of the family, hence the patronage job. In 1938, when Dies got authorization for HUAC, Stripling offered to serve without pay as committee secretary. Soon he was earning a salary as HUAC's chief counsel and principle interrogator. For Stripling, Communism was a "cancerous growth" operating "astutely within the texture of our Constitution and the resilient borders of our native tolerance."[4] For the next ten years, except for an interregnum in the army during World War II, he dedicated himself to its surgical removal. His friends called him Strip.

With Thomas as chair and the notorious John Rankin as the ranking Democrat, the rest of the committee was relegated to the role of background extras. In terms of the Hollywood-minded hearings mounted by Thomas, John S. Wood (D-GA), the once and future HUAC chair, was mainly missing in action, dropping in and out and, finally, out. John McDowell (R-PA) and Richard B. Vall (D-IL), undistinguished backbenchers who attended most of

HUAC Chairman J. Parnell Thomas (*right*) and committee counsel Robert E. Stripling (*left*) examine celluloid evidence of Communist "boring from within," May 28, 1947.

the sessions, were dutiful and forgettable. Karl E. Mundt (R-SD), J. Hardin Peterson (D-FL), and Herbert C. Bonner (D-NC) were total no-shows.*

The last member of the committee, the freshman congressman from the twelfth district of California, might not have been picked from the line up as the most likely to succeed, but he proved the only star to emerge from the humdrum supporting cast. Richard M. Nixon (R-CA), a thirty-four-year-old Navy veteran and lawyer, aspired "to win recognition as a 'movie expert' because of his California background," opined the *People's Daily World*, the Los Angeles-based paper of record for the CPUSA, little knowing how often it would have occasion to typeset the name. "He demands that films show 'the evils of communism.'"[5] Nixon believed that the authentic fifth columnists in the motion picture industry would hide behind the First Amendment,

---

* Both Wood and Mundt would have their own moments in the postwar anti-Communist limelight: Wood as chair of HUAC in 1949–1953 and Mundt as chair of the Senate Permanent Subcommittee on Investigations during the televised Army-McCarthy hearings of 1954.

but that the rest of the accused were garden-variety bleeding heart liberals "tinged with pink" rather than the "bright red" of the Communist Party.[6]

At full strength, the HUAC staff was composed of ten men and thirty women, the latter mostly secretaries and stenographers. "Although there was considerable jealously among the ten men, the 30 girls worked in harmony and we seldom had any trouble with them," Thomas recalled. He took pride in the multicultural spectrum represented by his employees. "I did not care whether a person was a Republican or a Democrat, black or white, Jew or Christian—all I wanted was results," Thomas averred, boasting that his was "the only committee staff on Capitol Hill that had Jews and Christians, blacks and whites employed." Not all his colleagues were as open minded. "Our Negro staffer, Alvin Stokes, was a sincere, extremely loyal, always fine worker," Thomas noted. "He was, however, never popular with the dyed-in-the-wool Southerners on the team."[7]

Once manned and empowered, the Thomas version of HUAC hit the ground running. On January 22, 1947, two days after the swearing in of the Eightieth Congress, the committee met for the first time and voted to give a "good airing" to "Communist influences" in Hollywood. "I intend to make it the most active year in the committee's history," Thomas vowed, which in Hollywood sounded like a threat. "Before 1947 is finished, we hope to make disclosures which will astonish the nation."[8]

To cries of "witch hunt," the committee said it was but heeding the will of the people. Rankin claimed to have a list of "thousands of names" of Californians who demanded that a probe of Communism in Hollywood "head the list" of HUAC priorities.[9] "Let the chips fall where they may," Thomas said in a gesture to fair play, tossing off an alliterative quip. "It doesn't make any difference whether they fall on Columbians, or the Ku Klux Klan, or the Communists."[10]

Of course, no Columbians or Klansmen were on the studio payrolls.

J. Edgar Hoover: "Communist activity in Hollywood is effective."

On March 24, 1947, the curtain opened on a teaser for the most Hollywood-centric season in HUAC history. Though not exclusively concerned with Communism in the motion picture industry, the five days of hearings set the rules of engagement for a decade-long struggle between Washington and Hollywood.

The most important witness to be called was not a Hollywood star; he was bigger: J. Edgar Hoover, director of the Federal Bureau of Investigation.

Inseparable from the federal law enforcement agency built in his image, abetted by a lapdog media eager to print, broadcast, and project his legend, Hoover was at the zenith of a power that was as close to absolute as any unelected official in American history. The "nation's number one G-man" was serenely incorruptible, briskly efficient, and eternally vigilant, a button-down constable who burned the night oil running gangsters and kidnappers to ground. He took grim satisfaction in scratching the bad guys off a most-wanted list and measuring crime statistics with mathematical precision. Hoover's FBI was always more about data than gunplay.

The FBI racked up its most impressive statistic during the late war when not a single act of domestic sabotage by either the Germans or the Japanese disrupted the domestic tranquility. As the all-seeing guardian of the homeland, Hoover grew in stature even as the tentacles of his domestic intelligence apparatus spread to meet the wartime emergency. Virtually all of the suspected Communists in Hollywood already had bulging FBI files that would expand exponentially as the Cold War dragged on, the result of tens of thousands of federal man hours spent shadowing their activities, culling their press clippings, and bugging their telephones. By 1947, and throughout most of the next quarter century, Hoover was untouchable, a revered public servant whom few dared cross. When he spoke, it mattered; when he sent out a warning, Americans listened.

On March 26, 1947, in testimony before what was now known as the Thomas Committee, Hoover told a disquieting tale. In 1935, word had gone out from Moscow for American Communists to launch a "furtive drive on Hollywood" that called for collective action on two fronts: "to infiltrate the labor unions and to infiltrate the so-called intellectual and creative fields." The dual focus—on the workers who built the sets and the idea men who drew up the blueprints—neatly paralleled the distribution of labor in the Hollywood production plant. "Communist activity in Hollywood is effective," warned Hoover. "The party is content and highly pleased if it is possible to have inserted in a picture a line, a scene, a sequence, conveying the Communist lesson, and, more particularly, if they can keep out anti-Communist lessons."[11] Hoover did not name names, but he did, under questioning, name

FBI head J. Edgar Hoover tells HUAC that Communists have infiltrated both the Hollywood labor unions and the creative fields, March 26, 1947.

a film that parroted the Communist line. *Mission to Moscow* (1943), he said, "was a prostitution of historical facts."[12]

Hoover's seal of approval on HUAC's work—his assertion that Communism had been seeded in Hollywood and needed uprooting—was a crucial validation. With Hoover in his corner, Thomas had secured the only endorsement that really mattered. Moreover, by emphasizing how Hollywood Communists worked to keep *anti*-Communist plots and dialogue off the screen, Hoover signaled that HUAC might also indict the studios for sins of cinematic omission as well as commission.

Following Hoover was a myrmidon in spirit, California State Sen. Jack B. Tenney, who chaired a Golden State version of HUAC in the California legislature, the Joint Committee on Un-American Activities. In certain quarters of the motion picture industry, the Tenney Committee was as despised as the Thomas Committee.

Unlike the men of HUAC, Tenney boasted a background in the entertainment business. A former president of the Los Angeles branch of the American Federation of Musicians, he was in such good standing as a progressive union leader that in 1938 he was named as a Communist before the Dies Committee. Elected in 1936 to the California State Assembly as a liberal Democrat, he exposed Willie Bioff's racketeering in IATSE and investigated pre-war Nazi agitation in and around Los Angeles, a hotbed of activity for the German American Bund, the Silver Shirts, and sundry Jew-baiting vigilantes. In 1942, he transferred allegiance to the Republican Party and made Communist hunting his legislative priority. Prior to discovering the Communist menace in Hollywood, Tenney was best known for composing the pop standard "Mexicali Rose."

Tenney repeated his alarums about Communism in Hollywood in his testimony before the parent HUAC. Unlike the circumspect Hoover, he got specific by naming marquee names. Charles Chaplin and John Garfield were fellow travelers and Fredric March and Frank Sinatra were dupes active in Communist front groups.[13]

The next day MPAA president Eric Johnston, in the first of his two appearances before HUAC that year, stepped forward to defend the industry and, as an impressed *Daily Variety* reported, "hit back at FBI chief J. Edgar Hoover."[14] Johnston pointed out that the best proof of the all-American spirit in Hollywood was the fact that Hollywood films were blocked from import by the Soviet Union—and with good reason. "American films give the lie by visual evidence to totalitarian propaganda," said Johnston. No wonder "the Communists hate and fear American motion pictures. It is their No. 1 hate." Sure, there were "undoubtedly" Communists in Hollywood, but the tiny minority exerted no influence over film content.[15] Anyone could see that.

Recalling Hoover's point about the paucity of anti-Communist scenarios in Hollywood's programming, Nixon asked Johnston if the studios had made any anti-Communist pictures along the lines of the anti-Nazi pictures the studios had produced before and during World War II.

Johnston drew a blank. He sheepishly admitted none came to mind, but he assured Nixon that an example would be forthcoming. Afterward, trade press reporters with better memories upbraided the MPAA president for not being film-smart enough to mention Ernst Lubitsch's romantic comedy *Ninotchka* (1939), in which Greta Garbo plays a stiff-necked Soviet commissar loosened up by the champagne and chapeaux of Paris, or *Comrade X* (1940), King Vidor's pallid attempt to imitate the Lubitsch touch.* Johnston also confessed he had never seen *Mission to Moscow*.

However, Johnston's most serious blunder was to disagree with the opinion of the reigning authority on the topic at hand:

> I wish now to comment on an observation made before this committee yesterday by Mr. J. Edgar Hoover, Director of the Federal Bureau of Investigation. He described how the Communists have reached out to employ the radio and the motion picture in their propaganda activities. Mr. Hoover said that several years ago the Communist underground directed its agents, in effect, to infiltrate Hollywood and do everything possible to poison the screen.
>
> But if the Communists set out to capture Hollywood, they have suffered an overwhelming defeat.[16]

Johnston's uppity dissent did not sit well with the FBI director.

Nor was the irascible Rankin impressed with the blithe assurances from Hollywood's glib frontman. Unless Hollywood cleaned house—both below and above the line, in the unions and up on the screen—Congress would take matters into its own hands and force a "purge" by legislative fiat.[17] Rankin's rebuke was the first outright threat of retaliation against Hollywood from an official of the U.S. government.

"I do not think we are ready yet for concentration camps in America," Johnston shot back. "A man has a right to make a living."[18]

Thomas was no more mollified by the MPAA president than Rankin. "I was disappointed in Johnston's whole testimony," he said, deploring the admission that Communists existed in Hollywood "but that the industry had done nothing to eradicate them." Johnston's testimony was "one naïve statement after another."[19] Thomas was also disturbed that Hollywood had failed to bankroll a single anti-Communist picture. How passionate could the motion picture industry be about anti-Communism if it had not drafted its flagship product into the fight?

---

* In 1941, Nicholas M. Schenck had been more quick-witted before the Senate Committee on War Propaganda. Asked to name an anti-Communist picture, he immediately mentioned *Ninotchka*. Garbo fan Senator Charles Tobey (R-NH) chimed in, "that was a corking good picture!"

Nixon seconded Thomas's call for Hollywood to join the battle with a slate of anti-Communist pictures, but demurred about the need for a full-dress investigation into the industry. "There are more important places to direct our immediate fire," he said. "First, the government, and second, the labor unions."[20]

Heretofore, Hollywood had won all of its face-to-face confrontations with the amateur actors on Capitol Hill, but the hangover from the bout in March left a queasy feeling around town. "Thomas and his committee were not pleased with Eric Johnston's effort to whitewash the picture business," wrote Billy Wilkerson, eyeing the storm clouds from his desk at the *Hollywood Reporter*. "They laughed at his statements, intimating that there is no Communistic infiltration here, when everybody knows, or should know and can know, that our studio payrolls are loaded with Reds and their sympathizers."[21]

Roy M. Brewer also seized the chance to stick the knife in. The on-site representative of IATSE wanted it known that *his* union was the moderate, pro-business partner in the capitalist enterprise, that it was the radical, Communist-infiltrated CSU that incited disruptive strikes and manned violent picket lines. Accusing Johnston of being part ostrich, part dodo bird, Brewer called on the MPAA to "stop burying its head in the sand and look at the facts"—namely that Communists had made serious inroads in Hollywood and Hollywood was rewarding the traitors with fat paychecks.[22]

Sensing that fences needed to be mended, Johnston phoned the FBI to ask Hoover to lunch "some noon at your convenience . . . to discuss with you the whole problem of Communism in Hollywood and the motion picture industry." The call was taken by a Hoover aide who passed the invitation on to the director. The FBI head curtly rebuffed the MPAA head. "It would have been much better if he had gotten his facts first before popping off as he did at this Congressional hearing," Hoover scrawled on the aide's memo. "He has one view and I another and oil and water don't mix." Johnston tried again to make amends, repeating his invitation, and Hoover snubbed him again. "I don't intend to meet him," he wrote, leaving his aide the task of brushing off Johnston. "He pops off and deprecates Communism in films and now he wants my advice."[23]

Tangible proof of how seriously Johnston and the moguls took the threat from HUAC was not long in coming. Plans for an anti-Communist thriller were announced within days of the pointed questioning from Nixon and Thomas. On April 9, 1947, "inspired by J. Edgar Hoover's recent report to the Un-American Activities Committee," Twentieth Century-Fox chief Darryl F. Zanuck sent out a press release trumpeting the production of a semi-documentary film to be titled *The Iron Curtain*. It would be a ripped-from-the-headlines exposé of attempts by Soviet agents in the U.S. and Canada to subvert North America culture. Zanuck promised to supervise the picture personally.

Commenting on the first—but not the last—motion picture he inspired, Nixon expressed satisfaction. "I am greatly pleased to learn that one of the major studios is planning to produce a film based on the dangers of Communism and more particularly on the insidious infiltration of this revolutionary philosophy into the every-day lives of Americans."[24]

More tribute from Hollywood would soon be offered up.

Victor Kravchenko: "More than anything else, the Soviet fears the making of a film that portrays truthfully, in every detail, the conditions in Russia today."

From the moment Chairman Thomas was first given a gavel by the Eightieth Congress, he had promised a grand hearing into Communist penetration of the motion picture industry. Washington would provide the location, Hollywood the cast.

First, however, the groundwork had to be laid. For seven days, beginning on May 9, 1947, as if trying out a show on the road before opening on Broadway, a subcommittee of HUAC convened in Los Angeles for a run-through. As a preview of the dramaturgy to come, the session was not quite a full dress rehearsal—more like a first reading of the script to acquaint the actors with the dialogue and plot. It was a closed set, held behind locked doors, by invitation only.

Advance men had come to town to prepare the way. "FBI agents are busy combing Hollywood highways and byways relaying evidence for the forthcoming Congressional hearings but they are not paying much attention to the stars, directors, or other biggies," whispered *Daily Variety*, ear close to the ground. "It's those little anonymous characters who have been infiltrating key unions in the industry for the last half dozen years and you'd be surprised to hear how hard it is to locate them now. Most of them have gone back into the woodwork."[25]

The gossip was only half right: it was not just "those little anonymous characters" but the big famous characters who were being interviewed. Moreover, the FBI agents combing through the highways and byways were not always FBI agents; three of the investigators were dispatched by HUAC.

Daily Variety's confusion was understandable. To gain credibility and borrow an aura, HUAC hired ex-FBI agents to do its legwork, men whose manners and methods were indistinguishable from their former colleagues and who were often conflated with them. The distinction was sometimes lost on the press and anyone on the receiving end of a visit. To the people being interrogated and investigated, the polite, just-the-facts-ma'am men in off-the-rack suits and brown shoes, all came clothed in the vestments of the federal government.

Moreover, in 1947, an unusual overlap occurred between HUAC and the FBI. Though the FBI had kept a file on Hollywood and the CPUSA since 1942 indexed as "Communist Infiltration—Motion Picture Industry" (COMPIC), Hoover maintained a firewall between his executive branch men and the legislative branch investigators. Protective of his turf, he balked at sharing information.

Yet so urgent was the present emergency that Hoover permitted a departure from longstanding FBI practice. When Thomas came to Hollywood, he contacted Richard B. Hood, the special agent in charge of the FBI's Los Angeles field office, and requested assistance. Hoover, uncharacteristically, told Hood to channel information to HUAC, but with the stipulation that the FBI's sub rosa assistance be kept strictly confidential. "Expedite," Hoover wrote at the bottom of Hood's letter of inquiry, italicizing his order. "I want Hood to extend *every* assistance to this committee."[26]

Knowing the law enforcement hierarchy, Thomas's men—head investigator Louis J. Russell, who had made a previous site visit in summer 1945 for John Rankin, and the two-man road team of H. A. Smith and A. B. Leckie, both former FBI men—checked in regularly with the FBI. In turn, the FBI shared information with the HUAC men—but always on the QT. "Such material is furnished strictly for their confidential information and with the understanding that under no circumstances will the source of this material ever be disclosed," Hoover told Hood.[27]

Sometimes too, both sets of investigators fed information to favored journalists and informants. The former published specific and incriminating evidence on alleged Communist artists in Hollywood; the latter came before HUAC well briefed, supporting documents in hand. Not until decades later would Freedom of Information Act requests reveal the extent of the interlocking networks—if not always the identities, still redacted well into the next century, of the loquacious moguls, stars, screenwriters, journalists, and union leaders who, assured of confidentiality, free-associated about their colleagues and named names to Hoover's agents and Thomas's investigators.

With the advance team having prepared the way, the dignitaries arrived with due ceremony. On Thursday, May 8, 1947, Chairman Thomas, Representative McDowell, chief counsel Stripling, and committee investigator Russell rolled into town for what a front-page alert in the *Hollywood Reporter* called the "long threatened probe of Communists in Hollywood." Upon disembarking from the Santa Fe Chief at Union Station—luxury rail travel was still the preferred mode of transcontinental transportation—Thomas said he planned "an extensive and all-inclusive investigation." His purpose was simple. "We want the facts. We don't intend to make this a 'quickie' investigation." Georgia Democrat John S. Wood was reported to be arriving later by air, but never showed up.

While no public hearings would be held, Thomas promised to meet the press at least once before the group left the city, teasing that "he might have something interesting to say." In truth, Thomas would meet the press every day immediately after taking testimony.[28] The chairman was always very available to the press.

Thomas and Stripling got to work the next day. The base of operations was a conference room at the Biltmore Hotel, whose ornate Renaissance Revival digs served as the command center for the investigators. Over the next week, fourteen witnesses were called. The doors being closed to press and public, reporters relied on spontaneous press availabilities by the chairman, the witnesses, and the witnesses' attorneys for a sense of what went on in the shuttered but not very secret sessions. Thomas being Thomas, he also allowed the doors to be opened for a photo opportunity with an amenable and newsworthy witness.

The first two witnesses—called "friendly," a nomenclature that stuck—were James K. McGuinness, MGM producer and story editor, and John C. ("Jack") Moffitt, screenwriter and film critic for *Esquire*. Both were veterans

J. Parnell Thomas opens the closed-door sessions at the Biltmore for a photo opportunity with Robert Taylor. *Left to right*: Taylor, Thomas, Rep. John McDowell, and Robert E. Stripling. (Los Angeles Public Library).

of the Hollywood writers' wars of the 1930s, on the losing side of the battle between the SP and the SWG.

The pair spent a congenial ninety minutes discussing Communism in Hollywood with Thomas, McDowell, Stripling, and Russell.

Upon emerging from the committee room, McGuinness spoke to the waiting press. "This is no witch hunt and no innocent people would be hurt," he insisted, despite the crying out. "But anyone who says there are no Communists in the motion picture industry is either an ostrich or a fool."[29]

Over the weekend, though not in formal session, the committee interviewed willing informants. "The Thomas party shrouded its moves with much mystery," said *Daily Variety*, trying to shed some light. "Officially, the investigators no longer are registered at the Biltmore Hotel, although it is understood group is still housed there and all day yesterday [Sunday, May 11] interviewed members of the film colony who wished to report information on subversiveness within the industry."[30]

On Monday, the first witness was Roy M. Brewer, IATSE's international representative. Accompanied by two business agents for Hollywood unions, B. C. "Cappy" Duval, who represented the IATSE prop men Local 789, and Harry Shiffman, who represented Local 44, Brewer spoke at length about how the Communists had hijacked elements of a once all-American labor movement.

After the testimony, Thomas disclosed that Brewer had accused the NLRB of acting as "an accessory to the Communist party." Brewer confirmed Thomas's account, telling newsmen that he revealed how "the Communists had stuck their noses into the Hollywood strikes."

After Brewer's testimony, the prosaic representative of studio labor made way for a prestigious Hollywood artist. He was not exactly a marquee name, at least for his work in the motion picture industry, but he was prominent enough for a single-card on-screen credit: film composer Hanns Eisler. HUAC had labeled Eisler a "philosophical Communist" and announced in advance he would be brought in for questioning.[31]

Eisler was part of the thriving German-Jewish refugee community in Hollywood, a nomadic band of artists who had fled Nazism in the 1930s. After being put on a Nazi hit list in 1933, he had escaped to Great Britain and then, in 1938, moved on to New York, where he provided the soundtrack for Popular Front gatherings, Soviet-themed music recitals, and plays by his close friend and fellow exile Bertolt Brecht.

Prospering in exile, Eisler accrued the rewards of decadent American capitalism, receiving a twenty-thousand-dollar grant from the Rockefeller Foundation and a music professorship at the New School for Social Research. However, his residency status was precarious and the war in Europe made finding a secure berth imperative. In 1940, under circumstances HUAC found highly suspicious, he was granted a prized non-quota residency visa by the U.S. Department of State.

During the war, Eisler graduated from composing motion picture scores for politically *engagée* documentaries to conjuring the mood music for Fritz Lang's *Hangmen Also Die!* (1943) and Clifford Odets's *None But the Lonely Heart* (1944). At the time of his testimony, he was working for RKO on the score for Jean Renoir's oddball noir *The Woman on the Beach* (1947).

Such fame as Eisler possessed outside of Hollywood was by association. His brother was Gerhart Eisler, not just a known Communist but a known Communist superspy, "the guiding hand of Communism in the United

States," and "Moscow's number one political agent in this country," as he was regularly described.[32] Gerhart had been an influential apparatchik in the Communist party in Germany, a concentration camp prisoner in France, and, since his arrival in America, a shadowy figure of many aliases who ran espionage rings for the Soviet Union. Utterly ruthless, speaking with the lethal authority of an emissary from Stalin, Gerhart was the face of Soviet espionage in America, villainized in the Hearst press and lionized in Communist and fellow traveler circles.[33]

Over the weekend Stripling had driven out to Eisler's Malibu beach house to personally serve the composer with his HUAC subpoena.[34] Eisler claimed that only his Hollywood connections and "the coincidence of my family ties" had made him a political target.[35] In a puff piece in the *New Masses* by screenwriter Alvah Bessie, who by September would be handed a HUAC subpoena of his own, Eisler made the inevitable comparison. The prosecution of his brother Gerhart was "the beginning of a campaign against the liberal and progressive forces in this country. It does not surprise me. I have seen such campaigns before—in Germany. Before 1933."[36]

At 11:00 A.M. Monday morning, May 12, Eisler reported to the Biltmore as ordered. Thomas kept him cooling his heels while he chatted with Roy Brewer inside the conference room.

"Bald, bespectacled, and diminutive," cursed with a pair of outsized bunny ears, Eisler fit neither the image of a sinister Soviet spy nor a flamboyant European maestro. At his side was Ben Margolis, a civil rights lawyer who was to become a fixture on the defense teams of Hollywood artists subpoenaed by HUAC.

The session—on this everyone agreed—did not go well. Behind the locked doors of the Biltmore conference room, Eisler and Margolis engaged in "a heated verbal battle" with Stripling. They squabbled for about an hour before the questioning was cut short: Eisler was truculent and Thomas and Stripling were getting nowhere. An angry Eisler bolted from the room, with Margolis hot on his heels. "I am offended as a scholar, a scientist, and a composer," Eisler told the waiting press corps. "I am offended as a gentleman. I don't like to be pushed around."[37]

After the committee recessed, Thomas invited the press into the chamber for a post mortem. "We had Hanns Eisler here today as the result of a subpoena," he said. "We have voluminous evidence of all of Eisler's activities—evidence of his activities not only in the United States but also abroad." He said the composer pled "inability to remember when asked about numerous past jaunts in and out of the country, as well as his activities."[38] Thomas shook his head: "In my eight years on the committee, I have never seen a witness so evasive."[39]

The day's interrogations ended with lengthy sessions with James McGuinness and Jack Moffitt, who, having proven friendly and talkative, were both called back for additional testimony.

Moffitt was invited back for a *third* appearance the next day. Sequestered with the committee for most of the afternoon, he was the sole witness. To Thomas's delight, Moffitt dropped name after name. We're "getting some great stuff" from Moffitt, exulted the chairman. "He's giving us much more than we expected and he's really crowding our record."[40]

The fourth day finally brought some high-intensity star power to the Biltmore: screen heartthrob Robert Taylor; journeyman actor Richard Arlen; star-by-maternity Mrs. Lela Rogers, mother of Ginger; and non-star Henry Ginsberg, general manager of Paramount Pictures. Though all testified obligingly, it was a revelation from Taylor, then at the height of his matinee-idol-ness, that caused the first mini-sensation of HUAC's Hollywood year.

Emerging from the committee room, Taylor did not make the revelation himself, saying only "If there is anyone against Communism, it is I. I'm agin 'em."

Thomas was not so circumspect. Taylor's testimony had given him a piece of information that was both red meat and smoking gun. He couldn't wait to blurt out the news to the reporters waiting outside the hearing room.

"When Robert Taylor was asked in 1943 to take the lead role in the motion picture *Song of Russia*, he protested to the management of MGM studios on the grounds that the story was Communist propaganda," Thomas revealed. "The portrayal favored Russia, its ideologies, its institutions, and its way of life over the same things in America." However, the objections of the patriotic actor were overruled "primarily by the visit here of an agent of the [Roosevelt] administration who came here for the specific purpose of seeing that Taylor played the part."[41] Thomas quoted Taylor as saying "the ultimatum was laid down to him in the presence of Louis B. Mayer by 'a War Production Board agent.'" Later, when the head of the wartime agency in question, Donald P. Nelson, denied the charges, Thomas identified the "agent of the administration" as Lowell Mellett, who had headed up the Motion Picture Bureau of the OWI from 1942 to 1943.[42]

From Washington, Mellett labeled Thomas's charges "too damned silly to deny" and then denied them. He insisted he "certainly didn't compel Taylor or anyone else to do anything."[43] Mellett wasn't alone in finding Taylor's coercion scenario dubious. "Joe Skeptic wants to know who forced Taylor to appear in *Undercurrent*," snarked Red Kann at *Motion Picture Daily*, referring to the tepid melodrama then in release.[44]

In damage control mode, MGM released a statement from Louis B. Mayer. "I am assuming that the excitement brewing out of Robert Taylor's testimony before the House Un-American Activities subcommittee was due to the mistaken belief that the film, *Song of Russia*, was Communistic in plot and action," stated Mayer. "The film is at the studio unchanged since it was released in 1943 [sic] and subsequently shown throughout a large portion of the world." Not yet hip to the postwar ethos, Mayer explained that Hollywood was but a harmless entertainment machine. "*Song of Russia* is simply a love story about an American symphony conductor who was invited to Russia to direct a series of concerts," Mayer said. "It is true, of course, that Russia was our ally in 1943, and that our government was very friendly to the Soviets. But that is not why *Song of Russia* was made."[45]

Of course, being friendly to the Soviets was precisely why *Song of Russia* was made. Mayer's simply-a-love-story line—the fallback stance that had always served the industry so well when confronted with the real-world impact of its product—had been obliterated by Hollywood itself. The war had given every GI and home front moviegoer an education in how Hollywood shaped and transformed American values, in how cinema might be marshalled for political ends. *The Best Years of Our Lives, Crossfire, Gentleman's Agreement,* and a dozen other films on the marquee that very year were proving that the disingenuous pose was no longer a protective shield.

HUAC fixated on *Song of Russia*—and soon the other two pillars of the pro-Soviet troika, *Mission to Moscow* and *The North Star*—because their ideological currents required no special film smarts to navigate and because government pressure from the Roosevelt administration had unquestionably been brought to bear on the industry. Unspooling Exhibits A, B, and C allowed the Republicans on HUAC not only to tarnish Hollywood but to indict the Democrats for being too cozy with Moscow then and too casual about the threat from Communism now. No matter that the first indictment was all ex post facto: to make the case stick required only a willful act of historical amnesia.

On May 15, Jack L. Warner, actor Adolphe Menjou, director Leo McCarey, screenwriter Rupert Hughes, and a special surprise witness testified.

Warner was accompanied by Blayney Matthews, chief of studio police at Warner Bros., another sign that labor unrest no less than celluloid subversion was on the committee's mind. "I think that the Un-American Activities Committee is doing an excellent job here and I am happy to have had the opportunity to cooperate with its members," Warner said after testifying. "Whatever I may know about subversive elements in Hollywood, I shall tell the committee." In fact, Warner had named a number of subversive elements, forgetting that, during his allegedly secret testimony, a stenographer was taking down every word he said, words that would be read back to him during a future appearance before HUAC.

The debonair Menjou spent about an hour huddled with the committee. Voluble and quotable, he was in fine fettle, speaking to newsmen both before and after his testimony. "I believe that Hollywood is one of the main centers of Communist activity in America due to the fact that our greatest medium of propaganda—the motion picture—is located here and that it is the desire of the 'Masters in Moscow' to use this medium for their purpose—which is the overthrow of the American government."[46] Menjou's ambition was "to be the Paul Revere who sounds the alarm because Communism is out to destroy America."[47]

After Warner and Menjou testified, Thomas revealed that "both of these men named names," a phrase soon to enter the lexicon.[48]

The afternoon session was led off by director Leo McCarey, who remained closeted with the committee for only half an hour. The usually garrulous Irishman was tight lipped upon emerging, saying only, "I have nothing to say. I came down only because I was glad of the opportunity to cooperate with the committee."

The day's fourth witness, Rupert Hughes, another veteran of the defunct SP, was still fighting the battle of 1937. The SWG was "lousy with Communists today," he told reporters before walking into the conference room. He dredged up a turning point in history that, for him, was still a vivid memory. "When the Hitler-Stalin pact was in force, the Communists in the United States opposed all ideas of conscription and Lend Lease, but as soon as Hitler invaded Russia, they demanded immediate conscription and Lend-Lease."

Thomas saved his prize catch of the day for last, a witness who had more symbolic value in the twilight struggle between America and the Soviet Union than anyone on a studio payroll: Soviet defector Victor Kravchenko.

Kravchenko had come to the United States at the outbreak of World War II as a representative of the Soviet Purchasing Commission assigned to the Soviet embassy in Washington, D.C. Seduced by American freedom, he broke with the party and his country and, in 1946, published a best-selling memoir, *I Chose Freedom*. He was the most famous defector in the nation, reassuring proof that, when given the chance, any Russian would risk all to embrace the land of liberty. Kravchenko had nothing to do with Communism in Hollywood (or almost nothing: he had come to town in hopes of getting his book made into a "realistic" motion picture by an "honest Hollywood producer"), but rumors of Soviet assassination squads dispatched to prevent his testimony lent his appearance the *frission* of a spy thriller.* Not since Leon Trotsky, murdered on Stalin's orders in 1937, had the Soviet dictator so wanted a man dead, bragged Kravchenko.[49]

Kravchenko testified in the final session, accompanied by screenwriter Howard Emmet Rogers, who hoped to adapt *I Chose Freedom* for the screen. "More than anything else, the Soviet fears the making of a film that portrays truthfully, in every detail, the conditions in Russia today," Kravchenko told the press. "This they will go to any lengths to stop."[50]

After Kravchenko testified, Thomas brought HUAC's site visit to a close. "It is only fair to say that the subcommittee members are amazed at revelations made by all witnesses, particularly those connected to the Hollywood angle," he said by way of summation. "The situation is serious. I've been on many field trips for [HUAC] and the Military Affairs Committee but on none of them have I received such a voluminous amount of revealing testimony as this subcommittee has received in the last ten days."[51]

However, despite Thomas's upbeat self-evaluation, the reviews for his road show were brutal. "The best low burlesque to come out of Hollywood since Mack Sennett was in his prime," taunted *New York Post* film critic Archer Winsten. *Variety* also went with the reliable metaphor: "In toto, the Hollywood hearings wound up as a 'B' production, according to major opinion here."[52]

---

* Despite trade press reports in 1947 that *I Chose Freedom* was "in production," a film version was never made.

Even at *Motion Picture Herald*, a bastion of conservative opinion, editor Terry Ramsaye was cynical about HUAC's motives: "Perhaps it would have been expecting too much of a Congressional investigating committee to overlook and pass [up] an opportunity to get publicity attention by the involvement of the motion picture and the magic of a Hollywood dateline."[53]

A genuine Hollywood star also added her voice to the jeering section. Speaking at a rally for left-wing darling and soon to be presidential candidate Henry A. Wallace, Katharine Hepburn decried the secret session at the Biltmore. "Today, J. Parnell Thomas of the Un-American Activities Committee is engaged in a personally-conducted smearing campaign of the motion picture industry," she declared. "He is aided and abetted in this effort by a group of Hollywood super-patriots who call themselves the Motion Picture Alliance for the Preservation of American Ideals. For myself I want no part of their ideals or the ideals of Mr. Thomas."[54]

Ominously, though, few others in Hollywood were as outspoken as Katharine Hepburn. The arrival of federal investigators and aggressive congressmen had knocked the town off kilter: the Dies Committee had never managed to mount a major on-site visitation, never corralled a brand-name mogul and top stars, and never turned the screws on a suspected Communist with major screen credits.

Chapter 5

SMEARING HOLLYWOOD WITH THE BRUSH OF COMMUNISM

After being grilled by HUAC in March 1947, Eric Johnston concluded that a grand public hearing in Washington, with Hollywood as the defendant in the docket, was inevitable. Taking the high road, the MPAA president asked that the committee conduct "a fair and dignified investigation" and stop "making vague blanket charges that Communists have captured the American screen." Despite the fact that a congressional hearing was not a judicial proceeding bound by the rules of law, Johnston turned instinctively to the language of the courtroom to plead his case: "In the best American tradition, Hollywood is entitled to a fair trial before it is convicted. We know there are Communists in Hollywood as in other American industries. They would like to capture the American screen as they would like to capture the screen of any free country. But we are alert to this threat. Awareness is the first step to combat Communism, and Hollywood is aware."[1]

Johnston knew better than to expect a fair trial: the motion picture industry was guilty until proven innocent. Like any suspect fearing indictment, he began lining up a legal team and formulating a defense strategy. On June 2, 1947, he retained James F. Byrnes to represent the industry and "to champion the screen's right of freedom of expression."[2] A former Senator, Justice of the Supreme Court, director of the Office of War Mobilization, and Secretary of State under Truman, Byrnes oozed powerhouse Washington credentials. However, not wanting to trade on his dignity (or to have it diminished),

Byrnes stipulated that his role was to be strictly behind the scenes: he would not appear at the witness table during the hearings or before the newsreel cameras to defend the industry.

With Byrnes placing himself on the sidelines visibility-wise, Johnston needed a savvy lawyer to whisper advice in his ear and appeal to the court of public opinion. He chose Paul V. McNutt, another consummate Washington insider, who certainly looked the part: white-haired, immaculately dressed, patrician in bearing, leading man handsome. If the Hollywood actors who would testify before HUAC tried to look like button-down attorneys, McNutt fit the Central Casting model of a distinguished mouthpiece. His résumé was not quite as illustrious as Byrnes's, but it was impressive: former head of the Federal Security Administration, former High Commissioner to the Philippines, former governor of Indiana, and former National Commander of the American Legion. "We have nothing to fear, nothing to hide," said McNutt, upon his appointment, already using the plural pronoun. "Our record is an open book. The proof is in the pictures themselves."[3]

As Johnston was lining up legal talent, he was plotting another defensive measure, not announced to the trade press and kept secret from all but the highest levels of the motion picture industry: an attempt to preempt HUAC by raising the white flag of surrender before the hearings even commenced.

On June 2, 1947, the day the hiring of Byrnes was announced, Johnston convened a meeting in Hollywood of the AMPP, the West Coast branch of the MPAA. Representatives from all the major studios attended.

Johnston proposed a three-point plan of action. The first was a resolution that articulated the position of the MPAA toward the upcoming HUAC hearings. "Nothing can be accomplished by smearing Hollywood with the brush of Communism," it read in part. "Script burning and head hunting are un-American techniques. We want the facts, hard specific facts, and that kind of investigation we invite."[4]

The resolution was adopted unanimously, as was the third motion, which proposed the retention of Byrnes as counsel. It was the second of Johnston's three motions that shocked the assembled executives: "Agreed: not to employ Communists in Hollywood jobs where they would be in a position to influence the screen. Hollywood producers recognize the responsibility to keep the American screen free from Communist or any other subversive propaganda. . . . We emphasize that in agreeing not to employ proven Communists we mean just that. The proof must be conclusive and it is the responsibility of the Un-American Committee to furnish proof and the names." Johnston stressed that only the neon-lit Reds were to be tossed to the streets: "I am not interested in the pastel shades, the parlor pinks, or salmon colored zealots. They are just plain dupes and fools. My concern is the Red conspirator, the man who uses the freedoms of democracy to destroy democracy."

The proposal included some lip service to the principles of fair play and due process ("We must be scrupulous to avoid indiscriminate labeling. Every time you tag an innocent person with a red label you play into the hands of the Communists"), but it was a dramatic departure from long-standing practice: the first official consideration of an anti-Communist blacklist. If HUAC named the names and provided the proof, Hollywood would take corrective action.

The studio executives rebelled. Eddie Mannix, MGM's plant manager, spoke out first against doing HUAC's dirty work. "I wanted to play no part in it," he recalled, under oath, in 1948. "If there was an investigation to be carried on, I welcomed the Congress of the United States to carry on an investigation, but it was their responsibility to do it, and it wasn't our responsibility to have a witch hunt, [to determine] who and who was not a Communist." His colleagues agreed: they resented congressional interference in hiring decisions and they felt quite capable of keeping Communist propaganda off the American screen. From their point of view, they were exploiting the Communists: benefiting from the alienated labor of talented Reds, filming what was suitable, and rejecting what was subversive.

Johnston's proposal was voted down unanimously.[5]

By July 14, 1947, when Johnston convened another meeting of the West Coast producers, his understanding of the legal and political pitfalls anent a blacklist had advanced considerably. Now he believed: "We must have legal proof that a person is a Communist or otherwise subversive before this office will recommend that he be fired, because most persons in the industry are working under contract, which would result in legal suits and damages. We will cooperate with responsible agencies of the government to unearth subversive activities, but we are not in agreement with some of their methods."[6]

At that very moment in fact, responsible agents of the government were driving around Los Angeles making house calls. Thomas's two field investigators—former FBI agents H. A. Smith and A. B. Leckie—were back in town culling the Friendly from the Unfriendly. Thomas's investigators and J. Edgar

Hoover's on-site agents rubbed shoulders with and may well have bumped into each other interviewing potential witnesses.

Thomas's men deferred to Hoover's men, keeping the FBI's Los Angeles field office in the loop about their agenda and appointments. Upon arriving in Los Angeles, Smith made a courtesy call on the FBI to pay his respects. "Smith indicated that he would keep the Los Angeles Office of the Bureau fully informed of his activities and that he is desirous of letting the Bureau know of anything pertinent to our investigation which may come to his attention," special agent in charge Richard B. Hood informed Hoover.[7]

Thomas's emissaries were not the only visitors making courtesy calls on the FBI that summer. A stellar cast of Hollywood stars, screenwriters, and producers sought to head off trouble with a pilgrimage into the FBI office in downtown Los Angeles to offer information, clear the air, and suck up. Screen Actors Guild president Ronald Reagan and his wife, actress Jane Wyman, "on their own accord," dropped by to share the names of suspiciously left-of-center SAG members. Louis B. Mayer spoke at length to agent Hood to complain about how the HUAC hearings in Hollywood were conducted and to explain the true circumstances behind Robert Taylor's casting in *Song of Russia*.

Unprotected by the aura of the FBI, Thomas's men were not always greeted with the same reverence as Hoover's. In September 1947, HUAC investigators Smith and Leckie visited Eddie Mannix at MGM. Mannix, a gruff broad-shouldered Irishman who began his career as a bouncer at Nicholas and Joseph Schenck's Palisades Amusement Park, was not a man to cringe before factotums. Suspecting that the pair had brought along recording devices, he told them to leave their briefcases outside his office door and then launched into a twenty-minute tirade: Thomas was a publicity hound, HUAC was a witch hunt, and the policing of the MGM screen was his business not theirs. He didn't give a damn whether MGM screenwriters Dalton Trumbo or Lester Cole were Communists: "All I am looking for is getting people to write scripts for me and my responsibility, if he is a Communist or Democrat or Republican, [is] that the ideology is not put on the screen, [that nothing] except entertainment is put there."

The investigators brought up *Song of Russia*. Mannix scoffed at the notion that the wartime musical was Communist propaganda. He offered to show Thomas's gumshoes anything in the MGM catalogue. Smith took him up on the offer and watched *Song of Russia* in the MGM screening room. Upon exiting, Smith told Mannix he considered the film Communistic.

"The hell with you," barked Mannix. "I left him in the hall," Mannix recalled, having "no patience with a man who would tell me that [picture] was Communist propaganda."[8]

Howard Hughes: "Laughter is contagious."

J. Parnell Thomas understood that the track record of Hollywood-centric hearings on Capitol Hill was not good, that somehow the motion picture industry had always managed to come out on top—not only against the flat-footed Dies Committee hearings in 1938 or the ham-handed Clark Committee hearings in 1941 but from another more recent congressional spectacle involving a part-time mogul with a high-flying persona.

From July 28 to August 11, 1947, a special Senate committee investigating the National Defense Program launched a probe into Hughes Aircraft Company and Kaiser-Hughes Corporation. The charge was not Communist infiltration but capitalist corruption. In the hot seat was the strangest, richest, and most erratic motion picture producer in the annals of Hollywood, the industrial tycoon and aviation visionary Howard Hughes.

Hughes was the Texas-born heir to an oil drill-bit fortune, Hughes Tool Company, that he parlayed into an aviation and manufacturing empire. In 1925, as a raffish nineteen-year-old pilot, he landed in Hollywood with 3 million dollars to invest in the local economy, the kind of liquid assets that sent a stampede of producers and starlets into his arms. A wildcat independent in the by-the-numbers studio system, Hughes bankrolled and sometimes directed his own brand of don't-give-a-damn fare: *Hells Angels* (1930), the Great War aviation epic; *Scarface: The Shame of the Nation* (1932), the most controversial of the protean gangster films; and, *The Outlaw* (1943), an erotic western whose salacious ad campaign defied the straight-laced Production Code with a marvel of suspension engineering named Jane Russell. Hughes had money to burn, which he frequently did, and tolerated—even demanded—cost overruns that would have sent Louis B. Mayer or Jack Warner into anaphylactic shock.

Hughes had always made good copy, but as a subpoenaed suspect in a Washington corruption scandal he was front-page news for weeks. Sen. Owen Brewster (R-ME), chairman of the full Senate War Investigation Committee, and Sen. Homer S. Ferguson (R-MI), chairman of the special subcommittee investigating the National Defense Program, accused Hughes of war profiteering and his agents of seducing government contractors, sometimes literally, to funnel business to Hughes-owned companies. Before newsreel cameras, radio microphones, and a raucous crowd packed into every square inch of available space in the caucus room of the Senate Office Building, the two senators planned to double-team Hughes in an attempt to expose a juicy story of greed, corruption, and pandering.

On August 6, 1947, a furious, loaded-for-bear Hughes sat at the witness table poised to defend his company and his honor. To the delight of the reporters and newsreel boys, he lectured, bantered, and openly laughed at the committeemen. "Senator Brewster's story is a pack of lies, and I can tear it apart if given the opportunity," he declared. Against his virile defiance, laconic manner, and ready expertise, the senators came off like flustered schoolmarms. Outclassed at every turn, Senators Ferguson and Brewster fumed and fulminated.

On August 8, 1947, the hearings descended into semi-hilarity when Johnny W. Meyer, Hughes's publicity agent, skipped town ahead of a subpoena. Meyer had already spent five days on the stand testifying about the lavish entertainment parties—and occasional party girl—he had provided for government contractors.

Asked to account for Meyer's whereabouts, Hughes played dumb.

"Do you know where Johnny Meyers is?" asked Ferguson heatedly.

Hughes, whose hearing was shot from a lifetime of airplane racket and a near fatal crash the previous year, had to hold an earpiece to his ear. "Do you mean Johnny Meyer?" he replied calmly.

"Meyer or Meyers, where is he?" demanded Ferguson, temperature rising.

"I don't know," shrugged Hughes.

"Well, he was supposed to be here this morning but now I am informed he cannot be located."

At the news that Meyer had outsmarted the committee, the Hughes claque in the gallery burst into laughter.

"This is nothing to laugh about!" shouted Ferguson.

Hughes feigned innocence. "Senator, that's someone back there laughing."

"You laughed too!"

"Laughter is contagious," said Hughes innocently.[9]

On August 11, after a marathon day-long session, Ferguson and Brewster abruptly adjourned the hearings. Brewster has "headed for the Maine woods," Hughes gloated, because the senator was "too cowardly to stay here and face the music." At least Brewster was enjoying the outdoors: no sooner had the hearing room been cleared than Ferguson checked into a hospital to be treated for "poison ivy."[10]

The rout was total, even more sweeping than the victory of the moguls over the Senate War Propaganda committee in 1941. "The special Hollywood version of the horse laugh, the needle, and the hot foot had Subcommittee Chairman Homer Ferguson redly sputtering with rage and banging an ash tray," reported Mary Spargo, reviewing the show for the *Washington Post*.[11] In Hollywood, watching newsreels of the fracas, audiences hissed the senators and cheered Hughes.[12]

For the witnesses in the upcoming HUAC hearings, Hughes's cocksure defiance was offered as an exemplary model. "Perhaps Hughes, who couldn't be scared, has given Hollywood a much-needed lesson in how not to be kicked around," declared the legendary publicity man (and Hughes flack) Russell Birdwell.[13] " 'The movie industry should be mighty grateful to Howard Hughes,' one Washington wag has remarked," reported *Motion Picture Herald*. "What he meant was simple. The fiasco that the Hughes hearings developed into and the way they backfired on the committee have been a warning to the Un-American Activities Committee."[14]

Thomas and his fellow committeemen seemed to heed the warning. "You can definitely expect an improvement over past Hollywood investigations," Richard Nixon assured the *Film Daily*. "These hearings will be on a high plane and very factual—that's why we've employed [former] FBI men to help prepare evidence."[15] A HUAC spokesman said every possible step was being taken to prevent the hearings from "getting out of hand like the Howard Hughes Senate Investigation did."[16]

By "out of hand," he meant letting the accused get the upper hand.

America's Town Meeting of the Air: "Is There Really a Communist Threat in Hollywood?"

Throughout the summer of 1947, spurred by the past and future HUAC investigations, the red-hot topic of Communism in Hollywood was debated in fierce point-counterpoints across the media, moving through the mass-com food chain from trade press reports, to metropolitan dailies and newsweeklies, to popular monthly magazines, to radio news and commentary. The rush to publish and broadcast confirmed the new truism in postwar American culture: Hollywood had become the arena of choice for playing out the ideological contests of the day.

Radio aired all sides of the Communism-in-Hollywood controversy with surprising frankness. Despite commercial constraints and censorship codes, the primal need to fill air time allowed a chorus of disparate voices to be heard. By 1947, having come to maturity during World War II, the news and commentary functions of the medium were in full flower. The result was that Communism was not just debated by mainstream voices left and right, but that oddball dissenters, sometimes authentic Communists, were also handed a microphone.

In truth, radio was only too happy to air the dirty laundry of a rival medium. Local shows and network broadcasts alike corralled critics, politicians, and, when they were lucky, Hollywood personalities to debate how far Communism had bored into the motion picture (but certainly not the radio) industry. Soon enough, radio—and later television—would have reason to stifle the smugness.

Screen Writers' Guild president Emmet Lavery kept a busy on-air schedule defending the guild—a good thing too, because Lavery's calm voice and sane temperament served as a salutary counterweight to the stridency of so many of his colleagues, left and right. On July 6, 1947, on Los Angeles station KMPC, he joined with like-minded screenwriter Garret Graham to face off against long-time SWG nemesis Rupert Hughes and right-wing radio commentator Upton Close for an hour-long debate on the question "Should We Belittle Communist Influence in U.S. Pictures?" Lavery and Graham duly belittled the notion that Communist propaganda had crept into U.S. pictures what with patriotic capitalists like Louis B. Mayer, Darryl F. Zanuck, and Jack L. Warner manning the guard posts. "The industry is just as much a big business as General Motors and U.S. Steel," said Graham. "Until the *Wall Street Journal* starts whooping it up for Moscow, America need fear nothing worse from Hollywood than death by boredom."[17]

On August 26, 1947, *American Forum of the Air*, moderated by Theodore Granik, hosted a roundtable on alleged Communist infiltration in Hollywood featuring a matched pair of film critics on either side of the issue: Eileen Creelman of the *New York Sun* and Terry Ramsaye of *Motion Picture Herald*, who were "pretty sure of an existing Red Menace," and Irene Thirer of the *New York Post* and John T. McManus of *PM*, who were dubious.

"McManus was in there swinging hard for the rights of Hollywood to enjoy the same freedom of speech and expression that is accorded by the Constitution to other arts and communications media," observed *Variety*. "But he also wanted the name-callers to put up or shut up and he couldn't get to first base."[18]

The fiercest point-counterpoint on radio that year occurred on the political forum *America's Town Meeting of the Air*, a weekly public affairs show carried on 226 stations by the ABC network. Debuting in 1935 and broadcast from New York's Town Hall, the series was modeled on the freewheeling give and take of an old-time New England town meeting. Moderated by George V. Denny Jr., creator of the show and president of Town Hall, home to the famed New York chautauqua, the debates were held before a live audience who hissed, booed, cheered, and applauded in the raucous spirit of a fearless citizenry in a democratic Republic.

On September 2, 1947, broadcast live from the Philharmonic Auditorium in Los Angeles, *America's Town Meeting of the Air* addressed the question of the hour, "Is There Really a Communist Threat in Hollywood?" Mrs. Lela E. Rogers, mother of Ginger, and California State Senator Jack B. Tenney, chairman of the state's Joint Legislative Committee on Un-American Activities and author of *The Report on Un-American Activities in California, 1947*, argued for the affirmative. Emmet Lavery, SWG's hardworking president, and Albert Dekker, actor and former member of the California state assembly, took the negative. "We chose the topic," moderator Denny explained, "because of the widespread public interest in the subject, the impending Congressional investigation, and the tremendous influence of Hollywood films on the public mind."[19]

After a welcome from Los Angeles Mayor Fletcher Bower, Denny opened the show with his trademark folksy greeting ("Good evening, neighbors!") and introduced "a very important question in the life of this nation," namely "have the advocates of Communism, either party members or their sympathizers, gained sufficient influence in the film capital to constitute a threat to our America way of life?" He reminded listeners in the Philharmonic and at home that "a congressional committee on un-American activities will pursue its investigation on this subject in Washington on September 24th." Insisting on fair play, Denny forbade rude interruptions. "One person speaks at a time," he ordered, vowing to enforce decorum.

Lela Rogers, "former screenwriter, dramatic coach and mother of Ginger Rogers," spoke first. "The Communist threat is everywhere," she declared. Are we to believe that "it hasn't reached Hollywood yet?" Quoting Lenin on the importance of cinema to Communist indoctrination, Rogers charged that the SWG is "loaded with Communists." She then launched into a screed about a recent stage play that was unadulterated "un-American propaganda," a play written by none other than—Emmet Lavery. Rogers did not indict the play by name, but she meant his forthcoming stage production *The Gentleman from Athens*, in which Lavery had allegedly snuck "commie bits" into the dialogue.

Hoots of derision from the crowd greeted Rogers's accusations. The Philharmonic Hall was packed with SWG partisans.

Lavery replied that the brouhaha about Communism in Hollywood was "much ado about nothing" and defended his play as not being "about a man who lost his faith in Congress, but a man who found his faith in Congress." He resented the "outright libel and slander against the vast majority of 985 active members" of the SWG and ridiculed the notion that Communism could ever infiltrate the American screen. "Now the truth of the matter is that a Communist has about as much a chance of slipping a revolutionary idea into a Hollywood film as a Roosevelt Democrat has of slipping some New Deal ideas into Hedda Hopper's column," he quipped, to gales of laughter. As for himself, he freely admitted he was not a Communist. "In politics I am a Roosevelt Democrat and in religion I am a Roman Catholic."

Tenney was up next, introduced by Denny as "a gentleman who has locked horns with Mr. Lavery before," a reference to the face-off between the two before the California Committee on Un-American Activities on October 7, 1946. On that occasion, Lavery had testified that Communists in Hollywood were "actually a very small minority, but crusades like [Tenney's] magnify the Communist menace and increase the chances of our having a World War III."[20]

The Philharmonic audience gave Tenney a smattering of polite applause. When it subsided, he remarked, "I am very happy to hear a few Americans present." Some in the crowd booed. "I notice we have a lot of comrades," he sneered.

Tenney asserted that "the threat of Communism has been gaining momentum since 1930" and "the Communist threat is real and sinister, alarming and obvious." He quickly got personal, naming the screenwriters John Howard Lawson and Albert Maltz, the pioneering film educator Robert Gessner, and the actors Edward G. Robinson and Katharine Hepburn as part of a Hollywood party cell peddling "Marxist pipe dreams." He grouped his two debate opponents with the worst of the subversives, calling Lavery and Dekker "strict party liners."

Struggling to keep his cool, Dekker reminded Tenney and Rogers that actors have a right to express their opinions in a democratic society. He then introduced a new element into the conversation. "Antisemitism still threatens Hollywood and the world," he noted by way of praising *Crossfire* and *Gentleman's Agreement*, the two social problem films that year speaking out against antisemitism, the latter of which he was proud to have appeared in. "If these be Communism, make the most of it!" Dekker's exclamation received long and sustained applause from the Philharmonic crowd.

The speakers then joined Denny around the microphone for "a little give and take" before taking questions from the audience.

Rogers demanded to know whether Lavery, in accordance with a provision in the recently passed Taft-Hartley Act, would affirm that the SWG was not Communist run. Not sure if the law would be upheld, Lavery dodged the question, whereupon a brutal back-and-forth between Lavery and Tenney ensued.

"I said tonight I am not a Communist," Lavery insisted. "I can't answer for other members of the Guild. For myself I say now I'm not and never have been a Communist. I am not even bashful about it."

Tenney was having none of it. If Lavery were not a Communist, why hadn't he thrown the Communist screenwriters out of the guild?

Lavery was ready with a comeback: "The reason that we don't throw the Communists out is the same reason that we don't throw the Republicans out. [Applause] Under the prevailing decisions of the Supreme Court of the United States it is not seditious *per se* to be a member of the Communist party any more than it is to be a member of the Republican Party and so we do not have a political test for membership in the Screen Writers' Guild."

Moderator Denny struggled to keep order and steer the conversation into calmer waters, but an agitated Tenney was relentless in his attacks on Lavery and Dekker. Tenney wondered why Lavery embraced Communists in the SWG when Catholics like Lavery would be ousted from the Communist party.

"The senator is quite right," conceded Lavery to widespread applause. "I would be thrown out of any Communist society. But then I don't want to be in any Communist society."

As was customary, after the two sides tangled, members of the studio audience got into the act by asking questions. At that point, any pretense of civil discourse degenerated into bouts of name calling from the affirmative side. When Tenney tried to interrupt Dekker, the actor snapped. "We're not in one of your hearings now. Everyone gets a chance here."

Tenney muttered that Dekker was spouting "the usual party line covering up a group of fifth columnists working for the destruction of our country."

Denny stepped in to try to lower the temperature. "I would like to get out of this personal discussion of personalities. We are not here trying to smear or defend individuals whether you think they are or are not followers of the Communist party line."

Undeterred, Tenney continued to attack Lavery as a party liner:

Lavery: I take my social conscience not from the essays of Karl Marx—I take them from the gospel of the apostles and the encyclicals of the pope.
Tenney: He's hiding behind the Catholic Church!
Lavery: Catholics don't have to hide behind anything to have a social conscience.

Denny tried again to establish a modicum of civility. At the end of the hour, after each of the four had made brief summations, the shell-shocked moderator seemed relieved that a fist fight had not broken out.

For Hollywood, the coast-to-coast shouting match was a public relations disaster: almost no one liked what they heard. The whole sad spectacle, wrote a disgusted Pete Harrison in a detailed blow-by-blow in *Harrison's Reports*, "was a disgrace, not only to the individuals themselves, but also to the entire industry, for the debate was not confined to Hollywood; it was broadcast over more than two hundred and fifty stations."[21] *Variety* also called the show "a disgrace" for trafficking in "a shocking assortment of irresponsible charges, reckless smearing of reputations, appeals to religious bigotry, personal abuse, and what amounted to street-corner brawling."[22]

Appalled that free-floating slurs on his faith and character had been broadcast to a national audience, Lavery retaliated in a different forum. In addition to being president of the SWG, he was a lawyer, a member in good standing of the New York State Bar. After the show aired, Lavery brought a libel and slander suit against Lela Rogers for 1 million dollars claiming that her comments about his purportedly Communist play had caused financial backers to pull out.[23]

Unlike testimony before HUAC, accusations broadcast over the air were not immune from American libel law.

Charles Chaplin: "I am not a Communist. I am a peace monger."

On September 20, 1947, with his ducks finally in a row, J. Parnell Thomas announced that HUAC had subpoenaed forty-three Hollywood and would-be Hollywood personalities.[*] The list included some of the biggest names in the motion picture industry—moguls, stars, directors, and even a few recognizable screenwriters. "The mere fact that they are being called to testify before the committee should not be considered a reflection in any way upon their character or patriotism," said Thomas, pretending to assuage the panic he was causing. "Some of the witnesses are friendly to the committee's purpose. Others are undoubtedly hostile. The committee wants to hear both sides."[24]

But not both sides from everyone. In a pattern repeated by each successive iteration of HUAC, the subpoenas were launched like unguided missiles. Some obvious suspects dodged the bullet and some peripheral players found themselves looking at a federal marshal handing over a pink summons. Who was tagged—and who was ultimately called to testify—was a roll of the dice. A few on the list never received the promised subpoena while a few not on the list did receive a subpoena.

---

[*] The official press release from Thomas was dated September 19, 1947, with the italicized admonition that the statement was for release in the "Sunday morning newspapers, September 21, 1947," to assure maximum play. Listed alphabetically the original list was composed of Alva [*sic*] Bessie, Roy E. Brewer, Herbert Biberman, Berthold [*sic*] Brecht, Lester Cole, Gary Cooper, Charles Chaplin, Joseph E. Davies, Walt Disney, Edward Dmytryk, Cedric Gibbons, Samuel Goldwyn, Rupert Hughes, Eric Johnston, Howard Koch, Ring Lardner Jr., John Howard Lawson, Louis B. Mayer, Albert Maltz, Thomas Leo McCarey, Lowell Mellett, James McGuiness [*sic*], Lewis Milestone, Adoph [*sic*] Menjou, Sam Moore, John Charles Moffitt, Robert Montgomery, George Murphy, Clifford Odets, Larry Parks, William Pomerance, Ronald Reagan, Lela E. Rogers, Howard Rushmore, Morrie Ryskind, Adrian Scott, Dore Schary, Donald Ogden Stewart, Robert Taylor, Waldo Salt, Dalton Trumbo, Jack L. Warner, and Sam Wood.

The targeted subgroup of the subpoenaed—those who were not friendly, thus unfriendly, a label they cherished—brought together nineteen Hollywood artists who had to be coerced, under penalty of arrest, to appear in front of HUAC. Screenwriters Alvah Bessie, Herbert Biberman, Bertolt Brecht, Lester Cole, Richard Collins, Gordon Kahn, Howard Koch, Ring Lardner Jr., John Howard Lawson, Albert Maltz, Samuel Ornitz, Robert Rossen, Dalton Trumbo, and Waldo Salt; directors Edward Dmytryk, Lewis Milestone, and Irving Pichel; producer Adrian Scott; and—the only familiar face in the group—actor Larry Parks, who had recently rocketed to stardom in the title role in *The Jolson Story* (1946). Ten were Jews, which may or may not have been significant, and none had been in uniform during World War II, which certainly was.[25]

By far the brightest star in HUAC's sights was Charles Chaplin, still the most famous silhouette in cinema, a high-value target due to his long history of fellow traveling and his off-putting refusal, after thirty-five years in the nation that had made him rich and famous, to apply for American citizenship. The widespread public resentment over Chaplin's citizenship status reflected a perennial American schizophrenia: insulted when the live-in foreigner did not want to join the American family and suspicious when he did.

Chaplin rather liked the idea of making a showstopping appearance before the committee. In July, he had chided Thomas for not having subpoenaed him for the May hearings in Los Angeles and, in anticipation of being served for the main event, he telegraphed Thomas to say that he would gladly accept the "invitation" to appear in Washington. "I am not a Communist," insisted Chaplin. "I am a peace monger." To gain insight into his thinking, Chaplin suggested Thomas and company see his current picture, *Monsiour Verdoux* (1947), a dark comedy about a charming serial killer, whose subversive message, teased Chaplin, was "against war and the futile slaughter of our youth." To arrange a preview, Thomas could telephone him "collect" in the interest of "economy."[26]

To further needle Thomas, Chaplin booked *Monsieur Verdoux* into five theaters in Washington, D.C., where committeemen would be sure to see his name on the marquee. "If I am to be called to Washington there might just as well be a harbinger of my arrival," joshed Chaplin. He invited all the committee members to a free screening.[27]

Thomas told reporters that Chaplin was "definitely" scheduled to appear at a preliminary hearing in September that would also investigate the composer Hanns Eisler.[28] In the end, though, Thomas did not take the bait. The weekend before the October hearings commenced, Thomas announced to the disappointed press corps that Chaplin would not be called then either.

Eric Johnston would not be so lucky. Putting up a good front, Johnston pledged the cooperation of the MPAA, but he resented the slur upon a great, patriotic industry. "The motion picture industry has been accused of putting subversive propaganda on the screen," he wrote Thomas after the subpoenas were issued. "We deny that charge without reservation." The best brief for the defense was up on the screen: "The pictures themselves are proof of its complete falsity."[29]

The pictures themselves could also offer proof of Hollywood's unsullied patriotism. With an eye to the upcoming hearings, the MPAA sponsored a two-reel short entitled *Power Behind the Nation*, released simultaneously to two hundred theaters on October 11, 1947. Produced by Warner Bros. in Technicolor, it was the first in a planned series on the American way of life, with all profits going to charity.

Stuffed with stock shots from industrial films and reenactments lifted from patriotic Warner Bros. shorts from the late 1930s, *Power Behind the Nation* plays like a parody of postwar triumphalism. In a stilted prologue, Johnston rhapsodizes about the abundant resources of a great nation. "Increased production is the key to America's power and world recovery," he declares, grateful to be reciting nostrums from his Chamber of Commerce days. "What we need is new faith, new enthusiasms, and a new crusading spirit for America, its present, and its future."[30]

No less than coal, lumber, and water, "the power of a free press" guaranteed by the Constitution also fuels the American dynamo. Perhaps the greatest power behind the nation is unspooling before the viewer's very eye. Americans should always treasure "the ever-expanding scope of motion pictures that by penetrating the barriers of language and nationality unites the world with the blending of entertainment, the brotherhood of melody, and the background of education."

Exhibitors who balked at playing the pedantic short were advised to wise up. "*Power Behind the Nation* offsets in many quarters some of the sniping by enemies of the industry that knows no ending. For example, the forthcoming hearings by the House Un-American Activities Committee," noted *Motion Picture Daily*. "It is also one industry antidote for the poison that is constantly circulated about your business."[31]

Unstated was the queasy feeling that the poisonous cloud circulating about the business was only going to get thicker.

Hanns Eisler: "I must say, Mr. Rankin, these songs are not filth. They are great songs."

Thomas backed off from a confrontation with a scene-stealer of Charles Chaplin's caliber, but in the case of Hanns Eisler he was as good as his word. Beginning on September 24, 1947, as a sort of appetizer for the main course, HUAC held three days of public hearings devoted solely to the composer that HUAC counsel Robert Stripling alternately referred to as "the foremost musical figure in the Soviet revolutionary movement" and "the Karl Marx of communism in the field of music."[32] Eisler's nominal offenses were that he had stayed in the country illegally after his visa expired and lied on a subsequent visa application when he denied being a Communist. Of course, what spurred the investigation into Eisler's immigration status was his incriminating bond with his brother Gerhart, the Soviet agent.

Eisler's four hours at the witness table began with Eisler's lawyers, Herman Greenberg and Joseph Forer, asking to cross-examine witnesses. The request was denied. They then asked permission to submit questions for the chairman to ask. That request too was denied.

Eisler asked if he might read an opening statement.

Thomas gave the statement a cursory once-over. No, Eisler may not read it.

The request by an unfriendly witness to read an opening statement and the denial by the chairman to grant him a platform set a pattern. Also setting a pattern: the statement was handed out to the press and accrued more news value by being suppressed at the public hearing.

"This hearing is both sinister and ridiculous." Eisler's statement began. Thomas need not have, and probably didn't, read any further, certainly not to the concluding lines: "It is horrible to think what will become of American art if this committee is to judge what art is American and what is un-American. This is the sort of thing that Hitler and Mussolini tried. They were not so successful, and neither will be the House Committee on Un-American Activities."[33]

The Eisler hearings focused on the decision in October 1941 by the Department of State to allow Eisler into the United States for permanent residence on a nonquota visa. He had been in and out of America since 1932, but in 1939 the Department of Labor deported him to Mexico. From the other side of the border, Eisler angled to reenter the United States. To prove that Eisler had perjured himself on the immigration form when he denied membership in the Communist party, the committee called in Sumner Welles, former undersecretary of state; George Messersmith, former assistant secretary of state; and Robert G. Alexander, a former State Department employee who had prepared a background check on Eisler in 1938.

Welles and Messersmith were berated for allowing into the country "an international Communist agent" who had been "of extreme importance to the Soviet Union for many years." The committee looked more favorably on Alexander, who had reviewed Eisler's case and concluded that the composer was "anti-Nazi and pro-Communist" and had obtained "non-immigrant visas through fraud."[34]

The committee unearthed some interesting tidbits. Eisler had friends in very high places. Columnist Dorothy Thompson, critic Malcolm Crowley, playwright Clifford Odets, and director William Dieterle had all petitioned the State Department in support of Eisler's admission to the United States, warning that he faced certain death if deported to Germany.

The most prominent name among Eisler's petitioners belonged to the former First Lady of the United States, a revelation that allowed HUAC to indict the Roosevelt administration for its lax—or was it welcoming?—attitude to Communist artists. In 1939, Eleanor Roosevelt had written two letters on Eisler's behalf to Undersecretary of State Welles, a longtime friend, to grease the skids for Eisler's entry into the United States. Responding to the revelations in a public statement, Mrs. Roosevelt denied remembering the letters or knowing Eisler. In the desperate 1930s, she had received hundreds of requests for help each month which she "simply passed on for consideration." That was precisely "the thing that was so frightening about Eleanor Roosevelt helping Hanns Eisler into this country," scowled Hedda Hopper. "None of us will live long enough to know how many like Eisler received Eleanor's help."[35]

Composer Hanns Eisler (*right*) with attorney Herman A. Greenberg (*left*) testifying at HUAC's three-day hearing devoted to his immigration status, September 24, 1947.

Of all the HUAC congressmen, John Rankin was most incensed by the sight of the fifth columnist in front of him. "I'm as familiar with poetry as any member of either House of Congress," he claimed. "I think these songs are filth."

Eisler kept his cool. "I must say, Mr. Rankin, these songs are not filth. They are great songs."[36]

Eisler did himself no favors by dodging and dissembling. He initially denied being a member of the Communist Party, but then admitted that he had joined the party in 1926. He insisted however that he had never been an active member and had never been a tool of the USSR.[37] Did Eisler remember a letter from his sister saying he and Gerhart were Soviet agents who were trying to contrive a natural death for her? He could not remember—and then he could. "Let's say for the record that I got it," he conceded.[38]

On Eisler's Communist background and dishonesty on his immigration papers, the committee had the witness dead to rights. Stripling waved a picture from the *Daily Worker* showing Eisler giving the clenched fist salute—"the Red salute"—that was a universal sign of Communist solidary. Eisler lamely insisted that the gesture had been a symbol for the workers in Germany for a hundred years. Stripling asked Eisler to demonstrate the salute. Smiling wanly, Eisler raised his right arm and clenched his fist.

The composer might as well have signed his own deportation order.

After the Eisler hearing adjourned on September 27, HUAC turned its evidence over to Attorney General Tom Clark, who prosecuted Eisler for violations of U.S. immigration law.[39] "I recall, when I read in a French paper in 1933 Hitler had put a price on my head and the heads of other progressive artists, I was not surprised," Eisler said after posting bail in the case. "But I never dreamed I'd experience the same thing in the United States, a country that I love."[40]

Facing either jail or deportation, Eisler opted for a strategic exit. On March 26, 1948, from LaGuardia Field in New York, he left the United States under an agreement with the Department of Justice. "This is my second exile," he said as he prepared to board a plane for London. "The first exile was by the government of Adolf Hitler." Once safely overseas, he described Hollywood as "a city in a terrible state of hysteria. Old friends regard each other with suspicion; you don't know whether you can trust your neighbors. People whisper. There are prying eyes."[41]

Good riddance, snarled columnist Westbrook Pegler, with more venom than even he was wont to spit. "Hanns is a noisy Hollywood parasite," Pegler wrote by way of bon voyage, happy that the Justice Department had tossed the composer back to Europe—though, unfortunately, it was "too late for Hitler to gas him."[42]

John Huston: "You have my word for it that none of us are even sympathetic to Communism."

That September, as Eric Johnston consulted with lawyers and subpoenas were handed out like leaflets around Hollywood, liberals in the motion picture industry watched with alarm: if not HUAC's primary targets, they would surely be collateral damage. Most had worked closely with the alleged Communists, both at the studios and in the Popular Front. Out of a sense of moral outrage and self-preservation, they mounted a counteroffensive against HUAC, banding together under an unimpeachable, all-American masthead: the Committee for the First Amendment (CFA).

The ad hoc alliance of topline directors, screenwriters, and actors sought to coordinate opposition to the upcoming hearings, to refute the charge that Hollywood was a hotbed of Communist subversion, and to combat the modus operandi of the Thomas Committee: the reckless allegations, the guilt-by-association insinuations, the venting of career-killing accusations without giving the accused the opportunity to explain or cross-examine. At once glamourous and grass roots, it would be the animating center for the campaign against HUAC from Hollywood's besieged liberals.

A few members of CFA had long records of political activism, but most were neophytes who signed up instinctively to defend their profession in its hour of crisis. The membership included some of the best known and most accomplished motion picture artists: the name-above-the-title directors William Wyler, fresh from a heroic wartime record and the after-glow of the seven Oscars awarded to *The Best Years of Our Lives* (1946); John Huston, scion of Hollywood royalty, director of *The Maltese Falcon* (1941), and a wartime documentarian of equally courageous service; and Billy Wilder, the Ernst Lubitsch protégée who gave European cynicism an American accent; the screenwriter Philip Dunne, one of Hollywood's highest paid scribes, who during World War II served as chief of produc-tion for the Motion Picture Bureau of the overseas branch of the OWI; and the radio auteur Norman Corwin, the poet laureate of wartime values and postwar aspirations.[43]

A constellation of the brightest stars in the Hollywood firmament made up the headline attractions: Danny Kaye, versatile comedian and song and dance man; Gene Kelly, the hoofer who had just broken his ankle on the set of *Easter Parade* and was hobbling around, quite nimbly, on crutches; the raven-haired goddess Ava Gardner, who had vaulted to stardom playing the lethal minx in *Ernest Hemingway's The Killers* (1946); pin-up girl Rita Hayworth, whose luxurious mane of red hair had recently, perversely, been cut and dyed blonde by husband-director Orson Welles for *The Lady from Shanghai* (1947);*

---

* Welles himself, though an activist in progressive causes since the 1930s and a signatory to CFA manifes-tos, was conspicuously absent from CFA's higher profile actions. Trade reporters speculated that he was steering clear of controversy while contemplating a run for Congress in 1948.

and an actress-comedienne who would, in a new medium, surpass Hayworth's fame as a red-headed gamine, Lucille Ball. A lineup of corn-fed girl-next-door types like June Havoc, Marsha Hunt, and Evelyn Keyes balanced out the femmes fatale and bombshells.

Floating above even this rarefied ensemble was Hollywood's reigning golden couple: screen tough guy Humphrey Bogart and his ravishing young wife, Lauren Bacall. All and all, dazzling candlepower notwithstanding, these stars were not known for latching on to the *cause celebre* of the moment. They might lend their names to worthy charities, war bond drives, and a Democratic presidential candidate, but they tended to steer clear of controversial picket lines and out-of-the-mainstream rallies.

As with so much else in Hollywood history, memories diverge on the origins of the group. When and where the idea was first hatched is hazy—some say over a table at Lucey's Restaurant, the popular star hangout across the street from Paramount Pictures, others after a round of frenzied cross-town phone calls.[44] John Huston, who should know, credited himself and four others with the idea. "The original founders were: William Wyler, Philip Dunne, Norman Corwin, Billy Wilder, and myself," the director stated in April 1948, when memories were still fresh. "We five collaborated on every written line, I believe, from the original manifesto to the last paid advertisement appearing in the trade papers." Huston also credited his four colleagues and himself with conceiving the two highest profile actions taken by the committee: "We were also entirely responsible for the trip to Washington, and for the various radio programs."[45] Huston, however, was too generous with the credit. Corwin never claimed to be a principal organizer and said he took his cues from Huston. Wilder lent his name to the group but took no leadership role, opting out of the radio shows and the trip to Washington.[46]

Once the idea for an anti-HUAC committee circulated around town, a flurry of glitzy volunteers signed on: first numbering in the dozens, soon in the hundreds, with the original membership put at 135. A steering committee was formed, composed of Huston, Wyler, Dunne, actor Shepperd Strudwick, and talent agent M. C. Levee. To handle publicity for the committee, Colin Miller, an assistant to Charles Einfield, president of Enterprise Films, put his entire staff at CFA's disposal, a crew that included David Hopkins, son of FDR advisor Harry Hopkins.[47] Restaurateur David Chasen lent his landmark place-to-be-seen eatery as an informal command center; scores of people met at Chasen's every day to plot strategy, with Ava Gardner pouring coffee. Sam Jaffe, the prominent agent, lent his offices at the Sam Jaffe Talent Agency to Norman Corwin for writing scripts for two planned coast-to-coast radio broadcasts.[48] As remembered by its core membership, the pitch-in, can-do spirit partook of the let's-put-on-a-show spontaneity of a vintage MGM musical.

In New York, theater actors and playwrights formed a branch of their own to impede any incursion of HUAC into Broadway. Despite Chairman Thomas's professed uninterest in tracking red lines on the Great White Way, veterans of the socially activist and sometimes outright Communist productions mounted by the Federal Theater Project and the Group Theater in the 1930s knew that HUAC might find more likely suspects on stage than on screen.[49] The activist-actor John Garfield, who had a foot in Broadway as well as Hollywood, was point man for the New York contingent.

Had CFA been formed ten years earlier, the coalition might have been called a Popular Front group, but in one crucial aspect it was not at all like a Popular Front group. Though backed by a broad spectrum of liberals and progressives, and outraged at the tactics of the congressional anti-Communists, it was not Communist inspired or Communist controlled. The founding members of CFA had bitter memories of the supine submission of the anti-Fascist groups of the 1930s to the CPUSA line, especially the turnabout of the Hollywood Anti-Nazi League after the announcement of the Hitler-Stalin Pact. The selfsame ideological somersaults had been performed by most of the members of the Unfriendly Nineteen.

With that experience as background, CFA was determined not be branded a fifth column auxiliary of Soviet policy. Again and again, Wyler, Huston, Dunne, and the other members emphasized a key distinction between the postwar CFA and the prewar Popular Front. "You have my word for it that none of us are even sympathetic to Communism," Huston declared in 1948. "I am able to speak with such authority as I have been close friends with all of these men named [the original founders] over a good many years. We are simply outraged at the spirit which animated the Thomas Committee, and by its perverted use of the power of Congress."[50] Desperate to avoid any hint of a kinship with Moscow, CFA sought to steer clear of the Unfriendlies while, at the same time, condemning the tactics of the Thomas Committee. It would prove to be a difficult needle to thread.

If Wyler, Huston, and Dunne were the founding fathers and chief strategists of the group, Bogart was its public face. Although Bogart had signed pro-FDR petitions for the Hollywood Democratic Committee, his out-front role was a rare foray into politics for an actor who preferred to spend his down time drinking, sailing, and playing chess, who, while entertaining guests at his home, wore a button on his lapel reading: "No causes, politics, or religion discussed here."[51] Bogart's only brush with an anti-American smear had occurred in 1940, when he was named as a Communist by CPUSA secretary John L. Leech before the Buron Fitts grand jury. At the time, he was given a clean bill of patriotism by Martin Dies. Perhaps the lapel button was a reminder of the close call. The affection for the actor as the embodiment of hard-boiled but at heart decent masculinity had not yet blossomed into a full-blown cult, but the legend of the man known to gossip columnists and readers alike as Bogie was already being printed.

With Bogart in the spotlight and Wyler, Huston, and Dunne pulling strings offstage, the show business professionals did what came naturally—held press conferences, staged photo ops, and produced radio shows. No strangers to public relations ploys, the group settled on a coordinated three-pronged campaign against HUAC.

First, the Committee published a series of declarations in the trade press and select metropolitan newspapers articulating its principles, signed by prominent members, a gesture designed to attract new membership and boost fundraising. Second, Norman Corwin began work on a pair of radio shows that would showcase the celebrity roster and articulate the issues at stake. Third, in what was to be its most controversial gambit, the group planned what seemed like an inspired pseudo-event: a cross-country plane trip by Hollywood stars who would descend on Capitol Hill to protest HUAC's methods and rationale. Once in Washington, they would stand in line with average citizens, sit in the hearing room to bear witness, and roam the halls of Congress lobbying their representatives. Their very presence would siphon publicity oxygen away from the camera-hogging J. Parnell Thomas.

All of the prose emanating from CFA—the press releases, telegrams, ads, and pamphlets—was calm and considered, thoughtful and non-incendiary. It was, after all, crafted by some of the best wordsmiths in the business—mainly Huston, Dunne, and Corwin. The rhetoric sought a balance between sweet reason (of course Congress had the right to investigate Communist subversion) and steely defiance (but not at the expense of the Bill of Rights of the U.S. Constitution).

At one point, having promised to put on "a better show than the hearings," the group had considered staging a series of mock investigations to be mounted concurrently with the congressional hearings. Upon reflection, the steering committee rejected the notion as disrespectful. In the fraught atmosphere of 1947, no one wanted to appear disrespectful to Congress.[52]

(*right*): At the movies with John Rankin (*left*) and J. Parnell Thomas (*right*), as depicted by *Washington Post* cartoonist Herbert Block, October 22, 1947. (The Herb Block Foundation)

Part II
ON LOCATION IN WASHINGTON

"If You Ask Me, It's Un-American"

Chapter 6
SHOWTIME

The white marble caucus room on the third floor of the Old House Office building had been transformed into a fair semblance of a motion picture soundstage. Along the right side of the room a bank of six newsreel cameras—hefty three-lens 35mm Mitchells with their distinctive "mickey mouse" ears—rested on sturdy tripods, each with a camera operator, sound man, and producer in tow. A mobile cameraman holding a compact 16mm Eyemo, a workhorse deployed for combat photography during wartime, wandered to the far back of the room and off to the side, to capture panoramic shots of the hall. At the dais in front presided the congressmen, across from whom sat the subpoenaed at the witness table, "the hot seat," and stage right, akimbo, the table for the committee counsel and investigators. A cluster of outsized "fatboy" microphones had been set up at the tables for all three sets of interlocutors. Angling for position, and trying to keep out of the sightline of the newsreel cameras, eleven still photographers jostled each other, checking light meters and palming flash bulbs. Wags joked that the hearings must have been sponsored by Eastman Kodak: three days in, the man from *Life* magazine alone had taken more than one thousand shots.[1]

Three crystal chandeliers—back, center, and front—hung from the high ceiling, giving the cavernous space the incongruous feel of a grand ballroom: for the benefit of the newsreel cameras, the incandescent bulbs had been replaced by high-intensity orbs. "The illumination was as sharp and shadowless as that of an operating theater," shuddered screenwriter Gordon Kahn, one of the Unfriendly Nineteen, attending under duress.[2] A trade reporter in town, taking in the hubbub and squinting at the glare, conjured a more familiar association: "It's worse than a Hollywood premiere."[3]

The print press was granted privileged access at a bank of tables adjacent to and slightly behind the witness table. An estimated 150 reporters sat vigil for the major metropolitan newspapers, the national newsmagazines, and the three wire services (Associated Press, United Press, and, the Hearst syndicate's outfit, International News Service). Working a strange beat in drab surroundings—and rubbing shoulders with huffy "straight" reporters—were the representatives of the motion picture trade press. When the veteran industry reporter Maurice "Red" Kann, covering the hearings for *Motion Picture Daily*, was hailed by a colleague ("Hey, Red!"), the room went still. A few of the print reporters had come prepared—donning sunglasses to shield their eyes from the blinding lights set up for the newsreels. "They must be stars in disguise," whispered a breathless onlooker not in the know.

A few members of the press were expected to be called to the witness table. *PM*, the high-minded but low-circulation New York daily, had sent

A panoramic shot of the packed Caucus Room of the Old House Office Building, as the Thomas Committee investigation into alleged Communist subversion in Hollywood gets underway October 20, 1947. The arrow points to Jack L. Warner, the leadoff witness.

Quentin Reynolds to cover the hearings. The author of *The Curtain Rises*, published in 1944, a memoir of his time as a war correspondent, and a book to be quoted by chief counsel Robert Stripling, Reynolds was prepared to move from observer to participant. Lowell Mellett, the former wartime head of the OWI's Motion Picture Bureau and currently a columnist for the *Washington Evening Star*, was considered an "almost certain" witness due to having been named by Thomas as the government mastermind behind MGM's *Song of Russia*. Elmer Davis, CBS radio commentator and wartime chief of the OWI, was also considered a likely witness.[4]

The men in the docket—the Unfriendly Nineteen—and their lawyers had been granted reserved space in the front row of spectators. Covering the hearings for the *Nation*, the left-wing journalist I. F. Stone scanned the lineup and observed: "In the front rows left sat the most affluent-looking group of alleged 'reds' in modern history: earnest men, mostly young—only rich America could provide its alleged revolutionaries with such sleek clothes and Sulka ties."[5]

A core group of thirteen Unfriendlies—Alvah Bessie, Herbert Biberman, Lester Cole, Gordon Kahn, Howard Koch, Ring Lardner Jr., John Howard Lawson, Albert Maltz, Lewis Milestone, Samuel Ornitz, Larry Parks, Irving Pichel, and Dalton Trumbo—were faithful attendees. From his seat at the press table, *New York Mirror* columnist George Dixon eavesdropped on the men he called "pinko lice." He didn't like what he heard. "These downtrodden serfs managed to smile though it all," wrote the disgusted Hearst scribe. "In fact, they giggled and grinned. It wouldn't be going too far to say they smirked. They did."[6]

Mixed in with the players with an assigned role were recognizable faces from Washington's version of celebrities—politicians, lobbyists, and hostesses around town, calling in markers to make the scene at the hottest ticket in town. The socialite Alice Roosevelt Longworth, daughter of Theodore Roosevelt, wife of the late Speaker of the House Nicholas Longworth and a quipstress deemed second only to Dorothy Parker, attended every day of the hearings but seems to have left to history no HUAC-related *bon mot*.

Behind the press tables, jostling for the four hundred or so seats allotted to average citizens, a packed house waited for the curtain to rise on a performance with an estimated three-week run. From back in the gallery, the line of sight was awful: spectators had to stand to catch a glimpse of a star. Most of the time they just stared at the back of a head as the witness hunched over the microphones. On the first day, actor Larry Parks was the only face in the room a civilian might have recognized, but the industry-wise noticed MPAA president Eric Johnston ducking in forty-five minutes late.

For concerned citizens not on site, the media offered plenty of options for vicarious attendance. In addition to blanket coverage in the print press, radio transmitted the testimony both live and via recording for broadcast in the evenings. The Mutual network carried a live pick-up at 10:30–11:00 A.M. and aired playbacks at 4:30–4:45 P.M. and 11–11:15 P.M. ABC broadcast selections from the hearings each evening at 11:35 P.M. to 12:00 midnight, Monday through Friday, except Thursday from 10:30–11:00 P.M. It also aired interviews with committee members and witnesses on the nightly news program *Headline Edition* at seven o'clock each evening. CBS broadcast live coverage daily at 10:30–11:00 A.M. over its Washington affiliate WTOP and recaps nationally at 11:15–11:45 P.M. or 11:30 P.M. to 12 midnight.[7] Washingtonians were especially fortunate in their listening options: independent station WWDC broadcast the complete testimony on its sister station, WWDC-FM.

Thomas also welcomed the transmission belt of the not-so-distant future. In what would have been an unprecedented coup, he granted the upstart medium of television permission to broadcast the proceedings live, allowing two television cameras to be installed alongside the newsreel cameras on the platform behind the dais. In 1947 fewer than 2 percent of American families owned a television set, a device still watched mainly in saloons, but Washington and New York television stations were enthused about broadcasting live coverage to daytime drinkers and early adopter couch potatoes. While setting up over the weekend, however, the television cameramen discovered that the electric outlets in the caucus room were wired only for direct current. "Most tele equipment operates with alternating current," explained *Daily Variety*. "Cost of installing converters was too high, so broadcasters settled for films for later transmission."[8]

But though blacked out from live coverage, NBC television deployed its own newsreel crew to film the proceedings for half-hour nightly compilations of highlights. Granted space on the dais shoulder to shoulder with the five commercial newsreel crews, the television boys felt confident that parity would ultimately give way to ascendancy. "Though newsreels are highly popular, you seldom see as much as two minutes of any news event in a movie house, whereas TV can give you the whole show," bragged the medium-boosting newsletter *Television Digest*, delighted at the "top grade shooting"

NBC was doing at the hearings.[9] For the moment, though, the newsreels were the medium of record. Appropriately, for this most cinematic of congressional investigations, the images would be screened and preserved on 35mm film, the last Washington show to be the sole province of the motion picture newsreel.

Thomas was not alone in welcoming the spotlight. The Unfriendly Nineteen relished the chance to take the stage and do battle with their nemesis. Two weeks before the opening, the lawyers for the Nineteen had notified Thomas on behalf of their clients that "we will object to the holding of closed hearings from which the press, the radio, and the public are barred." They wanted their voices heard and they wanted to turn things around on HUAC, to make Thomas the villain of the play.[10]

The media scrum covering the HUAC hearings differed from the pilot fish who usually trailed after Hollywood. The congressional show trial was not a celebrity marriage, a scandalous divorce, or a shocking indiscretion; it was the serious stuff of Communism versus democracy, national security versus freedom of expression. Every major newspaper in the country headlined the daily face-offs and weighed in editorially. Gossip columnists and trade reporters prone to cynicism vied with name-brand columnists whose fallback position on Hollywood was condescension. The dissonance in the coverage reflected the double edge to the Washington-Hollywood matchup: breathless headlines, snarky asides, and, on occasion, tempered and sober analysis of what was, in truth, the ritual enactment of a great Constitutional conflict.

In a sign of the times, a good deal of the media coverage was meta-media in outlook, with one eye on how the players played in the media. "The hearings were brought to an avid public by newspaper banner headlines, nightly half-hour recordings of the testimony broadcast coast-to-coast by the American Broadcasting Company; television via films, broadcast nightly by the National Broadcasting Corporation, and the newsreels," reported *Motion Picture Herald*, in a tally of the coverage that also noted Thomas's savvy manipulation of same. "As the parade of witnesses moved to and from the stand in the House caucus room, it became clear that the committee was spotting the more sensational moments so as to obtain the best headline breaks in the late afternoon editions of the country's press. And they were getting them."[11]

Thomas savored the limelight and kept a wide-open door policy toward the print press, the radio, and the newsreels. He even allowed himself to be interviewed and baited by Virginia Gardner, reporting on HUAC for the

Communist weekly, the *New Masses*. "Mr. Thomas and I have a professional interest in each other," Gardner jested. "From what he has told me loudly and with delight, I infer that I am the only live, breathing, and sensate Communist Party member who has ever been a visitor in his office."[12]

Yet for all the buzzing in the gallery and among the press, the tribunal was undermanned: a prominent player was not on stage. On May 16, 1947, when the road show left Los Angeles, the expectation was that the full committee would meet in Washington a month later on June 16 for the long-threatened public hearings. But the date kept being pushed back, said Thomas, so his agents in the Hollywood field could make a thorough investigation. Besides, before raising the curtain on the main event, the chairman had a serious casting problem to solve in the person of John E. Rankin.

To all but a small constituency of like-minded xenophobes who looked upon Hollywood as a viper's nest of Bolshevik Jews, Rankin was a toxic presence. Critics of HUAC incessantly linked his name by hyphen with the present iteration of HUAC—"the Rankin-Thomas Committee," it was dubbed, and not just by the *Daily Worker*. In addition to wounding the chairman's ego, the label sullied the reputation of the committee. Thomas well understood that "the temperament of the renowned Southern gentleman John Rankin" was a severe "headache" for HUAC. "Further, he was unduly narrow-minded on certain subjects, bitter against the Jews, and never hesitated to show his disgust for Jews," the chairman recalled in 1957. "This presented acute problems both in executive sessions and in public hearings."[13] With Rankin on the dais, HUAC could rightly be considered a front for antisemitic troglodytes.

Yet Rankin was the senior Democrat on the committee, a former interim chairman, and a power among the blue dog Southern Democrats crucial to President Truman's coalition. He could not be dislodged and he could not be silenced.

Fortunately for Thomas, fate intervened. On August 21, 1947, Rankin's only rival as a congressional racist and antisemite, Sen. Theodore G. Bilbo (D-MS), died.[14] The death of Bilbo, a proud Klansman and author of *Make Your Choice: Separation or Mongrelization*, left his Senate seat open. A special election was announced for November 4. Rankin threw his hat into the ring.[*]

---

[*] Both Bilbo and Rankin are called out by name in Elia Kazan's anti-antisemitism social problem film, *Gentleman's Agreement*, released November 11, 1947. By that date, Bilbo was dead and Rankin had lost the Senate election to replace him.

Thomas seized the opportunity. The hearings had already been rescheduled from June to an announced starting date of September 29, when Hanns Eisler was to be interrogated, but by pushing back the date of the main event to October 20, Thomas made certain that Rankin would not sit on the dais to discredit the committee and draw headlines away from the chairman. Thomas explained that the postponement would "permit all committee members to attend."[15] This was transparently false. Delaying the hearings to October 20 meant that Rankin would be far away from Capitol Hill, in the Mississippi Delta, campaigning for Bilbo's Senate seat. "The wisest thing the Thomas investigating committee has done yet is shove Rankin (allegedly electioneering at home) to the background," commented Rankin's old enemy Walter Winchell. "He is Congress's worst ad."[16]

After maneuvering Rankin off the dais, eight remaining members were left to serve. On that momentous first day, however, only five showed up— Thomas, McDowell, Nixon, Vail, and Wood. Wood, the former (and future) committee chair, popped in late and attended only intermittently. That left four members—not a full quorum. Technically, the tribunal would be a subcommittee of the House Committee on Un-American Activities.

The soundstage ambiance in the normally sedate chamber coexisted with the kinetic *frisson* of a high-stakes criminal trial. Yet the caucus room was no courtroom. While the hearings had the trappings of a legal proceeding— subpoenas, swearing in, testimony from witnesses, the presence of lawyers, and prosecutorial interrogations—they had none of the strict rules of evidence, attention to due process, and protection of civil rights that marked a proper American trial. Congressional testimony being immune from American libel laws, witnesses and congressmen alike might accuse by name and fire off charges with impunity.

Moreover, the ersatz judge who presided over the faux courtroom lacked a judicial temperament. An urban Irishman with a short attention span and a shorter fuse, Thomas handed down brusque, off-the-cuff rulings punctuated by thunderclap gavel whacks. He refused to permit lawyers to coach or advise their clients, although consultations between attorneys and clients were usually permitted in congressional hearings. He allowed some witnesses, usually the Friendlies, to read opening statements, but denied the right to others, usually the Unfriendlies. The hearing was too public to be a star chamber and too open-ended to be a kangaroo court, but it was not a judicial proceeding either. It was a bastard hybrid, part show, part trial.

Bartley Crum: "This is certainly un-American."

Before the hearings came to order, as the technicians checked sound levels and electrical connections, Thomas walked out on the floor to supervise the placement of cameras and lights, or pretend to. The stage management was all for show: the layouts and sight lines had been scoped out over the weekend. The previous Saturday, during a technical run-through, a kind of dress rehearsal had taken place. A cooperative subject, Thomas amiably took direction from the newsreel boys. On cue, he stepped out and walked to his seat on the dais. A short man, he sank down in the chair to an undignified level. A red pillow and a telephone book were fetched to elevate him on the makeshift throne. A cameraman took a tape measure and calculated the distance from his nose to the cameras. "Thank you, Congressman," said a newsreel man. "That's fine."[17]

Gavel at his right, Nixon at his left, Thomas looked into the cameras and made a statement that would be screened in motion picture theaters with the next newsreel issue, released that Monday upon the start of the hearings:

> I want to emphasize at the outset of these hearings that the fact that the Committee on un-American Activities is investigating alleged Communist influence and infiltration in the moving picture industry must not be considered or interpreted as an attack on the industry itself nor should our investigation be interpreted as an attack on the majority of persons associated with this great industry. I have every confidence that the vast majority of movie workers are patriotic and loyal Americans.[18]

Signaling that the battle was to be joined, Eric Johnston replied via the same medium. "As the hearing gets under way, we bring you a statement on behalf of the film industry by Eric Johnston, president of the Motion Picture Association," announced MGM's *News of the Day*, pairing Johnston with Thomas in the same issue, and allotting him more screen time to explain himself:

> The motion picture industry has been accused of putting subversive and un-American propaganda on the screen. We deny that without any reservation. The pictures themselves are complete proof of its falsity. We are accused of having Communists and Communist sympathizers in our employ. Undoubtedly, there are such persons in Hollywood, as you would

find elsewhere in America. But we neither shield nor defend them. We want them exposed. We're not responsible for the political or economic ideas of any individual. But we *are* responsible for what goes on the screen. We guard that with great care. If Communists have attempted to inject their propaganda into the motion picture, they have failed miserably. We would never permit them to succeed.[19]

Back to back on newsreel film, Thomas and Johnston would soon enough be face to face in a bout that was billed as mortal combat but that would, in the end, be a meeting of the minds.

Finally, after nearly ten months of buildup and ballyhoo, the warm-ups gave way to the big show. At half past ten in the morning, Thomas called the hearings to order. The first important piece of business was an opening statement from Chairman Thomas.

Thomas was "well aware" of the grave and momentous task his committee was undertaking. "The motion picture industry represents what is probably the largest single vehicle of entertainment for the American public. With such vast influence over the lives of American citizens as the motion picture industry exerts, it is not unnatural . . . that subversive and undemocratic forces should attempt to use this medium for un-American purposes." In turn, it was not unnatural for the House Committee on un-American Activities to investigate the medium.

As soon as Thomas finished his opening remarks, Robert W. Kenny and Bartley C. Crum, lawyers for the Unfriendly Nineteen, stepped forward. Kenny moved that the subpoenas be quashed, an appeal that Thomas summarily dismissed.

"This is certainly un-American," muttered Crum.

It was "a pretty loud mutter," remarked *PM*'s Quentin Reynolds, listening from the press table.[20]

The featured attractions were two of Hollywood's brand names: Jack L. Warner, vice president of production at Warner Bros. Pictures, and Louis B. Mayer, vice president in charge of production at MGM. The moguls testified as friendly witnesses, eager to demonstrate cooperation and to deflect criticism away from the executive suites and onto a tiny cell of malcontent screenwriters. Warner Bros. and MGM wanted it known that, no less than HUAC, the studios maintained a vigilant watch over the American-ness of the Hollywood screen.

By happenstance—the congressional investigators were too ignorant of studio style to have premeditated the juxtaposition—the two moguls represented opposite ends of the art and ethos of Hollywood cinema. Warner Bros. cultivated a gritty, street-level look with films that trafficked in socially conscious and politically edgy material. MGM draped itself in a glossy sheen of celestial glamour and went first class all the way. The definitive Warner Bros. film was *I Am a Fugitive from a Chain Gang* (1932), a bleak portrait of a chain gang convict, unjustly accused, who escapes from prison but not fate, ending up caught in the shackles of Great Depression America. The trademark MGM film was *Love Finds Andy Hardy* (1938), the fourth in a fifteen-part series of family romances set in a placid, pure-white neighborhood practicing an unspecified brand of Protestantism. Warner was a prominent Democrat, a staunch FDR man, and supporter of the New Deal, except when it came to regulating Warner Bros. profits and executive salaries. Mayer was a rock-ribbed Republican whose idea of a great president was Calvin Coolidge.

Jack L. Warner: "Subversive germs breed in dark corners."

Jack L. Warner was given the dubious distinction of being chosen as the leadoff witness. Fifty-five years old, slickly mustached and nattily dressed, he somehow managed to look gruff and dapper at the same time. He was accompanied by Paul V. McNutt, the lawyer who had been retained by the MPAA to advise and defend the industry.

Given all that had been done for America and Americanism under the Warner Bros. shield, Warner was understandably rattled by the congressional onslaught. Just the previous March at a special ceremony at March Field in Riverside, CA, General of the Army H. H. "Hap" Arnold had presented him the Medal for Merit "for extraordinary fidelity and meritorious conduct" during World War II along with a citation signed by President Truman.[21] Now the legislative branch of that same government was calling him on the carpet for coddling Communists.

Warner could expect no help from the lawyer at his side. Before Warner was even sworn in, Thomas had curtly informed McNutt that he might advise his client on his constitutional rights, but he could not interject to cross-question Warner or the committee members. The jowly, bald, pear-shaped chairman seemed to resent the chiseled good looks of the courtly MPAA attorney he sneered at as "pretty boy Paul McNutt."[22] "You are no different from all the other attorneys who have appeared before this committee," snapped Thomas.

After being sworn in, Warner was permitted to read a prepared statement—a privilege not accorded all the witnesses, certainly not all the Unfriendlies. Stumbling over some of the multisyllabic words in his ghostwritten remarks, he likened the Communists in Hollywood to "ideological termites," a phrase that perfectly captured the sense of invasive infestation abroad in the land: Communists were like insects burrowing into the architecture of American life. Warner argued for an exterminationist policy:

> Wherever they may be, I say let us dig them out and get rid of them. My brothers and I will be happy to subscribe generously to a pest removal fund. We are willing to establish such a fund to ship to Russia the people who don't like our American system of government and prefer the Communistic system to ours. That's how strongly we feel about the subversives who want to overthrow our free American system.

No Warner Bros. picture, he asserted, could "fairly be judged hostile to our country or Communistic in tone or purpose." Indeed, the interest of Warner Bros. "in the preservation of the American way of life is no new thing with our company. Ever since we began making motion pictures we have fostered American ideals."

On that last point, the witness was on solid ground: no Hollywood studio had done more than Warner Bros. to promulgate made-in-America democracy. Since entering the ranks of the majors with *The Jazz Singer* (1927), an all-American tale of a Jew melting into the mainstream to make good on Broadway, themes of good-natured comradery and casual equality had infused the studio's slate of biopics, melodramas, and action adventures. During World War II, Warner Bros. provided facilities and personnel for military training films, morale-boasting home front shorts, and war-minded melodramas and combat films that taught the teamwork and tolerance necessary to wage modern war.

Warner concluded his statement with a defense of freedom of expression that even the Unfriendly Nineteen might have saluted. "We can't fight dictatorships by borrowing dictatorial methods," he declared. "Nor can we defend freedom by curtailing liberties. But we can attack with a free press and a free

Jack L. Warner (*left*), lawyer Paul V. McNutt (*center*), and Louis B. Mayer (*right*) listen to the opening statement of HUAC Chairman J. Parnell Thomas on the morning of October 20, 1947.

screen." So as not to appear too liberal-minded, he returned to his pesticide metaphor at the close of his remarks. "Subversive germs breed in dark corners," he warned. "Let's get light into those corners. That, I believe, is the purpose of this hearing and I am happy to have had the opportunity to testify."

If Warner thought his patriotic preamble would endear him to the committee, he was mistaken. Thomas took the first shot. "You admit that there are, or were, Communists or Communist sympathizers in your own industry?" he asked.

Warner blandly admitted that screenwriters sometimes tried to inject un-Americanism into studio scripts but it was his business to see that it didn't get in. "If it eventually does creep in, I cut it out."

During HUAC's road trip to Los Angeles back in May, Warner—testifying behind closed doors at the Biltmore and assuming his testimony would be secret—had offered up the names of fifteen screenwriters he suspected of un-American leanings, names immediately leaked to the press. When Warner seemed reluctant to repeat the accusations in public, Stripling refreshed his memory by reading his earlier statements aloud.

Warner could not very well recant his previous sworn testimony, but he backtracked and equivocated. Asked if he stood by his statements, Warner replied he could not say for certain the people he listed were Communists but "I could tell from what they were putting in scripts, they were 'un-Americans.'" He confessed to having been somewhat "emotional" during his earlier testimony and, upon calmer reflection, felt that a few of the names he blurted out should be excised from his list. "There are several men whom I don't recollect as having written subversive propaganda," he admitted.

"You'd better name those," ordered Thomas.

Warner absolved Guy Endore, Sheridan Gibney, and Julius and Philip Epstein. In portraying rich men as villains, the screenwriters had simply followed a populist plotline "as old as the world is itself."

The single undeniable blot on Warner Bros.'s record of all-American productions inspired an extended back and forth. A counterfactual hallucination as cravenly pro-Stalin as *Mission to Moscow* was impossible to explain away, but Warner reminded his interrogators that the film was made to fulfill a wartime purpose. "If producing *Mission to Moscow* in 1942 was a subversive activity, then the American Liberty ships which carried food and guns to Russian Allies and the American naval vessels which convoyed them were likewise engaged in subversive activities. The picture was made only to help a desperate war effort, and not for posterity." In the days when a played-out print was put on a warehouse shelf and forgotten, Warner could not have suspected that *Mission to Moscow* would come back to haunt him.

Visibly squirming under Stripling's grilling, Warner denied what was, in fact, true: that the White House, in the person of FDR himself, had pressured the studio to make the pro-Soviet film. The charges, Warner insisted, were a "fantasy."[23] He testified that his brother Harry had personally and independently negotiated the screen rights for *Mission to Moscow* with Ambassador Joseph E. Davies.

Stripling asserted that the historical inaccuracies in the film amounted to nothing less than cinematic "fraud."

"As far as I'm concerned," Warner replied nonsensically, "I considered it true as written in Davies' book."

Thomas was getting bored with the back and forth. "I think we have gone into this *Mission to Moscow* at some length," he told Stripling, cutting short the film analysis.

When Nixon broke in to suggest that the MPAA could act as a clearing house for politically suspect employees, Warner demurred. "I don't think it would be legal to have an association banded together for this purpose," he said. "I would not be a party to it." Representative Vail picked up on the point and asked whether it would be advisable for the MPAA to prepare a list of directors and writers with Communist ties and refuse to employ them. "Absolutely no!" shot back Warner, who, unlike the congressman, had been tutored on conspiracy statutes by studio lawyers.

However, when Thomas asked whether he favored legislation to outlaw the Communist party, Warner quickly concurred. "I am in favor of making it an illegal organization." He also said that Warner Bros. was in preproduction on an anti-Communist film, but would not say what the title was.[24]

A few lighter moments served to relieve the tension in the room. When Stripling referred to the unfriendly screenwriters as "rich men," Warner put things in Hollywood perspective. "They're not rich men," he insisted. "They only earn $2,000 to $3,000 a week." Later, when Warner resisted attempts to interrupt him during a lengthy panegyric on his studio's patriotic films, Nixon drily commented, "We can see now, Mr. Warner, why you've been so successful selling your pictures to the American public."[25] Warner drew his biggest laugh when, in answer to a long-winded question from Nixon, he replied, "Well, I agree with everything you say."

During his time at the microphone, Warner ventured only one subtle jab at the committee. Asked if he would recognize a Communist, he said he had never seen one. "I wouldn't know one if I saw one," he insisted. But Fascists? "Yes, I've seen them." He hastened to add, "Not in America. I mean in Europe."

After nearly two hours, Thomas had heard enough. He glanced at his watch and said it was time for lunch. The hearing was adjourned until two o'clock.

At the noon recess, Kenny and Crum held an impromptu press conference outside the hearing room: the first of a regular series of instant rebuttals from the legal rapid response team for the Unfriendly Nineteen. Kenny noted that "the great bulk" of the writers Warner had allegedly cashiered "have been offered jobs by Warner time and time again." For the record, Gordon Kahn had not been dismissed by Warner but paid the studio ten thousand dollars to get out of his contract. Robert Rossen had three of his pictures re-issued by Warner Bros. that very year. Trumbo had resigned at the request of the SWG.[26] Judging from the record, Warner applied no ideological litmus test to the hiring or firing of his schmucks with Underwoods.

Sam Wood: "I know there are Communist writers in Hollywood."

Samuel Grosvenor Wood was a successful Hollywood director whose vocation was nearly swallowed up by his politics. "He's so far to the right, he's coming around again on the left," cracked Groucho Marx, not really joking.[27] So great was Wood's anti-Communist volatility that even the HUAC investigators harbored doubts about his stability. In his pre-testimony report on Wood, committee investigator H. A. Smith said the director would "make a satisfactory witness," but that he "is not too articulate, and to some extent gets excited."[28,*]

A founding member and president of the MPA-PAI, Wood came to Hollywood in 1910 to try his hand at acting after going bust in gold mining, farming, and real estate. By 1914, he was serving as an assistant to his ideological soulmate Cecil B. DeMille, and by 1916 he was sitting in a director's chair under contract for Paramount. He spent the silent era polishing the luster of Rudolph Valentino, Gloria Swanson, and Marion Davies. By 1931, he had moved up the ladder to MGM, the top rung of the studio hierarchy. When Wood took the oath before HUAC, he had over seventy motion pictures to his credit.

Wood was a job-of-work craftsman, not a stylist with a personal touch. Still, as a ringmaster in the greatest show that was MGM, he had helmed enough big-budget hits to lend him plenty of heat: the Marx Brothers comebacks, *A Night at the Opera* (1935) and *A Day at the Races* (1937); and the heart-tugging melodramas *Goodbye, Mr. Chips* (1939), *Kings Row* (1941), and *The Pride of the Yankees* (1942). He also made pivotal and uncredited contributions to the biggest of all MGM epics, *Gone With the Wind* (1939).

Wood despised Communist and fellow-traveling screenwriters and the feeling was mutual. "98 percent of all screenwriters with the hammer and sickle brand on their rump are nothing but mechanics," he was wont to say.[29] Dalton Trumbo responded that it was Wood who was the mechanical hack. While Wood's contemporaries—D. W. Griffith, F. W. Murnau, Eric von Stroheim, and so on—had revolutionized the art of cinema, "the curious fact [is] that most standard volumes on the theory and practice of motion pictures fail to take his work into account. Lewis Jacobs's *The Rise of the American Film* [1939], for example, doesn't even mention his name."[30]

---

* Prior to being called to the witness table, most of the friendly witnesses were given extensive pre-testimony interviews by Smith. The interviews also served as coaching sessions.

Producer-director Sam Wood, president of the Motion Picture Alliance for the Preservation of American Ideals, testifying on October 20, 1947.

In his testimony before HUAC, Wood made Jack Warner look close-mouthed. Names tripped off his tongue—the directors John Cromwell, Irving Pichel, Edward Dmytryk, and Frank Tuttle; and the writers Dalton Trumbo, Donald Odgen Stewart, and John Howard Lawson. Wood was most emphatic about Lawson. If he wasn't a Communist, "then I haven't any mind." Gesturing toward a section of the gallery that would not dissent, he said, "I suppose there are 19 gentlemen back here that say I haven't."

Wood's own union, the Screen Directors Guild (SDG), had also fallen prey to the conspirators. Past president John Cromwell "with the assistance of three or four others, tried hard to steer us into the Red river."

Yet Wood rebuffed the notion of government censorship, insisting that Hollywood be allowed to make pictures on every facet of American life. When Stripling suggested the dangers in exporting John Ford's bleak Dust Bowl saga *The Grapes of Wrath* (1940), Wood said he figured the Russians would find little use for it as propaganda. In America, after all, even dirt-poor Okies owned their own jalopies.

In Wood's eyes, any Hollywood organization that was not the MPA-PAI was suspect. He assailed the Free World Association, an internationalist group "dug up by Walter Wanger," the liberal independent producer, and the Emergency Council of Hollywood Unions, headed by Emmet Lavery, both of which were constantly blocking the good work of his own outfit.

Worst of all was the SWG, which was a cauldron of Communist subversion. "What group must be watched more carefully than the rest?" he asked himself, promptly answering: "Writers. I know there are Communist writers in Hollywood." Once again, the subaltern scribes tolerated by the studios as a necessary evil had been transformed into the vanguard of the Revolution.

Before excusing the witness, Thomas bestowed a benediction. "Mr. Wood, to use the slang expression, you really lay it on the line. If the great, great majority of persons in industry, labor, and education showed the same amount of courage that you show, we would not have to worry about Communism or Fascism in this country. In other words, you've got guts."

Wood assured Thomas that all the members of the MPA-PAI were similarly equipped.

After Wood's testimony, the SDG immediately telegrammed Speaker of the House Joseph W. Martin and Chairman Thomas to deny Wood's charges that it had ever wanted to navigate into the Red river. Wood's remarks were "without foundation," said a special committee made up of the guild's heaviest hitters—president George Stevens, backed by John Ford, Merian C. Cooper, John Huston, George Sidney, and William Wyler. The men were not only prestigious directors but, except for Sidney, veterans with sterling war records. "Every signatory of this telegram is an American citizen opposed to Communism," read the message. "But we firmly believe that an American citizen should not have his reputation attacked by anyone without the rights which we believe were the intent of the Constitution to give."[31]

Louis B. Mayer: "I will not preach any ideology but Americanism."

As the last letter in Hollywood's most famous initials, Louis B. Mayer presided over Technicolor adventure films, opulent costume dramas, and heartwarming paeans to prosperous American families. Not even the Great Depression could tarnish the gleam of Hollywood's most glamorous and profitable studio, or the Midas touch of its helmsman, long the highest-paid salaryman in the nation. MGM's celestial slogan ("more stars than there are in heaven") and the Leo the Lion symbol that roared as its logo, befit the alpha male status of its chief executive—the prowling, man-eating king of the Hollywood jungle.

At the witness table, however, facing the HUAC tribunal, Mayer did not roar. He purred like a kitten.

During the preliminary questioning to establish his identity, Mayer gave his birthplace as Russia. "This bit of intelligence brought a score or more of random spectators forward in their seats," noticed Gordon Kahn, who did not budge.[32]

Mayer had traveled far from his roots in Minsk: he lived the American dream his studio so lavishly and lovingly projected. Brought by his parents to St. John, New Brunswick, at age three, he spent his childhood selling junk from a little red wagon he pulled along behind him. By his teens, he was in the ship salvage business, which brought him to Boston, where he had the epiphany that was to reshape American entertainment. In 1907, Mayer refurbished a rundown theater and programmed good, clean Christian-centric entertainment. He was soon the most powerful exhibitor in New England.

By 1919, Mayer was in Hollywood, the new motion picture frontier, where, with a brilliant young executive named Irving Thalberg, he designed the industrial infrastructure of the studio system. He seldom let a trace of his own background—foreign born, Jewish, reeking of the shtetl—muss up the manicured lawns in the restricted-covenant neighborhoods of MGM-world.[33] In Mayer's office were two pictures that summed up his assimilationist instincts and conservative politics: Roman Catholic prelate Richard Cardinal Spellman and newspaper publisher William Randolph Hearst.[34]

Like Warner, Mayer was given permission to read an opening statement. Picking up on his rival's theme, he called on HUAC to recommend legislation "establishing a national policy regulating employment of Communists in private industry." He expressed the "earnest hope" that HUAC perform a "public service" by declaring that Communists "should be denied the sanctuary of the freedom they seek to destroy." Presumably, he meant prison or deportation.

"Like others in the motion picture industry, I have maintained a relentless vigilance against un-American influences," Mayer said. "We can't be held responsible for the political views of each individual employee. It is, however, our complete responsibility to determine what appears on the motion picture screen." Knowing the industry was on firmer ground defending its pictures than its personnel, Mayer wanted all eyes fixed on the end product.

The industry's hatred of Communism, Mayer pointed out, was "returned in full measure" because "few if any of our films reach Russia. It hates us because it fears us." Not to be outdone by Warner, Mayer seized every opportunity to shill for MGM's Americanism. As an example of MGM's commitment to the American dream, he cited *An American Romance* (1944), King Vidor's rags-to-riches tale of a Czech immigrant who rises from the iron mines to become a wealthy industrialist. Asked to repeat the title, he happily obliged, adding—he couldn't help himself—"in Technicolor."

Just as Warner had to defend *Mission to Moscow*, Mayer had to explain away *Song of Russia*. "Mention has been made of the picture *Song of Russia* as being friendly to Russia at the time it was made. Of course it was. It was made to be friendly," Mayer admitted. He reminded the committee that before World War II, his studio had taken satiric shots at the USSR. "In 1938, we made *Ninotchka* [1939] and shortly thereafter *Comrade X* [1940] with Clark Gable and Hedy Lamarr—both of those films kidded Russia."

H. A. Smith asked Mayer if MGM were producing any anti-Communist films "at the present time."

Mayer replied, "I think we are going to start shooting promptly"—an inadvertent laugh line.

Thomas leaned forward, grinning. "Mr. Mayer, these hearings haven't had anything to do with that promptness, have they?"

Still on defense, Mayer insisted that the field agents from the OWI "were coordinators and at no time did they attempt to tell us what we should or should not do. We made our decisions on production." Though a Republican, Mayer did not want to tar the legacy of FDR any more than Warner, not with the Department of Justice, suing the studios under the Sherman Anti-Trust Act. His public testimony contradicted what he had told investigator A. B. Leckie in a private interview prior to testifying: that the OWI had pressured MGM into making *Song of Russia* and even suggested the plot. MGM was "requested to make the picture in order to pet the Russians," Mayer told Leckie. "The government gave them the idea of the music conductor in Russia and having him meet a girl, etc."[35]

In its wartime context, Mayer reminded the room, *Song of Russia* "could not be viewed as anything other than for the entertainment purpose intended and a pat on the back of our then ally, Russia." The Soviets were hard pressed at Stalingrad and a cinematic kudos from Hollywood might inspire the Russian Army to fight more heroically against the Wehrmacht. Mayer himself had chosen Robert Taylor as the ideal lead for the film, but Taylor demurred, because he did not like the story. "At the time, Taylor mentioned his pending commission in the Navy, so I telephoned the Secretary of the Navy, Frank Knox, and told him of the situation." Recalling the good that had been accomplished by *Mrs. Miniver* (1942) and other morale-boosting pictures, the secretary called back and agreed that Taylor could be given time to make the film before being called to service.

Stripling asked Mayer if he felt *Song of Russia* was pro-Communist. "It had no political implications," he insisted. "I am convinced of that and I am under oath. If I went to meet my God, I would still say so." To support his case, Mayer read from a sampling of reviews that described the film purely as "light entertainment." Mayer claimed to have personally cleansed *Song of Russia* of any pro-Communist implications. In the first draft, Mayer said, "they had farm collectivism and I threw it out. I will not preach any ideology but Americanism. I had it [re]written and that is why Robert Taylor was delayed in getting into the service." Since then, Mayer deadpanned, "our relationship with Russia has changed."[36]

Prodded by Smith, Mayer spilled the names of three suspect screenwriters in his stable: Dalton Trumbo, Lester Cole, and Donald Ogden Stewart.

Representative Vail then asked a question that was on the minds of a lot of average Americans. "What motivates these writers and these actors whose income is in astronomical figures to embrace Communism?"

"I think they're cracked," replied Mayer, genuinely befuddled. "It can't be otherwise."

The gallery erupted in laughter.[37]

Ayn Rand: "I have never seen so much smiling in my life except on the murals of the World's Fair Pavilion of the Soviet!"

The last witness of the day, following Mayer to the stand, was Ayn Rand, another Russian not inclined to sing the praises of her birth country. Who could have predicted that the fame and impact of the little woman would rival—or surpass—the big men who preceded her that day?

Born as Alissa Rosenbaum in 1905 in St. Petersburg, Russia, Rand witnessed the October Revolution—and the funerals of its first victims—from the balcony of her family's apartment. Bookish and brilliant, she was enthralled by philosophy, history, and the movies, publishing a booklet on the Polish actress Pola Negri and a monograph with the dreamy title *Hollywood: American City of Movies*. In 1925, she secured a visa to the United States and, upon disembarking in New York, began the immigrant's act of metamorphosis, first with a new name, then with a credo molded to fit her self-absorbed personality.[38]

In 1926, Rand lit out for the American city of movies, aspiring not to stardom but to work with Cecil B. DeMille, and found employment as a screen extra and screenwriter. Returning to New York, she worked as a file clerk and wardrobe executive at RKO, and then—"nursing a yen to write," as *Variety* put it—moved "from dresses to scripts" with a screenplay development deal at MGM.[39]

Hopscotching back and forth between MGM, Paramount, and Universal, Rand struggled—her plays flopped, her scripts either died in pre-production or on the screen—but in 1943, after nine years of labor, she scored her first best seller, *The Fountainhead*, a will-to-power tale of an architect who would rather blow up his building than see his vision corrupted by philistines. At 754 pages, the doorstop of a novel was a clunky explication of her philosophy of Objectivism, a system of "rational selfishness" that helped shape, if not define, the libertarian strain in postwar American life.

Described by H. A. Smith as a "Russian-born Jewess," Rand warranted an especially thorough pre-testimony profile. "Ayn Rand is a very brilliant woman and understands the Communist Party line," wrote Smith. "She is well read and can handle herself very well in answering questions." On the debit side, however, "she does speak with an accent and it is a little difficult to understand her, and her appearance is slightly detrimental in that she has a semi-mannish haircut." Also—oddly, for HUAC's designated film critic—"she has not seen very many pictures in the last year."[40]

Despite Rand's negligent moviegoing habits, a month before her testimony, on behalf of the MPA-PAI, she wrote the *Screen Guide for Americans*, a guidebook for patriotic filmmakers and spectators. Like the rest of the world,

Hollywood faced a "narrowing choice between freedom and slavery." The Communists had already joined the fight; loyal American filmmakers must rise up to confront the challenge. Too often had Hollywood depicted industrialists, bankers, and businessmen as "villains, crooks, chiselers, or exploiters." Too seldom have moviegoers seen robust capitalism and individualism celebrated on the screen. "Let us put an end to the use of our pictures, our studios, and our money for the purpose of preaching our expropriation, enslavement, and destruction," she demanded. "Freedom of speech does not imply that it is our duty to provide a knife for the murderer who wants to cut our throat."[41]

At the witness table, Rand was a diminutive but riveting figure, erect and dynamic, tightly wound, staring into the men on the dais with her piercing dark eyes, sporting the close-cropped jet-black hair that Smith found so unladylike. Speaking in clipped rhotic-accented English, she might have stepped out of a Parisian salon for exiled Russians as imagined by Ernst Lubitsch. "A White Guard Russian," hissed the *New Masses*, knowing a mortal enemy when it saw one.[42]

Rand was called before HUAC not as a screenwriter but as an expert witness: a survivor of the Soviet system who had made exposing Stalin's crimes part of her life's work. At the request of the committee, she had recently watched *Song of Russia*. "She ripped into the picture and its angles as though she was trying to prove that Mayer's views of its purity were vapid and that he wouldn't know a Communist angle if he fell over it," reported *Variety*.[43]

As the only person in the room with a ready mastery of the text, Rand spoke with authority: she could call up visual details, dialogue exchanges, and thematic through-lines. In MGM's screening room at Culver City, she had watched the martial musical with mounting disgust; waves of nausea soon gave way to fits of fury. The opening of *Song of Russia*—a dissolve from the American flag to the Russian anthem and the hammer and sickle—"made me sick." It got worse. "There are montages of scenes in Moscow," reported Rand. "I don't know where they got them, but I never saw anything like it. It shows a Moscow restaurant such as never existed. If there were such restaurants, they would be for commissars and profiteers and girls from villages would not be permitted." Rand mocked MGM's bountiful fantasyland. "In that Moscow there were no food lines. The streets were clean and prosperous. There were no homeless children such as I have seen. In this picture you see people on excursion boats in satin blouses such as you see only in Russian restaurants in this country." A peasant family served up a table laden with food—described in the dialogue as "a simple country meal." The sumptuous feast was "such as anybody would be murdered for in Russia." According to MGM, peasant huts were equipped with radios while tractors were treated as private property. "This type of thing was to create a picture of how favorable life was under a totalitarian Soviet."

Rand continued her slashing film review by decrying a line spoken by Robert Taylor, as the handsome American conductor, to Susan Peters, as the gorgeous Soviet ingénue: "You are a fool, but a lot of fools like you died on the village green at Lexington." Rand was appalled. "I submit that it was blasphemy because the men at Lexington were not fighting just a foreign invader. . . . To compare them to somebody, anybody, fighting for a slave state is, I think, dreadful."[44]

After two decades working in Hollywood, Rand still managed to sound shocked that Moscow, MGM, bore no resemblance to Moscow, USSR. "There is a park where you see happy little children in white blouses running around," she scoffed, her voice rising in indignation. "I don't know whose children they are, but they are really happy kiddies." The bright toothy grins on the faces of a people she knew to be downcast and glum infuriated her. "I have never seen so much smiling in my life except on the murals of the World's Fair Pavilion of the Soviet!"

Representative McDowell liked what he heard, but even he questioned the total absence of childish glee in the Soviet Union. Was Rand really certain children didn't smile in Russia?

She was certain. "If they do, it is privately and accidentally. Certainly it is not social. They don't smile in approval of their system."

As Rand testified, Quentin Reynolds looked over at a flummoxed Louis B. Mayer, who was blinking in astonishment.[45]

Thomas thanked Rand for her comments and adjourned the hearing at four-thirty that afternoon. The curtain line for the day was left to attorney Robert Kenny: "This is the first time in history that the government has hired its own critic."[46]

Robert W. Kenny: "The thing we feared most has happened."

After Thomas gaveled the proceedings to a close, Kenny held a press conference. Dueling press conferences—by the congressmen, the witnesses, their

In rapid response mode, Robert W. Kenny (*left*) and Charles J. Katz (*center*), attorneys for the Unfriendly Nineteen, hold an impromptu press conference during a recess in the hearings, October 20, 1947.

lawyers, and various bystanders and surrogates—followed each day of hearings, indeed were held during breaks in the testimony, at the noon recess, and sometimes, to the consternation of the chairman, during the testimony itself.

"The thing we feared most has happened," Kenny warned. "The committee is trying to censor. . . . They are censoring by intimidation." The strange spectacle of a kowtowing Louis B. Mayer stuck with him. "Mr. Louis B. Mayer, producer of *Song of Russia*, was made uncomfortable. From now on Mr. Mayer's range will be limited. He knows that if he ever produces another picture like it, he will be brought before the committee again."[47]

In the evening hours, the campaign for the Unfriendly Nineteen moved away from the corridors of the Old House Office building to the auditorium of the National Press Club. At a rally jammed with eight hundred supporters, Irving Popper, vice president of the National Lawyers Guild, introduced each of the Nineteen and their lawyers, Kenny and Crum. All proclaimed that their goal was to "break up" the Thomas Committee. Director Edward Dmytryk declared that "if the Thomas Committee its successful in is purpose, no more films like *Crossfire* will be seen on the American screen. Suppression, once begun, will not end with one film."

If a Fascist terror was descending upon the nation, the prospect did not silence Bartley Crum. As a collection plate was passed among the crowd, Crum delivered an unlawyerly screed. "During Crum's remarks he unmercifully tongue-lashed Mr. Thomas, making numerous derogatory remarks concerning his appearance as well as his method in chairing the un-American Activities Committee," reported an FBI agent in attendance. "In concluding his remarks, Bartley Crum stated that he never appeared before such a nauseating individual as Mr. Thomas, and as the day went on he found it difficult for him to control himself to prevent being sick to his stomach."[48]

Rightly suspecting that not all of his listeners were partisans of the cause, Crum passed on a special message. "He said if there were any FBI agents present in the auditorium," reported the FBI agent present in the auditorium, "he wanted them to go and tell Thomas what he said and then both Thomas and the agents could 'go to Hell.'"[49]

Chapter 7
LOVEFEST

Unimpressed by the regal moguls, who were quite docile away from their own domains, the members of the Thomas Committee seemed positively smitten during the testimony of Adolphe Menjou, the first screen figure to walk in to the caucus room backlit by the glow of motion picture stardom. A "love-fest" is how *Variety* described the mutually admiring back and forth that opened the second day of hearings.[1] The mood was almost as cozy during the testimony of two exceptionally friendly screenwriters, one a name-dropping blabbermouth, the other a slightly more discreet elder statesman.

Adolphe Menjou: "I'd move to the state of Texas if they came over here, because I think the Texans would kill them on sight."

Adolphe Menjou's career in film predated Hollywood, not to say the Third Reich, which otherwise would have necessitated a name change. Suavely urbane—or too slick by half depending on taste—the fifty-seven-year-old actor cultivated a screen persona built around a to-the-manor-born, unctuous European sophistication. Offscreen, he kept in character—or maybe it was the other way around. Known as the best-dressed actor in Hollywood, he had to keep up appearances. His closets bulged with tailor-made suits imported from Saville Row. "Everybody is looking under beds for Reds," quipped Walter Winchell. "But fashion plate Menjou keeps looking in his clothes closet!"[2]

The waxed moustache, clipped diction, and Continental airs belied an all-American upbringing. Menjou was born and reared in Pittsburgh, the son of a French father, a prosperous restaurateur and café owner, and an Irish mother. When Charles Chaplin was looking for someone to play "the most sophisticated man in Paris" for *A Woman in Paris* (1923), he picked Menjou for the part. The actor was typecast forever after as an elegant swell, but he also played against type, showing his range as the fast-talking, whiskey-gulping newspaper editor in *The Front Page* (1931), for which he won an Oscar nomination, and the cynical bookie in *Little Miss Marker* (1936), where he was the paternal foil to the scene-stealing Shirley Temple, whom, he admitted, knew his lines better than he did. "My identifying traits were the roving eye, the cynical smile, and the immaculate dress suit," Menjou reflected, with the wry

Adolphe Menjou poses for photographers prior to his testimony, October 21, 1947.

self-knowledge of a self-made man.[3] He was currently featured in a made-to-order role in *The Hucksters* (1947), playing a venal ad agency executive, just the kind of unscrupulous businessman that anti-Communists accused Hollywood of purveying to discredit capitalism.

The committee knew that Menjou, who had testified in closed session back in May, was a prize catch. "He is probably as well read on the subject [of Communism] as anybody," wrote H. A. Smith. "He has a brilliant memory, and can quote from books and articles on the subject at length." Smith was concerned that Menjou was too much of a right-winger even for HUAC, but with the proper coaching, "he will take the stand, testify in a brilliant manner, and materially help our side." For all his eagerness to play Paul Revere sounding the alarm about Communism in Hollywood, Menjou worried that his testimony might interfere with his role in Frank Capra's forthcoming production, *State of the Union* (1948). Smith assured him that "we will do everything we possibly can to make his appearance timely with his acting."[4]

At the witness table, Menjou dressed for the part. "Mr. Menjou wore a beautiful De Gez (544 Fifth Ave.) brown pin-striped suit which was well worth the $200 he paid for it," observed *PM*'s Quentin Reynolds, displaying a sartorial eye suited to the fashion plate. "He wore a Sulka tie ($8), and his moustache was carefully waxed." Looking owlish behind thick, oval shell-rimmed glasses, Menjou chain-smoked Pall Malls as he delivered what even detractors acknowledged was a "splendid performance."[5] The thin moustache twitched as he spoke.

Articulate, at ease, and well-versed in the topic of the hour, Menjou knew about Communism from more than slogans and pamphlets. He began his study as a doughboy in the Fifth Division during World War I while stationed in Karl Marx's birthplace in Trier, Germany. Of the 350 books on the Soviet system he claimed to have read, he urged the American people to bone up on Max Eastman's condensed version of Marx's *Das Kapital*, William Z. Foster's *Towards a Soviet America*, T. S. Eliot's *The Dark Side of the Moon*, and Karl Volk and Julian Gumperz's *Pattern for World Revolution*. With the possible exception of several members of the Unfriendly Nineteen, he was likely the only person in the caucus room who had done the assigned reading. "He is so het up about un-Americanism that he practically stutters," joked his friend Hedda Hopper, but Menjou would not muff a single line before HUAC.[6]

Menjou broke the ice with a bit of self-deprecation that charmed the gallery. Asked his occupation, he declared in a loud clear voice, "I'm an actor."

Then, sotto voce, but not so sotto voce that the microphone could not pick it up: "I hope."[7]

"I am not here to smear," declared Menjou. "I am here to defend the industry that I have spent the greater part of my life in. I'm here to defend the producers and the motion picture industry."

Thomas took the cue. "I might also say that we are not here to smear the industry or the people working in it. We're here to get the facts and only the facts."

Remembering who signed his paychecks, Menjou condemned Communist efforts to infiltrate Hollywood but praised the vigilance of producers for keeping Red dialogue off the soundtrack. Didactic proselytizing from the screen was not the only danger, however. Communism might seep into cinema in a thousand devious ways. Exposing a few secrets of the trade, he revealed how a crafty actor could inject a subversive sentiment into a film with a gesture, a sidelong glance, or an arched eyebrow.

Fortunately, HUAC and his own Motion Picture Alliance for the Preservation of American Ideals had already prevented "a great amount of subtle and sly propaganda" from getting into films. Theirs was no easy task considering how freely Communists roamed the studio lots. "I know a great many people who act an awful lot like Communists," he stated. Although not quite as effusive as the fluent name droppers who had preceded and would follow him, he was not circumspect in identifying suspects.

Among the Communists Menjou knew to be working in Hollywood, director John Cromwell, whom Sam Wood had accused of trying to lead the Screen Directors Guild "into the Red river," was an unabashed zealot. "Mr. Cromwell, in his own home, said that capitalism was through in America and that I would live to see the end of it." Menjou paused for effect. "That is a strange statement from a man who earns more than $250,000 a year and who owns a large amount of real estate in Hollywood."

Playing to the gallery, Menjou laced his testimony with colorful language and blunt opinions, lambasting the "political idiots" and "crackpots in Hollywood" who had fallen for the "oriental tyranny" of Communism. "I'd move to the state of Texas if they [the Communists] came over here, because I think the Texans would kill them on sight."

Menjou admitted that the writers who had already been named as Communists represented some of the ablest wordsmiths in the business and that, in their pictures at least, he could not detect an iota of subversive influence.

"These men can write," he conceded. "Let them write, but make them come into the open. Then they can be closely watched and their stuff closely screened." He rejected the notion of a blacklist, saying that Communists should not be deprived of their right to work, only exposed and monitored. As for the Communist Party USA itself, it was a fifth column that should be outlawed.

Menjou singled out *Mission to Moscow* and *The North Star* as "dishonest" pictures that should never have been made. "Fortunately, both pictures were unsuccessful," he said. "They stank."[8] Their dismal quality was a stroke of luck. "The better the entertainment the more dangerous it is."

The conversation turned to Herbert K. Sorrell, head of the CSU and the culprit behind the strikes that had been disrupting the studio assembly line since 1945. Menjou called the present strike "disastrous," and said he suspected Sorrell of being a Communist under the nom de guerre Herbert K. Stewart.

Menjou then did something curious and all too revealing of the back-channel lines of communication between the government and its allies within the motion picture industry: he entered into the record a photostatic copy of Sorrell's CPUSA card and a supporting affidavit from "the world's greatest handwriting expert," verifying the signature.

How Menjou had obtained the photostat was not revealed, but it could only have come from collusion between the committee investigators and the MPA-PAI or from Billy Wilkerson at the *Hollywood Reporter*. The congressional investigators leaked their findings to the MPA-PAI, and the MPA-PAI leaked to the press. Counsel Stripling, of course, was familiar with Sorrell's party card and said that "Stewart" was Sorrell's mother's maiden name.

Menjou held Sorrell responsible for "the most incredible brutality, beatings, and overturning of cars" during the strike in 1945. Had the strike been settled under Sorrell's terms, Menjou claimed, "Every union would have been under the dominance of the Communist party." Worse was the fact that so much above-the-line talent lent their prestige to the radical workers. Among those who shared a platform with Sorrell, Menjou recalled, were the actors Edward G. Robinson, Hume Cronyn, Paul Henreid, and Alexander Knox.

Menjou's testimony marked the first time the issue of the Hollywood strikes had come up, but the animosity between studio management and radical labor, between the International Alliance of Theatrical Stage Employees and the Conference of Studio Unions, and between the Screen

Writers' Guild and the defunct Screen Playwrights. Inc., was a steady sub-surface hum. The battle lines were as schematic as the refrain from a labor anthem from the 1930s: on one side of the picket line, the moguls and their supporters in the MPA-PAI and IATSE; on the other side, the CSU, the liberals, and the Communists. With the former sitting pretty, the time was nigh for settling scores.

"Do you believe the motion picture industry is doing everything it can to rid itself of Communists?" asked Stripling.

"Yes, I do," replied Menjou. "I believe it has been that way for a year or a little more than a year now."

Though pleased by Menjou's testimony, Thomas had a less-compliant group of Hollywood stars on his mind: the CFA, scheduled to descend on Washington by plane that Sunday. The group had fired off a telegram to Thomas that day, throwing down the gauntlet. The barb had its intended effect: Thomas saw red. Asked to comment on the telegram, Menjou obliged by dismissing his colleagues as "innocent dupes." "They just haven't read about Communism," he shrugged. "I feel sorry for them." Thomas asked Menjou what he thought about the critics of the committee who had charged that HUAC's investigation amounted to "censorship" of the movie industry.

Before answering, Menjou gave a fair demonstration of how a practiced thespian, with gesture and pacing, could milk a scene. He leaned back in his chair, took a sip from a glass of water, inhaled a Pall Mall, blew the smoke through his nose, and spat out his lines. "I think that's juvenile. It's infantile . . . I don't see how that statement could be made by any man with the intelligence of a louse."[9]

The committee members beamed: finally, a Hollywood star who was eloquent, passionate, and sympathetic. Representative McDowell looked across the table and bestowed his blessings. "In addition to being a great actor, Mr. Menjou is one of the greatest American citizens I have ever met," he said with feeling. "He knows more about Communism than anybody I have ever known."

If J. Parnell Thomas was offended, he didn't say so.

When Menjou left the stand, the packed hearing room broke into a loud and sustained round of applause, the first such outburst accorded any of the witnesses. Menjou, uncharacteristically, was momentarily at a loss. He then turned around and made a formal bow to the crowd. The applause did not subside until he exited the hearing room.

Jack Moffitt: "I think there is a touchstone by which you can identify a Communist."

The second witness of the morning was a visual contrast to the debonair Menjou, the corpulent, threadbare forty-five-year-old John Charles ("Jack") Moffitt, *Esquire* movie critic and screenwriter. Moffitt was a veteran of the Screen Playwrights, Inc., still embittered by the defeat, still bearing the scars of the old battles, still ready to flail at his adversaries from the 1930s. He was a no-holds-barred witness who not only named slews of names but, for the benefit of the congressional stenographer, spelled them out: M-A-L-T-Z, K-A-H-N, C-O-L-E. . . .

A former motion picture editor for the *Kansas City Star*, Moffitt had come to Hollywood in 1930 to work at Universal. In 1936, he earned his most intriguing writing credit by collaborating with Sinclair Lewis on a stage version of Lewis's dystopic *It Can't Happen Here*, a production underwritten by the Federal Theater Project.[10] Though a good enough journeyman screenwriter, Moffitt had never quite broken into the top tier of his profession. "John C. Moffitt offers an imposing list of pictures nobody remembers," sneered film critic Archer Winsten at the *New York Post*.[11]

An ardent anti-Communist, Moffitt lobbied hard for a starring role at the witness table from the moment he heard of HUAC's plans to investigate Hollywood, sending several "I'm available" messages to Thomas via his congressman, Norris Poulson (R-CA). "I think I am qualified to unmask the techniques by which Communist thought has been concealed in specific pictures," he wrote. "I will be happy to put my professional abilities, as a critic and screen writer, at the disposal of Mr. Thomas to show him how the job is done." At the May hearing in Hollywood, Moffitt had rattled off so many names and film titles that he was invited back for two additional appearances. Moffitt was thrilled with the attention and his growing reputation as a Red-slayer. "Hollywood really is scared because of its Red record," he wrote Poulson. "Every studio in town is trying to figure out a way to whitewash itself."[12]

Yet over the summer Moffitt had second thoughts. The negative reaction to his testimony in May had sensitized him to the downside of besmirching the studio system he sought to work within. "We have spent considerable time with Mr. Moffitt in attempting to convince him to testify, inasmuch as he seems very opposed to appearing in Washington," wrote H. A. Smith that September. "He makes the statements that if we require him to testify, we are actually taking food out of the mouths of his children, he would lose his job at *Esquire*, and probably would be unable to obtain employment anywhere else." Hungry children or not, the committee needed Moffitt to repeat in public the names he had recited at the May hearings. To reassure Moffitt, Smith recruited influential Hollywood conservatives such as James McGuinness and director Victor Fleming to encourage his cooperation. "We are spending a lot of time with this individual, as we feel [his testimony] is important," Smith emphasized.[13]

Smith's efforts paid off. Moffitt fingered screenwriters Frank Tuttle, Herbert Biberman, Donald Ogden Stewart, and John Howard Lawson for luring him into joining the Hollywood Anti-Nazi League in 1937. The outfit, Moffitt claimed, was a classic Communist front group—an organization that suckered in good-hearted liberals and anti-Nazis but whose true agenda was dictated by the Comintern in Moscow. "I thought the purpose of the organization was stated in its title, the Anti-Nazi League," he said, expressing a misunderstanding that was not his alone. Moffitt proposed a litmus test that had proven all too reliable. "I think there is a touchstone by which you can identify a Communist. I think if you look at their attitude during the period of the Berlin-Moscow pact and you find that they approved of everything Nazi Germany did at the time, and then reversed themselves on the very day that the Germans invaded Russia, you will find that the person is a Communist and followed the Communist party line."

Moffitt said the SWG was dominated by the Communist Party and its in-house magazine, *The Screen Writer*, was "filled with Communist propaganda." At membership meetings, writers who dared question the party line were heckled down.

Moffitt reserved a special dose of venom for John Howard Lawson, who had been instrumental in founding the SWG in 1933 and resurrecting it in 1937. Lawson was the commissar of Hollywood's Red Guard, said Moffitt, an agent who had come out west "for the express purpose of organizing Hollywood for Communism."

Though not exactly on point, Moffitt veered from subversion on screen to subversion on stage. The theater people of Broadway, he said, were more dedicated than their counterparts in Hollywood. Veterans of the Federal Theater Project, the New Deal agency that was a make-work program for destitute actors and playwrights, and the Group Theater, a left-wing ensemble dedicated to social realist theater and Soviet-style agit-prop, had staged innumerable pro-Soviet productions. By Moffitt's precise calculations, forty-four of the one hundred plays that New York critics had selected as the "best plays" between 1936 and 1946 were "out and out Communistic" and two hundred thirty-three in the same period "favored the party line." On this point, Thomas, who had first made a name for himself in 1939 by chairing HUAC's hearings on the Federal Theater Project, needed no convincing.

Asked to name more "Communistic screenwriters," Moffitt obliged, ticking off a list of by now familiar bylines: Albert Maltz, Robert Rossen, Dalton Trumbo, Gordon Kahn, Ring Lardner Jr., Richard J. Collins, Harold Buchman, Lester Cole, Henry Meyers, William Palmer, Maurice Rapf Jr., John Wexley, and Harold J. Salemson, the last an organizer for the SWG.

After a lunch break, Moffitt opened his afternoon testimony with an attack on a little-known union called the Screen Story Analysis Guild, a cohort of gatekeepers who read scripts pitched to the studios. Moffitt charged that the guild skewed its reports to support Communist writers at the expense of non-Communist writers. Asked to be specific, Moffitt named Frances Millington, Paramount's chief script analyst and head of the group; her assistant, Simone Maise; and Bernie Gordon, also a Paramount analyst; Dave Robinson at Warner Bros., and Robinson's wife Naomi, whom he said was the Communist Party treasurer in Hollywood; Michael Uris at Enterprise; and, at MGM, Jesse Byrne and Lona Packer.[14]

At this point, Charles J. Katz, one of the lawyers for the Unfriendly Nineteen, who also represented the Screen Story Analysis Guild, had heard enough. Rising from his seat in the front row and striding down the aisle, he called out, "Mr. Chairman, Mr. Chairman, I represent a number of persons—"

"You are out of order!" bellowed Thomas.

"I demand the right of cross-examination—," Katz yelled back, matching Thomas's decibel level.

"Out of order, out of order!" screamed Thomas, pounding his gavel.

When Katz showed no inclination to get in order, Thomas barked, "Throw him out!"

From the press table, *New York Mirror* columnist George Dixon snarled, "Get a blackjack and slug him."

Four beefy cops and three plainclothesmen converged on Katz from all sides. A policeman and a committee investigator grabbed him by the arms and forcibly escorted him out of the hearing room. As the trio reached the door, Katz took a parting shot: "I thought this was to be a fair hearing!"

In the corridor outside of the hearing room, Katz told reporters he wanted to challenge Moffitt to name one film script suppressed by the Screen Story Analysts Guild, but before he could complete the point his escorts hustled him to an elevator and, with the press in tow, deposited him outside the building on the sidewalk.

Reporters clustered around Katz. "I only wanted to cross-examine Mr. Moffitt to show that everything he said was based on hearsay evidence and rumor," he said, now speaking softly. "The Supreme Court has said that the right of cross-examination is necessary to conduct a fair trial."[15]

Katz's ouster was the first physical altercation in a drama that so far had been short on action sequences.

While Katz was speaking to reporters, Bartley C. Crum was holding a mini-press conference inside the hearing room to comment on Katz's forced exit. The chattering carried on up to the committee bench.

"Break up that conference," demanded Thomas. "We must have order."

Crum rose from his chair and began to shout, "We just want the same right [of cross-examination] accorded to Howard Hughes"—at which point he noticed the Capitol police bearing down on him. Photographers rushed in anticipating another photogenic scuffle. "Get away from that man and come back here!" Thomas bellowed at them, as the galley erupted in laughter.[16] Rather than follow in Katz's footsteps, Crum sat down, muttering and red-faced, but obedient.

Moffitt tried to lighten the mood, saying that the outbursts reminded him of how the gallery had tried to dominate the sessions of the Commune during the French Revolution.

Thomas didn't want any talk of anarchy and revolution at his hearing. "If you are referring to what is taking place, I don't want you to refer to it," he ordered.

With Katz bum-rushed and Crum silenced, Moffitt resumed his meditations on the wily ways of Communist infiltration, telling how agents employed "the drop of water technique in injecting Communist propaganda on the screen and gradually conditioning American minds along Communist lines." Nonetheless, despite all he had said and all whom he had named, Moffitt estimated that "film producers were 98 percent successful" in eliminating any Red taint from the silver screen.

Among the Communist techniques of "water dropping" dollops of anti-Americanism into Hollywood scenarios was the incessant depiction of bankers as coldhearted skinflints who refused to loan money to worthy GIs, a reference to a scene in *The Best Years of Our Lives* (1946) where a banker questions the wisdom of a business loan to an undercapitalized veteran. Yet Moffitt defended Frank Capra's *It's a Wonderful Life* (1946), a film whose bloodsucking moneylender Mr. Potter already ranked as one of the most repellent incarnations of soulless capitalism in all of Hollywood cinema.

Moffitt then flung out a truly bizarre charge. Hollywood, he claimed, was undercutting religion by portraying clergymen as the mouthpieces of rich parishioners and "reactionary" old women. Of course, since Joseph I. Breen had taken the reins of the Production Code Administration in 1934, the clerics of all denominations—above all, the priesthood of the Roman Catholic Church—had been depicted by Hollywood as God's representatives on earth.

Moffitt's most explosive charge created an excited buzz in the hearing room. He claimed that several alleged Communists in Hollywood were implicated in an attempt to obtain restricted military information. Moffitt charged that John Weber, head of the west coast branch of the William Morris agency, had been sent out to Hollywood by CPUSA headquarters in New York. Weber and "other persons of left-wing tendencies" had tried to trick Chalmers "Slick" Goodlin, the famed test pilot, into revealing military secrets in a film script. According to Moffitt, Weber told Goodlin that "he must have a wonderful story to tell." A draft of a story with restricted information was ultimately put into Weber's hands.

The accusation went beyond anything that even J. Parnell Thomas had charged: not "boring from within" with subversive screen content or financing the CPUSA with donations, but outright espionage for the Soviet Union, an act of treason that might put an American in the electric chair. Scenting blood, Thomas promised to take up the matter in executive session.

After his lengthy and incendiary testimony, Moffitt was approached by Broadway columnist Earl Wilson, who wanted further details about the Red currents on the Great White Way. It was, after all, Wilson's beat: how could he have been so oblivious to the menace under his nose? Moffitt said he had discerned the subversion when he worked at the *New York Sun* . . . twenty years ago. "In other words, the fresh, crisp, crackling, up-to-the-minute viewpoint!" exclaimed Wilson.[17]

Asked to respond to Moffitt's charges, composer Richard Rogers insisted that Broadway "isn't dominated by Communists or anyone else"—though with five hits currently playing, he might have exempted himself and Oscar

Hammerstein. Rogers gave plaintive voice to the liberal's dilemma in the either-or year of 1947: "The way I see it, if you come out against Jim Crow in the theatre, they call you a Commie. And if you don't, you're called a Fascist. What happened to the middle of the road?"[18]

Rupert Hughes: "You can't help smelling them."

Moffitt was followed by another emotionally scarred veteran of the Hollywood writer's wars, Rupert Hughes, former president of the SP. The chubby, cigar-chomping seventy-five year old was the uncle of Howard Hughes but that was the least of his credit lines. A prolific author of novels, short stories, plays, and scholarly works; lecturer, radio commentator, and silent-era film director; and former Army intelligence officer in the Great War, he had been around longer, and plied more trades, than any other witness called before the Thomas Committee. In his spare time, he was a tinkerer and inventor who held a patent for a prototype of the modern switchblade.[19]

Longevity had made Hughes plenty of enemies. As a founding member not only of the non-filmic Author's League of America but of the original SWG formed in New York in 1920, a proto-version of the Hollywood arm, in which he had served as president, Hughes had been a staunch advocate of author's rights and an opponent of motion picture censorship all his life.[20] In 1924, invited to speak on behalf of the motion picture industry to a convention of dowdy matrons at the General Federation of Women's Clubs, he told the ladies to take up a broom if they were interested in cleaning—and not try to censor motion pictures.[21]

An early and principled anti-Nazi, anti-Fascist, and anti-Communist, Hughes opposed the SWG and its "cultural commissars" as an expression of his libertarian antagonism to all centralized authority. "I know of no tyranny more cruel than that of many labor organizers and no oppressions more devastating," he wrote in 1936. "Fascism, Communism, Nazism all start with cries of liberty and end with that word hushed and complete tyranny in the saddle."[22]

Hughes had witnessed a lot of literary history, but HUAC was interested in the more recent past, the Hollywood writers' wars of the 1930s. Hughes thought the lot of the screenwriter had been just fine "until John Howard

Lawson and some of his people revived [the SWG] in order to make it an instrument of Communist power." The Unfriendlies, he believed, were self-deluded. "I think those nineteen gentlemen have labeled themselves as Communists, but I don't think any one of them is now," he said, as if he understood the ideology better than they. How could he tell a Communist? "You can't help smelling them." Hughes's nostrils detected Communism at the highest levels of the despised SWG. Emmet Lavery, he charged, was "a Communist disguised as a Catholic."

Hughes said the studios balked at making anti-Communist films because exhibitors were intimidated by threats of vandalism. In 1935, he recalled, he was paid fifteen thousand dollars for a five-thousand-word plot satirizing the Communist Party. Hal B. Wallis, head of production at Warner Bros., told him that Jack and Harry Warner nixed the idea because party members "would put stink pots in the theaters." Producer Sol Lesser was threatened in like manner when he was considering a story on life in Russia called *Caput* (in the USSR everything was caput). Hughes alleged that "the wife of Hollywood's leading Communist" told Lesser: "If you show the picture, we will cut up the upholstery in every theater where it plays." (Presumably Hughes meant either the actress Gale Sondergaard, wife of Herbert Biberman, or the journalist Ella Winter, wife of Donald Ogden Stewart.)

While denouncing the laxness of studios that rewarded Communists with cushy salaries of two thousand or five thousand dollars per week, Hughes offhandedly referred to the University of California at Los Angeles as a "Communist-dominated institution." At that, the gallery tittered.

Unexpectedly, Thomas intervened and ordered the remark about UCLA be stricken from the record on the grounds that Hughes could not prove it. "This was the first time that charges were ordered stricken in this probe on the grounds of lack of factual evidence," *Variety* archly noted.[23]

When Hughes left the stand, he got a loud round of applause from the gallery. In the corridor outside the hearing room, however, he was confronted by a skeptical journalist. "*Ninotchka* didn't seem to turn loose any violence in theaters," the reporter pointed out, reminding him of Ernst Lubitsch's romantic comedy about a frosty Soviet commissar melted by the charms of Paris and Melvyn Douglas. "Correct," Hughes admitted. "Maybe it was because Greta Garbo was in it."[24]

After the hearings adjourned, MPAA counsel Paul V. McNutt held a press conference mobbed by some fifty reporters. Turnabout being fair play, he challenged HUAC to name pictures not people: to provide the titles of the films alleged to have undermined American values. "As I listened to the evidence the last two days, even the most damning evidence shows that they are 98 percent pure," he pointed out, referring to the percentile Jack Moffitt had used. "That is as good as Ivory soap."[25]

Away from Capitol Hill, Slick Goodlin, the heroic test pilot Moffitt had accused of treason, was appalled to hear his name had been sullied. Goodlin telegrammed Thomas to deny Moffitt's "malicious assertions" and demand the right to testify to refute the charges. "I, as a patriotic American, feel it is only just that the committee records contain my rebuttal and that the press be advised accordingly," wrote Goodlin. "If need be, I will gladly place myself along with documentary evidence at your disposal."

Goodlin was never called.[26]

Chapter 8

FRIENDLIES, COOPERATIVE AND UNCOOPERATIVE

D
ay Three would be a good day for the committee. Men with real expertise, pertinent backgrounds, and verifiable memories—an executive, a screenwriter, and a former film-minded Communist—would speak clearly and sanely about Communist infiltration in the motion picture industry. A major star with an admirable war record would lend his prestige, leaving the room to giddy cheers from fans. A disinterested spectator—presuming such a creature existed in 1947—might well have concluded that Chairman Thomas was on to something, smoking out an enemy within Hollywood, maybe even exposing Hollywood itself as the enemy.

James K. McGuinness: "These men charged with production are primarily showmen and not men deeply informed on the dialectics of Communism."

James Kevin McGuinness, producer and story editor at MGM, was the leadoff witness. Like Jack Moffitt, McGuinness had testified at great length—though twice not thrice—during HUAC's road trip to Hollywood in May. Thomas was charmed enough to invite McGuinness back for the public forum.

An Irish Catholic welcomed into the executive suites at MGM, McGuinness started out as a script doctor on *Tarzan and His Mate* (1934) and rose steadily up the ranks of the most solvent studio in town. A founding member and past chairman of the executive board of the MPA-PAI, he had fought against Communist influence in Hollywood since the writers' wars of the 1930s. As a principal organizer and spokesman for the SP, he still bore a grudge against the SWG for trouncing the company union.

The feeling was mutual. Remarks McGuinness made during a debate on ABC radio's *America's Town Meeting of the Air*, broadcast on September 6, 1945, caused the *Screen Writer*, the house organ of the SWG, to castigate him. The show addressed the question "Should Hollywood Make Pictures Designed to Influence Public Opinion?" Actress Constance Bennett and screenwriter Robert Riskin, former head of the Film Division of the Overseas Branch of the OWI, argued for the affirmative; actor Donald Crisp and McGuinness argued the negative. "Mr. McGuinness and his followers have tended toward bitterness and anti-writer organizations," observed screenwriter Paul Trivers, who covered the debate for the guild. "To no one's surprise, [he] took the position that films shouldn't influence anyone." Miffed, McGuinness resigned as an associate member of the SWG. His resignation was accepted, so said the guild, "with regret."[1]

McGuinness found more simpatico listeners on the Thomas Committee. "We are very well pleased with Mr. McGuinness, and feel that he has his feet on the ground as well if not better than any of our witnesses, that he does not get excited and go off to the Right, but looks at the question from a very sane and sensible point of view," observed H. A. Smith in his pre-testimony evaluation. McGuinness was also valued for his ability to recruit and coach like-minded screenwriters. The paunchy forty-six-year-old was not in the best of health, but Smith hoped he would be able "to help us in lining up the testimony of the various witnesses."[2]

Thomas greeted McGuinness like an old friend. Under gentle questioning, the writer said in public what he had said behind the closed doors of the Biltmore. Hollywood was thick with Communists.

However, McGuinness was not ready to indict the industry, and his studio, for following orders during World War II. Defying expectations, he defended the production of *Mission to Moscow*, *The North Star*, and *Song of Russia* with a felicitous phrase, calling the troika "a form of intellectual

Lend-Lease." Moreover, "we profited by reverse Lend-Lease," since Communist writers were given permission by the Comintern to write pro-American pictures during wartime. He open-mindedly pointed to an archrival, Dalton Trumbo, who wrote two "magnificent" wartime pictures for MGM, *A Guy Named Joe* (1943) and *Thirty Seconds Over Tokyo* (1944). McGuinness failed to mention Trumbo's *Tender Comrade* (1943), either because of the subversive title or the RKO imprint.

To illustrate the tactics of the Communists, McGuinness dredged up the case of MGM's *Tennessee Johnson* (1942), a turgid biopic of President Andrew Johnson. Appalled by the unflattering portrait of African Americans and radical Republicans during the Reconstruction era, the Communists had opposed the release of the film. Backed up by the *Daily Worker*, a group of five screenwriters—Donald Ogden Stewart, Hy Kraft, Richard Collins, Jules Dassin, and Ring Lardner Jr.—tried to derail the picture. "We had apparently done the commies a disservice" by representing "in his true light" Thaddeus Stevens, the radical Republican senator who led the movement to impeach Johnson and championed the rights of former slaves. MGM released the picture but, in the interests of wartime unity, did not vigorously promote it. The studio took a heavy loss.[3]

Representative McDowell felt compelled to speak up for the native son of the Keystone State. "Just to keep the record straight," he interjected. "Thaddeus Stevens was a great American patriot and citizen. Pennsylvania is very proud of Thaddeus Stevens and the role he played in American history."

Undistracted by home state chauvinism, Thomas brought up the allegation by Rupert Hughes that exhibitors were wary of booking anti-Communist films due to the threat of vandalism in the theaters. "The industry as a whole, if confronted with the threat, might not have the courage to face it," McGuinness admitted, considering the vulnerability of theaters to vandals. A week's receipts, once lost, cannot be regained.

But, wondered Representative Nixon, wouldn't the resulting publicity actually *help* a picture's grosses?

"Yes, there would be local embarrassment, but nationally it would help," responded McGuinness. "[The production of anti-Communist pictures] would be a good business gamble and I think it is a necessary moral obligation."

Thomas pressed the point about the dearth of anti-Communist pictures. "Why is it they are not being made?"

McGuinness replied that "it is not so long ago that Russia was our ally." Also, a motion picture takes time to make.

"Has the industry the will to make anti-Communist pictures?" Thomas asked, suspicious it did not.

"I think the industry is acquiring it," McGuinness replied evenly.

As an example of MGM's newfound willpower, McGuinness mentioned Bruce Marshall's anti-Communist novel *Vespers in Vienna*, "written by a Catholic," whose screen rights MGM had recently purchased.* MGM must not seem less vigilant than Twentieth Century-Fox, which was already well along into the production of *The Iron Curtain*.

Perhaps to lighten the air of intimidation, McDowell hastened to add that he thought Hollywood should not be forced to make any pictures "either anti or pro" Communist.

"I think I'm solid in saying that the Committee is not urging you to make any kind of pictures," McDowell insisted. "That is a matter for the producers to determine."

H. A. Smith asked McGuinness whether an employee who had been fired from one studio for Communist activity would be able to find work at another studio. He responded ruefully that "he's generally rehired at an increased salary at another studio." He estimated that if studios were to purge all Communists from the payrolls they would lose ten to fifteen top-flight men and ten to fifteen films per year "if they were not more productive than they are now."

If the loss was so small, wondered Smith, then why didn't the studios terminate the suspect employees?

"These men charged with production are primarily showmen and not men deeply informed on the dialectics of Communism," explained McGuinness. "They are most concerned with getting the best possible script than with anything else." McGuinness seemed to be conceding that the un-American Communists somehow had their fingers on the pulse of the American public.

In an odd out-of-character moment, as McGuinness rattled off the names of screenwriters who "consistently followed the Communist party line at every twist and turn," Thomas interrupted to caution the witness, noting that McGuinness did not have the documented evidence or investigatory powers

---

* Released in October 1949, MGM's screen version was called *The Red Danube*.

held by the committee. "We have a very complete record of at least 79 persons active out in Hollywood," Thomas revealed. "The time will come in these hearings when this documented evidence will be presented . . . either sometime this week or sometime next week."[4]

The mathematical precision of the accusation would be a common tactic for anti-Communist crusaders throughout the Cold War, a means of giving statistical credibility to any charge of institutional subversion. "These 79 persons that I named before are not just the run-of-the-mill; they are very prominent persons, prominent in the industry, and those are the people that we have the records on," said Thomas. "Those are the people whose records are going to be brought out before this hearing is over."

The unveiled threat was a preview of coming attractions: when the Unfriendlies came before Thomas next week, he would have the goods on them.

In the caucus room, and back in Hollywood, minds were concentrated on the number of people whom Thomas had omitted. Everyone could do the subtraction: sixty more names were being readied for the target range.

After Thomas called the noon recess, MPAA counsel Paul V. McNutt wasted no time in speaking to reporters. The questioning of McGuinness by Thomas and Nixon made clear that HUAC was trying "to dictate and control, through the device of the hearings, what goes on the screens of America." In high dudgeon, he declared, "It is no concern of any Congressional committee what goes on the screen."[5] Getting quicker on the uptake, McNutt was also becoming bolder in his comebacks. "You don't need a law to impair the Constitutional rights of free speech. It can be done by coercion. That is the why of totalitarian regimes, which we all hate." Eying the reporters clustered around him, McNutt asked, "How would your editors like to be told what should be put on the editorial page?"[6]

During his press conference, McNutt had implied that McGuinness was part of HUAC's campaign of coercion. The next morning a furious McGuinness confronted McNutt and told him he favored no such thing and resented being singled out. The lawyer hastily backtracked, issuing a statement saying that he never meant "to indicate in any way that Mr. McGuinness might favor censorship."[7]

While McNutt was lecturing the reporters, Thomas and the committee were meeting in executive session to discuss the charge of espionage brought out in Jack Moffitt's testimony the day before: that test pilot Slick Goodlin had been gulled by John Weber of the William Morris Agency into divulging top-secret information on a supersonic bomber, the XS-1 plane. "We have a large amount of additional material not developed yesterday," said Thomas at a press conference after the session. "We will have a witness to develop publicly the information we have in connection with this case and the tie-in between this case and some other disclosures on the same line."

Asked if the committee had hard evidence of espionage in Hollywood, Thomas was emphatic. "My answer is yes." The revelations, Thomas promised, would be "sensational."[8]

Robert Taylor: "If I had my way about it, they would all be sent back to Russia or some other unpleasant place and never allowed back in this country."

The afternoon session featured the appearance of the first swoon-worthy matinee idol to sit before the microphones—the tall, dark, and handsome Robert Taylor. Attired in a brown suit with red and white pin stripes, radiating studly glamour, the actor was at the peak of his virile charisma and box office bankability.

Taylor boasted an enviable screen and military record. Born in 1911 in small-town Nebraska, he ditched his effete-sounding birth name— Spangler Arlington Brough—and collided with destiny in a stage production of *Journey's End* at Pomona College. A looker even by dreamboat standards, he was spotted by Ida Koverman, Louis B. Mayer's right-hand woman, and offered a seven-year contract. Once the studio—and the girls—caught sight of the actor in bit parts, MGM promoted Taylor to the leading man status he retained until the collapse of the studio system. From *Magnificent Obsession* (1935) to *Waterloo Bridge* (1940) to *Song of Russia* (1944), he specialized in mushy romances tugging at the heartstrings of what trade reporters called "the distaff side."

The soft-focus image belied Taylor's hard-nosed character. Itching to get into uniform during World War II, he served stateside as a Navy pilot and flight instructor; he also narrated combat documentaries. In 1939, he had married Barbara Stanwyck, who shared his political opinions but far surpassed his thespian range. As a Hollywood golden couple, Taylor and

Stanwyck were outshone only by Bogart and Bacall. His most recent film was a changeup: *Undercurrent* (1946), with Katharine Hepburn, where he played a homicidal husband.

Though publicly friendly, Taylor was privately furious with Thomas for blurting out the contents of his closed session testimony in May. The actor had been assured the testimony would be secret and felt double-crossed by the headline-hunting chairman. Learning he would be subpoenaed for the October hearings, he wrote a blistering letter to H. A. Smith outlining his grievances. "At the recent hearings in Los Angeles I was asked—not subpoenaed—to testify," he pointed out. "I did so willingly under the *assurance* that my testimony was confidential. My testimony was *not* kept confidential and I must confess that, when certain people on the 'other side of the fence' saw fit to ridicule said testimony, I had to agree with them—it did look pretty silly!"

Having testified once, Taylor saw no need for a reprise under the Klieg lights. "Whatever good was to be done *has* been done—even to the extent of having garnered some free *publicity* for Mr. Thomas and his Committee." Taylor had a lot more to get off his chest:

Which brings me to another point. I've never cared a whole helluva lot for politicians, whether they be Republican or Democrat. And I've certainly never believed it inherent in my job as a motion picture actor to aid in feathering any of their nests for them via publicity from my name—a name, by the way, which I worked Goddam hard to build and maintain without any blemish.

My last appearance to testify was valuable only insofar as publicity was concerned; my appearance in Washington can be valuable purely for the same reasons. I firmly believe this to be utterly ridiculous and a waste of time, both for me and for the Committee.

Thomas's preening before the cameras disgusted Taylor. "These investigations, the way they're being run in Washington at the moment, remind me more of a 3-Ring circus than of a serious effort to rid the country of a real threat," he wrote. "When the subject matter gets juicy enough and the names involved are capable of getting 'space,' it's awfully hard for a dyed-in-the-wool politician to stick to the subject."

Of course, if subpoenaed, the actor would have no choice but to heed the summons. However, "I will feel utterly ridiculous and shall resent every minute of the whole thing. I shall, moreover, kick myself for ever having gotten myself into such a position by having testified previously." His official designation as a "friendly," he made clear, was a misnomer. "Moreover, as a 'friendly' witness, I shall be friendly only to the *cause*; as far as being friendly to the Committee itself is concerned that possibility went out the window the last time I was 'crossed up.' " Taylor was not threatening to go over to the other side—only signaling his surly truculence. "I assume one uncooperative friendly witness won't be much of a stumbling block."

Taylor concluded his poison pen letter to HUAC by restating his firm opposition to Communism *and* to testifying in Washington. "You'll seldom find a guy who hates Communism as much as I—nor one who is so adamant about going to Washington to testify. Sorry but that is the way I feel about it." If worse came to worse—"God forbid it is actually necessary"—the actor would prefer to fly to Washington—"in case I am unsuccessful in ducking the U.S. Marshall."[9]

Smith tried to mollify Taylor. Promising to forward the letter to Thomas and Stripling, he explained that the subpoena was a legal formality issued for the witness's own protection. He hoped that what the actor and HUAC had in common would override the recent unpleasantness. "I regret that you feel so keenly about not testifying at the forthcoming hearing in Washington, as I sincerely feel that it is necessary for all of us to cooperate in fighting this vicious enemy," Smith wrote Taylor.[10]

True to his word—and the subpoena—Taylor showed up. Though he may have bit his tongue, he proved a compliant prop for J. Parnell Thomas.

To hear the press tell it, fully one half of the population of Washington, D.C. was all-a-flutter with palpitations at Taylor's proximity. "It was gals, gals, gals, everywhere from adolescent bobby soxers to gray-haired grannies who were obviously bobby soxers in soul," chuckled Florence S. Lowe at *Daily Variety*. "At the rear entrance, through which the committee entered the chamber, the mass of girls—largely Congressional secretaries—was also something to resemble Macy's basement during the pre-Christmas week shopping."[11] Outside the caucus room, standing eight abreast in the hallways, women jammed the corridors. "Capitol police were almost helpless in the face of the feminine onslaught," reported the *Washington Post*. For the first time, beset police allowed some of the overflow to stack up on a platform behind the dais where the newsreels cameras were mounted.

Before sitting down at the witness table, Taylor posed with Thomas for the photographers. "Now we'll allow another ten minutes for taking pictures; the hearings must begin," said Thomas, all smiles, as a fusillade of flash bulbs popped.[12] Before Taylor was sworn in, Thomas announced that he had received a telegram from director Sam Wood, who had testified on Monday. Wood wanted the record amended. While at the witness table, he had drawn a blank about the name of an un-American director. Now he remembered: "His name is Lewis Milestone," said Thomas, reading from Wood's telegram. The Russian-born director of *All Quiet on the Western Front* (1930), *Of Mice and Men* (1939), *The Purple Heart* (1944), and the radioactive *The North Star* (1943) was the most illustrious Hollywood name in the Unfriendly Nineteen. The allegedly un-American director was also a veteran of the Great War.

As Taylor raised his hand to take the oath, a photographer hollered, "Get your hand back! You're hiding your face." Accustomed to taking direction, Taylor obliged.

Flanked by police and followed by a crowd of smitten fans, MGM star Robert Taylor walks away from Capitol Hill after testifying before the House Committee on Un-American Activities, October 22, 1947.

After the hubbub settled down, committee counsel Stripling asked, "How long have you been an actor, Mr. Taylor?"

Taylor paused for effect. Emphasizing the verb, he got an appreciative laugh from an audience he held in the palm of his hand. "I have been *employed* as an actor since 1934."

Each of the committeemen took turns tossing softball questions to Taylor.

Nixon asked if the actor had been subjected "to ridicule and abuse" by the left-wing press after his friendly testimony in May.

"I am afraid I was, but that certainly didn't bother me."

And for his testimony today?

"I suppose so," shrugged Taylor. And then firmly: "I take any attacks from the left-wing press or individuals as compliments. I really enjoy their dislike."

Nixon asked if Taylor's outspoken anti-Communism might hurt him at the box office.

"I happen to believe strongly enough in the American people to feel that they will go along with anyone who prefers the American system," replied Taylor.

Stripling asked whether Taylor thought the CPUSA should be outlawed. Loath as he was to disagree with J. Edgar Hoover, Taylor thought it should be. He then uttered one of the biggest applause lines of the entire hearings. "If I had my way about it, they would all be sent back to Russia or some other unpleasant place and never allowed back in this country."

Cheers and cries of "Hurrah for Robert Taylor!" broke out from the gallery.

Thomas dutifully rapped his gavel for order and admonished the spectators against further demonstrations. "This is not a show or anything like that," he insisted, evidence to the contrary notwithstanding.

Conspicuously not part of Taylor's cheering section were the members of the Unfriendly Nineteen in attendance. *New York Mirror* columnist George Dixon seethed as he watched their antics. "Every time the actor expressed his opinion of Hollywood Communists they nudged each other, whispered, and giggled," he wrote. "They practically rendered themselves cross-eyed winking at each other."[13]

Alarmingly, in the past four to five years, Taylor had detected "more indications" of Communist activity in Hollywood. As a member of the Screen Actors Guild, he believed there were members "who, if not Communists, are working awfully hard to be so." Asked for specific examples, Taylor offhandedly mentioned Karen Morley, a "disrupting influence" at SAG meetings, and

Howard Da Silva, who always "seems to have something to say at the wrong time." They were "the only two I can think of at the moment." Incongruously, he added, "I don't know whether they're Communists." He also hedged on the third name he named. "Lester Cole, who is reputedly a Communist. I wouldn't know personally."

Inevitably, *Song of Russia* came up again. Repeating his testimony from the previous May, Taylor labeled the film Communist propaganda and said he had objected "strenuously" to playing the lead role. Reminding everyone of the wartime context, Taylor insisted he did what he could to eliminate overt pro-Communist dialogue while denying the obvious, namely that the film was made at the behest of the U.S. government to buck up a besieged ally. He recalled attending a five-minute meeting with MGM executives and Lowell Mellett, head of the Motion Picture Bureau of the OWI, where they discussed deferring his induction in the U.S. Navy so he could star in the picture.

However, Taylor wanted to correct an impression left from his earlier testimony; he had not been coerced into making the film. "If I gave the impression that I was forced to make the picture—I wasn't forced, because they can't force you to make any picture," he said, doubtless to the surprise of studio contract players.

Taylor said he had not knowingly worked with a Communist and would not do so. Along with 99.9 percent of Hollywood, he regarded the Communists as "the rotten [apples] in the barrel."

At that point Robert W. Kenny passed a note to the press table pointing out that Lester Cole, whom Taylor had named as a suspected Communist, was one of the writers of Taylor's forthcoming release *High Wall* (1947). "This is difficult to reconcile with Taylor's statement that he would not work on any picture with anyone suspected of 'communistic tendencies,' " said Kenny's note.

In twenty-five minutes, Taylor was gone, trailed by applause and another cry of "Hooray for Robert Taylor!" by a middle-aged woman wearing a red hat.[14] Thomas instructed everyone, including photographers, to stay in their seats as his star witness was escorted from the caucus room.

Investigators Smith and Leckie were given the plum assignment of accompanying the witness from the chambers. As Taylor exited the building, only one lucky fan—a three-year-old cutie named Patti Borgiasz—managed to nab an autograph. Photographers saw the pretty girl waiting with her mother and asked Taylor to pose for pictures with her. He smiled and signed her comic book.[15]

Howard Rushmore: "The general line would be the stars are, 99 percent of them, political morons."

The star power—and the female claque in the gallery—diminished appreciably with the swearing in of the next witness, the reformed Communist Howard Rushmore. Despite his patriotic surname and all-American lineage (a southerner with Confederate ancestors, proud of his heritage and hillbilly roots, but fiercely committed to racial justice), he had been a member of the CPUSA from 1936 to 1939, leaping into the arms of the party after witnessing a lynching.[16] At a hulking six-foot-five, Rushmore looked like he could serve the Revolution best by manning the barricades instead of a typewriter, but as the film critic for the *Daily Worker*, he dutifully wrote party line reviews

Ex-Communist film critic Howard Rushmore and friendly screenwriter Morrie Ryskind testify, October 22, 1947.

flaying the opiates of the studio system, decrying Hollywood escapism, and praising Soviet social realism.[17]

In 1939, however, Rushmore had an epiphany. He broke with the party not over the Hitler-Stalin Pact but *Gone With the Wind* (1939): Rushmore found the film admirable in parts—who could deny the gorgeous Technicolor registration and jaw-dropping spectacle?—while the party line dictated a blanket condemnation and a call for universal boycott. When he refused to toe the editorial line and "blister" the film, he was fired.

The termination of the Communist film critic for speaking his mind was widely reported in the press. Rushmore became an instant cause célèbre, a martyr for freedom of thought when liberal sympathy for American Communists was at a low ebb. "If MGM has an ounce of gratitude, it will give Howard Rushmore a job at once," suggested James Dugan, Rushmore's erstwhile counterpart at the *New Masses*, who claimed that "no cables came in from Stalin asking to read my copy before it went to press." Dugan blistered *Gone With the Wind* as four hours of "reactionary art."[18]

Defecting wholeheartedly to the other side, Rushmore found employment not at MGM but at the *American Mercury* and *Reader's Digest* and, currently, as a writer for the *New York Journal-American*, the Hearst daily that was as far from the *Daily Worker* as American journalism traveled. Committee counsel Stripling considered Rushmore a "great reporter" for the investigative journalism that helped lead to the identification of the slippery Soviet agent Gerhart Eisler. By 1947, Rushmore was one of the most famous once Communist, now anti-Communists in America. *Variety* described him as a "professional Commie-baiter."[19] Perhaps—but Rushmore was an authentic inside-dopester: he had logged long hours at the office of the *Daily Worker* and knew the innermost workings of the CPUSA.

Rushmore revealed how deeply the CPUSA had burrowed into the Hollywood studio system. Party headquarters in New York had studio informants, above and below the line, who gave a heads up on potentially anti-Communist films in the studio pipeline. The information was passed on to V. J. Jerome, head of the Communist cultural commission, who orchestrated preemptive campaigns against the reactionary releases. In 1939, Jerome got an early look at the script to Paramount's *Our Leading Citizen* (1939), a melodrama—written by Jack Moffitt—about an industrial strike that faulted greedy capitalists and violent revolutionaries alike. Jerome passed the script along to Rushmore. "I reviewed the picture and called for a boycott of it," Rushmore testified. "A letter and telegram barrage against Paramount started immediately. We had prepared in advance for things like this. The party uses every organization that they control or have any influence with."

Rushmore ticked off the names of loyal Communist apparatchiks in Hollywood: actor Howard Da Silva, labor leader Herbert K. Sorrell, and screenwriter Albert Maltz. He knew John Howard Lawson had been "assigned to head the party in Hollywood." He saw playwright-screenwriter Clifford Odets "many times at Communist party headquarters" and heard Donald Ogden Stewart referred to as "comrade Stewart." He also named Hebert Kline, former editor of *Theater Arts* and co-director of the anti-Franco Spanish Civil War documentaries *Heart of Spain* (1937) and *Return to Life* (1938) and the anti-Nazi documentary *Crisis* (1939), as a "party member." He knew for a fact Lawson and Kline were Communists because they were admitted into the ninth floor of CPUSA headquarters, located on 35 East Twelfth Street in New York City—the "inner sanctum" for deep-dyed Reds.

As Rushmore spoke, Robert Kenny turned to one of his clients and whispered, "Rushmore doesn't look like a rat, does he?"[20]

Picking up on McGuinness's earlier testimony about Communist intimidation tactics, Stripling asked Rushmore about party-instigated vandalism in theaters. Rushmore knew of no instances. Compared to Europe—where stink bombs and seat slashings were common tactics—politically inspired violence in American theaters was virtually unknown. The last significant disruptions were the scattered incidents of bomb threats phoned in by the German American Bund, who had sought to shut down Warner Bros.'s *Confessions of a Nazi Spy* (1939).

Rushmore revealed that a select group of actors and screenwriters, though perhaps not Communists, were always rewarded with good ink in the *Daily Worker* due to their progressive politics and willingness to lend their names and wallets to Communist front groups. Charles Chaplin and Edward G. Robinson were foremost among the "sacred cows," Rushmore claimed, although he figured "sacred red cows" might be a more accurate term. V. J. Jerome instructed him "to always defend Robinson, even if he was in a bad picture, with a bad performance."

Rushmore not only named names, he name-called. Hollywood recruits were ripe examples of Lenin's notion of useful idiots. "The general line would be that the stars are, 99 percent of them, political morons," said Rushmore. "The Communist party per se had great contempt for the movie stars of Hollywood. Jerome once told me: 'Their only use to the revolution is in their bank accounts.' I heard Lawson at New York headquarters cite Lionel Stander as a perfect example of how a comrade should not act in Hollywood." Apparently, Hollywood seduced Communists as easily as Communism seduced Hollywood:

> Joe North, editor of the *New Masses*, went out [to Hollywood] on one occasion to raise funds. He raised $20,000 in one week, but said that some stars did not give much. He complained particularly about one star, John Garfield, who wouldn't give him any money. Joe said, "That's what happens to our comrades when they went to Hollywood."

Rushmore's testimony left plenty of names on the record and re-imprinted the popular image of motion picture stars as simpletons with open checkbooks, but his testimony that Hollywood was littered with CPUSA agents who gave early warning signals to Communist activists was jarring, "a stick of dynamite" tossed into the testimony as *Daily Variety* low-whistled.[21] It certainly explained how the CPUSA seemed to be better wired into Hollywood's secrets than Hedda Hopper and Louella Parsons.

Morrie Ryskind: "We didn't get the Bill of Rights in order to protect quislings."

Unlike the other friendly writers—Moffitt, Hughes, and McGuinness, who were past their prime or had been less than prime in their prime—Morrie Ryskind was a hugely successful, much-honored, and in-demand scribe. He had written with George S. Kaufman the Pulitzer Prize winning play *Of Thee I Sing* (1931); conspired with the Marx Brothers to unleash anarchy on stage and screen; cowritten or touched up two immortal screwball comedies, *My Man Godfrey* (1936) and *His Girl Friday* (1940); and earned two Oscar nominations. He was esteemed around town as an all-purpose script doctor and dialogue writer, making pivotal and often uncredited contributions to dozens of films.

Born in 1895 to Russian-Jewish immigrants in Brooklyn, Ryskind may have shared an ethno-religious lineage with many of his fellow screenwriters but not a political allegiance. Though a socialist in his youth (while attending Columbia University, he had boarded with the anarchist icon Emma Goldman) and a liberal in adulthood, he moved steadily rightward due to disenchantment with the servility of the Popular Front to the Soviet Union.[22] During the Hollywood writers' wars, Ryskind had been a staunch advocate for the Screen Writers' Guild not the Screen Playwrights, Inc., and in 1939, he had testified before the NLRB about how the studios had attempted to intimidate him into abandoning the SWG. By 1944, however, he was a member of the executive council of the MPA-PAI, signing, and perhaps authoring, its affirmation of purpose:

> We seek to make a rallying place for the vast, silent majority of our fellow workers; to give voice to their unwavering loyalty to democratic forms and so to drown out the highly vocal, lunatic fringe of dissidents; to present to our fellow countrymen the vision of a great American industry upholding the American faith.[23]

Testifying before HUAC, Ryskind now made common cause with the writers he had done bare-knuckled battle with in the 1930s—and spoke against the men he had worked with to build the SWG. At the time of his testimony, Ryskind was troubled with a stomach ulcer, and no wonder.

H. A. Smith judged Ryskind "a very level headed and brilliant strategist, and one who can materially assist us." The committee valued Ryskind's inside knowledge of how Communism had slithered into the SWG. Moreover, "he is a man who is capable of adding a bit of humor here and there, [and] is well respected by all of the others."[24]

Sure enough, upon being sworn in, Ryskind cracked wise. Handling the biographical preliminaries, investigator Smith listed a couple of Ryskind's impressive stage and screen credits and asked, for the record, "Is that correct?"

"Yes," Ryskind replied, "and a couple of flops in between, which I am glad you didn't mention."

Was there Communist infiltration in the motion picture industry, asked Smith, not interested in bantering.

"You'd have to be deaf, dumb, and blind not to observe those activities," exclaimed Ryskind. By way of detection, he felt the olfactory method suggested by Rupert Hughes was a reliable indicator. "And even if you lost all those [senses] and still kept your nose, the odor would tell you."

Ryskind revealed how his wife had innocently joined the League Against War and Fascism, thinking it a civil rights group. She resigned when she discovered its true Communist agenda. "I want to say one thing in fairness to her," Ryskind interjected, to keep peace at home. "My wife arrived here today and I want to say that joining that league was the only mistake she has made in the 18 years we have been married."

Ryskind declared that the SWG, under the leadership of Emmet Lavery and Gordon Kahn, editor of the *Screen Writer*, was Communist controlled. He noted that Kahn and he lived next door to each other, and, although they were nice to each other's children and "our dogs are very good friends," relations had become strained since the HUAC investigations. Labeling Kahn a Communist "will not increase neighborly relations," Ryskind understated. As for another member of the Unfriendly Nineteen: "Well, if Lester Cole isn't a commie, I don't think Mahatma Gandhi is an Indian."

Ryskind recognized that eliminating Communism from Hollywood was a difficult task, that the balance between freedom of thought and freedom from subversion was hard to gauge. "I think we believe in and want to protect our civil liberties," he said, but "we didn't get the Bill of Rights in order to protect quislings." He understood fully the risk to his career that might result from his forthright testimony, but the stakes were life and death. The Communists "use the techniques of character assassination, and if they ever get control of the screen or the country, it won't be just characters they'll assassinate."

A favorite technique the Communists employed to reel in the unwary was the creation of front groups—"for suckers," Ryskind said ruefully, for he numbered himself among them.

Chapter 9
HOLLYWOOD'S FINEST

On Day 4 the stars came out. The packed caucus room buzzed with the electric current of imminent proximity to celluloid celebrity. A quartet of marquee talent had come to Washington, under duress, but game for the performance, roles rehearsed, lines memorized, dressed for the part.

The queues started long before the scheduled opening at 10:30 A.M. Though unaccustomed to Standing Room Only attendance for a congressional hearing, Capitol police were getting better at crowd control, putting up barricades to hold back fans who hadn't arrived early enough to score one of the four hundred or so seats reserved for the public. An extra detail of police augmented the survivors who had been bruised and battered the day before by the "stampede of sighing women to see Robert Taylor."[1] "Squealing [bobby] soxers and elderly hausfraus" is how *Variety*'s Herb Golden described the predominately female spectators. "Once the femmes do get in, they still can't see much from the flat floor, especially since the witness is seated with his back toward them. They're all on their feet and on the chairs when their heroes pass in front of them on the way out. This is accompanied by the usual noises of swooning."[2] Frustrated stargazers locked out of the morning session kept their place in line for the 2:00 P.M. session. Elsewhere on Capitol Hill, the normal work of government ground to a halt: seemingly every congressional secretary in the building had left her post to gawk at the star witnesses.

The stars were not just at the witness table. At the afternoon session, Brooklyn-bred hunk John Garfield sat in the third row next to actor-singer-composer Joseph Calleia. Also in attendance were the screenwriting twins Julius and Philip Epstein, best known for *Casablanca* (1942) and recently exonerated from subversive activities by Jack Warner; Larry Parks, the only recognizable face in the Unfriendly Nineteen, an up-and-coming triple, or double, threat sensation on the strength of his lip-synching performance in *The Jolson Story* (1946); high society dancer Paul Draper; actress and drama teacher Uta Hagen; singer Bernice Parks; Broadway producer Oscar Serlin; and the African American actor Canada Lee, Garfield's co-star in Robert Rossen and Abraham Polonsky's brutish boxing film *Body and Soul* (1947), currently in release, a thinly veiled metaphor for the cutthroat fisticuffs of American capitalism.

Never in the history of Washington, D.C. had so much Hollywood glamour been corralled into a hearing room, the talent of the two cities sharing the same stage, under the glare of newsreel lights and before hot radio microphones.

Prior to eyeballing the main attractions, the gallery had to endure two relative nobodies, the screenwriters Fred Niblo Jr. and Richard Macaulay. For years, both disaffected veterans of the Screen Playwrights, Inc. had been fighting a hopeless rearguard action against Communist influence in the Screen Writers' Guild. HUAC gave the pair a platform that the guild had always denied them.

Fred Niblo Jr.: "The whole atmosphere suggested a Moscow purge trial."

Despite his lack of star power, Fred Niblo Jr. sprang from showbiz aristocracy. He was the son of silent film director Fred Niblo, who brought *Ben Hur: A Tale of the Christ* (1925) to the screen for MGM, and the nephew of composer-star George M. Cohan, the Broadway multi-hyphenate and subject of the Warner Bros. musical biopic *Yankee Doodle Dandy* (1942). In 1928, after several years working with his uncle on Broadway, Niblo Jr. embarked on a busy career as a screenwriter, first at Warner Bros., and then at Twentieth Century-Fox. Along the way, he earned an Academy Award nomination for the embryonic gangster film, *The Criminal Code* (1930). His name was associated with enough crowd-pleasing money makers—*Hell's Kitchen* (1938), *The Fighting 69th* (1940), and *Four Jills in a Jeep* (1944)—to keep him steadily employed. Nonetheless, to *New York Post* film critic Archer Winsten, Niblo's resumé was further evidence of the marked "disparity in talent" between the friendly screenwriters and their unfriendly colleagues. "Fred Niblo, Jr. seems to have written for the movies from 1928 to 1942 without accomplishing anything worth mentioning," he jeered. "Then he came up with *The Falcon in Danger* [1943] and *Tampico* [1944], and if you saw either of those, no more comment is necessary."[3]

Odd man out in his own union, Niblo Jr. had waged a long, fruitless, and frustrating campaign against Communist influence in the SWG—speaking out (and being drowned out) at meetings, running unsuccessfully for the executive board, and trying to get published in the *Screen Writer*. In 1945, he introduced a resolution to make a loyalty oath mandatory for executive board members and new members: it went down to defeat when opponents walked out on the vote and the membership failed to muster the necessary quorum. A founding member of the MPA-PAI, he was also, like so many of Hollywood's passionate anti-Communists, a devout Roman Catholic.

Describing the SWG as the "spark plug and spearhead" of the Communist engine in Hollywood, Niblo quickly got down to specifics. John Howard Lawson, Lester Cole, and Dalton Trumbo definitely "follow the party line" and the *Screen Writer* functioned as a "sort of a literary monthly supplement of the *Daily Worker*." Asked whether Gordon Kahn was a Communist, Niblo replied, "That is my opinion, though I cannot prove it any more than Custer could prove that the people who massacred him were Indians." The Communist party, Niblo believed, "no less than the Ku Klux Klan," should be outlawed.

Niblo made an interesting exception to his blanket indictment of the red spark plugs firing up the SWG. He disagreed with Howard Rushmore and Morrie Ryskind about the Communist leanings of SWG president Emmet Lavery, whom Niblo said "has associated himself with the moderate movement" among guild members to wrest control away from the Communists. Perhaps Niblo had seen Lavery at Sunday mass too often to think of him as a party liner.

Niblo seemed a poignant figure, a man authentically hurt about the years of mistreatment and ostracism from his colleagues. A frequent target of criticism at SWG meetings ("the whole atmosphere suggested a Moscow purge trial," he said of a public dressing down he got for casting his lot with the

MPA-PAI), he was especially galled by the refusal of the *Screen Writer*, under the editorial reins of Dalton Trumbo in 1945–1946 and Gordon Kahn in 1947, "Tweedledum and Tweedledee," to publish his letters in the open forum section. Attacked in the guild's magazine by screenwriter Garrett Graham, Niblo was not allotted space to respond. He still chafed at the snub.

None of the committeemen had much to ask Niblo. He was brushed away from his moment in the spotlight in less than thirty minutes. Like the spectators in the gallery, the congressmen were eager to get to the bigger attractions waiting in the wings.

Richard Macaulay: "Possibly, they would like to cut my throat . . . "

Prior to the portion of the programming lineup all had come to see, the congressmen and the crowd had to listen to another tepid turn by an obscure screenwriter.

Following and backing up Niblo was his longtime ally in the SWG, Richard Macaulay. A former magazine and radio writer, Macaulay was a much-credited screenwriter in the Warner Bros. stable (his script for *The Roaring Twenties* [1939] helped define the motion picture memory of the previous decade), a reliable adaptor, and an all-purpose assignment man. Among his many credits with Jerry Wald, his frequent collaborator, was *Brother Rat* (1938), a title that invited a too-obvious insult.

For years, Macaulay had been in the trenches fighting Communism in the SWG, running for office on an anti-Communist slate and proposing anti-Communist resolutions that were invariably voted down. Like Niblo Jr., he was incensed to have been blackballed from the pages of the *Screen Writer*. Investigator A. B. Leckie was impressed with the "very courteous" Macaulay, judging him a "young man of sound ideas and thinking," who "very readily admitted that he would be glad to testify provided he was given the general questions that would be asked prior to the hearing in Washington."[4]

On the eve of his testimony, Macaulay took out a full-page ad in *Daily Variety* to share his musings on the social and psychic cost of the current and most momentous battle in the Hollywood writers' wars. "Dalton Trumbo, Ring Lardner Jr., Lester Cole, and Richard Collins and others all speak to me," he noted. "Possibly they would like to cut my throat, but at least they don't stand around in sullen silence, hating for some obscure reason not even faintly clear to themselves."[5]

With Macaulay set to name names in public testimony before HUAC, the reason was not so obscure. A grudge-holding Irishman with a long memory, he was the most name-dropping witness yet.

"I might possibly be doing an injustice to some of them," Macaulay admitted prior to spilling forth.

Handling the questioning of the B players before the congressmen took over with the stars, H. A. Smith hastened to interject, "we prefer you name only those in the guild whom you feel are Communists."

"I am morally certain of all of them," said Macaulay. "I merely say if they habitually consort with bank robbers and the bank on the next street is knocked off, they can't holler if someone blows the whistle."

Macaulay then blew the whistle on twenty-eight screenwriters who followed the party line, joined front organizations, and abused anti-Communist writers like himself. Unlike Hughes and Ryskind, he did not use the smell test. "Primarily, these men have followed—no matter how ridiculous it got— the party line of the Communist Party."

In at least one instance, however, Macaulay was tripped up by his own criterion. Screenwriter Ranald MacDougall, one of the men Macaulay tagged, telegrammed Thomas to deny the "irresponsible falsehood" and demand the right to testify to rebut the charges. MacDougall told the committee that he could easily pass the crucial litmus test:

> I wish to point out a matter of available record: during 1940 and 1941, prior to Russia's entry into the war and at a time when the so-called party line was apparently friendly toward Hitler and bitterly opposed to any thought of American entry into the war, I was employed by the National Association of Manufacturers as writer and editor of their weekly NBC radio program *Defense for America*. Among many other public expressions of my beliefs I refer you to the numerous wartime radio programs I wrote for the government.[6]

MacDougall was never called.

Like Niblo Jr., Macaulay recited a long train of abuses and personal slights: of being hissed down at SWG meetings, denied space in the *Screen Writer*, and denigrated by "a well-organized clique."

Macaulay was dispensed with in less time than Niblo. The documents he submitted—rejection letters from the editorial board of the *Screen Writer* and the rejected article in question, which he eventually published in *Variety*— were put into the record but not read aloud. No need to eat up any more time.

Robert Montgomery: "I gave up my job to fight a totalitarianism called Fascism. I am quite willing to give it up again to fight a totalitarianism called Communism."

Finally, the dowdy scriveners of the SWG ceded the spotlight to the charismatic leading men of SAG. Klieg lights switched on, flashbulbs popped, and spectators stood up. Rep. John Wood, an irregular attendee who had skipped the two screenwriters, was now seated at the dais ready for action.

The first witness did not disappoint. One of the most versatile talents in Hollywood history, Robert Montgomery possessed sterling credentials as an actor, director, producer, and patriot.

Born in 1904, private school educated and Princeton bound, Montgomery came from money but his plans for the Ivy League were dashed when his father died along with the family fortune. The callow youngster went from patrician privilege to hardscrabble hustling overnight. Thrust into manual labor, he worked cleaning locomotives and wiping down oil tankers. In the early 1920s, landing in New York intending to become a writer, he got small acting parts on stage. He was soon signed by MGM, which could always spot a star in embryo. "Standing over six feet tall and weighing 185 pounds, Montgomery looked and acted like the men in the audience wanted to look—handsome, debonair, rich," wrote *Los Angeles Times* reporter Keith Love.[7]

At MGM in the 1930s, Montgomery played the sophisticated, flippant leading man opposite the most desirable partners in the studio stable— Greta Garbo, Joan Crawford, Irene Dunne, Norma Shearer—but he bristled at being typecast as a tuxedoed mannequin. "The directors shoved a cocktail shaker in my hands and kept me shaking it for years," he groused.[8] Against the wishes of Louis B. Mayer, he broke out of the mold to play a psychotic killer in *Night Must Fall* (1937), proving he was more than a pretty face.

George Murphy, Robert Montgomery, HUAC counsel Robert Stripling, and Ronald Reagan pose for a publicity shot prior to testimony, October 23, 1947. (Courtesy of Arnie Reisman)

An early and activist member of SAG, Montgomery served as president four times, from 1935–1938, when he helped negotiate a closed shop policy for the guild, and again, for a period of three months, in 1946, when he kept SAG from getting embroiled in the jurisdictional strikes besetting Hollywood. Montgomery had lately produced, directed, and starred in a quirky version of Raymond Chandler's *The Lady in the Lake* (1946), in which a camera's-eye-view perspective kept him off screen for most of the running time, a visual self-effacement that pointed ahead to his future as a behind-the-scenes producer rather than top-billed front man.

Montgomery's wartime service record was as heroic as an ad-pub man at MGM might have cooked up: even before America entered the war, he joined the battle as a self-financed ambulance driver for the American Field Service in France. In 1941, prior to Pearl Harbor, he was commissioned as a lieutenant, junior grade in the U.S. Naval Reserve. Soon on very active duty, he saw action at Guadalcanal, the Marshall Islands, and Normandy on D-Day, where he was on the deck of the first destroyer to enter Cherbourg harbor. He retired from the service a full commander in the U.S. Navy and, unlike so many Hollywood commissions, the rank was earned. In John Ford's *They Were Expendable* (1945) he played a version of himself with his credit line, above that of non-veteran John Wayne, certifying his military bona fides: Robert Montgomery, Commander, U.S.N.R.

As a patriot-star, Montgomery was the best Hollywood had to offer, but his courage was not confined to the combat zone. During his first three terms as SAG president, he fought hard to keep both the Communists and the mobsters from infiltrating the guild. In 1937, when gangland thug Willie Bioff tried to expand his union empire by muscling in on SAG, Montgomery led the counteroffensive. "These weren't movie tough guys," recalled musical star George Murphy. "These were the real thing." Taking on the most dangerous roles in their motion picture careers, Montgomery and Murphy teamed up to keep the mob out and the guild clean. "You're playing with fire," warned MGM production manager Eddie Mannix, himself no weak-kneed desk jockey. "They'll think nothing of smashing your brains out." He was not being melodramatic. Murphy received threats that his children would have acid thrown in their faces. Stuntmen volunteered to act as bodyguards for Montgomery, Murphy, and members of the SAG executive board. When the actors threatened a nationwide strike that would expose the extent of union racketeering, Bioff backed down.[9]

Seated at the witness table in a modest double-breasted brown suit, Montgomery radiated calm authority and seasoned professionalism. Asked his occupation, he picked his most recent and said, "I am a director."

Montgomery was neither defensive nor deferential. "We have had in the Screen Actors Guild, as have other labor unions, a very militant, very small minority [of Communists], well organized and well disciplined," Montgomery admitted, but he insisted that the minority was "never successful under any circumstances" or at any time in dominating SAG policy.

Montgomery got the biggest round of applause of the day—probably of the entire hearings—with a heartfelt declaration: "Mr. Chairman, in common with millions of other men in this country in 1939 and 1940, I gave up my job to fight against a totalitarianism which was called Fascism. I am quite willing to give it up again to fight against a totalitarianism called Communism."

Representative Nixon interjected to say that "although no applause can be allowed from the audience," he believed he spoke for everyone when he said how very encouraging it was to find an actor-patriot of Montgomery's caliber speaking "articulately, intelligently, and firmly on a matter which is of great interest to this country at the present time." Representative McDowell chimed in: "You are as good a citizen as you are an actor."

When, at the end of his brief testimony, Montgomery asked permission to make a comment, no one on the dais would have dared refuse.

The actor ventured a mild rebuke. "I have been watching and hearing via the press and radio the proceedings here in this committee," he said. Unfortunately, the general impression given was that only "a small minority within Hollywood" was "fighting Communism and Fascism. This is actually the reverse of the true picture." Montgomery was proud to have spent twenty years in a business where only a small minority was fighting *for* Communism.

"Thank you very much, Mr. Montgomery, for coming here today," said Thomas, not bothering to conceal his admiration.

American moviegoers echoed the sentiments and found an appropriate way to register their approval during the actor-director's current motion picture release. "Robert Montgomery gets applause every time his pic *Ride the Pink Horse* is shown on the screen," noted Louella Parsons, adding her own. "That's because he was a popular witness at the Washington investigation of the un-American Activities committee."[10]

George Murphy: "There are an awful lot of good, honest, liberal people who are being used by the Communists."

George Murphy was also a former SAG president. A song and dance man, inevitably described as a hoofer, he exuded a buoyant fun-loving personality. It was deceptive: the son of a prominent athletic coach who trained track and football greats at Yale and the University of Pennsylvania, Murphy was raised in a lace curtain Irish atmosphere but never traded on his connections and prided himself on his wide-ranging experience in life and work: as a bouncer, auto plant worker, coal miner, runner on Wall Street, and, during Prohibition, bootlegger.[11]

Murphy was earning a good living as a legitimate—that is, Broadway—performer when Hollywood beckoned. After debuting in *Kid's Millions* (1934) with Ethel Merman and Eddie Cantor, he was put under contract by MGM for a streak of splashy boy-meets-girl etc. musicals, from *Broadway Melody* (1935) to *For Me and My Gal* (1942). On the soundstage dance floor, he twirled a teenage Lana Turner in *Two Girls on Broadway* (1940), a teenage Judy Garland in *Little Nellie Kelly* (1940), and a thirtyish Ginger Rogers in *Tom, Dick, and Harry* (1941). He spent the war years selling bonds and making martial musicals like *The Navy Comes Through* (RKO, 1942) and *This Is the Army* (Warner Bros., 1943), where squadrons of rifle-bearing men in khaki replaced chorus girls with parasols.

Murphy put the brakes on a hyperactive screen career to serve as SAG president for two terms from 1944–1946, a tumultuous time in the history of the guild. He played a hands-on role in assuring that SAG would take a hands-off policy during the first acidic IATSE/CSU strike. He also pushed through a significant change in guild policy designed to diminish the influence of the Communists: rewriting the bylaws to require a vote from the full membership, and not just members who attended meetings in person.[12] Die-hard Communists were notorious for attending union meetings en masse, stalling with procedural questions, and yammering into the wee hours until less radical actors with a family life bailed—and then calling a vote when their members dominated the hall. By having the full membership vote by secret ballot, Murphy transformed SAG into a more democratic and middle-of-the-road outfit.

As befit his Broadway roots, Murphy dressed a bit flashier than Montgomery, donning patriotic colors for the occasion, a double-breasted blue suit, a white shirt, and a blue tie speckled with red. He gave his profession as "actor-dancer."

H. A. Smith took over to conduct a perfunctory interrogation—more a conversation, really. Much of the questioning focused on internal SAG politics and the relationship of the guild to the CSU strikers. As SAG president, Murphy had guided his membership away from meddling in the strike, an action confirmed by 97.3 percent of the membership in a secret ballot vote. He also mentioned the curious fact that when he assumed his office he began to receive unsolicited copies of the *Daily Worker* in the mail.

"I think there is Communism in the motion picture industry as there is in practically every other industry in our nation today," Murphy testified. "I think the screen has been very successful in keeping any attempts to propagandize off the screen. It is natural that the Communists would be active in working into the movie industry because it is a communications medium."

To be sure, Communists were a "constant irritation" and, yes, front groups would occasionally exploit the natural generosity and good will of Hollywood personalities. "There are an awful lot of good, honest, liberal people who are being used by the Communists and who are sometimes suckered into these things." Nonetheless, he reckoned that the Communists accounted for less than 1 percent of the Hollywood community.

Despite coaxing by Smith, Murphy declined to name names. He obliquely referred to a union leader who did not want to settle the IATSE/CSU strike ("here was a man who had his neck bowed, who was mad, and was not interested in settling the strike"), but he did not name the man as Herbert Sorrell. Nor did he name any actor who opposed the anti-Communist resolution agreed to by SAG during Montgomery's presidency.

McDowell was uplifted by what he had heard. "It is fortunate for the American film industry—producer, actors, workers, painters, everybody else—that there has been a group of you fellows are out there, men and women, who have had the courage of your convictions and stood up and fought."

"Don't forget," put in Murphy, "we have the backing of the great majority of our members."

Now that all the actors could vote, Murphy spoke with some authority.

Ronald Reagan: "Jefferson put it a lot better than I can—but if all the American people knew all the facts, they'll never make a mistake."

On a marquee, Ronald Reagan was not in the same league as his fellow actors and predecessor SAG presidents Robert Montgomery and George Murphy, but his quiet demeanor, dreamy good looks, and Midwest ballast gave him a fiercely loyal fan base.

The gee-willikers front masked a more complicated interior. Reagan later described his prairie childhood as "a rare Huck Finn idyll," but an alcoholic father and extreme poverty was the other side of the Huck Finn experience. The darker backstory informed his two best-known performances: as George Gip in *The Knute Rockne Story* (1941), the ill-fated quarterback whose death-bed request to his teammates to "win one for the Gipper" bequeathed a nickname and a catchphrase, and Drake McHugh in *Kings Row* (1942), who wakes up after his legs have been amputated and screams, "Where's the rest of me?!"

In 1942, Reagan enlisted in the U.S. Army and was assigned to the Signal Corps. He spent the war making morale-boosting shorts and training films, fighting the "Battle of Beverly Hills," as the Hollywood-based veterans dubbed their soft assignment. In 1946, a marine took a cheap shot at Reagan in the pages of the *Hollywood Reporter*, calling him a "Cutting Room Commando at Fort Roach."* The trade paper distanced itself from the smear with an item proving how popular the actor was around town:

> Personal to Ronald Reagan: It would have done your heart good to know (as we discovered yesterday) how many friends you have in Hollywood—and whose fury at the injustice done you in the letter carried in these pages under Open Forum, kept our phone ringing incessantly. We already knew, as they did, what a fine job you did during the war; that without your glasses you're "blind as a bat": how you tried for overseas duty time and again; how you (as a Reserve Officer) were one of the first to report for duty and put on "limited service."

The next day Reagan got further vindication in a letter, signed by nine combat veterans with Hollywood pedigrees, that took up a full page of the trade paper. Reminding readers of the wartime ethos, it stated the obvious:

> The attack on Ronald Reagan is an attack on all in our community who served during the war in work for which their valuable motion picture training best fitted them, work which had to be done at home.

Among the signatories was Audie Murphy, the most decorated soldier of World War II.[13]

H. A. Smith was not immune to the Reagan charm. Reagan "has no fear of any one, is a nice talker, well informed on the subject, and will make a splendid witness," Smith wrote, in the most affectionate of all his pre-testimony reports. "He is of course reticent to testify, because he states that he is a New Deal Liberal, and does not agree with a number of the individuals in the Motion Picture Alliance." Though Reagan "states he never was a leftist," the

---

* During wartime, production at the Hal Roach Studios was given over almost exclusively to military training films.

actor had "got tangled up with a few committees that he thought were all right," but as soon as he learned their true nature, "he got out of them." Smith personally vouched for Reagan's integrity. "I happen to have been raised in the same town with Reagan [Dixon, Illinois], and know him very well, and because of that fact he opened up and talked to me very freely, and he will go to Washington if we request him to do so." Concluded Smith: "I think we should have him there."[14]

As head of SAG, Reagan was in a difficult position: he needed to protect the guild from HUAC, keep the Unfriendlies at arm's length, and avoid alienating the moderates and the liberals. The Communists were another matter. Feeling no obligation to shield actors and actresses he felt comprised a de facto fifth column, Reagan spoke regularly with the FBI, passing along the names of suspected subversives in the guild.

As with many of the friendly witnesses, Reagan was briefed in advance and fed questions by the committee. The night before his testimony, Robert Stripling visited his hotel room to rehearse their lines. The run-through, Reagan later told the FBI, prepared him to make what he considered a "pretty good defense of the industry." Reagan was annoyed, however, that Stripling failed to ask him all the agreed upon questions.[15]

Reagan was one of the few witnesses, friendly or unfriendly, who did not secure legal representation before walking into the hearing room. "What do I need a lawyer for?" he asked *PM*'s Quentin Reynolds. "I have nothing to conceal. I am not on trial. . . . Me, I'm proud of the industry I make my living in. It's a good American industry. We in Hollywood aren't afraid of Communists. As a matter of fact, I've never seen a picture which I felt advocated un-American sentiments."[16]

Casting aside the thespian's vanity for an aura of gravitas, Reagan wore a pair of horn-rimmed glasses for his severe nearsightedness. A reporter for the *New York Times* heard "a long drawn-out 'oooh' from the jam-packed, predominately feminine audience as the tall Mr. Reagan, clad in a tan gabardine suit, a blue knitted tie, and a white shirt," walked to the witness chair.[17] He might have been an exceptionally handsome and congenial college professor, the kind the co-eds in the lecture hall sighed over. Today, however, he was all business.

Like his predecessors, Reagan acknowledged that a small group of Communists existed in Hollywood, as everywhere, but within "the bounds of democracy we have done a pretty good job in blocking their activities" and have been "eminently successful" in stymieing "their usual tactics of running an organization by minority [rule]." He expressed "great pride in the film industry and I will match its record for social welfare with that of any other industry in the United States."

"I abhor the Communist philosophy but more than that I detest their tactics, which are the tactics of the fifth column," he testified. "However, as a citizen, I hope that we are never prompted by fear or resentment of Communism into compromising any of our democratic principles in order to fight them." Applause filled the room.

Reagan's eloquent avowal of the consensus liberal position—respect for the committee and the necessary job it was doing, but concern that the fear of Communism might erode civil rights—endeared him to wide swaths of the media. He made no mention of the Unfriendly Nineteen, neither to condemn nor defend. He named no names.

Also, unlike Jack Warner, Adolphe Menjou, and Robert Taylor, Reagan refused to call for the outlawing of the Communist party, choosing to put his faith in the common sense of the American people. "I would not like to see the Communists outlawed unless they are proven agents of a foreign power or not a legitimate party," he stated. "Fundamentally, I would say in opposing those people that the best thing to do is to make democracy work. In the Screen Actors Guild we make it work by assuring everyone of a vote and by keeping our members informed. And Jefferson put it a lot better than I can—but if all the American people knew all the facts they'll never make a mistake."

After Reagan's testimony, Thomas adjourned for the noon recess. The three actors left the caucus room together, a swarm of fans and reporters on their heels. Outside the Old House Office Building, the trio was set upon by newsreel cameramen who had them pose against the Capitol dome, to the delight of onlookers who cheered and applauded. "This is the most expensive set we've ever worked in," joked Murphy. "And it isn't the initial cost either. It's the upkeep."[18]

Reagan received some of the best reviews of his career for his performance before HUAC. "If any single member of the Hollywood delegation stole the show with the weight of his testimony, it was Mr. Reagan," wrote Carl Levin in the conservative *New York Herald-Tribune*. Levin's opposite at the left-leaning *PM* echoed the sentiments. "Intelligent Ronald Reagan stole the show from his better known colleagues," commented Quentin Reynolds, who ventured the opinion that the personable, forthright actor ("merely a decent citizen who likes his country and who is very willing to say so") might well "have a future beyond show business."[19]

Gary Cooper: "I don't like it because it isn't on the level."

As if pumping up the excitement for the main act on a vaudeville bill, the last of the Hollywood leading men to testify was the showstopper—in his soft-spoken, understated way. Murphy, Montgomery, and Reagan were stars, but Gary Cooper—"Coop" to his friends and legions of fans—occupied that rarified realm reserved for screen immortals, already an icon.

Contrary to persona, Cooper came from a big ranch not a sodbuster's shack. Montana born and bred, the son of a judge, he was privileged enough to attend grammar school in England but home enough on the range to earn a living as a working cowboy. He had come to Hollywood to be a stunt man, but producers took one look and fell in love: he was often cast without a screen test. Clad in buckskin, riding tall in the saddle, slinging a rifle, he was the lanky American frontiersman come to life, a man of few words, steely integrity, and sure-shot vision, the screen incarnation of the myth conjured by his namesake, James Fenimore Cooper. His breakthrough role was made to order: the title character in the film version of Owen Wister's *The Virginian* (1929), the first great sound western. Whether a cowboy (*The Westerner*, 1940), combat marksman (*Sergeant York*, 1941), or baseball hero (*The Pride of the Yankees*, 1942), he looked every inch the part.

Cooper came before the committee reluctantly. With director Leo McCarey, for whom he was starring in *Good Sam*, a whimsical comedy of manners and morals currently in production, he tried to wiggle out of an appearance. Cooper "is in the middle of completing a production of a motion picture in which over two million dollars is invested," entertainment lawyer Loyd Wright telegrammed Thomas. Wright respectfully requested that his clients—both Cooper and McCarey—be excused. If their testimony was essential, perhaps an affidavit or other written statement would suffice?[20]

No, it would not. Thomas was not about to let either man off the hook: a subpoena was a subpoena. "Their presence will be required only for that day," he telegrammed back. "The committee will be glad to arrange for air transportation both ways which should only require their being away one or two days. Regret that I cannot comply with your request but this investigation requires their presence."[21]

H. A. Smith's pre-testimony interview with Cooper confirmed what casting directors had known since 1926. "Mr. Cooper presents a very excellent appearance, and will testify in a smooth, even, soft-spoken, unexcitable manner," observed Smith. The investigator also discerned a principled reticence, an attitude that was, under the circumstances, no act. Cooper confided that in 1936 he had been approached by a missionary for the Communist cause. "Mr. Cooper will not name the individual with whom he had this conversation," Smith stated. Nor would he identify by name any other person he might suspect of Communist leanings. Cooper was "convinced that there are a number of people who are either Communists or fellow travelers of the Party line," wrote Smith, but "he cannot prove it, nor will he wish to name specific names, but he can state an overall opinion."[22]

True to type, and Smith's prediction, Cooper was a man of few words at the witness table, laconic, tight-lipped, and polite: if there had been a woman on

A tight-lipped Gary Cooper testifies, October 23, 1947.

the dais, he would surely have addressed her as "ma'am." Unlike Montgomery, Murphy, and Reagan, he held no position in SAG. Unlike Menjou, he never shot his mouth off about politics. Why the actor had been called before HUAC was something of a mystery until one looked at the rapt gallery, hanging on his every one-syllable response.

A striking contrast to the alert and articulate intelligence evinced by his fellow actors, Cooper appeared tongue-tied and abashed, well out of his comfort zone. A film actor used to a boom mike, he seemed discomforted by the bank of table microphones, which he bobbed around uncertainly. He had to be told to speak up twice.

The opening banter was pure Coop. When asked to name his profession, he blushed and admitted sheepishly, "An actor." Chuckles rippled across the caucus room.

H. A. Smith asked Cooper if he had been offered any Communist-minded scripts. Cooper said he had turned down "quite a few scripts because I thought they were tinged with Communism."

Pressed for titles, Cooper claimed to draw a blank.

Thomas was skeptical. "I say, you haven't got that bad a memory, have you? You must be able to remember some of those scripts you turned down because you thought they were Communist scripts." As always, the chairman wanted names and titles.

Cooper stuck to his guns: he couldn't think of a specific title.

Cooper was startled when the committee asked him to read a pair of outlandish documents disseminated by Communist parties in Eastern Europe. One claimed he had spoken before a crowd of ninety thousand in Philadelphia for something called the Philadelphia Communist Federation. "You would have a hard time getting 90,000 people out in Philadelphia for anything," he observed. The other document claimed he was imprisoned for his Communist beliefs and that the screen actor Buster Crabbe was machine gunned to death on the corner of Seventh Avenue. "Humph," muttered a puzzled Cooper, who explained that not only was Buster Crabbe alive but "Mr. Crabbe is a very healthy specimen of American manhood."

Cooper's opinion about Communism was frontier-saloon blunt: "I've never read Karl Marx and I don't know the basis of Communism—beyond what I've picked up from hearsay. What I've heard, I don't like it because it isn't on the level."

All in all, Cooper was on the stand for less than twenty minutes.

In private, away from the microphone, the actor was more eloquent. Asked by *New York Mirror* columnist George Dixon why so many wealthy Hollywood types seemed to be in thrall to Marxism, he responded with a thoughtful psycho-economic analysis that belied his aw-shucks persona:

> I think it's some kind of guilt complex. On the set we work side by side with hundreds of people who are vitally important to the picture. They are at work when we get there and they're still working when we leave. Yet most of them are grossly underpaid by any comparison. We rub elbows with them pretending equality, but we know things aren't equal. We know in our secret hearts that we are getting twenty times as much as we are worth while they're getting peanuts. So there are temptations to try to salve the conscience by bleeding out loud for the "underdog."[23]

Cooper said nothing as insightful before the committee. He dummied up and kept faith with the code of a born Westerner.

Leo McCarey: "Pictures should be entertainment."

In 1947, the producer-director Leo McCarey was riding the crest of one of the greatest streaks in motion picture history. Even by the hype-filled exclamation points of Hollywood ballyhoo, McCarey's success was astonishing: the year before, the easygoing Irishman had surpassed Louis B. Mayer as the highest paid salary man in America.

Born in 1898, a rare native of Los Angeles, Thomas Leo McCarey came of age with the industry. His father Thomas J. ("Uncle Tom") McCarey was a well-known fight promoter—gloved fisticuffs are a recurrent motif in the McCarey *oeuvre*—who wanted his son to enter a more respectable racket, the law. McCarey hated it. An accomplished amateur pianist, he tried his hand at songwriting, flopped, and, in 1918, got a job at Universal Pictures as a "script clerk" for director Tod Browning. He was chagrined to discover the gig was only for women. Forever after, McCarey said that he broke into show business as a script girl.

When the studio learned McCarey had gone to college, he was promoted to assistant director. In the next decade, he shaped the careers of many of the great comedians of the golden age of silent comedy. From 1923 to 1928, at the Hal Roach Studios, he directed over three hundred shorts. "Everything was completely original," he recalled wistfully of the madcap methods of his salad days. "We never knew what it was to buy one sheet of paper from anybody."[24] He teamed up an overweight America extra and a British music hall mime to create Laurel and Hardy; he helmed the zaniest of the Marx Brothers comedies, *Duck Soup* (1933); and he escorted Mae West in *Belle of the Nineties* (1934), Eddie Cantor in *The Kid from Spain* (1932), and Harold Lloyd in *The Milky Way* (1936).

By the time of the assimilationist comedy *Ruggles of Red Gap* (1935), McCarey had perfected the improvisational brushstrokes that defined his touch—a unique blend of humanistic comedy and gloopy sentimentality. In 1937, he directed two masterpieces that showed his creative range: the screwball comedy *The Awful Truth* and the multiple hankie not-just-a-woman's weepie *Make Way for Tomorrow*. In the former, Cary Grant basically did an imitation of the director, and a screen persona was born. In the latter, a heart-wrenching tale of the treatment of the elderly in America, McCarey walked a tightrope between the lachrymose and the tragic. Of all his films, *Make Way for Tomorrow* was his personal favorite.

McCarey's two most recent films were *Going My Way* (1944) and *The Bells of St. Mary's* (1945), each about an Irish-Catholic priest, played by Bing Crosby, who was more at home with pop lyrics than sacred liturgy. His version of a laid-back nonjudgmental brand of Irish Catholicism was a balm to moviegoers of all faiths and a landmark in the mainstreaming of Catholicism in American culture. McCarey was "the eminent impresario who ran a rosary bead into 15 million slugs," joshed his good friend, the writer Mark Kelly.[25] "Certainly, there is more humanity in his pictures than in those of any other movie maker," wrote AP reporter Bob Thomas in a review that called *The Bells of St. Mary's* "a Christmas gift to the nation."[26] Like the rest of the Irish-Catholic mafia in Hollywood who convened on Sunday mornings and Holy Days of Obligation at the Church of the Good Shepherd in Beverly Hills, McCarey despised the godless specter of Soviet Communism.

To attend the hearings, McCarey was forced to shut down production on *Good Sam* (1948), starring Gary Cooper, his HUAC warm-up. As promised, HUAC arranged to have the pair testify on the same day to cut down on the expenses incurred from the hiatus in production. Taking no chances,

RKO, which was to distribute *Good Sam*, insisted McCarey and Cooper fly to Washington on separate airplanes.

McCarey's testimony was brief and nonsensational. A bit surprisingly, he said he opposed the production of anti-Communist motion pictures. "I don't think pictures should be made that have much more than what the medium stands for. It is a great art. Pictures should be entertainment," he opined. "I believe it only tends toward causing more enmity if we are partisan and take sides in our pictures."

"Do you mean," interjected Thomas, "we would be doing the same thing Soviet Russia is doing?"

"That's right," McCarey said, despite the fact that the Communists had conspired to prevent "pro-American" films "from seeing the light of day." However, thanks to HUAC, it was "getting a bit unpopular now" to be a Communist in Hollywood.

Though McCarey's total appearance went by faster than a Hal Roach short, he managed to get off one of the best lines of the hearings.

Stripling played straight man, asking whether McCarey's double-barreled paean to all things Irish Catholic, *Going My Way* and *The Bells of St. Mary's*, had been successful at the box office. As everyone in the room well knew, both films were gold mines.

McCarey admitted that the pair had been money makers.

"How did they do in Russia?" Stripling asked.

"We haven't received one ruble from Russia on either picture," said McCarey. "I think I have a character in there that they do not like."

"Bing Crosby?" ventured Stripling.

"No," deadpanned McCarey. "God."

At that, the hearing room—the committeemen, the press, the gallery— rocked with laughter.

John Garfield: "No official, high or petty, can prescribe what can be considered orthodox."

Hollywood had rolled out its best players before HUAC and the reviews were ecstatic. The calm demeanor of the director and the actors—and their refusal to blurt out names—sat well even with opponents of the committee.

The *New York Herald Tribune*, which had been sharply critical of the hearings, admitted, "Five members of the motion picture industry brought momentary dignity this week to the hippodrome being staged in Washington by the House Un-American Activities Committee. Their testimony was free of insinuation, long lists of suspicious characters, and hysterical denunciation of vague enemies."[27]

The day saw one other major star turn in the person of a sturdy leading man who came to Washington of his own volition and at his own expense. After the hearings adjourned, John Garfield, besieged by press and autograph seekers in the caucus room, asked that everybody follow him out into the corridor for a press conference. He led the group to the elevator alcove down the hall, climbed halfway up the adjacent stairs, and began to read from a prepared statement.

Garfield had come to Washington that day as the head of a delegation representing the New York branch of the Committee for the First Amendment,

The New York branch of the Committee for the First Amendment, arriving in Washington D.C., October 23, 1947. *Left to right*: Julius Epstein, Canada Lee, Oscar Serlin, Bernice Parks, Irving Pichel, John Garfield, Larry Parks, Uta Hagen, Philip Epstein, and Paul Draper. Garfield embraces two members of the Hollywood Nineteen. (Courtesy of Leslie Epstein)

a contingent composed mostly of entertainers from the Broadway stage.[28] The New Yorkers may have commanded less star power than their screen colleagues on the opposite coast, but they were more blunt spoken and contemptuous of the HUAC hearings. They were also openly in solidarity with the position of the Unfriendly Nineteen.

Flanked by Paul Draper and Canada Lee, Garfield denounced Thomas and the inquiry, and declared that he and others had formed a committee to defend the Unfriendly Nineteen. That declaration blandly contradicted the position of CFA's Hollywood branch, which strived to straddle the space between HUAC and the Unfriendlies. Not yet fully coordinated with developments on the West Coast, Garfield said the committee was be called the Committee for the Defense of the First Amendment of the American Constitution.[29] The New Yorkers promised to send representatives to the caucus room each day to swing publicity away from Chairman Thomas.

"No official, high or petty, can prescribe what can be considered orthodox," declared Garfield, quoting Justice Robert Jackson. Draper added that their mission was to assure "that the spirit of free creativeness is not stifled by [the] individual ambition of Congressional committees." The dancer also denounced McCarey as "uninformed" and Gary Cooper as "stupid."[30]

Skeptical newspapermen asked Garfield point blank if his group were a Communist front. "So far as we know, there are no Communists in our group," Garfield and Draper insisted. "The committee is certainly and absolutely not a Communist front." Lee, Uta Hagen, Bernice Parks and the Epstein twins all chimed in and likewise asserted their anti-Communist sentiments. Garfield then handed out the statement drawn up by the Hollywood branch:

> We hold that these hearings are morally wrong because any investigation into the political beliefs of the individual is contrary to the basic principles of our democracy. Any attempt to curb freedom of expression and to set arbitrary standards of Americanism is in itself disloyal to both the spirit and letter of our Constitution.

Draper was asked if he knew any Communists on Broadway. He did not tap-dance around the answer. No, he said, not a one.

"Not one?" scoffed a cynic.

"Not one on Broadway. In fact, I don't know any Communists!"

At that, members of the press corps snickered.[31]

Chapter 10

DOLDRUMS

As star witnesses, Mrs. Lela Rogers, Oliver Carlson, and Walt Disney were no match for the headline-grabbing matinee idols of the day before. No smitten matrons or swooning bobbysoxers crowded the corridors of the Old House Office Building hoping for a glimpse or an autograph. On the last day of the first week of the hearings, a morning-after calm settled over the room, all eyes on the weekend. Thomas had contemplated a special Saturday session, but opted against it "because some people have to attend football games."[1] Mindful of the priorities, he called only three witnesses and ended the day early.

The diminution in star magnitude was reflected in the erosion of the gallery. The press seats were half filled, the spectators half interested. Thomas had to gavel repeatedly for order, not to quiet fan hubbub or partisan outbursts but because of the restless chattering of bored reporters. "The final day of the week was so dull, it should have been left on the cutting room floor," kvetched Florence S. Lowe, wringing more juice from the showbiz metaphor. A committee clerk scanned the empty seats and cracked, "Now we almost got room enough for the lawyers." Behind the dais a newsreel soundman was snoozing contentedly.[2]

In Hollywood, the city awoke to more stirring news. The Committee for the First Amendment formally announced itself in a tandem series of full-page ads published in *Daily Variety* and the *Hollywood Reporter*. The ads were part of a venerable industry tradition: any Hollywood group with an agenda took to the pages of the trade press to post gripes, settle scores, and speak its piece. Along with the splashy advertisements for a studio's slate of current releases, the advertisements gave a fair reading of the political temperature of the community in any given season.

The ad simply reprinted the text of the First Amendment, under which were the names of 139 Hollywood personalities—and a plea for support and funding.[3]

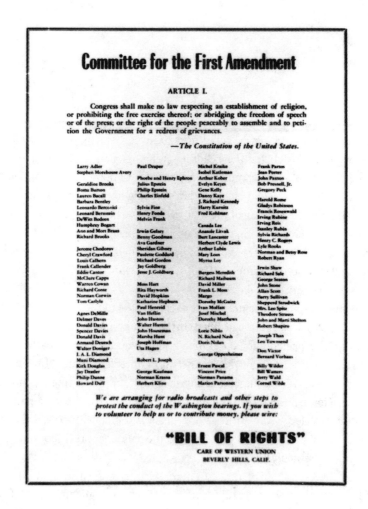

The Committee for the First Amendment formally announces itself in *Daily Variety* and the *Hollywood Reporter*, October 24, 1947.

In Hollywood, the response to the ad was electric. "We've had many calls from people complaining that their names should have been added to ours," an excited Jane Strudwick, wife of actor Shepperd Strudwick, told the *Daily Worker*.[4] The need for a support group to coalesce around was palpable. "It was a disturbing and frightening period in Hollywood," recalled Lauren Bacall. "Everyone was suspect—at least, everyone to the left of center."[5]

Lela Rogers: "I would suggest that the Congress of the United States immediately enact such legislation as will preserve the Bill of Rights for the people for whom it was designed."

The first witness was a celebrity by parentage, Mrs. Lela E. Rogers, a staunch Republican in a Democrat stronghold, a founding member of the MPA-PAI, and the mother of screen star Ginger Rogers. Rogers *mater* seemed to be, and was often portrayed as, the Central Casting incarnation of an overbearing stage mother, a harpy channeling her energies into the career of her multi-talented daughter, who, unlike her mother, steered clear of roughneck political combat.

But though infinitely caricature-able, Rogers was no clinging appendage; she was a force of nature in her own right. Born in 1891 in Council Bluffs, Iowa, she married at nineteen, gave birth to her famous daughter, jettisoned a beta-male husband whose ambition did not match hers, and lit out to become a newspaper reporter. By 1916, Rogers was in Hollywood working as a screenwriter. When America entered the Great War, she was one of the first ten American women to enlist in the U.S. Marines. In uniform, she served as a press officer, edited training films, and rose in the ranks to become editor in chief of *Leatherneck*, the official monthly of her beloved Corps.

Retiring as a sergeant, Rogers returned to the motion picture business— for herself and the bundle of talent under her wing. In Hollywood, while her daughter danced from the chorus line into the spotlight, she established a theatrical school, worked as in-house dramatic coach at RKO, and freelanced as a theater producer, director, playwright, and manager. She also made a brief, in-joke appearance as Ginger's mother in Billy Wilder's screwball comedy *The Major and the Minor* (1942). Close, mutually nurturing companions, mother and daughter were also bound by religion. In a town thick with Jews and strewn with Catholics, Lela and Ginger stood out as observant Christian Scientists.

In the presidential campaign of 1944, Rogers backed FDR's opponent and served as vice chairman of the Hollywood for Dewey Committee. Like many self-made success stories, she had scant sympathy for the little guy who hadn't pulled himself up bootstrap-wise and deeply resented a federal government siphoning off her hard-earned income to support layabouts on the dole.

Rogers was widely quoted—and in leftist circles widely ridiculed—for her contention that a line from *Tender Comrade* (1943), the Edward Dmytryk-directed, Dalton Trumbo-scripted home front melodrama with a communitarian subtext and red-flag title, was evidence of the insidious "boring from within" practiced by Communist screenwriters. Emerging from her testimony during the HUAC hearings in May, she told newsmen that Ginger had balked at the subversive sentiment in the line "Share and share alike—that's democracy!" Said Rogers: "Ginger refused to speak the line and it was put into the mouth of Kim Hunter, and it appeared in the picture!"[6]

Little wonder that H. A. Smith was dubious about Rogers's usefulness as a witness. She "has considerable contempt for the Committee based again on the alleged unfavorable manner in which she feels Taylor was treated," he noted, speaking delicately about Thomas's double-cross of the actor. Smith worked to reassure her on that score. "If we can confine her testimony to brief, concise opinions, she will be of value. However, if she goes off and testifies to 'share and share alike,' it will do us more harm than good." Rogers was scheduled to make her litigious appearance on ABC radio's *America's Town Meeting of the Air* the very night Smith wrote his report. "If she is able to hold up, then she should make a good witness," figured Smith. "If not, it would be best not to call her."[7] Apparently, she passed the audition.

A graying blond in black-rimmed glasses, Rogers owned the room. It was evident where Ginger had gotten her looks. Ungraciously forgetting her sole female predecessor, the *New York Herald-Tribune* identified Rogers as "the first woman so far called before the committee" and noted that HUAC "had purportedly been calling only male Hollywood celebrities so it cannot be charged with conducting a beauty show."[8] She brought a spark of feminine flash and the whiff of perfume to the witness table, which could not be said of Ayn Rand.

Ronald Reagan and Lela Rogers listen to testimony, October 22, 1947.

Thomas was not so ungentlemanly as to deny a lady permission to read an opening statement. "Some of our executives have been deceived by the party liners they hired," Rogers declared. "As a free people, we have no experience with such intrigue and conspiracy. Our executives were no more asleep [to Communism] than were our people or our government or the whole world in fact. The Communist is a trained propagandist, a highly disciplined operator, as is revealed by the testimony of former Soviet officials and ex-members of the Communist party. His ways are devious and not easy to follow." Fortunately, Hollywood had been slapped to its senses by HUAC. "I think that once our executives see this, and know it for itself, they will be most happy to clean it out of their pictures. In the first place there have been very few pictures ever made with Communist propaganda in them that were successes at the box office."

Having been prepped by the committee, Rogers rustled through her crib sheets as she spoke. "Well, uh, I would suggest that the Congress of the United States immediately enact such legislation as will preserve the Bill of

Rights for the people for whom it was designed," she said. "That precious bill was never intended to protect enemy agents, saboteurs, and spies, whether they're American or alien born."

Stripling asked whether Rogers would favor the outlawing of the Communist party.

"I favor the outlawing of the Communist party as an agency of a foreign government."

"You consider them to be the agents of a foreign government?"

"I do, sir. Yes, sir."

Unexpectedly, Representative McDowell interrupted to make a point about something that had been bothering him. The only Communist propaganda alleged to have seeped into the films themselves was the occasional instances of a banker depicted as a "no-good." As evidence of Communist hegemony in Hollywood, wasn't that pretty thin gruel? "Well, of course, I know many fine bankers, many patriotic men," McDowell hastened to add. "I also know stinkers that should have been in jail 30 years ago. That doesn't necessarily constitute Communist propaganda."

"I can't quote you the scenes exactly, but I can give you the sense of them," Rogers said defensively. "When a Communist secures a firm footing in a picture, he surrounds himself only with other Communists." As proof, she added a new film to the pro-Soviet slate: *None But the Lonely Heart* (1944), a Marxist critique of capitalism. The film was "moody and gloomy, in the Russian manner," she said, quoting from a review. "I think this is a splendid example of what type of propaganda Communists like to inject into the motion pictures." The film's anti-capitalist centerpiece showed a son telling his mother, the owner of a second-hand store, "You're not going to work here and squeeze pennies out of little people who are poorer than I am!" The line was unnecessary, she explained, "because in life there are always people richer or poorer than ourselves."

Rogers had opposed the purchase of the property by RKO and the selection of playwright Clifford Odets to write and direct it. The reason was simple: Odets was a Communist. "For years I had heard that Mr. Odets was a Communist," Rogers said, and he had never denied it. Confirming her birds-of-a-feather theory of infiltration, Odets had hired Hanns Eisler to compose the soundtrack.

Rogers admitted that the percentage of Communists in Hollywood was very small—perhaps smaller than 1 percent—but no matter. "The Communists don't want numerical superiority, they want small, disciplined cells." So insidious was their boring from within that Ginger herself may have unwittingly served the red cause by starring in *Tender Comrade*. Doubtless to Smith's relief, she did not repeat her indictment of the "share and share alike" motto.

Rogers's testimony—perhaps her very presence and personality—put Thomas in a good mood. "Thank you, and just go back to Hollywood and make a little more money so you can pay off that libel suit," he joked, referring to the lawsuit pending against Rogers filed by SWG president Emmet Lavery, who was suing her for calling him a Communist on *America's Town Meeting of the Air*.

Oliver Carlson: "The Communist attitude is, 'Why worry about Moscow gold, when you can get Hollywood greenbacks?'"

The forty-eight-year-old, Swedish-born, Michigan-reared Oliver Carlson, a college teacher and self-styled expert on Communism, was best known, to the extent he was known at all, for working the Communism-in-Hollywood beat for the anti-Stalinist labor magazine the *New Leader*. Though Carlson had testified before the Tenney Committee in Los Angeles in 1941, and lectured as an authority on Communism, he was a bit player plucked from the crowd of extras for a brief close-up. He had recently authored a pamphlet for the Catholic Information Society entitled *Red Star Over Hollywood* warning that "few cities and few areas of American life have been so thoroughly 'captured' by Stalin's agents as Hollywood and the movie industry."[9]

Another former Communist in full repentance mode, Carlson said he had joined the party "when I was a kid," but broke with it soon after. He maintained contacts in the party apparatus, however, and told a harrowing tale of fifth column subversion, not just in the Hollywood studios but in the Los Angeles school system (the American Federation of Teachers was "dominated by Communists"). The man behind the educational outreach was Eli Jacobson, an emissary from the New York branch of the CPUSA, who had been sent out to Hollywood in 1938 to set up the People's Education Center, a school for subversion that had been "extremely effective for training in Communist ideology." Jacobson had confided to Carlson that he was "sent to Hollywood by the party to conduct classes and educational propaganda among the film folk, not the rank and file but the elite." Jacobson's job "was to see to it that many important persons were softened up so as to agree to join front organizations the Communist party was forming in Hollywood."

Carlson plied the conventional wisdom: that Communists targeted Hollywood because it was a propaganda powerhouse with a reservoir of gullible stars willing to fill party coffers. "I don't have to tell this committee," he told the committee, "that the motion picture industry is not exactly a sweat shop industry. Here is a treasure chest which is important. The Communist attitude is, 'Why worry about Moscow gold, when you can get Hollywood greenbacks?'" Carlson re-imprinted the popular image of easily duped—and sometimes consciously sinister—Hollywood stars opening their checkbooks to bankroll international revolution.

Carlson scoffed at the notion that HUAC was an agent of "thought control," as critics claimed. "The thought control is all on the other side. There's something sadly amusing about people who endorse the Soviet government's control of press and radio talking about thought control in this country."

Representative Vail asked Carlson—"as a propaganda expert"—what he thought of the charges by MPAA president Eric Johnston and newspaper columnists that the HUAC investigation was but a veiled attempt to assert government control over Hollywood.

Carlson began a lengthy, convoluted answer, but Thomas cut him off. "I think we have gone too far afield," decreed the chairman, as bored as everyone else.[10]

Carlson praised the committee and likened Communism to a cancerous growth that had to be cut out to save the organism "even though I know some good innocent people would be destroyed." The former Communist had taken to heart the Leninist maxim about how an omelet couldn't be made without breaking a few eggs.

Walt Disney: "We must keep the American labor unions clean."

Walt Disney was not yet a signature—if not *the* signature—brand name of the American century, a man of lands, kingdoms, and synergistic empires, not yet the crinkly avuncular figure with an animated fairy flitting about his shoulders. Only after 1955 would the double-barreled marketing juggernauts of Disneyland and the ABC television show *The Wonderful World of Disney* make his visionary dreamscape and soothing persona as famous as the creatures that sprang from his drawing board. He was simply the father of the animated feature film, the premiere independent producer in Hollywood, and a certified genius.

Disney was also the creator and voice of Mickey Mouse, of course, and the sorcerer behind scores of cartoons and singalongs, most famously *The Three Little Pigs* (1933), whose Depression-resonant chant "Who's Afraid of the Big Bad Wolf?" suggested we all were. In 1937, *Snow White and the Seven Dwarfs*, a quantum leap forward into feature-length animation and depth psychology, propelled Disney into a select pantheon with Griffith and Chaplin. What followed—the symphonic hallucination *Fantasia* (1940); the night-sea journey of a prevaricating marionette, *Pinocchio* (1940); the aerodynamic pachyderm *Dumbo* (1941), and the traumatic tale of an orphan fawn, *Bambi* (1942)—put him in a class by himself. The instructional work Walt Disney Pictures performed for the U.S. military during World War II—using the pliant medium of animation to help GIs read sonar, identify aircraft, and understand ballistics—earned his studio the distinction of being the only motion picture plant designated as an essential wartime industry.

Even before television stardom, Disney affected an image as a kindly overseer with a call-me-Walt managerial style. Long removed from the dronework of cel animation, he assumed that his animators were like the seven dwarves—whistling while they worked, happy to be hunched over their drawing boards, singing hi-ho, hi-ho.[11]

In 1937, a man with a familiar name—Herbert K. Sorrell—entered the edenic forest to torment its benevolent game warden. Sorrell had quietly organized the Disney proletariat into the Screen Cartoonists Guild (SCG), a trade union dubbed "the Mickey Mouse Guild," but as usual there was nothing Mickey Mouse about Sorrell's hardball tactics.[12] On May 27, 1941, the Disney family was torn apart when the SCG voted to strike and picket theaters showing Disney cartoons. Waving the best-illustrated picket signs in the history of organized labor, they demanded better wages and working hours. "I am positively convinced that Communistic agitation, leadership, and activities have brought about this strike," Disney told his employees, it being the only possible explanation for their rejection of his "fair and equitable settlement" offer.[13] Ultimately, after a bitter nine weeks, an arbitrator from the U.S. Department of Labor brokered a settlement. Disney signed a closed-shop agreement with the SCG and agreed to pay back wages to the strikers. He never forgot what he considered a betrayal from a pack of ungrateful trolls.

H. A. Smith carefully vetted and coached Disney prior to his testimony. "Mr. Disney is a gentleman, presents a nice appearance, talks well, and certainly will be an asset as a witness on our behalf," Smith reported. But though a dedicated anti-Communist and an original officer of the MPA-PAI, Disney was a reluctant witness. "He has no fear of testifying, however he states that his story is an old one and that he is doubtful whether it would be of any value," wrote Smith. Given the Disney demographic, the animator-mogul was considered an especially valuable catch. "We feel that in view of the type of picture which he makes his statements opposing Communism would be of material value so far as the younger generation is concerned."[14]

Before taking the oath at the witness table, Disney endeared himself to two fathers on the dais. While waiting to testify, he drew cartoons of Mickey Mouse and Donald Duck for a pair of delighted children who just happened to be Bunny Stripling, daughter of the chief counsel, and Jerry Wheeler, son of committee investigator William Wheeler. Bunny sat perched on Uncle Walt's lap.

At the witness table, Disney was the factory owner not the visionary artist. He still bristled at what he saw as the plot by the Sorrell-led Communists to destroy his life's work. According to Disney, Sorrell said "that he did not want an election and threatened a strike. He said I couldn't stand a strike and he would make a dust bowl out of my place. I believe he was a Communist. When he pulled the strike, the first group to put me on the unfair list was the Communist front organizations."

Disney vouched for all his current employees who, unlike the malcontents in the past, were "100 percent American." Asked to identify the suspected Communists, Disney named David Hilberman, a former Disney artist and SCG activist; William Pomerance, former chief field officer for the NLRB and business manager for the SCG; and Maurice Howard, who in 1944 succeeded Pomerance as business manager.

"I think the industry is made up of good Americans, just like in my plant, good, solid Americans," Disney said by way of closing. The main thing, always, was to keep the Communists from disturbing the serenity of the workers. "They get themselves closely tied up in this labor thing, so that if you try to get rid of them, they make a labor case out of it," he said. "We must keep the American labor unions clean."

Disney had performed as hoped and Chairman Thomas was delighted. "There is no doubt that movies are the greatest medium of entertainment in the United States and in the world," he gushed. "You, as a creator of entertainment, are one of the greatest examples in the profession."

At 2:30 P.M., Thomas gaveled the day to an early close.

As the dog-tired investigators and bored-to-tears spectators shuffled out of the caucus room, they could look back on an eventful week. The testimony had revealed the emergence of two camps of witnesses. Both were friendly, or pretended to be. One group—the members of the MPA-PAI and anti-Communists activists like Ayn Rand, Howard Rushmore, and Oliver Carlson—saw Communists in Hollywood as a real and present danger. The fifth columnists needed to be identified, purged, and outlawed. The other group—the moguls, the SAG presidents, past and present, and, as yet from off stage, MPAA president Eric Johnston—saw the Communists as a minor problem that Hollywood's watchful sentinels were wise to. They were protective of Hollywood's prerogatives and insulted by the notion that Communists had made serious inroads in the unions (thanks to IATSE) and the guilds (excepting maybe the SWG). Moreover, the minuscule percentage of Communists working in the industry had certainly gained no influence over Hollywood cinema thanks to the vigilance of the producers and the good sense of American moviegoers.

The second week, when the Unfriendlies were scheduled to take the stage, would introduce a third camp. First, however, the weekend intermission would allow all sides to regroup. The break also gave critics the chance to review the performance of the cast.

Chapter 11
CRASHING PAGE 1

I n 1947, the verb "spin"—meaning to twist the news and lie bald-faced for political advantage—had not yet entered the vernacular, but spinning was what the congressmen, witnesses, and lawyers in the HUAC pageant were doing over the weekend break. The three combatants on the Hollywood side of the caucus room—the Motion Picture Association of America, the Committee for the First Amendment, and the Unfriendly Nineteen—all moved out of the insular confines of the trade press into the civilian media for public declarations of principles. They gave interviews in print and on air, published advertisements, held rallies, and, in a singular instance of vocal defiance, Hollywood's liberals produced a radio show to take their case to the nation.

The journalists covering the proceedings also weighed in. Reporters, commentators, and editorial cartoonists from across the political spectrum digested the first full week of the show and mulled the odd spectacle that had just transpired. The confrontation between Howard Hughes and the U.S. Senate in August had been about alleged criminal conduct—a familiar story of greed and corruption, of government-industry collusion and influence peddling. The HUAC hearings were about the First Amendment: the other committee from Hollywood had that right. Watching the clash of a popular art and an unpopular ideology, onlookers joined the debate over the place, if any, of Communism under the U.S. Constitution and negotiated the fine points of a postwar contract balancing national security and freedom of expression.

The trade press reporters who analyzed show business for a living were convinced that the five-day serial drama had been exposed as a naked bid for headlines. "As of now, Rep. J. Parnell Thomas & Co. already have been paid off—in spades—if they're after publicity," wrote *Variety* editor Abel Green in a rare boxed-off editorial. "What's more natural than latching onto Hollywood to crash P. 1?" Green saw the hearings not as a serious investigation into Communist subversion but a cynical ploy by obscure politicians to grab above-the-fold coverage. "By the nature of the subject it's a set up for the headlines. . . . No amount of brass can compete with Hollywood marquee names for printer's ink glamour," he continued. "Thomas and his Un-American Activities Committee know it. The picture business knows it. The press knows it—and no one ever accused the U.S. press of being backward in attaching itself to a Hollywood name for generous space. Wotta parlay—s.a. and USA!* How can it miss the headlines when glamour and a neo-patriotic cause are involved?"[1]

Other observers suspected motives and feared implications darker than mere ballyhoo. *New York Daily News* columnist Ed Sullivan—still years away from the television variety show that would carve his stone face into American memory—expressed a common foreboding. "This is a star chamber proceeding that not only exempts the investigators from the intervention of a jury, but also exempts them from observing the telltale bearing of accused and accuser, when brought face to face," he wrote. "Such a trial, or hearing, can establish a dangerous precedent."[2]

Sullivan's "star chamber" barb was the mildest of the rebukes. Intemperate language and hyperbolic overkill were reflex reactions on both sides: HUAC was an Inquisition presaging an American Reich; Reds were vermin eating into the foundations of America. Each side saw a totalitarian future on the horizon, one filtered through the Nazi past, the other projected as a nightmare vision of Stalinist things to come.

The Nazi precedent—so recent, so vivid—was the incessant fallback metaphor for the Communist, the left wing, and the liberal press, all of which conjured the imagery, the personalities, and the tactics of the Third Reich to forecast the descent of Fascism upon American soil and to warn that the HUAC hearings were but a step away from Gestapo thugs herding dissidents

---

* S.A. was *Variety*ese for sex appeal, a cutesy holdover from the 1920s.

into American concentration camps. The Communist party hacks seemed positively thrilled at the chance to roll out the heavy rhetorical artillery. "In Washington the Kliegs burn brilliantly—like a bonfire of books, or an open-door oven. There's even an Adolph," shivered Joseph North in the *New Masses*. "Truly, it is the Nuremberg book burning—in Technicolor."[3]

The predictions of Gotterdammerung were not limited to the pages of the *New Masses* and the *Daily Worker*. "The Un-American Activities Committee seems to me to be better for a police state than for the U.S.A.," opined Eleanor Roosevelt in her syndicated column.[4]

Seasoned reporters from the trade press took a less apocalyptic view, but saw good reason for concern. Looking back on the Senate War Propaganda hearings of 1941, when things had gone so well, Hollywood's tribunes wondered why things were going so badly now. "The contrast is immediately perceptible," wrote Herb Golden in *Variety*. "Then the industry was confident of its strategy and immediately took the offensive away from the investigator." Now, facing the Thomas Committee, the industry was nervous and vacillating, split between compliance and resistance.

Much of the blame for the poor showing fell on the industry's attorney Paul McNutt, who displayed neither the wit nor firepower of Wendell Willkie. "Comparison between McNutt and Wendell Willkie, who served so brilliantly in the 1941 probe, is as inevitable as the comparison of strategy," Golden observed. To be sure, McNutt was relegated to a sideline role by Thomas's autocratic decrees, unlike Willkie, who was granted wide latitude to make his case and deferred to by the senators. Even so, the feeling that Hollywood had hired a B-lister as its wing man deflated industry supporters. "The only chance he gets to say anything publicly is when reporters crowd around him after the hearings," complained Golden. "In those sessions, if they can be used as any criteria, he shows little of the vigor and deep feeling for civil liberties that made Willkie the dominating figure of the pre-Pearl Harbor sessions."[5]

In HUAC's corner, the most vocal cheerleaders wrote for the tabloid press of William Randolph Hearst, the media mogul who had harbored a grudge against Hollywood since Orson Welles's film à clef *Citizen Kane* (1941). In shrieking headlines and scaremongering ledes, the Hearst press kept up a steady drumbeat of criticism and alarums. "Anyone knows why the *Daily Worker* is opposed to the Hollywood investigation," editorialized the *Los Angeles Examiner*. "It simply does not want Hollywood Communism to be exposed."[6] Likewise, the *New York World Telegram* believed that "those who are expressing the fear that the present Hollywood probe is a black effort at censorship seem to overlook the fact the Communist slanting of film entertainment now under fire amounts to the same thing in Red."[7]

In the *New York Sun*, Hearst's flagship tabloid, George E. Sokolsky defended HUAC against "those hoofers and literary hacks and imitators of gangsters [who] for so long have been above the law." Sokolsky believed that "the only protection the United States has against a Russian fifth column and a vast body of American Quislings is such an investigation as the Thomas Committee is conducting and the work of the FBI."[8] Sokolsky's support for the committee was significant. As the son of a rabbi, the widely syndicated commentator helped insulate HUAC from charges of antisemitism.

But Sokolsky and his Hearst brethren were outliers. Liberal, mainstream, and even conservative newspapers sided with Hollywood not HUAC. Two legacies of World War II—the goodwill the motion picture industry had accrued from doing its bit and the memory of state-run media under Joseph Goebbels—worked to Hollywood's advantage. Thomas's crass preening and visible glee in the spotlight also predisposed the press, itself in the First Amendment business, to speak out against the hearings.

The opposition against HUAC extended to the pages of the *New York Herald Tribune*, a moderate Republican newspaper and a reliable bellwether of conservative opinion. It lambasted the hearings as a "witch hunt" conducted for Chairman Thomas "to seek personal aggrandizement on the taxpayer's funds." In an editorial that might have been penned by the leadership of the Committee for the First Amendment—or the Unfriendly Nineteen for that matter—the paper stated flatly that "the beliefs of the men and women of the screen are, like the beliefs of any ordinary men and women, nobody's business but their own, as the Bill of Rights mentions."[9] With the Hearst press raining down a daily bombardment of invective, Hollywood took special solace from the editorial support in so unexpected a quarter. CFA republished the editorial in full page ads in *Daily Variety* and the *Hollywood Reporter*.

The preeminent Hollywood-Washington gossip columnist—the man who virtually invented the hybrid of celebrity news and political commentary—was Walter Winchell, currently presiding in a daily *New York World* column ("In New York") and from Table 50 at the Stork Club, where he planted himself evenings to get tips and receive obeisance. An early anti-Nazi, an ardent anti-Communist, and a confidant of J. Edgar Hoover, Winchell was not as keen on HUAC as one might expect. His patented "slanguage"—the patter of glib coinages for which he was famous—was deployed to demean the Communist cadre—"punkos" for "pinkos," "yellow travelers" for "fellow travelers"—but he had seen too much of Hollywood to believe it was a hotbed of anything other than hubris and chutzpah. "The level of Americanism is as good any day in the week at Hollywood and Vine as it is at Pennsylvania and F. Street," he figured. "And so is the level of morals."[10] Unlike so many media circuses Winchell had lived through, he did not attend the hearings in person, and mentioned them only intermittently. "Isn't it typical of Congress?" he smirked. "They're worried more about the Reds in Hollywood than the Reds in Moscow."[11]

The judgments of the professional observers in the press were augmented by commentary from the actors on the stage. Many of the witnesses, those who had already testified and those waiting in the wings, massaged and manipulated the media to shape coverage of their testimony, expanding, glossing, and underscoring, saying to the press what they did not, or could not, say into Thomas's microphones.

Eric Johnston, who had not yet testified but who was scheduled to be the leadoff witness first thing on Monday, sent a letter to the congressional leadership suggesting "that the time has come for the Congress to overhaul its procedure in committee investigations to clarify and make secure the rights of individual citizens." Too often, Johnston charged, have individuals and institutions been "slandered and libeled by hostile witnesses not subject to cross-examination and immune from subsequent suit or prosecution." Though well aware that a congressional investigation was "a fact-finding inquiry and not a trial," in practice, the committee had become "prosecutor, judge, and jury, and the individual becomes the defendant."[12] It was Johnston's strongest statement to date, addressed over Thomas's head to his superiors on Capitol Hill.

The Unfriendly Nineteen: "Keep America Free!"

Activist by nature, adept at organizing support networks and orchestrating media coverage, the Unfriendly Nineteen used the weekend hiatus to rally anti-HUAC sentiment. None had yet been called to the witness stand but a foretaste of their rhetoric rang out in interviews, seminars, press conferences, and a blow-out rally.

In New York, anti-HUAC forces took advantage of Saturday and Sunday to mount a two-day forum billed as the Conference on Cultural Freedom and Civil Liberties. Sponsored by the Progressive Citizens of America and held at the Hotel Commodore, it was a hybrid of academic conference, consciousness-raising session, and pep rally consisting of discussion panels, press conferences, and performances. It was highlighted by a huge nighttime rally to "Keep America Free!"

Among the panelists, novelist Howard Fast spoke on "Thought Control and the First Amendment," Larry Parks on "What Is Loyalty to America?" and Albert Maltz on "The Meaning of the Un-American Activities Committee." The great African American singer-actor-activist Paul Robeson lent his formidable presence to a talk on "Politics and Civil Rights." In addition to many of the Nineteen and supportive fellow artists, the panels featured eminences from politics, the press, the law, and academia. Victor Bernstein, foreign correspondent and author of *Final Judgment: The Story of Nuremberg*, explained "How Fascism Grows," Dr. Walter O. Roberts of the Harvard College Observatory contemplated "The Atomic Crisis," and O. John Rogge, former assistant U.S. attorney general, gave a history lesson entitled "The Alien-Sedition Laws—1947."[13] Rogge was one of many who raised the familiar specter. "In these dark times, what we have in our midst is incipient fascism."[14]

Robert W. Kenny came up from Washington to warn the delegates of a "cold censorship" of films, but he was heartened by the tide of editorials directed against HUAC. "I think it is safe to say that no official body in the history of our country during the past two decades has brought so much discredit to Congress." Dr. Harlow Shapley, director of the Harvard College Observatory and chairman on the conference, read a radiogram from former Vice President Henry A. Wallace, in which the darling of left liberals and future presidential candidate asked, "Has America really gone crazy? Is the un-American Activities Committee evidence that America is traveling the road to fascism?"

A radio and film panel warned that the Thomas Committee was seeking to intimidate the media and thereby make "trained seals" of the American people. "We're already subject to censorship which is partially responsible for the insipid artificiality of so many of our pictures," said Ring Lardner Jr., referring to the Production Code. "When Thomas is given the right of script approval, any resemblance to American life or democratic notions will be strictly an oversight."[15]

After the (relatively) decorous academic panels, the friends of the Unfriendlies staged a rollicking Saturday night rally at the St. Nicholas Arena, often a venue for prize fights, with top seats going for $1.80. Billed as a "Keep America Free" rally "for the 19 Hollywood progressives subpoenaed by Thomas-Rankin," the festivities included speeches from Kenny, Dr. Shapley, John Garfield, Paul Draper, Frank Kingdon, Lillian Hellman, and Sen. Claude Pepper (D-FL). Some seventy-five hundred supporters attended with fifteen hundred more turned away at the door.

As usual, playwright-screenwriter Lillian Hellman did not mince words. "This has been the week of turning the head in shame; of the horror of seeing politicians make the honorable institution of Congress into a honky tonk show; of listening to craven men lie and tattle, pushing each other in their efforts to lick the boots of their villifiers; publicly trying to wreck the lives, not of strangers, mind you, but of men with whom they have worked and eaten and played, and made millions." Hellman, who would herself soon be in the crosshairs of the committee that inspired her remarks, lamented "a sickening, sickening, immoral and degraded week" and derided Adolphe Menjou, Gary Cooper, and Robert Taylor as "craven men, lying and tattling." She couldn't figure out why HUAC was targeting Hollywood since there was "never a single word about Communism in any American film—in fact, there's seldom an idea of *any* kind in films."[16] Hellman's snide put-down was rank misdirection: there were always ideas in Hollywood films and Hellman and the Unfriendly Nineteen had worked overtime to put them there.

Larry Parks read a prepared statement from Bartley Crum, who was ill in Washington. Crum commented on a number of "coincidences" about the hearings that led him to believe the probe was antisemitic in cast, "particularly the fact that all of the subpoenaed had something to do with pictures against racial discrimination." Parks, director Irving Pichel, and actor Sam Wanamaker lightened the mood with a sketch entitled "Drums of Silence," parodying the supine postures of Jack L. Warner and Louis B. Mayer.

An adulatory account of the evening in the *Daily Worker* singled out a favorite son. "The fighting spirit of the aroused conference was summed up by actor John Garfield at the rally when he shouted, 'I'm sore, damn sore. We say 'No' and that 'No' has become the fighting slogan of thousands of people who love this country and want to see it free."[17]

The presence of Garfield and the dancer Paul Draper at the Keep America Free rally—two prominent members of CFA's New York contingent—undercut the strategy of the Hollywood branch. Even as Houston, Wyler, and Dunne were trying to keep the Unfriendly Nineteen at arm's length, Garfield and Draper were embracing them.

John Huston, William Wyler, and Billy Wilder: "THIS IS MORE IMPORTANT THAN ANY PICTURE YOU EVER MADE."

That same weekend, as the Unfriendlies and their friends rallied to the anti-HUAC cause, another group of concerned citizen-artists with a direct interest in the outcome of the hearings intervened bodily into the fray. On Sunday, October 26, twenty-three members of the Committee for the First Amendment appeared on the ground in Washington to confront the Thomas Committee face to face.*

Two days earlier, in Hollywood, directors John Huston, William Wyler, and Billy Wilder had sent out an urgent telegram announcing a meeting at the home of lyricist Ira Gershwin.

THIS INDUSTRY IS NOT DIVIDING AGAINST ITSELF. UNITY MUST BE RECAPTURED OR ALL OF US WILL SUFFER FOR YEARS TO COME. YOUR AID IS REQUIRED IN THIS CRITICAL MOMENT. PLEASE BE AT 1021 ROXBURY DRIVE, BEVERLY HILLS, TONIGHT, FRIDAY, OCTOBER 24, AT 8:30 P.M. THIS IS MORE IMPORTANT THAN ANY PICTURE YOU EVER MADE.[18]

The meeting was also important to people not on the invitation list. Outside Gershwin's home that night, the attendees were being watched—not by the FBI but by Warner Bros., who placed men in the vicinity of the house to write down the license plate numbers of cars parked on the street. The numbers were furnished to the FBI, who, with ready access to the California Department of Motor Vehicles, matched the plates to the drivers.[19]

---

* The official passenger manifest lists twenty-three celebrity souls on board, not counting Sterling Hayden's wife, press agent Henry Rogers, a stenographer, and a TWA representative. Press tallies of the number of CFA celebrities attending HUAC sessions and press conferences vary.

Even without the supplementary manpower from Warner Bros., the FBI was keeping a close eye on liberal Hollywood. From the first hours of its inception, informants on the committee—and their spouses—funneled information to Hoover's men about CFA's moves, strategy, and membership. "Liberals in Hollywood are of [the] opinion that the motion picture invest[igation] is a move to smear Roosevelt and his policies," an early teletype from the Los Angeles office alerted FBI headquarters in Washington, D.C. "Allegedly, many local liberals are taking part in this movement. Many liberals who consider Communism a threat feel that the Thomas Committee is playing in[to] the hands of the Communists by showing itself to have political designs rather than the desire to expose Communism. This causes liberals to unite with the Communists in protest."[20]

The FBI analysis was wrong: the leadership of CFA and the bulk of its membership strived to avoid the onus of Communist fellow traveling. The public embrace of the Unfriendlies by a few of its members—especially John Garfield—was a constant irritation.

At the Gershwin meeting, and around tables at Lucey's and Chasen's, the favorite restaurants-to-the-stars in Hollywood, the guiding hands of the committee settled on two high-profile ways of fighting back against HUAC: "on the air and in the air." They would fly to Washington to strut their celebrity stuff and they would herald their in-person visitation with a broadcast over the medium that was still, but not for long, the central artery for information and entertainment in American culture.

Radio, not the newsreels or the tabloid press, was the keyhole at which Americans eavesdropped on the HUAC hearings—both live broadcasts and recaps recorded on transcription disks. "Radio is doing a most thorough job covering and broadcasting the current hearings of the House Un-American Activities Committee on Capitol Hill," judged Bryson Rash, broadcasting critic for the *Washington Evening Star*.[21]

Thus it was to radio that CFA turned to raise its loudest voice of protest with a pair of thirty-minute shows entitled *Hollywood Fights Back!* Originating at WJZ in New York, the broadcasts aired over the ABC network on two successive Sunday afternoons from 4:30–5:00 P.M., with the network making the program available via transcription disk at 8:00 P.M. for affiliate stations unable to carry it live. CFA paid ABC eight thousand dollars for the air time and preserved the broadcasts in a set of three twelve-inch vinyl records, which it sold to spread the word and finance future activities. "Five dollars per set post paid," read the order form. "All proceeds used to defray cost of the recordings, and to further the work of the Committee for the First Amendment."[22]

The prestigious radio scripter Norman Corwin wrote the copy and produced the shows. The poet laureate of Allied triumphalism—his famed V-E Day broadcast *On a Note of Triumph* had been hailed as the definitive expression of wartime values and postwar aspirations—Corwin coined the term "radiowright" for his unique oeuvre. "One might ask what an assault on the freedom of the film industry has to do with a radio man," he asked. "A threat to the freedom of expression of Lewis Milestone and Larry Parks is a threat to the freedom of the radio industry, the printed page, and the spoken word, a threat to the rights of conductors and painters."[23]

Corwin served as on-site producer for the Los Angeles side of the broadcasts; CBS radio producer William N. Robson for the New York end. The show bears all the hallmarks of Corwin's ethereal touch: clarion rhetoric, orchestral bombast, and a chorus of voices speaking in the many accents of the common man—or, in this case, Hollywood star.

The first show aired on Sunday afternoon, October 26. The episode begins with a defiant *crie de couer* yelled by Edward G. Robinson—"*Hollywood fights back!*"—and a musical fanfare trumpeting the call to arms. The conventions of radio drama (musical transitions, a guiding narrator, dramatic reenactments) are subsumed to what is mainly a series of direct address exhortations from a cavalcade of stars, each of whom delivers a brief statement and then cedes the microphone to a fellow patriot. All in all, forty-five speakers—stars, directors, screenwriters, and four United States senators, speaking from Los Angeles, New York, and Washington D.C., both live and via transcription disk—vent their outrage at HUAC.* Fourteen in the lineup—in transit even as the show was being broadcast—recorded their parts in Los Angeles before taking off for Washington.

---

* In Washington, D.C., the show aired at 8:00 P.M. over WMAL, just as the stars were landing in the city. The speakers in order were Charles Boyer, Judy Garland, Gene Kelly, Lauren Bacall, Joseph Cotton, Peter Lorre, June Havoc, John Huston, Danny Kaye, Marsha Hunt, Walter Wanger, Cornel Wilde, Melvyn Douglas, Richard Conte, Evelyn Keyes, Burt Lancaster, Paul Henreid, William Holden, Robert Ryan, Florence Eldridge, Myrna Loy, Robert Young, Lucille Ball, Van Heflin, Henry Morgan, Keenan Wynn, Humphrey Bogart, John Beal, Edward G. Robinson, Paulette Goddard, Norman Corwin, Audie Murphy, William Wyler, Fredric March, John Garfield, Deems Taylor, Dr. Harlow Shapley, Artie Shaw, Arthur Garfield Hays, Sen. Albert Thomas (D-UT), Sen. Harvey Kilgore (D-WV), Archibald MacLeish, Sen. Claude Pepper (D-FL), Glenn Taylor (D-ID), Judy Garland (again), and Vincent Price.

In Los Angeles, Fredric March, Paulette Goddard, Edward G. Robinson, and Audie Murphy speak out on the Committee for the First Amendment's radio show, *Hollywood Fights Back!*, October 26, 1947

The first voice to be heard on the broadcast—a sly defiance of expectations—is un-American in accent: the mellifluous French tones of Charles Boyer, the vocal timbre redolent of Gaelic romance. A matinee idol since enticing Hedy Lamarr into the Casbah in *Algiers* (1938), Boyer had become a naturalized American citizen in 1942. "This is the greatest honor of my life," he said upon taking the oath of allegiance. "I took out my first papers when this country was at peace, and now that she is at war, I want to do my part as an American citizen."[24]

Boyer still wanted to do his part:

This is Charles Boyer. The reason why parts of this program are transcribed is that fourteen of the fifty stars you are about to hear are at this moment in a special plane flying to Washington to carry on in person the fight for our rights as American citizens. If it weren't for studio commitments, all of us here today—and dozens more—would be "in the air" as well as on it.

A musical bridge leads to the second star, who affects the chirpy tones of her days as MGM's house ingénue:

This is Judy Garland. Have you been to a movie this week? Are you going to a movie tonight or maybe tomorrow? Look around the room. Any newspapers lying on the floor? Any magazines on the table? Any books on your shelves? It's always been your right to read or see anything you wanted to—but now it seems to be getting kinda complicated. For the past week in Washington, the House Committee on Un-American Activities has been investigating the film industry. Now I have never been a member of any political organization, but I've been following this investigation and I don't like it! There are a lot of stars here to speak to you. We're show business, yes, but we're also American citizens. It's one thing if someone says we're not good actors—that hurts, but we can take that. It's something else again to say we're not good Americans. We resent that!

Garland was followed by Gene Kelly who in turn was followed by Lauren Bacall and so on. The only break from the sing-song pattern of statements from the stars was a sonic montage that delivered the most damning indictment of HUAC's proceedings: a recitation of insinuations and charges, performed by actor Keenan Wynn and comedian Henry Morgan, that evoked the modus operandi of the Thomas Committee.

To remind listeners that the First Amendment was not just the concern of pampered celebrities, the broadcast recruited the voice of a real-life hero. "Here now is one of the famous veterans of that war, America's most decorated soldier—Audie Murphy," says Norman Corwin. Murphy gives a ringing endorsement of the creed of the committee:

You know during the war every guy in uniform dreamed of the day when he could stop squeezing triggers and come home. You get so fed up on fighting that you never want to do it again. There's one kind of fighting that has to go on always. You can't ever take a furlough from this fight to preserve human liberty. I think the methods used by the Thomas-Rankin Committee are a challenge to those liberties and I think we should use every fair and constitutional means to fight those methods.

Throughout the broadcast, many of the stars refer to "the House Un-American Committee," shortening the name to tag the members of HUAC as the true un-Americans. A few also call it the "Thomas-Rankin" Committee to conjure the visage of the bigot absent from the dais.

Toward the end of the show, Judy Garland returned to appeal to listeners to "let Congress know what you think of this *un-American* committee. Tell them how much you resent the way Mr. Thomas is kicking the living daylights out of the Bill of Rights!" Then, in bathetic tones, "I ask you, when they put words in concentration camps, how long will it be before they put men in there too?"

Stirred by the passion and eloquence of the united Hollywood front, anti-HUAC partisans took heart. "ABC's 'Hollywood Fights Back' airer has topped all previous events, except V-J Day, in bringing mail and phone calls to the various outlets for the web," marveled the *Hollywood Reporter*. "Local [switchboard] was jammed for hours and things have been complicated by supporters sending in cash to create a fund for continuance of such broadcasts."[25] Stan Anderson, the radio-TV critic for the *Cleveland Press*, telegrammed Norman Corwin with imperative words of encouragement: "Today's show was moving [and] to the point and should be repeated as given."[26]

Yet not everyone liked what they heard. Hedda Hopper printed a response from a Mrs. Smith of Milwaukee, Wisconsin, who claimed to speak for some fifty like-minded listeners, "plain American citizens . . . all movie loving folks." On behalf of her neighbors, Mrs. Smith vowed to boycott the movies until she was satisfied that Hollywood's stars were not closet Communists. "Hedda, I do hope that I have conveyed to you in this wire how strongly we feel about this matter, and that said broadcast was a farce," wrote the voice from the heartland. "And I hope you will convey our sentiments to Judy Garland and the others who want to know how we feel."[27]

Hedda Hopper correspondents notwithstanding, the cast of *Hollywood Fights Back!* had good reason to feel the show was a hit. On radio—a congenial medium for a generation of stars trained in selling their vocal persona along with their screen presence—CFA presented a well-spoken and harmonious front. Actors, writers, directors, politicians, and a certified World War II hero had joined together for an eloquent defense of a great American art. Performing in their comfort zone with no interruptions, no feedback, and no backtalk, the actor-activists were in full command.

The next media gambit—an in-person appearance on Capitol Hill by twenty-three motion picture personalities—was not to be as felicitous.

Danny Kaye: "If you say 'they went left,' the first thing you know you're up before the House Un-American Activities Committee."

No face-off against HUAC by the Committee for the First Amendment left a more scorching backfire than the decision to airdrop a planeload of Hollywood stars onto the field of battle in Washington, D.C. Air travel in 1947 was still an adventurous mode of civilian transportation and the charter plane trip initially seemed a stroke of ad-pub genius, a mediagenic gesture underscoring the urgency of the mission and the need for a speedy response to an imminent threat to the Republic. Not least, it exuded the high drama of that most venerable of Hollywood tableaux, the showdown. Though a stage-managed pseudo-event, the cross-country pilgrimage had real consequences—and though labeled a junket, it was no pleasure cruise.

The scheme to go airborne and the itinerary for the trip were hastily planned. Only two days before, over drinks at Lucey's, the restaurant-waterhole outside the gates of Paramount Pictures, Bogart, Bacall, Houston, and Wyler tossed around the idea of a cross-country plane trip. What better way to publicize their cause, demonstrate Hollywood's solidarity, and draw press attention away from the Thomas Committee?

When Howard Hughes heard of the group's plans, he offered to make a plane available, free of charge. Hughes was no friend to liberal activism, but his run-in with the Senate committee that August still rankled. He was happy to support any endeavor that stuck it to Congress.

Colin Miller, the Enterprise Studios PR man doing pro bono work for CFA, passed along Hughes's overture, but the steering committee declined the offer to avoid seeming a tool of a big money producer. Instead the group opted to charter a plane from Hughes's airline, Transcontinental and Western Air, Inc. An appeal was made to the membership for funds for the trip; pledges to cover the charter fees came forward immediately.

When the passenger list was being made up, nervous Hollywood agents pressured stars not to go, fearing their clients might alienate portions of the moviegoing public. To little avail: a few faint souls sat on the sidelines, but the trip was a hot ticket. The seats were quickly filled, indeed oversubscribed. "Everyone wanted to go but we had to limit it because of the size of the plane," Bogart told reporters.[28]

Throughout the trip, Bogart was to get top billing in all of the group's actions. In the days leading up to departure, ad-pub man Miller blanketed the media with press releases, all of which highlighted the actor. Bogart was also chosen to deliver a pre-boarding announcement to the press. Under the heading "What's this trip about?" he declared, over his handwritten signature:

This [trip] has nothing to do with Communism. It's none of my business who's a Communist and who isn't. We have a well organized and excellent agency in Washington known as the F.B.I. who does know these things.

The reason I am flying to Washington is because I am an outraged and angry citizen who feels that my civil liberties are being taken away from me and that the Bill of Rights is being abused and who also feels that nobody in this country has any right to kick around the Constitution of the United States, not even the Un-American Activities Committee.

In the early morning of Sunday, October 26, 1947, with a small band of well-wishers and gawkers seeing them off, the self-appointed ambassadors from Hollywood gathered at the Los Angeles airport for a jaunt reminiscent of the cross-country bond tours during World War II. Prior to takeoff, Wyler briefed the group. "I told them to stay away from the 'unfriendly' witnesses,"

At the ticket counter at the Los Angeles airport, members of the Committee for the First Amendment prepare to board a charter flight to Washington D.C., October 26, 1947. *Left to right*: June Havoc, Marsha Hunt, Humphrey Bogart, Lauren Bacall, Evelyn Keyes, and Paul Henreid. Danny Kaye is rear left.

he recalled in 1956. "I told them the newspapers would say they were there to defend the Communists, but they were going to Washington to attack HUAC and not defend any Communists."[29]

Joining Bogart aboard the plane were twenty-two producers, directors, writers, and—the headline-grabbing cargo—fellow actors. The passengers claimed to represent some five hundred other Hollywood personalities who either had prior commitments or for whom there was no room on board. Before the plane took off, Miller handed out a statement to the press:

> We are protesting the nature of the hearings of the Committee because we defend the rights of individuals to be free from political inquisition, and because we resent any attempt to censor by law or intimidation the motion picture screen as a medium of expression.[30]

While not united in their opinions, the passengers agreed on what today would be called talking points, with certain phrases recurring in the public statements each made.

After a forty-five-minute delay due to fog, the plane took off at 7:45 A.M. PST. Most of the passengers were already exhausted, having stayed up until the wee hours the night before going over strategy. Wyler had instructed them to dress appropriately. "We must not look like slobs," Lauren Bacall recalled. "We were representing a lot of people in the industry, we must make a good impression—the women were to wear skirts, not slacks; the men shirts and ties."[31] For outerwear, the women wore mink, the men, overcoats.[32]

Bacall did not mention, but Philip Dunne did, that the night before the flight William Wyler instructed the group on a matter more urgent than fashion. He told anyone "who was in the slightest degree vulnerable" to a charge of Communist affiliation to bow out so as not to discredit the mission. "You don't have to tell us about it," said Wyler, who was himself staying behind on doctor's orders. "Just don't show up at the airport tomorrow morning."

Recalled Dunne: "Two individuals, for reasons that have never been clear to me, chose to ignore the warning." Thirty-three years later, he was still not naming names but the two former Communists were actor Sterling Hayden and humorist Arthur Kober.[33]

The plane flew west to east, puddle-jump style, with stops in Kansas City, St. Louis, and Pittsburgh, the itinerary planned to gain publicity momentum as the delegation approached its final destination. At each of the stops, fans and reporters greeted the envoys from Hollywood. In Kansas City, a United Press report observed "autograph hounds were all over the place, but nobody was overheard asking any of the stars what they thought about civil liberties."

Unlike the fans, however, the press was eager to hear what the stars thought about civil liberties. Had you ever seen a subversive script or picture, Danny Kaye was asked. "No, sir," he responded politely. "I haven't." Then why did the "smear" of Communist affinities settle on Hollywood? "Big names," replied Kaye. "And big names make news." Kaye went on to describe the "censorship of fear" pervading Hollywood:

> It's reached the place where you have to be careful even shooting Wild West pictures. Say you have a bank holdup and the sheriff comes running up wanting to know which way the bad men went. If you say "they went left," the first thing you know you're up before the House Un-American Activities Committee.[34]

At the stopover in St. Louis, the group was met by a crowd of two thousand. "I don't know what a Communist is," Bogart commented. "I wouldn't know a Communist if I saw one."[35]

That evening, shortly after ten o'clock, its reputation having preceded it, the jet-lagged and stiff-legged delegation landed on the tarmac of National Airport. At a press conference at the Statler Hotel, which would serve as command center for the group, Huston repeated the line that the hearings had "instituted a censorship of fear" in Hollywood and warned that "mature films are becoming out of the question." Huston's favorite leading man saw a bigger picture. "They have permitted witnesses on hearsay to call people Communists yet the people so called have no opportunity to defend themselves or to ask questions," said Bogart. "That isn't right."[36] The other pilgrims were described as "sleepy-eyed and travel weary" and short on quotable copy.

However, after the formal press conference broke up, while mingling with reporters over drinks in the hotel bar, the stars loosened up. "All I know," said Danny Kaye, "is that this Congressional committee doesn't give anybody a chance to talk for himself. If I got up on the stage and the audience yelled 'You stink,' I'd ask for a chance to sing a song, or tell a joke, to show them whether I stink. If they still yelled 'You stink,' and didn't give me a chance to show my stuff, they'd be acting like the Committee on Un-American Activities. That's what I'm here to protest."[37]

Chapter 12
CONTEMPT

The first week of the hearings had showcased representatives of official Hollywood, men who—if sometimes opposing HUAC's methods and the assertion that Hollywood was anything other than a fount of Americanism—accepted the committee's right of oversight and investigation. They had come to placate and cooperate and, occasionally, though gently and respectfully, to reprove and contradict.

The second week—what the *Hollywood Reporter* billed as "the second reel of the Hollywood red story"—would be dominated by a single-minded and truculent defiance of HUAC's operating rationale: that a body of Congress had the right to ask American citizens their political associations and beliefs.[1] Of the original Unfriendly Nineteen subpoenaed to testify, only eleven would be called to the witness table. Of that eleven, ten would stand shoulder to shoulder, united by their resistance to the committee—and their adherence to the Communist party line.

The legal strategy had been developed collectively in Hollywood and hammered out again at the Shoreham Hotel in Washington, D.C., where the Nineteen and their lawyers had huddled since the hearings began. The men were not killing time; they coordinated talking points, planned rallies, gave interviews, and composed statements to be read before the committee. Attorney Robert Kenny grandiosely called the command center at the Shoreham the "headquarters for the most magnificent operation a little band of nineteen men ever undertook." On the eve of the hearings, Bertolt Brecht, the last of the Nineteen to arrive in Washington, looked in at the other eighteen, the lawyers, the publicity men, and the stenographers and smiled. "Zise did not happen in Germany," he said. "In Germany nobody got together. I am very happy."[2]

The cadre agreed not to break ranks or defy party discipline. The Unfriendly Nineteen would be a cohesive, unified front, a phalanx of loyal foot soldiers determined to hold fast against the enemy.

The strategy involved a broad principle and a legal technicality, the second of which was often lost in the shuffle. That is, the first line of defense was to invoke the protection of the First Amendment: HUAC had no right to inquire into the political beliefs of an American, period. The second line was a legalistic, almost Jesuitical ploy: the witnesses were not refusing to testify, so they claimed, but merely answering the committee in their own way. The convoluted dodging, bobbing, weaving, and filibustering the Unfriendlies performed at the witness table was designed to sidestep an outright refusal to answer and thereby avoid grounds for a contempt of Congress citation. Kenny gambled that the nonresponsive but non-refusal testimony "would create a jury issue as to whether they had actually refused to answer or been prematurely removed from the witness stand by the short-fused chairman."[3]

On the first point, the Unfriendly Nineteen stood on firm Constitutional grounds. They based their case on the 1942 Supreme Court ruling in *West Virginia v. Barnette* and what attorney Charles Katz called the "Olympian— and electrifying" decision of Justice Robert Jackson, writing for the majority.[4] Justice Jackson's words were to be quoted endlessly in anti-HUAC editorials and at rallies to buck up the resolve of the Unfriendlies:

> Freedom to differ is not limited to things that do not matter much. That would be a mere shadow of freedom. The test of its substance is the right to differ as to things that touch the heart of the existing order. If there is any fixed star in our constitutional constellation, it is that no official, high or petty, can prescribe what shall be orthodox in politics, nationalism, religion, or other matters of opinion or force citizens to confess by word or act their faith therein.

The precedent seemed utterly apt, the case precisely parallel, and the ultimate verdict certain. As Dalton Trumbo mused years later, "We thought we'd win."[5]

The other legal option, the obvious one, was for the Unfriendlies to stand on their Fifth Amendment rights against self-incrimination. This strategy was rejected—"without much discussion" as attorney Ben Margolis recalled—because it would not allow the Unfriendlies to speak at all. To take the Fifth was to accept a self-imposed gag order that would prevent the men from berating Thomas to his face. Also, though a legal shield against prosecution, taking the Fifth was tantamount to an admission of guilt in the court of public opinion. Only by confronting Thomas head on and speaking their piece could the Unfriendlies undermine or destroy the committee.[6] They refused to sit as mute dummies before a blustering J. Parnell Thomas.

The group had hoped to recruit an important ally to their cause. On Sunday night, October 19, 1947, the eve of the hearings, the lawyers for the Hollywood Nineteen attended a clandestine three-hour meeting with MPAA president Eric Johnston in the rooms of Paul McNutt, who was also staying at the Shoreham.[7] According to Kenny, Johnston offered assurances that, though he could not publicly lock arms with the Nineteen, he had their backs. He had emphatically not, as Kenny suspected, made a backroom deal with Thomas to blacklist the Nineteen. "As long as I live I will never be a party to anything as un-American as a blacklist, and any statement purporting to quote me to agreeing to a blacklist is a libel on me as a good American," he told Kenny. "We're not going totalitarian just to please this committee."[8] Kenny did not know, and Johnston did not tell him, that the MPAA president had already proposed a blacklist to the studio heads back in June. Fearing legal blowback, the executives had balked.

The Unfriendlies called to the witness table hardly needed rhetorical cover from the MPAA head. To a man, they were articulate and impassioned polemicists, champing at the bit to trample over their accusers in a public forum. Unlike the ghostwritten boilerplate read by Jack L. Warner and Louis B. Mayer, the manifestoes they composed—with two exceptions they were not permitted to read their statements aloud during the hearings—were their own work product. Literary by vocation and argumentative by nature, quick on the uptake and never at a loss for words, the subpoenaed artists—fifteen of whom worked at the writer's trade for a living—were eloquent and unflinching, sarcastic and insulting. The Unfriendlies were just that: unfriendly to Chairman Thomas, unfriendly to the agenda of the committee, and unfriendly to the whole anti-Soviet temper of postwar America. Their antagonism was not just political but personal: returning the favor, they held the congressmen, the chief counsel, the investigators, and the friendly witnesses in utter contempt. During the first week of testimony, as the group sat together in the front row of the gallery and made snarky comments, snickered, and rolled their eyes, *New York Sun* columnist George Dixon watched, listened, and seethed.

The verbal brawls between Thomas and the Unfriendlies that week were captured by the radio microphones and recorded by the newsreels—and replayed forever after in archival documentaries on Hollywood's blacklist era. The shouting matches, with each side yelling over the other, bequeathed a montage of sound-bitten images that became audiovisual shorthand for the repression of speech in Cold War America: an unhinged, red-faced Thomas furiously banging down his gavel and hollering "No! No! No! No! No! No! No! No! No!" until his defiant interlocutor was hauled away from the witness table by Capitol police.

The most explosive exchanges were described in pugilistic terms—a fishwife brawl, a donnybrook, a knock-down drag out.[9] But on any fight card there is a main event, and the *mano a mano* that opened the second week of hearings was the money-card matchup. By the end of the encounter, Thomas had literally pounded his gavel into two pieces, if not quite to smithereens.

John Howard Lawson: "I'm not on trial here! The committee is on trial before the American people!"

The man who would strike the first blunt-force rhetorical blow against HUAC from the witness chair was the personification of the "ideological termite" the committee had come to flush out and step on: not only a card-carrying Communist, but a Communist organizer, a contributor to the *Daily Worker* and the *New Masses*, and the unofficial "cultural commissar of Hollywood." Neither the FBI nor HUAC was needed to expose John Howard Lawson's true colors. The screenwriter was a proud, strident, and very public Red. For Lawson, it wasn't a double life but the same life: worker, writer, union activist, agitator, and Communist party apparatchik.[10]

Born in New York in 1894, Jewish, college educated, a radical in politics and literature, Lawson experienced his class-conscious epiphany during World War I while serving as a volunteer driver in the Italian Ambulance Service with novelist John Dos Passos, who converted him to Marxist-Leninism. Dos Passos ultimately veered hard right; Lawson never strayed from the faith. In 1927, he was arrested in Boston for protesting the death sentence of Sacco and Vanzetti; in 1934, he was arrested in Birmingham for protesting the death sentence of the Scottsboro Boys.[11]

Lawson brought the same ideological commitment to his writing. In 1928, his play *The International* was blurbed as "the FIRST COMMUNIST play to be produced in an American theater" with "the red blood of Revolution" flowing in its veins.[12] As experimental in his art as he was orthodox in his politics, Lawson pioneered Brechtian techniques before they were named after his Unfriendly Nineteen comrade: Lawson's characters broke the fourth wall and directly addressed the audience as playwright mouthpieces.

In 1929, Lawson earned his first screenplay credit for *Dynamite*, directed by, of all people, Cecil B. DeMille, a lavish extravaganza about exploited coal miners and high society swells, in which DeMille's pagan epicureanism smothered Lawson's Marxist earnestness. In 1932, Lawson scored an eponymous success with *Success Story*, a play about a ruthless Jewish businessman who sells his soul to the devil—that is, forsakes his radical ways—for pieces of silver. *Success at Any Price* (1934), the Hollywood version, de-Judified the unscrupulous protagonist, but took advantage of its pre-Code license to inject an element of prostitution, the metaphor of choice for all capitalist labor. By then, Lawson had signed a generous three-picture deal with RKO, for ten thousand dollars per picture, allowing him to write from his Long Island home. Perhaps the radical playwright was suspicious that the high life in Hollywood would corrupt him.[13]

Fat chance. Luxury Lawson enjoyed—by 1938, in addition to the twenty-two-acre summer home in Moriches, he owned plush digs in Hollywood—but he never lost his spiritual solidarity with the workers of the world.

The studio moguls must have regretted ever luring Lawson out west. No sooner had he arrived in town than he began agitating for a screenwriters union. As founder and first president of the SWG, he was on the front lines in the Hollywood writers' wars of the 1930s, taking advantage of the labor-friendly policies of the New Deal and bargaining hard for a closed shop. When he was not typing, he was likely walking a picket line in support of trade unions, civil rights, or the Spanish Republic. In 1937, in testimony before the NLRB, Howard Emmett Rogers recalled hearing Lawson explain "that the Soviet system in Russia would ultimately be adopted by the U.S.

government. He said 'I hope it comes without bloodshed.' "[14] In a city of lackadaisical fellow travelers, Lawson was a hard-core party member and a strict enforcer of ideological purity, considered extreme even by CPUSA standards—hence the "commissar" sobriquet. A few of his comrades referred to him behind his back by a nastier nickname: the Gauleiter, after the Nazi group leaders.[15]

Commissar or Gauleiter, Lawson earned the reputation. He insisted on lockstep party loyalty from his screenwriter comrades, manipulated screenwriter credits to the advantage of himself and other party members, and looked forward, come the Revolution, to the day when his ideological enemies could be dispatched in the prescribed Soviet manner. "The Soviet Union has set a brilliant and necessary example to the world of cleaning out those who are committing acts of treason," he told the League of American Writers in 1943, speaking of the fifth column "loudmouths" who dared criticize the veracity of *Mission to Moscow*.[16]

Lawson's most ambitious attempt to bore from within was his screenplay for Walter Wanger's *Blockade* (1938), a war-torn melodrama covertly celebrating the Republican side in the Spanish Civil War, a depiction so compromised that the uniforms of the combatants were tailored so as not to be identified with any actual nation. "It is certainly falsely charged that the picture is a brief for Marxist government," Lawson said with a straight face.[17] His current screen credit was the edgy social problem film, *Smash-Up: The Story of a Woman* (1947), a portrait of a female alcoholic, a plotline that the Breen office found distasteful on principle.

Before Lawson was sworn in, the two lead lawyers for the Nineteen, Robert Kenny and Bartley Crum, stood up and made a request to argue Kenny's petition to quash the HUAC subpoenas on the grounds the committee was "illegal both in its powers and its use of those powers." Kenny had two arguments: first, that HUAC was trying to dictate the content of films; and second, that it was trying to intimidate producers into creating "a blacklist of those who should not be hired by the industry, in violation of the First Amendment." As Kenny addressed Thomas, he stood behind his client, his hands on the back of the witness chair, rocking nervously.

The previous time a lawyer for the Unfriendly Nineteen had risen to challenge the chairman, Thomas had the offender tossed from the hearing room, a high-handed act that attracted widespread editorial criticism. This time, if only for appearance's sake, the committee withdrew into executive session to consider Kenny's arguments. Fifteen minutes later it returned. "This is the unanimous decision of this sub-committee," Thomas informed the room, the "sub" an acknowledgment of the three members comprising its bench strength—McDowell, Vail, and himself. "No committee of Congress has the right to establish its own legality or constitutionality. A committee of Congress cannot disqualify itself from the provisions of the law." He eyed Kenny evenly. "As a former attorney general of the state of California, you certainly know that your remedy, if any, is in the courts."

Crum interrupted with a petition asking to cross-examine witnesses from the previous week, "to show that these witnesses lied!" That motion too was denied.

Short and stocky, dressed in modest brown tweeds, and beset by a slight limp, Lawson took his seat flanked on either side by corner men Kenny and Crum. After being sworn in, he pulled out a statement to read. Thomas asked to look it over. He glanced at it for a few minutes, noted that on the basis of the first sentence alone it should not be read, and handed it back to Lawson.

"You have spent one week vilifying me before the American public—"

"Just a minute—," Thomas broke in, banging his gavel for silence.

"—and you refuse to let me to make a statement on my rights as an American citizen!" Lawson shouted.

Thomas repeated that the statement was not pertinent.

Pausing just a moment, Lawson continued: "The rights of an American citizen are important in this room here, and I intend to stand up for those rights, Congressman Thomas."

Lawson calmed down and answered some innocuous questions about his name and place and date of birth.

Asked if he were a member of the SWG, Lawson again raised his voice indignantly. "Raising the question of any political belief or affiliation is beyond the purview of this committee—"

Thomas interrupted with shouts of "order!" "More gaveling with Thomas, a red-faced man, growing redder all the time," observed *Daily Variety*, savoring the color coordination.

Lawson repeated the phrase and then wearily conceded, "but it is a matter of public record" that he was a member of the Screen Writers' Guild. Inadvertently, so it seemed, Lawson had answered the first question.

"Have you ever held office in the Guild?" asked Stripling.

Lawson was determined to testify on his own terms. "Last week you permitted witnesses to answer questions in three, four, and five hundred words—and you want brief answers from me?"

"You'll be responsible!" hollered Thomas, whacking the gavel.

"I'm not on trial here! The committee is on trial before the American people!" Lawson shouted. "It is outside the purview of this committee to inquire into what organizations I belong."

"Now, you're just making a big scene for yourself and getting all 'het up,'" cooed Thomas, as if talking to a child. Parts of the gallery chuckled. "Be responsive to the questioning just the same as all the witnesses have. You're no different from the rest."

"I'm being treated differently from the rest!"

Thomas interrupted the interruption and the two yelled over each other in a furious, schoolyard-style shouting match.

"If you're trying to force me to put you in contempt of Congress, you won't have to try much harder!" barked Thomas.

Stripling broke in with the second question: "Are you now or have you ever been a member of the Communist party in the United States?"

For a beat, the room went silent.

"The question of Communism is in no way related to this inquiry, which is an attempt to get control of the screen and to invade the basic rights of American citizens in all fields," declared Lawson. The sole purpose of the committee was to smear the motion picture industry.

"You have learned your lines well," scoffed Thomas.

Undeterred, Lawson accused the witnesses from the previous week of perjury and demanded the right to expose their "tissue of lies." Thomas—face flushed, neck bulging—wielded his gavel jackhammer style. "We're gonna get an answer to that question if we have to stay here a week!"

"It's unfortunate and tragic that I have to teach this committee the basic principles of Americanism," responded Lawson.

"That is not the question! That is not the question!" screamed Thomas. "The question is: have you ever been a member of the Communist party?"

"I am framing my answer in the only way in which an American citizen can frame his answer to the question which absolutely invades his rights." The American people, said Lawson, knew where he stood from what he had written.

"Stand away from the stand!" ordered Thomas.

Screenwriter John Howard Lawson, the first of the Unfriendlies to testify, leaves the witness table, October 27, 1947. HUAC's William A. Wheeler stands at right.

Lawson was not going anywhere. "I have written Americanism for many years, and I shall continue to fight for the Bill of Rights, which you are trying to destroy."

Thomas called in his muscle. "Officers, take this man away from the stand."

Six uniformed members of the Capitol police closed in around Lawson, but he returned to his seat in the first row under his own volition. As Lawson was escorted, first applause—for the defiant witness? for the police?—then boos went up from the gallery. The whole round had lasted about twelve minutes.[18]

At one point amid the bedlam, a flood light for the newsreel cameras exploded with a soft "plop" and showered slivers of glass down on the crowd. "I thought they had me for a minute," cracked a Capitol policeman.[19]

The denouement was quieter but for many in the gallery more bracing. Committee investigator Louis J. Russell, making the first of what would be eleven appearances at the witness table that week, was sworn in to submit evidence against Lawson into the record. An ex-FBI man, thirty-five years old, Russell would be far more than a spear-carrier in the ensuing drama:

it was he who introduced the only evidence that mattered—more important than sneaking Communist dialogue into Hollywood films, making speeches at radical rallies, or writing checks to Communist front groups. The HUAC hearings were a game of cards, as Broadway columnist Earl Wilson pointed out, and the ace in the hole was the Communist party card that Russell dealt face up on the witness table. Russell introduced a nine-page memorandum containing thirty-five items, all related to Lawson's Communist activism, but the smoking gun was a photostat of Lawson's CPUSA card issued in 1944—card number 47275 made out to John Howard Lawson, a writer, in Los Angeles.

Speaking in his Broadway patois, Wilson described how the poker-faced Russell shuffled the deck:

Get the drama, Pally. Sitting at the witness table investigator Russell opens a manila folder. The radio lanes and the telegraph wires are his as he flips through his 15 or 20 Commy cards, hunting the right one. He cups them so carefully in his hand you can't see them. Ahhh, now then. "I have a photostatic copy of a Communist Party registration card made out in the name of——."[20]

After Russell filled in the blank, Stripling interjected to say that the committee possessed over one hundred exhibits "showing Mr. Lawson's affiliation with the Communist party." The long list of writings and activities proved beyond a reasonable doubt that "Mr. Lawson had publicly avowed allegiance of the line of the Communist Party during four distinctly divergent periods"—before the Hitler-Stalin Pact, during the Hitler-Stalin Pact, after the Hitler-Stalin Pact both before and during American entry into World War II, and after the pro-Soviet wartime alliance. The documents itemized the anti-American record of "one of the most active Communists in the Hollywood movie industry."[21]

Thomas informed the hearing room that the subcommittee considered Lawson in contempt of Congress for refusing to answer questions about his membership in the CPUSA and that a recommendation would be made to the full committee to so affirm. The citation would then be certified by the Speaker of the House and voted on by the full House. Afterward, the citation would be turned over to the United States District Attorney for the District of Columbia for prosecution. Conviction could carry a penalty of a fine of one thousand dollars and a year in jail.

At the news of Lawson's contempt citation, a smattering of applause erupted from a small quarter of the gallery—the same quarter, noticed Gordon Kahn, "where earlier was heard in a sort of ventriloquist croak the word 'Jew!'"[22]

Even as Russell was reading the record of Lawson's Communist activities, Lawson and his lawyers were circulating mimeographed copies of his opening statement to the press in the hearing room. Thomas's suppression of the statements from the unfriendly witnesses had the predictable consequence of making the statements more quotable in the press.

Lawson's statement came right to the point. "For a week, this committee has conducted an illegal and indecent trial of American citizens, whom the committee has selected to be publicly pilloried and smeared," it began. Chairman Thomas had read no further, but Lawson continued:

> Rational people don't argue with dirt. I feel like a man who has had truckloads of filth heaped upon him. I am now asked to struggle to my feet and talk while more truckloads pour more filth around my head.
>
> No you don't argue with dirt. But you try to find out where it comes from. And stop the evil deluge before it buries you—and others. The immediate source is obvious. Let these people live with their consciences, with the knowledge that they have violated their country's most sacred principles.

Lawson ended his lengthy indictment by calling Thomas "a petty politician, serving more powerful forces" who were "trying to introduce Fascism into this country." Thomas and his henchmen understood "that the only way to trick the American people into abandoning their rights and liberties is to manufacture an imaginary danger, to frighten people into accepting repressive laws which are supposedly for their protection."[23]

Lawson may have been prevented from reading his statement, shouted down, and escorted away from the witness table, but he was not silenced.

After the morning session broke up, Crum and Lawson answered questions from eager reporters who clustered around. Crum said his client had refused to answer "because his Constitutional rights were being violated." Was Lawson a Communist? Crum shrugged and said, disingenuously, that he neither knew nor cared whether Lawson was a Communist.

Lawson was ebullient, still exhilarated by the adrenaline rush of the confrontation. "Nothing is more sacred to me than my sacred allegiance to this country," he told reporters, smiling broadly, rather than keeping a straight face. Asked whether the Communist Party card was his, he grinned and said, "I'll leave that to the American people."[24]

Gene Kelly: "We're not sitting in judgment on Lawson or Communists, but on censorship that will not only kill films but murder people's careers."

In the back rows of the caucus room sat a "particularly alert and handsome audience," twenty-five members of the Committee for the First Amendment, who were profoundly rattled by Lawson's raucous performance. The shouting match between a defiant Hollywood screenwriter and an enraged gavel-thumping congressman was terrific theater for Washington but terrible public relations for Hollywood.

Worse was what followed: irrefutable documentary evidence of Lawson's long-time worker bee activity for the CPUSA—his incendiary statements, his lockstep devotion to the party line, and, most damning, his Communist party card. Worse yet: the celebrities seemed to have come out in force not to support the respectful and patriotic Robert Montgomery, George Murphy, and Ronald Reagan, but to lend their star power to an obnoxious and disrespectful Communist. Had Thomas set a trap or was it just happenstance?

The Hollywood delegation—dubbed "the glamour brigade" even by friendly reporters from the *Daily Worker*—had planned things differently.

For the first full day on the ground, the group kept to a hectic schedule. The day began with an early morning press conference in the Statler Hotel suite that served as command headquarters. The Californians were joined by members of the New York contingent, headed up by John Garfield.

John Huston zeroed in on Richard Nixon, the home state congressman on the committee. He had prepared a bill of particulars with a list of questions for Nixon. "Is it true in an unguarded moment you told a newspaperman that the object of this committee was to 'give Hollywood a dose of preventative medicine?'" Huston wanted to know. "If you say this, what do you mean by 'preventative medicine?'"[25]

"That's what we came here to ask Mr. Nixon," said Bogart. "But we can't find Nixon. He apparently went back to California the evening we got here." That was true: sensing the diminishing returns from being a supporting player in Thomas's show, Nixon had left for his home district over the weekend. He would be absent for the remainder of the hearings.

Gene Kelly, with one leg in a plaster cast, told reporters that "the essence of our trip is 'give a man the good old American right to answer back.'"[26]

After the early morning press conference, the group (absent the hobbled Kelly) made the pilgrimage up to Capitol Hill—to pose for still photographers and the newsreel cameras with the Capitol dome looming in the background. Traffic was blocked off for fifteen minutes as the stars posed in a walking lineup. When the delegation arrived outside the Old House Office building, about one hundred reporters gathered around them. Huston again handed out the questions for the missing-in-action Nixon.

After the on-the-pavement press conference, the stars waited in the long visitor's queue. Upon reaching the door of the hearing room, a non-starstruck guard snapped, "Are you the show people?" They were escorted past empty seats in the front to the back rows, where they were surprised to find Thomas had reserved space for them. Spied by the earlier arrivals in the gallery, the stars were greeted by a round of applause. John Garfield arrived late; more applause.

Sometime later, a friendlier guard moved June Havoc and Jane Wyatt nearer the front. The actresses chatted with two elderly matrons who worked as cleaning women in the Old House Office Building. "We old biddies are just as mad as we can be," one confided. "Why it was plain orneriness of them to seat you in the back of the room."[27]

MPAA president Eric Johnston was slated to be the first witness that morning, and the plan was for the stars to form a wall of support and solidarity for Johnston—but Johnston's testimony was moved back to the afternoon. The changeup meant that on the first day the stars attended the hearings, they were seen as the cheering section for the first of the unfriendly witnesses to be called, the cantankerous John Howard Lawson.

Lawson's defiant backtalk and boisterous ejection from the witness table has played in retrospect as a heroic artist-activist speaking truth to power. At the time, however, his antics alienated Americans who saw no reason why a loyal citizen should refuse to answer questions about membership in the Communist party. In seeming to be in Lawson's corner, the Committee for the First Amendment found itself on the wrong side of Hollywood's most important constituency—the moviegoing public.

After Lawson's removal from the witness table, CFA held a tense noon press conference back at the Statler in the sitting room of a suite that served as the group's command center. Danny Kaye tried to lighten the mood with an introduction. "Gene Kelly is a hoofer with a broken leg," he said. "And I'm a comedian with no jokes today."

"How about a wisecrack?" coaxed a reporter.

"Not today," replied Kaye. "I don't feel funny now."

Kelly was also dead serious. "It doesn't make any difference to me if Lawson is or is not a Communist," he said. "We're not sitting in judgment on Lawson or Communists, but on censorship that will not only kill films but murder people's careers."[28] Kelly had been asking everyone from "10 years up" if they had ever seen a Communist film from Hollywood. "Nobody has ever seen such a film and nobody ever will," he said. "The movies are a big business owned by Wall Street and bankers and all sorts of people who aren't Communists. Propaganda pictures won't make money—look at the awful egg *Mission from Moscow* laid."[29]

Cecelia Agar, film critic for *PM* and former reporter for *Variety*, was impressed by the informality and eloquence of the group. "Their behavior at their mid-day press conference was a movie fan magazine writer's dream of folksiness," she wrote. Kaye, Bogart, Sterling Hayden, Richard Conte, John Garfield, and Larry Adler sat on the floor; Paul Henreid sloped against a wall. Since the room was too crowded for the reporters to see who was talking at any given moment, and since the Washington reporters wouldn't have recognized the off-camera faces anyway, each speaker began by introducing him or herself, "This is Humphrey Bogart," "This is Sheridan Gibney," and so on. "None of the 25 interrupted each other or their press questioners," wrote Agar. "John Huston and writer Philip Dunne (*Forever Amber*) were the ostensible spokesmen for the group, but at some time or other almost every one of them spoke up, freely, earnestly, always seriously, always modestly."[30]

Still, the uproar of the morning session had left the group frazzled. "I think it's something that everyone should see," said Lauren Bacall, but she didn't say why. Screenwriter Sheridan Gibney appeared flustered and off message. He said he saw no reason why any member of the Communist party should refuse to admit it, but he also felt that anyone cited for contempt by HUAC would never work in Hollywood again.

After the midday presser, the delegation journeyed back uphill to hear Eric Johnston testify at the afternoon session. Democratically forgoing VIP treatment, the stars joined the hoi polloi in line and jostled for seats. "They did a lot of seat hopping to get close enough to hear Eric Johnston's testimony," reported *Variety*'s Florence S. Lowe. "It was definitely 'no special privilege day' for the stars."

Eric A. Johnston: "Expose Communism, but don't put any American who isn't a Communist in the concentration camp of suspicion."

Thomas, as was his wont, had promised a "surprise witness" for the afternoon session, but the witness was no surprise: Eric Johnston. The MPAA president had originally been scheduled to testify in the morning, after which he planned to board an afternoon train for Chicago. Annoyed by Johnston's broadsides at HUAC over the weekend, Thomas rescheduled the appearance for 2:00 P.M. so Johnston would miss his train from Union Station. Johnston was testifying despite being "painfully ill": he had been badly beaten in a street brawl during his days with the Marines in Asia and was never in top health afterward.[31]

The rescheduling had another consequence. Many of the stars from the delegation from CFA, who had attended Lawson's session in full force, were unable to get back into the hearing room. When the hearings reconvened, their seats were already taken by spectators who wanted to look at *them*.[32] Seemingly, fewer stars were in Johnston's corner than in Lawson's.

Some not-so-friendly banter preceded Johnston's formal testimony. As Johnston took his place at the witness table with MPAA counsel Paul McNutt, Stripling asked if Johnston felt the need for a lawyer. Thomas feigned concern. "Well, if it makes him feel any better. . . ."

Emboldened by the good showing the previous week by the steadfast Robert Montgomery, George Murphy, and Ronald Reagan; by the hundreds of screen personalities on both coasts who had signed on with CFA; and by an overwhelmingly critical reaction on the editorial pages of the non-Hearst newspapers, Johnston felt the tide was turning in Hollywood's favor. Jack L.

Warner and Louis B. Mayer were servile and polite. Johnston was defiant and caustic.

"Hollywood is weary of being the national whipping boy for Congressional committees," Johnston declared. "This must be the investigation to end all investigations"—by which he meant that enough was enough. HUAC had been slandering Hollywood since the days of Martin Dies. It was high time to put up or shut up and name the films riven with Communist subversion.

Unlike John Howard Lawson, Johnston was permitted to read an opening statement. He made four demands. First, he called on Thomas to correct the damaging and false impression that had "spread all over the country as a result of last week's hearings." To hear the Thomas Committee tell it, "the public would get the idea that Hollywood is running over with Communists and Communism."

Second, the committee must withdraw its claim that "some of the most flagrant Communist propaganda pictures were produced as the result of White House pressure." The charges were patently false, having been "completely refuted by the testimony before you." Hollywood had been no tool of the Roosevelt administration, he wanted it known, though this was a hard sell given that the locals had been so fully invested in the cult of FDR.

Third, the committee must provide "a list of all pictures produced in Hollywood in the last eight years which contained Communist propaganda." It must do what it demanded of its witnesses: name names. "Until the list is made public, the industry stands condemned by unsupported generalizations, and we are denied the opportunity to refute these charges publicly." He would be happy to arrange a special screening of the pictures. Give the titles and get down to specifics, else "absolve the industry from the charges against it."

Finally, Johnston draped his demands in a ringing defense of freedom of expression. He did so despite being advised by "some persons to lay off" on the ground that "I'd be playing into the hands of the Communists." Johnston was being disingenuous: a defense of freedom of expression would not be playing into the hands of the Communists but of right wingers who might twist an avowal of constitutional rights into an endorsement of the Communist party line.

"Nobody has a monopoly of the issue of free speech in this country," Johnston proclaimed. He then spoke words that were truer and more prophetic than he knew:

When I talk about freedom of speech in connection with this hearing, I mean just this: you don't need to pass a law to choke off free speech or seriously curtail it. Intimidation or coercion will do it just as well. You can't make good and honest motion pictures in an atmosphere of fear.

He brought home his point with a chilling metaphor: "Expose Communism, but don't put any American who isn't a Communist in the concentration camp of suspicion."

Johnston concluded his statement with a mesh of liberal bromides and patriotic uplift. "The real breeding ground of Communism is in the slums," he said, and not, presumably, on the manicured lawns of Beverly Hills. "If we fortify our democracy, we'll lick Communism here and abroad. Communists can hang all the iron curtains they like, but they'll never be able to shut out the story of a land where free men walk without fear and love with abundance."

After Johnston finished, boisterous applause and loud cheers broke out, led by the Unfriendly Nineteen and CFA. Squelching the outburst, Thomas pounded the gavel for order.

Johnston's aggressive defense was met with a strong pushback by Thomas and Stripling. "I wouldn't be surprised, from statements you made during the past few days, that you have been trying to run this committee," stated Stripling.

"When you hurt us, you hurt our pocketbooks and reputations abroad," retorted Johnston. "We believe that our pictures are the best emissary of good will the United States has in other countries." What was good for Hollywood was good for America.

Thomas shifted strategies with an explosive accusation. "It makes my blood boil," he said, to see "certain persons . . . perhaps of dubious character" trying "all the tricks of the trade" to get the committee to "lay off" or "postpone" the hearings. Thomas claimed that "a man" had given him "all signs of an offer" to bribe the committee into not calling certain witnesses.

Johnston vehemently denied that the overtures had come from the MPAA.

Thomas was also angry about the counteroffensive Johnston and McNutt had been waging in the press, on radio, and in the newsreels. "And your counsel has been giving out statements on the hour and off the hour critical of the committee," he charged. "Is that the kind of cooperation you promised?"

Motion Picture Association of America president Eric Johnston (*lower left*) clashes with Chairman J. Parnell Thomas (*upper right on dais*) and committee counsel Robert Stripling (*lower right*) during his testimony on October 27, 1947.

"I told you we'd give cooperation and we did," Johnston replied. "I never sought to get any witness off. When one witness did try to get excused, I had him write you a letter asking to be called."*

Taking a conciliatory tack, Rep. John McDowell said that the motion picture producers who had come before the committee last week had "done a noble job of acquitting the industry" of charges of Communist domination. "I think the motion picture industry will come out of this with a very fine reputation."

However, Johnston was not prepared for the next salvo. Apropos of nothing, except to make the information a matter of public record, Stripling jumped in to note that Edward T. Cheyfitz, an assistant to Johnston, had once been a member of the Communist party.

Johnston denounced the smear and asked Stripling point blank if he was implying that Cheyfitz was still a member of the CPUSA. Stripling backed down and admitted that this was not the case. But that was not the point:

---

* The reference was to Louis B. Mayer.

Cheyfitz's name was now in the public record; a man who had the ear of the president of the MPAA had been branded as a former Communist. "I am not here to defend Cheyfitz," said Johnston bitterly. "He's in town. Why don't you call him?"

Yet Johnston did defend Cheyfitz. He produced a sheaf of letters attesting to his associate's good name and affirming that Cheyfitz had left the CPUSA long ago.

Members of the Committee for the First Amendment listen to testimony, October 27, 1947. *Third row, left to right*: Evelyn Keyes, June Havoc, Humphrey Bogart, and Lauren Bacall. *Fourth row, left to right*: Joseph Sistrom, Ralph Alswang, unknown, Robert Ardrey, Richard Conte, Geraldine Brooks. (Courtesy of Arnie Reisman)

Surprised that Johnston was so well prepared for rebuttal, Thomas said, "You sort of had a suspicion this was coming up."

"Knowing Mr. Stripling," replied Johnston acidly, "I was prepared for anything."[33]

The meandering interrogation devolved into a discussion of the mechanics of Hollywood censorship. As everyone in the motion picture business well knew, the most powerful agent of ideological influence in Hollywood was not John Howard Lawson but Joseph Ignatius Breen, head of the Production Code Admistration since its inception in 1934. A devout Irish Catholic, a bureaucrat of ruthless efficiency, and a staunch anti-Communist, Breen wielded more power over the values promulgated in Hollywood cinema than anyone in town, including the heads of the major studios. There was no better proof of the cluelessness of HUAC to the real-world, on-the-ground operation of the studio system than the fact that Breen was not subpoenaed to testify: in fact, his name was not mentioned once in the nine days of testimony.

Struggling to understand the process of industry self-regulation—where the PCA vetted scripts before production and previewed final prints before granting a film the coveted Code seal necessary for national distribution—Representative Vail asked: "Isn't it true [that] scripts your organization passes are frequently rejected by state censors?"

"Yes, and frequently for ridiculous reasons," Johnston retorted. "In Memphis, for example, one film was rejected for having a colored boy playing with white boys."[*]

Vail made a lame attempt at humor. "He wasn't in the woodpile?"[†]

Johnson's curt response was nearly drowned out by hissing. "No, nor under a [wood]chip."[34]

Realizing his gaffe, Vail hesitated for a moment and then agreed. "Yes, that [decision] does seem a little ridiculous."

Thomas asked Johnston how many movies he saw a week.

"One, maybe two movies a week," figured Johnston.

"Why, I see more than that."

---

[*] The reference was to the banning of the Hal Roach production *Curley* (1947), a children's picture with an integrated cast of little rascals. The social equality between the races offended Memphis's notoriously racist censor, Lloyd T. Binford, who banned the film from his jurisdiction, an edict that made national news.
[†] Common American vernacular since the 1840s, the phrase "nigger in the woodpile" was an idiomatic expression meaning "something hidden or suspicious."

"I am glad to hear that, Mr. Chairman," said Johnston smoothly, "since you pay for yours. I don't."

Under a barrage of hostile questioning from Thomas and Stripling, the gracious businessman was becoming positively snippy. Asked by Stripling to explain the decency clause of the Production Code, he lost patience. "That's about sex," he explained. "You've heard of that, I presume."

After Johnston stepped down, Samuel Sillen, covering the hearings for the *Daily Worker*, approached the African American actor Canada Lee, who had been watching with the New York contingent from the back rows. He was still "boiling with rage" over Vail's racist allusion.[35]

Johnston's "stirring defense of the industry" received stellar notices. After the mealy-mouthed subservience of the moguls, his stiff-backed counterattack was a balm to an industry that had for so long played punching bag to a bully. "Eric Johnston was in rare form," gloated *Variety*. "His snappy comebacks frequently tossed committee members for a five-yard loss."[36]

Yet—reflecting the mixed feelings of the industry at large—*Variety* was of two minds. Why needlessly antagonize politicians who had such power to disrupt—and maybe dismantle—the way Hollywood worked? "Before Hollywood goes into another round with Congress, it's my humble opinion that the big boys ought to get a spokesman who can pour oil instead of vinegar on the troubled waters," suggested Florabel Muir.[37] Always in the background of the HUAC assault was the more momentous government prosecution of Hollywood practices, the Justice Department's case against the studios for violation of the Sherman Anti-Trust Act.

Following Johnston's testimony, before closing the day's proceedings, Thomas reserved a few choice words for a section of the gallery that seemed to gall him more than the Unfriendly Nineteen. Eyeing the celebrities in the back rows, he vowed to continue the investigation undaunted "no matter how many glamour girls you stack up in the rear of the room."[38]

Lauren Bacall: "You have no idea of the fear that has overtaken Hollywood."

After an exhausting day, the glamour girls—and boys—were observed in their suite back at the Statler Hotel sipping ice water and eating ice cream, taking their first breather since coming to town. The group felt some head-way had been made. A sympathetic account in the *Washington Evening Star* positioned the delegation just where it wanted, independent of the other two factions from Hollywood. "A flying squad of 26 film personalities who hold themselves aloof from both the witnesses and producers' representatives [sat] quietly in the back row of spectators," the paper reported. "Generally they are concerned at the committee's refusal to permit all witnesses to make statements and cross-examination and specifically they express alarm at the impression they fear has been given that Hollywood is Communist-dominated."[39]

After the late afternoon press conference, a reporter for the *Washington Daily News* managed to corner Lauren Bacall for an exclusive op-ed, dictated by the actress to a typist as she walked back and forth in her hotel room in her nylon stockings. "Well, I wanted you to know that I attended two sessions of the hearings and it frightened me," she said of her day's work. "When I left the House Office Building, I couldn't help but feel that every American who cares anything at all about preserving American ideals should witness a part of the investigations." Bogart poked his head in at the door to ask about supper, but Bacall was on a tear and shooed him away. "Before I go further, I want it clearly understood that I'm not defending or attacking any of the witnesses who have appeared or will appear. And I am not questioning the committee's right to ask any questions it sees fit. I am questioning its right to ask questions and allow only monosyllabic answers." She blurted out a final thought, almost in disbelief: "You have no idea of the fear that has overtaken Hollywood." Delighted with the star's byline, the paper assured readers that "every word of the story was" Bacall's. "No ghost writer or press agent had anything to do with it."[40]

The Hollywood delegation had originally planned to return home the next day. However, goaded by Thomas's insult and not wanting to seem intim-idated, the group decided to spend an extra day in Washington. No one wanted it said that the stars couldn't take the heat, that Thomas had run them out of town.

Chapter 13

$64 QUESTIONS AND NO ANSWERS

All the major strands of the HUAC show trial came together on the second day of week two: name calling and name naming, righteously indignant Unfriendlies, an unhinged gavel-banging chairman, a resentful representative from the MPAA, and, in the gallery and making the press rounds, the Committee for the First Amendment. The reporters at the press tables and the cameramen behind the dais could hardly believe their good luck.

Again, no quorum was present. Only Representatives McDowell and Vail sat on the dais with Chairman Thomas to form a subcommittee. If HUAC was a vehicle for publicity-hungry politicians to strut before the cameras, most members were shunning the spotlight. By contrast, the Capitol police were out in force; an extra detail had been put on to patrol the aisles of the caucus room.

Dalton Trumbo: "I note this is the beginning of an American concentration camp!"

The first witness of the day was as close to stardom as a mere screenwriter could come. None of the Unfriendly Nineteen had more to lose from a political purge than Dalton Trumbo, an obedient Communist who was extravagantly well rewarded by the capitalist machine. Trumbo embodied the contradictions that the American public found so hard to fathom: the Marxist-Leninist screenwriter as landed gentry. If anyone lived the life of the Hollywood raj, it was he.

Born in 1905 in Montrose, Colorado, Trumbo was a true character—droll, alternately good-humored and prickly, impossible to dislike. For his Communist comrades, he accrued added cachet by being the only member of the Nineteen who had labored long and hard in an authentically working-class job. Arriving in Los Angeles in 1925, he spent nine years making his living as a baker, a salt-of-the-earth trade beloved in Soviet social realist circles. He started the job at forty dollars a week. "When I quit, nine and one half years later, I was earning $18," he recalled in the *Daily Worker* in 1940, not needing to elaborate on the reasons for his radicalization. "During that time I wrote eighty-eight short stories and six novels, all rejected."[1]

In 1934, Trumbo finally landed a couple of literary jobs, editing the short-lived *Hollywood Spectator* and ghosting a novel. His first studio employment was as a script reader at Warner Bros.; his first screenwriting credit was for *Road Gang* (1936), a prison melodrama in the stark tradition of *I Am a Fugitive from a Chain Gang* (1932). His punctuality with a deadline and facility across genres propelled his rise up the salary scale.

In September 1939, as war broke out in Europe, Trumbo's antiwar novel *Johnny Got His Gun* was published. Though written before the Hitler-Stalin Pact, its bitter antiwar sentiments—the flashbacked narration is by an armless, legless, blind, deaf, and mute veteran immobilized on his hospital bed—were perfectly in sync with the current party line. By then, Trumbo, the once-militant anti-Fascist, was publishing articles in *Hollywood Now*, the official weekly of the Hollywood League for Democratic Action, formerly the Hollywood Anti-Nazi League, labeling support for interventionist policies such as Lend-Lease and national defense tantamount to treason.[2] In June 1941, after the Nazi invasion of the Soviet Union, Trumbo took up the new party line with equal enthusiasm, calling any *opposition* to interventionist policies such as Lend-Lease and national defense tantamount to treason. He also gave advice to the U.S. military on the absolute necessity of launching a second front in Europe, post-haste, to relieve the burden borne by the Russian Army.

Upon American entry into World War II, Trumbo adhered to the OWI playbook. He scripted two of the best-remembered wartime films, the proto-feminist home front melodrama *Tender Comrade* (1943) and the stirring combat film and rehabilitation story *Thirty Seconds Over Tokyo* (1944). "If this is not the best of the war pictures—and maybe it is—it is at least one of the top," wrote the *New York Sun's* Eileen Creelman of *Thirty Seconds Over Tokyo*, singling out Trumbo for keeping "the script apparently simple, a nice piece of deception, as the picture deals with so many moods and so many people and places."[3]

In 1944, Trumbo signed a five-year contract with MGM that was deemed the best screenwriting deal in Hollywood. The former baker, *Variety* couldn't help punning, was "still in the dough."[4] He knew how to spend it. In addition to a one hundred-thousand-dollar mansion in Beverly Hills, he lived with his wife and daughter on a marvelous ranch-cum-writer's retreat in the Tehachapi Mountains eighty-five miles north of Hollywood. "We have 320 acres, a mountain stream, four horses, two cows, two pigs, three dogs, and a cat named Homer," the gentleman farmer guilelessly boasted to the *Daily Worker*.[5] The luxury inside and outside dazzled Alvah Bessie, his far less prosperous comrade. "I noticed that there was a meadow as level as a billiard table and decided it would be possible to fly a light plane up sometime and land it on Dalton's front lawn."[6] Prolific, fast, and adaptable, Trumbo worked best under deadline pressure, wired on Benzedrine, in the bathtub, nude, typing out prose on a clunky Underwood, on a writing table that spanned the tub.

In 1945, Trumbo took over the editorship of the *Screen Writer*, and tilted the SWG forum markedly to the left. For Trumbo and the Communists, the guild was not just a trade union but a platform to advance a broader political agenda. The liberal guild president Emmet Lavery tried to steer a more middle-of-the-road course, seeing the outfit's main purpose as the protection of screenwriters' rights not the fomenting of a proletarian revolution.

Descending on Washington with the rest of the Nineteen on the weekend before the hearings, Trumbo had not kept silent. "The committee has in fact degenerated into a conspiracy against the American people and their government," he told listeners of WQQW radio on the afternoon of October 19, in a broadcast sponsored by the National Lawyers Guild. He and his eighteen fellows would not kowtow and they would not cooperate. "We do not come to Washington as the abject subjects of a police state. We come as citizens of a democratic republic."[7]

With attorneys Kenny and Crum in tow, Trumbo came to the witness table armed with his credentials, lugging a large box bulging with the scripts he had written, more as visual aids than as actual evidence to be submitted into the record. Under his chair were several canisters containing 16mm prints of his pictures.[8] He hunched over the microphones as he spoke, his heavy horn-rimmed glasses and bushy moustache giving him an owlish, curmudgeonly look.

Like Lawson, Trumbo politely asked to read an opening statement. Thomas refused. It was "not pertinent to the inquiry, therefore the chair will rule that the statement will not be heard."

Keeping cool, speaking in measured tones, Trumbo reminded Thomas that HUAC had once allowed Gerald L. K. Smith to read a statement into the record. Smith was a loathsome antisemitic demagogue who had testified in 1945.

Thomas's gavel whacked down. "If you conduct yourself like the first witness yesterday, you won't be given the privilege of being a witness before this committee of congress," Thomas snapped, not wanting a repeat of the performance by John Howard Lawson.

Trumbo's declarations were drowned out over Thomas's shouting and gavel-whacking.

Stripling broke in to ask Trumbo about his SWG membership. Soothingly, he suggested that Trumbo answer yes or no to the committee's questions, after which, he felt sure, the committee would let him speak his piece.

"Your job is to ask the questions and mine is to answer them," Trumbo responded. "I shall answer yes or no if I please to answer. I shall answer in my own words." A good many questions could be answered yes or no only "by a moron or a slave."

Trumbo requested permission to put into the *Congressional Record* twenty of his scripts as well as the commendations for his work by General H. H. "Hap" Arnold of the U.S. Army Air Force; by the chaplain in charge of motion picture projects for the U.S. Navy; and by the head of the motion picture division for the United Nations Relief and Rehabilitation Administration, so that the American public may see what the committee was trying to prevent it from knowing.

"Too many pages," muttered Thomas.

Stripling asked again about Trumbo's membership in the SWG.

"Mr. Stripling, the rights of American labor to inviolably secret membership lists have been won in this country by a great cost of blood and at great cost in terms of hunger," Trumbo lectured. "These rights have become

American tradition. Over the Voice of America we have broadcast to the entire world the freedom of our nation—"

Thomas cut him off. "Are you answering the question or are you making another speech? If you want to make another speech, we can find a corner right up here where you can make some of these speeches."

Trumbo said that if he answered the question, every American might be hauled before a committee and similarly coerced.

More snide remarks from Thomas, more dodging from Trumbo.

McDowell tried to mollify Trumbo. It was "no disgrace to identify yourself as the member of a labor union."

Trumbo asserted that labor unions have the right to keep their membership lists secret.

Having heard enough, Thomas ordered Trumbo excused, but Stripling stopped the dismissal: the chief counsel always remembered to ask the key incriminating questions in order to put the witness's refusal to answer on the record.

"Are you now or have you ever been a member of the Communist party?" asked Stripling, in his Texas twang.

Trumbo played coy. "First, I should like to know whether the quality of my last answer was acceptable, since I am still on the stand?"

"This has nothing to do with your last answer to the last question," interjected Thomas, playing along. "This is a new question now."

"Mr. Stripling," non-responded Trumbo, "you must have some reason for asking me this question. I understand that members of the press have been given an alleged Communist party card belonging to me. Is that true?"

"No, that's not true," replied Stripling, but as he did Thomas broke in angrily, gavel down, yelling, "You're not asking the questions!"

"I was," Trumbo put in, quickly.

"—the chief investigator is asking the questions."

"I beg your pardon, sir."

"Are you or have you ever been a member of the Communist party?"

Trumbo ignored the question. "I believe I have the right to be confronted with any evidence that supports this question," he said. "I should like to see what you have."

"Oh, well, you would!" smirked Thomas.

"Yes."

"Well, you will pretty soon!"

Guffaws and applause rippled across the room.

"The witness is excused," said Thomas, shaking his head. "Impossible."

Trumbo's genial manner instantly evaporated. He erupted in anger, becoming as loud and intemperate as John Howard Lawson.

"I note this is the beginning of an American concentration camp!" he screamed, as Thomas tried to gavel him to silence and Capitol police arrived to escort him away.

"Typical Communist tactics," snorted Thomas. "Typical Communist tactics."

As Trumbo was returned to his seat in the first row, loud applause, scattered cheers, and a few boos broke out.[9] His appearance had lasted no more than fifteen minutes.

Trumbo was followed to the witness table by Louis J. Russell, who duly produced a photostat of a Communist party registration card made out to "Dalt T." A long litany of Communist party and Communist front activities was also submitted into evidence.

At the conclusion of Russell's recitation, Thomas seemed impatient, remarking that the committee was "two days behind schedule already."

Thomas, Vail, and McDowell didn't bother to retire to a private conference room to consider the contempt charge against Trumbo. They put their heads together and conferred at the dais for a moment before Thomas announced the unanimous decision to cite Trumbo for contempt.[10] "The fact that he followed the usual Communist line of not responding to questions of the committee is definite proof that he is a member of the Communist party," said Thomas.[11]

Over the noon hour, the committee voted to allow the statements by the Unfriendlies to be entered into the *Congressional Record*: the press was getting copies from the defense team anyway. Trumbo's statement read in part:

> You have not exclusively attacked the principles of a free screen. In the past you have sought to intimidate workers in the radio industry. It clearly reveals your intention to establish a slave screen, subservient to the cultural standards of J. Parnell Thomas and the humanitarian precepts of John E. Rankin.

Conjuring the Nazi imagery that was the fallback rhetorical mode of the Unfriendly Nineteen, Trumbo said the Thomas Committee had produced "a capital city on the eve of its Reichstag fire. For those who remember German history in the autumn of 1932, there is the smell of smoke in this very room."[12]

Roy M. Brewer: "Hollywood unions have worked valiantly to prevent their unions from becoming an adjunct of Soviet foreign policy."

The very friendly Roy M. Brewer of IATSE followed Trumbo to the witness table. With the appearance of Brewer, two prongs of the pincer movement against Communist influence in Hollywood converged. Just as the above-the-line Communists in the SWG were thought to have subverted film content, the below-the-line Communists in the unions had infiltrated the patriotic ranks of American labor.

Officially, IATSE president Richard Walsh was Brewer's boss, but Brewer's alpha-male personality and fervent anti-Communism made him seem the more dominant half of the pair, the go-to guy when the studios wanted a problem on the shop floor solved or a radical stagehand eliminated (fired not killed). A former projectionist, Brewer knew where the levers of union power were located and how to put the screws to the moguls—but he was a partner not an adversary. No less than the producers, he wanted peace on the lots and a steady flow of studio profits. A rising box office, he reasoned, raises all salaries. Under the management of Walsh and Brewer, IATSE wasn't exactly pristine but compared to the naked corruption and brass-knuckled thuggery of the 1930s, it was law-abiding enough to avoid federal prosecution. Of course, Herbert Sorrell may not have detected a change in managerial tactics, having been shot at in 1945 and throttled to within an inch of his life in 1946.

Like the defeated screenwriters of the defunct Screen Playwrights, Inc., Brewer had come to Washington to settle scores. Unlike them, however, he held a trump card. The Taft-Hartley Act had given the anti-Communist IATSE the imprimatur of the federal government. The Conference of Studio Unions was in retreat and would soon be neutralized.

None of which meant that Brewer declined to use his platform to deliver a verbal coup de grace to his longtime rival. He charged that the jurisdictional strikes instigated by Sorrell were part of "a real Communist plot to capture the motion picture industry." As was so often the case in the annals of American labor, the animosity between the rival unions was as at least as bitter as the battle between labor and management.

Like Lawson and Trumbo, Brewer asked to read an opening statement, but, with a nod to evenhandedness, Thomas refused the request.

Unlike Lawson and Trumbo, Brewer had no objections to admitting his membership in a labor union. He was proud to belong to IATSE. However, he would not be proud to belong to CSU-affiliated unions such as the Painters Union Local 644, the Screen Cartoonists Guild, and the Screen Story Analysts Guild, all "completely controlled" by Communists.

Brewer named John Garfield, John Wexley, Sidney Buchman, Howard Koch, Larry Adler, Lewis Milestone, Dalton Trumbo, John Howard Lawson, Carey McWilliams, Frank Tuttle, Robert Rossen, and William Pomerance as "observers" of the strikes who were actually in cahoots with CSU. "Hollywood unions have worked valiantly to prevent their unions from becoming an adjunct of Soviet foreign policy," he declared. "Hundreds have suffered personal injuries. Homes have been bombed, automobiles destroyed, and children threatened. Intimidation and coercion have caused many to live for weeks in terror." Behind the reign of terror was his nemesis Sorrell, "the spearhead of Communist activities in the Hollywood labor field." According to Brewer, Sorrell was not the victim of union thugs; he *was* a union thug.

After hearing Brewer speak, Vail said, on second thought, the witness should be allowed to read his opening statement, which he found "relevant, comprehensive, informative, and of value to the intent and purpose of the committee."

Brewer's statement detailed "a real Communist plot to capture our union in Hollywood as part of the Communist plan to control the motion picture industry as a whole." The plot had come "dangerously close to success," but vigilant made-in-America unionists had prevented the revolution from catching fire.

The plot was begun by Jeff Kibre, an official of the United Studio Technicians Guild, an ally of Herbert Sorrell, and a Communist agent sent out to Hollywood in 1935. When Kibre proved ineffectual, the work of subversion was taken up by Sorrell. Meanwhile, "other Communist forces led by Mr. John Howard Lawson, whose activities have been effectively described here, were to infiltrate and control the talent guilds and the so-called cultural groups in the industry."

No sooner had Brewer left the witness chair than Sorrell shot off a telegram to Thomas. "Roy Brewer is an unmitigated liar, just as is Walt Disney, and I demand that I be subpoenaed and given the opportunity not only to refute their statements, but to tell what I know about who actually is responsible for Communism in the motion picture industry."[13]

Sorrell was never called.

Paul V. McNutt: "Insinuation and innuendo are never fair and are not facts."

After the lunch recess, MPAA counsel Paul V. McNutt was sworn in for a surprise appearance at the witness table. He had demanded the right to reply to charges Thomas had made during Eric Johnston's testimony the day before. Thomas had darkly insinuated that a mysterious man—presumably a bagman for the moguls—had approached him—presumably to bribe the chairman off the case.

McNutt wanted to read a statement, which he handed up to Thomas, who seemed taken off guard.

"Do Jack Warner and Mr. Mayer personally know about this statement?" asked Thomas. McNutt replied that Mayer had read it, but Warner had not.

Thomas took his time reading the statement as McNutt and the gallery waited. Finally, he announced, "The chair will reply later in a very full and detailed manner, but I would like to ask a question or two. Does your organization employ a Mr. Cahill?"

"We do," said McNutt.

Gerald Cahill was an assistant to Jack Bryson, legislative representative of the MPAA.

"Did you know that Cahill went to the committee chambers a number of times?"

"Yes."

"Do you know what he went for?"

"To get whatever information you were willing to offer."

"There," said Thomas triumphantly, "you said it yourself. He went to get information."

Thomas continued, "Do you know a Mr. Rosner who lives at the Shoreham [Hotel]?"

McNutt said he had never heard of him. Thomas dropped the matter.* McNutt went into his statement.

"Yesterday afternoon the organizations I represent were accused of having tried to stifle this inquiry," said McNutt. "This charge was made against

---

* Mickey Rosner was a shady underworld figure and scam artist who approached Thomas on September 21, 1947, claiming to be an emissary from Louis B. Mayer. He sought to deter Thomas from calling the reluctant Mayer to testify at the HUAC hearings in Washington.

us without proof and on the basis of insinuation and innuendo. This is a charge which does grave damage to our industry and seriously reflects on the personal integrity, loyalty, and patriotism of individuals associated with it. We cannot stand by and allow these vicious charges to go unchallenged before the public." How dare Thomas, without a scintilla of evidence, accuse the MPAA of trying to bribe him "to lay off or postpone [the inquiry]"?

Building up a head of steam, McNutt demanded, "Does the committee have any proof of these gratuitous insinuations? We want to know. The public is entitled to know. If the charges can't stand the light of day in open and above board discussion, they should not be made." Although McNutt well knew that HUAC trafficked in both, he cautioned against two rhetorical techniques: "Insinuation and innuendo are never fair and are not facts."

McNutt reminded Thomas that from the beginning of the hearings the motion picture industry wanted *all* members of the committee to be present at the hearings and "at no time did we want to stifle the inquiry. The truth is, we repeatedly asked for a full, fair and conclusive hearing because we want to see Communists exposed wherever they may be."

With this, McNutt made an insinuation of his own, one that everyone on the committee knew was true: that Thomas had himself postponed the hearings from their original starting dates until October 20, when John E. Rankin would be away from Washington, in his home state of Mississippi, campaigning for the U.S. Senate seat vacated by the death of Theodore Bilbo.

Albert Maltz: "I have answered the question, Mr. Quisling."

Following McNutt was the screenwriter Albert Maltz, who was even less friendly to HUAC than the MPAA lawyer.

Born in Brooklyn in 1908, Maltz came to Hollywood with a rare set of top-tier academic credentials: Columbia University graduate, 1926, and Yale School of Drama, 1932. For years he worked at the writer's trade, composing plays, short stories, and novels, getting the odd play produced, selling the odd story to Hollywood, publishing in everything from the *New Yorker* to the *New Masses*, making a name for himself as "one of the best and most considerable of the proletarian writers" for his sensitive depiction of "the woes of the underprivileged and downtrodden."[14]

In 1941, Maltz struck pay dirt when MGM bought his short story "The Happiest Man in the World," which had won the 1938 O. Henry Award for Best Short Story. The studio made it into a two-reel short, allowing the author to live up to the title.

During the war, Hollywood and Maltz continued to make each other happy. He attained A-list status, screenwriter-wise, counting among his credits hits such as *This Gun for Hire* (1942), *Destination Tokyo* (1943), and *Pride of the Marines* (1945). He won two Academy awards, one for co-writing the commentary to *Moscow Strikes Back* (1942), the American edit of the Soviet documentary, *The Defeat of German Forces Near Moscow*, and the other for *The House I Live In* (1945), a Mervyn LeRoy–directed short in which Frank Sinatra gives a tuneful lesson in tolerance to a gang of antisemitic street kids.

"Wherever I met injustice, wherever I saw it in my limited knowledge of society, I revolted against it just automatically, as though I were touching a hot stove," he recalled, explaining why he joined the Communist party in 1935.[15] The spirit informed all his writing, but he understood a revolution demanded stern measures. In 1945, in the *New Masses*, he voted with the majority in a literary roundtable on the question "Should Ezra Pound Be Shot?" (Consensus: yes.)[16] Like many of the Unfriendlies in the docket, he had a film in the pipeline, the gritty shot-on-location noir *The Naked City* (1947).

Thomas, who had refused John Howard Lawson and Dalton Trumbo permission to read their opening statements, surprised the hearing room, and the witness, by allowing Maltz to read his. Perhaps having just given Brewer the floor—and removing Trumbo from it—he felt a gesture to fairness was in order. Thomas had been criticized for the disparate treatment accorded the Friendlies and Unfriendlies, but, as usual, his decision to let Maltz speak was made on a whim.

Thomas asked to look over the statement first.

Maltz challenged the request. "May I ask whether you asked Gerald L. K. Smith to look at his statement first?" he asked.

"I wasn't chairman of the committee then," replied Thomas.

"You were a member," shot back Maltz.

"I asked a good many questions, some of which he had trouble answering," Thomas said.

Maltz may have looked like a mild-mannered clerk, but, of all the Unfriendlies, he unleashed the most eloquent denunciation of the committee, a righteous jeremiad spat right into the faces of his inquisitors. He made the most of his chance, reading quickly and passionately, as if afraid Thomas might cut him off at any second:

> I am an American, and I believe there is no more proud word in the vocabulary of Man.* I am a novelist and a screen writer and I have produced a certain body of work in the past fifteen years. As with any other writer, what I have written has come from the total fabric of my life—my birth in this land, our schools and games, our atmosphere of freedom, our tradition of inquiry, criticism, discussion, tolerance. Whatever I am, America has made me. And I, in turn, possess no loyalty as great as the one I have to this land, to the economic and social welfare of its people, to the perpetuation and development of its democratic way of life.
>
> Now at the age of thirty-nine, I am commanded to appear before the Committee on Un-American Activities. For a full week the committee has encouraged an assortment of well-rehearsed witnesses to testify that I and others are subversive and un-American. It has refused us the opportunity that any pickpocket receives in a magistrate's court—the right to cross-examine these witnesses to refute their testimony, to reveal their motives, their history, and exactly who they are. I maintain that this is an evil and vicious procedure; that it is legally unjust and morally indecent, and that it places in danger every other American, since if the rights of one citizen can be invaded, then the constitutional guarantees of every other American have been subverted and no one is any longer protected from official tyranny.

Maltz listed his patriotic credits as a screenwriter, highlighting the wartime submarine thriller *Destination Tokyo*, adopted by the U.S. Navy as an official training film, and the hybrid of combat film and rehabilitation melodrama *Pride of the Marines*, which premiered in twenty-eight cities under the sponsorship of the U.S. Marine Corps. "By cold censorship, if not by legislation, I must not be allowed to write," he said. "Will this censorship stop with me? Or with the others now singled out for attack? If it requires

---

* The original version of Maltz's statement continued: "I believe it despite the fact that other Americans, like Mr. Rankin, pour filth on the word by their hatred of the very idea of brotherhood." He probably decided not to read the line because Rankin was not in attendance.

acceptance of the ideals of this committee to remain immune from the brand of un-Americanism, then who is ultimately safe from this committee except members of the Ku Klux Klan?"

Maltz pledged to remain forever a stand-up guy, come what may. "I would rather die than be a shabby American, groveling before men whose names are Thomas and Rankin, but who now carry out activities in America like those carried out in Germany by Goebbels and Himmler," he rasped. "The American people are going to have to choose between the Bill of Rights and the Thomas Committee. They can't have both."

When Maltz finished, Thomas banged his gavel—but not to stifle applause. Maltz's closing was greeted with a long silence and Stripling needed to be startled back to attention.[17]

Unmoved, Stripling asked if Maltz were a member of the SWG.

Maltz didn't answer, spoke around the question, and insisted he had answered it.

Stripling tried again, and Maltz parried as before. "I would be a shabby American if I didn't answer as I have," he snapped. Asked if he were a member of the Communist party, Maltz replied, "Next you are going to ask what my religious beliefs are and you are going to insist before various members of the industry that since you don't like my religious beliefs I should not work in that industry."

Stripling tried yet again.

"I have answered the question, Mr. Quisling," sneered Maltz.

The reference to Vidkun Quisling, the Norwegian politician who collaborated with the Nazis during World War II and whose name had become a synonym for "traitor," was no Freudian slip.

"I object to that statement," interjected McDowell, but Stripling, not to be baited, ignored the insult.

"Excuse the witness," snapped a fed-up Thomas. "No more questions. Typical Communist line."

Compared to the raucous exits of Lawson and Trumbo, the departure of Maltz was almost decorous.

Again, investigator Louis J. Russell was sworn in to brand the witness as the Communist he would not admit to being. Russell submitted a fifteen-page précis of Maltz's subversive activities and a Communist party registration card made out to "Albert M." "I discovered a code and found that the Albert M. is Albert Maltz," Russell revealed.

Screenwriter Albert Maltz walks away from the witness table after refusing to cooperate, October 28, 1947.

"Clever code, hey? How do you think they ever manage to think up such tough codes?" cracked columnist Earl Wilson. Turning serious, Wilson watched the cardholder react as Russell spoke: "Albert Maltz, 39, one of this generation's most gifted writers, chews gum and smokes a cigarette simultaneously—perhaps he has thought to the last they didn't have 'a card on him.'"[18]

Buried in Russell's report was an illuminating interlude in the intellectual journey of the man who had just said he would rather die than be a shabby

American. In 1946, in a think piece on Marxist literature in the pages of *New Masses*, Maltz had advocated a deviance from the party line. "I have come to believe that the accepted understanding of art as a weapon is not a useful guide, but a straightjacket," he wrote. "Writers must be judged by their work, and *not* by the committees they join. It is the job of the literary critics to appraise the literary works only."[19] Maltz had given voice to a heresy that the CPUSA had tried to stamp out since the 1920s, the sin of judging art for art's sake not the party's.

The enforcers of party orthodoxy exacted speedy comeuppance. "Unhappily, the art which Maltz enthrones is the art of rejection, and, in the end, annihilation," responded the Communist novelist Howard Fast. Maltz's outlook "is an anti-Marxist position," stated *New Masses* editor Joseph North, who must have blamed an editorial assistant for letting Maltz's apostasy go to press. "He would, if his counsel were heeded, destroy the fruitful tree of Marxism."[20]

Two men whom Maltz currently sat with in the first row of the gallery also instructed him on how best to water the fruitful tree of Marxism. Maltz's thinking "is a product of the bourgeois concept that regards artists as sacred idiots who should not be protected from popular anger when they are fascist traitors," declared Alvah Bessie. "We need *Party* artists. We need artists deeply, truly, and honestly rooted in the working class who realize the truth of Lenin's assertion that the absolute freedom they seek 'is nothing but a bourgeois or anarchist phase.'"[21]

Hollywood's cultural commissar also weighed in to set Maltz straight. Quoting chapter and verse—Marx, Engels, and Lenin—John Howard Lawson berated him for ideological sins mortal and venial. Maltz was incapable of placing "the problem of the artist in its historical and social context"; Maltz appealed to a discredited "humanist tradition"; and, worst of all, Maltz did not "say one word about [the class] struggle, or suggest that the writer has any connection with the workers or their allies, or any obligation to take sides in the conflict."[22]

Chastened and humiliated, Maltz returned to the pages of the *New Masses* to recant:

> I consider now that my article—by what I have come to agree was a one-sided non-dialectical treatment of *complex* issues—could not, as I had hoped, contribute to the development of left-wing criticism and creative writing.

I believe also that my critics were entirely correct in insisting that certain fundamental ideas in my article would, if pursued to their conclusion, result in the dissolution of the left-wing cultural movement.

After the mea culpa, Maltz promised to sin no more, assuring his comrades that he fully understood that:

If the writer is to retain inner firmness, if he is not to sink into cynicism and despair, if he is to maintain his love for the people without which true art cannot flourish, then he must understand that events have a meaning, that history has a direction, that the characters he portrays are part of a social web based upon the life and death struggle of classes. For this understanding, for inner firmness, for the spiritual ability to retain faith in people and faith in the future, he must, in this epoch, turn to Marxism.[23]

The witness who refused to grovel before HUAC had gotten down on all fours before his Communist brethren.

Robert W. Kenny: "I would be disgraced before every one of a hundred thousand lawyers in the United States if I answered that question."

Sitting beside Maltz was his lawyer, Robert W. Kenny, former attorney general of the state of California and vice president of the National Lawyers Guild, lately cited by Attorney General Francis Biddle as a Communist front group. To the surprise of the attorney and the gallery, Stripling asked that Kenny be called as the witness right after Maltz, even before Russell made his indictments. He wanted Kenny to respond to newspaper reports that the lawyer had advised all his clients to refuse to answer the committee's questions, a legal strategy Thomas considered a conspiracy against the government.

The week before, in an interview in the *New York Post* with Earl Wilson, Kenny had confided the legal-political strategy of the Unfriendly Nineteen: a collective uncivil resistance. "Our men will be sworn and will testify on anything the committee has a right to know," Kenny revealed. "But, when they're asked what they think or believe or the contents of their mind or how they vote, they'll say no." Running with his scoop, Wilson spelled out the lede: "They've agreed to take that unified stand when called to testify, well realizing they may be cited for contempt."[24]

During the pro forma swearing in ceremony for Kenny, an awkward incident transpired. An eyewitness—Crossley Bowen, a top-notch journalist covering the hearings for *PM*—and the *Congressional Record* tell slightly different versions of what happened.

According to Bowen, when Kenny stood to be sworn in, he raised his left hand.

"Raise your right hand," Thomas ordered.

Kenny moved his right arm only slightly. The arm had been crippled from birth, dislocated during a difficult delivery.

"Raise your *right* hand!" barked Thomas, glowering.

Bartley Crum walked over to the chairman and whispered, "Everybody in Washington knows that Kenny's right arm is paralyzed."[25]

Apparently, not quite everybody—though Thomas's enemies took the incident as confirmation of his callousness. "Thomas had met Kenny a number of times previously, had conferred with him in meetings concerning his clients, and had seen him sitting in at the hearings for several days," fumed Bowen.

The *Congressional Record* is less dramatic:

The Chairman: Mr. Kenny, will you please take the stand? Raise your right hand, please.

Mr. Stripling: Your right hand.

The Chairman: Your right hand.

Mr. Crum: He cannot raise his right hand.

The Chairman: He cannot?

Mr. Crum: No; he is crippled.[26]

After Kenny swore in with his good arm raised, Thomas asked him if Wilson's report were true, if he had advised his clients not to answer and instead to "invite prosecution" and "walk the plank." Thomas reminded Kenny that section 37 of the Criminal Code dealt with conspiracy against the government.

Kenny played coy. He reminded Thomas that communications between a lawyer and his client were privileged. "I would be disgraced before every one of a hundred thousand lawyers in the United States if I answered that question."

Thomas was not about to be put off. If Kenny had advised the Unfriendly Nineteen to coordinate their refusals to invite prosecution, he might find himself "in more trouble than some of your clients."

Thomas rephrased his question: did Kenny tell a reporter that he had so advised his clients?

Kenny said that he hated to disavow a newspaper story, but the account by Wilson, which had gone out over the United Press wire, was not quite accurate.

Thomas wanted the last word. "You squirmed out of that one temporarily, but if the committee later determines a conspiracy was attempted, it will recommend action against you."

Kenny was having none of it. "And I might say that the committee has squirmed out of that one too. Lawyers don't divulge the nature of the advice to clients, and you know it, Mr. Thomas."[27]

"Oh, no, and neither would you want to commit conspiracy," sneered Thomas, leaning forward to eye Kenny.

"Shall we say that neither one of us has been intimidated, Mr. Chairman?" Kenny asked, satisfied to call it a draw.[28]

Thomas let the matter drop. He was keeping his eye on the high-value targets.

Alvah Bessie: "General Eisenhower himself has refused to reveal his political affiliations, and what is good enough for General Eisenhower is good enough for me."

Alvah Bessie was a true believer, a devoted soldier in the Communist ranks who wrote, lived, and breathed the party. In fact, he served as a literal soldier for the cause, putting his life on the line by fighting with the American volunteers of the Abraham Lincoln Brigade on the Loyalist side in the Spanish Civil War. He was prouder of his service in Spain than of any screen credit he earned in Hollywood.

Born in 1904 in New York, a son of the Jewish upper class, Bessie led a charmed literary-intellectual life: student at Columbia University, winner of a Guggenheim fellowship, author of a well-received first novel, *Dwell in the Wilderness* (1936), about the incursions of industrialism on rural life, and theater and book critic for the *Brooklyn Daily Eagle*. In 1937, inspired by an interview he conducted with the novelists André Malraux and Ralph Bates, both fierce partisans for the Spanish Loyalists, he decided to act on his workers-of-the-world principles and enlisted in the Abraham Lincoln Brigade.

George Orwell, another overseas recruit for the Loyalists, became disillusioned, but the Spanish Civil War did not break up Bessie's romance with Communism. Neither did the Hitler-Stalin Pact. A week after the signing, with Poland in flames, he wrote a letter to the *Brooklyn Daily Eagle* in defense of the USSR, still "the only country in the world that has consistently acted as a bulwark for world peace and an inspiration to those who would like to see our democracy succeed despite the aims of Fascist imperialism."[29]

In 1942, Warner Bros. brought Bessie out to Hollywood to work on a screenplay based on the Broadway play *Brooklyn U.S.A.*, a beat he knew well from his newspaper days. He spotted an item in *Variety* that described his good fortune. "Scribblers are so scarce in Hollywood these days—most having gone in the Armed Forces—that anyone who can write a simple declarative English sentence is being inked to long term contracts." Bessie circled the story and wrote "me" next to it.[30]

Bessie's best-known film credit was *Objective Burma* (1945), an action-packed wartime vehicle for Errol Flynn, but, as he freely confessed, he was not in the same league as his good friend Dalton Trumbo. While a hustling screenwriter, Bessie continued to write, under his own byline, for the *New Masses*, doing film, theater, and book reviews, his critical insights always in line with party orthodoxy. James K. McGuinness described him as "a Communist hatchet man."

Being a good Marxist-Leninist, Bessie did not believe in omens, but shortly before traveling to Washington to testify, he drove out to Trumbo's ranch for a visit. On the way, he witnessed a horrific automobile accident. Bessie stopped to help carry the female victim into an ambulance. The next day, looking in the *Los Angeles Times* for the names of the witnesses subpoenaed by HUAC, he came across the news that the woman had died. Her name was Bessie.

Bessie knew what to expect from HUAC, but he was looking forward to the encounter. Upon hearing his name called, he confessed to "a suddenly stepped-up heartbeat, dryness of the mouth and throat, shaking hands, sharp pain in the intestinal region," but—not unlike an actor or a solider—"the moment you step upon the stage—or onto the field of fire—the symptoms seem to disappear, and you are suddenly at ease and in sharp command of all your facilities—such as they may be."[31]

Again defying expectations, the inscrutable Thomas permitted Bessie to read the first and last paragraphs of his opening statement and agreed to put the full statement into the *Congressional Record*.

Bessie seized the opportunity:

> This body has no legal authority to pry into the minds or activities of any American who believes, as I do, in the Constitution, and who is willing at any time to fight to preserve it. . . . The understanding that led me to fight in Spain for that Republic, and my experience in that war, teach me that this committee is engaged in precisely the identical activities engaged in by un-Spanish committees, un-German committees, and un-Italian committees which preceded it in every country which eventually succumbed to Fascism. I will never aid or abet such a committee in its patent attempt to foster that sort of intimidation and terror that is the inevitable precursor of a Fascist regime.

The familiar tango proceeded: Stripling and Thomas asking the are-you-now-or-have-you-ever-been question, Bessie refusing to answer, and Bessie being led away from the witness table.

Unlike some his fellow Unfriendlies, Bessie did not filibuster or hem and haw: he refused flat out to answer. "I do not believe this committee has any more right to inquire into my political affinities than I believe that an election official has the right to go into the voting booth and examine the ballot which has been marked by the voter," he replied. Then, invoking the name of the most admired man in America, who was then being solicited by both major political parties to declare his allegiance, Bessie got off a good line, if he did say so himself. "General Eisenhower himself has refused to reveal his political affiliations, and what is good enough for General Eisenhower is good enough for me."

Laughter and applause—mixed with a few boos—greeted the rejoinder.

"It is very apparent you are following the same line as these other witnesses," said Thomas.

"I am following no line—" insisted Bessie.

"—which is definitely the Communist line."

"I am using my head, which I am privileged to do."

Thomas dismissed the witness with a curt, "You are excused. If you want to make a speech, go out there under a big tree."

Thomas's line got a bigger laugh than Bessie's.

Stripling could not permit General Eisenhower's name to be taken in vain. "I just want to make one observation for the committee," he said. "If General Eisenhower were a witness before this committee and he was asked the question 'Are you a member of the Communist party?' he would not only be very responsive to the question, but he would be absolutely insulted, and solely for this reason: A great man like General Eisenhower would not ever think or dream to ever being a low-down Communist."

Stripling's comeback got the loudest reaction of all: boisterous, supportive applause.

Louis J. Russell was then sworn in. He produced the witness's Communist party registration card bearing his full name—"Alvah Bessie"—and a seven-page report documenting his Communist activities.

Bessie's testimony was notable for bequeathing a catchphrase to the lingo of Cold War anti-Communism. While interrogating Bessie, Stripling referred, for the first time, to the question regarding Communist party affiliation, always asked with the same wording, as "the $64 question." The phrase caught on immediately, and why not? Like the radio quiz show that inspired it, the question from HUAC created an air of palpable tension as the listening audience waited for the answer, with the correct response either rewarding the contestant or sending him away from the microphone.* Of course, for the Unfriendly Nineteen, it was no brain teaser: they knew the question in advance and the only correct answer.†

After Bessie was cited for contempt and left the witness table, a spectator in the gallery muttered, "Four down and fifteen to go."[32]

---

* The highest dollar amount in the CBS radio quiz show *Take It or Leave It* (1941–1948), the phrase had entered the vernacular during wartime as shorthand for any momentous query, so much so that by 1947 it had become more of a cliché than a witticism.

† The classic phrasing was: Are you now or have you ever been a member of the Communist party?" The "have you ever been" was inserted to prevent a technical dodge: the wily CPUSA passed a resolution dismissing from membership any member asked that question at the moment of the asking—thus allowing the member to say, truthfully, that he was "not now" a member of the CPUSA.

Edward T. Cheyfitz: "Communism was like a religion. You couldn't lose it overnight."[33]

As the day's dramas unfolded, another display of emotional testimony was happening outside the caucus room. In what in years to come would be a familiar sight, an employee in the motion picture industry whose loyalty had been impugned went before the press for a ritual cleansing. During Johnston's testimony the day before, Edward T. Cheyfitz, an assistant to Johnston on labor issues for the past two years, had been dragged into the spotlight by Robert Stripling.

Cheyfitz held a press conference to tell his story. In 1932, at age eighteen, in the nadir of the Great Depression, he had joined the Communist Party. During 1934–1935, he had spent a year in the USSR, "just to see what was going on there," working as a laboratory technician in a chemical factory. His disillusionment with Communism began when he saw firsthand how ordinary citizens in the worker's paradise lived, "under very tough conditions with no freedom of expression or movement." As with so many American Communists, the scales finally fell from his eyes with the signing of the Hitler-Stalin Pact in 1939. Still, he anguished about making a clean break. "Communism was like a religion," he said. "You couldn't lose it overnight."[34]

Supported by Johnston, Cheyfitz weathered the controversy. However, back in Hollywood, members of the AMPP felt that Johnston had exercised poor judgment in selecting a former Communist as a special assistant. Y. Frank Freeman, vice president of Paramount, and Herbert Preston, counsel for Warner Bros., accused Johnston of "embarrassing himself and the Association before the American public when it became known that Cheyfitz had been associated with the Communist movement." Freeman was of the opinion—expressed to Cheyfitz's face—that "leopards never change their spots."[35]

Marsha Hunt: "We're all in a social studies class."

The Committee for the First Amendment had not planned to spend a second full day in Washington, but after Thomas's reprimand at the end of Monday's session, the group decided to stick around so as not to appear to have turned tail.

The second full day of CFA counter-programming began with two back-to-back press conferences early in the morning, one for the local film critics and one for the feature writers.

That same day, CFA published in the trade press a second full-page ad whose copy echoed the sentiments of the first. Under the bold all-caps headline "HOLLYWOOD FIGHTS BACK," the manifesto opened with a reprint of the First Amendment of the U.S. Constitution, punctuated with the declaration that the undersigned American citizens, "who believe in constitutional democratic government, are disgusted and outraged by the continuing attempt by the House Committee on Un-American Activities to smear the Motion Picture Industry."

In addition to 326 Hollywood personalities, the list of signatories included 4 U.S. senators: Harley Kilgore (D-WV), Claude Pepper (D-FL), Elbert Thomas (D-UT), and Glen Taylor (D-ID). Also prominently typeset was a plea for funds "to enable us to carry on the fight! Every dollar is important!" The popularity of the committee was on a rising arc: the list of signatories in the second ad had expanded exponentially. Once the pioneers had taken the first steps into the roiling waters, the more timorous waded in.

After the two press conferences, the group arrived in the corridors outside the hearing room at 9:30 A.M., an hour before opening, in order to get good seats.[36] Thomas was no longer reserving space for the glamour brigade. With growing alarm, they watched the surly defiance of Dalton Trumbo and the evidence submitted by Stripling and Russell.

In between the morning and afternoon testimony, members of the group convened in the office of Rep. Chet Holifield (D-CA) to draw up a petition to Congress for "redress of grievances." Filed with the clerk of the House, Speaker John W. Martin being absent that day, the petition charged that HUAC had switched its investigative functions "from fair and impartial to unfair and partial and prejudicial" and that "reputations had been besmirched" at the hearings.[37]

Strolling the hallways of the Old House Office Building between sessions, the stars chatted up reporters who were thrilled to be charmed. "I talked with Lauren Bacall, which is nice work when you can get it," reported Quentin Reynolds in *PM*. "She remembered studying the Bill of Rights at the New York City high school she attended. She talked convincingly and intelligently. Danny Kaye and Bogart chimed in. None of them liked Communism: they just couldn't understand how people became Communists in a country like ours. But they couldn't understand the arbitrary rights which the committee had taken unto itself."[38]

At the end of the day, back at the Statler Hotel, Huston announced the return trip to California to about fifty reporters at "a rather confused meeting during which the Hollywood delegation made clear that it stands off by itself, that it was not invented by John Garfield, and that it has no close connection with the 19 'unfriendly' witnesses," *Daily Variety* noted.[39] The reference to John Garfield was telling. An alumnus of the leftist Group Theatre in New York in the 1930s, a prominent spokesman for the Hollywood Anti-Nazi League, and an apologist for the Moscow Purge Trials, Garfield had too high a profile as a left-of-center activist cozy with Communists to be front man for a group trying to straddle a position between two extremes.[40] To the consternation of Huston, Wyler, and Dunne, Garfield had consistently muddled the position of the committee: the stars had *not* flown to Washington to stand in solidarity with the Unfriendly Nineteen.

Screenwriter Philip Dunne picked up Huston's theme, saying it was nobody's business whether a man was a Democrat or a Republican, and that CFA represented various political parties and persuasions. The diverse members of the committee agreed on only one thing, the principles highlighted in its name: HUAC threatened the freedom of opinion and association guaranteed by the First Amendment.

In the common suite area at the Statler, Marsha Hunt huddled with a group of earnest high school students, who had persuaded their principal to let them attend the hearings as a field trip for their social studies class. "You came here from high school for that purpose, and we flew from Hollywood for that purpose," she told them. "That's what the First Amendment's about. We're all in a social studies class. We're all learning you've got to *do* something to see that all people get an even break."[41]

The day's press conferences were all well-attended by the allegedly jaded Washington reporters, most of whom seemed grateful to be covering a beat with more beauty and charisma than usually walked the halls of Congress. Florence S. Lowe, the glib correspondent for *Daily Variety*, couldn't help but jibe at the "self-styled sophisticates of the Washington press corps" who nonetheless "made time on overcrowded days to attend all three of the press conferences" held by CFA. "Turnout for the final news conference, with cocktails, was a tribute to the star system," Lowe teased. "Few will admit it but the lure of the Bogarts, Gene Kelly, Lucille Ball et al. worked like sprinkling salt on the bird's tail."*

---

* Florence S. Lowe, "Washington Hullabaloo," *Daily Variety*, November 5, 1947: 6.

Chapter 14
JEWISH QUESTIONS

The morning of the penultimate day began with a prepared statement that Chairman Thomas permitted to be read into the record: the statement was by Chairman Thomas.

Overnight, realizing that MPAA attorney Paul McNutt had gotten the better of him in the exchange over the allegations that agents of official Hollywood had attempted to thwart or bribe the committee, Thomas had decided to double down. In what the chairman described as a statement of "recapitulation," he asserted, "we have not, and we are not, violating the rights of any American citizen, not even the rights of the Communists whose first allegiance is to a foreign government." Despite scrupulous attention to due process however:

> The committee is well aware that powerful influences have sought in every manner to divert this committee from its main course of inquiry. I am proud to say that this committee has not been swayed, intimidated, or influenced by either Hollywood glamour, pressure groups, threatened ridicule, or high-pressure tactics on the part of the high-paid puppets and apologists for certain elements of the moving picture industry.

The reference to "Hollywood glamour" was a swipe at the stars representing the Committee for the First Amendment, who had been sitting in the back of the hearing room for two days, lending moral support to the motion picture industry and causing a buzz from people more interested in getting a seat next to a celebrity than hearing the shouting matches between the obstinate screenwriters and gavel-whacking chairman. Like the rest of the attendees, the stars craned their necks for a good view and stood up to see what was going on when an obstreperous Unfriendly was escorted away from the witness table by the Capitol police. The presence of Bogart, Bacall, Garfield, Kaye, and other marquee faces, even more than the defiance of the Unfriendlies, seemed to gall Thomas.

"The people are going to get the facts, just as I announced on opening day," Thomas promised. "Last week we had before us over twenty witnesses, all of whom had been subpoenaed, all of whom were tops in their profession, and all from Hollywood. They are among our most prominent producers, directors, writers, and actors. Their names stand high, not only in Hollywood, but throughout the world, as great entertainers and producers of entertainment." He paused, unable to resist another dig at the delegation from Hollywood. "They certainly have more at stake in Hollywood than some of the actors who have descended upon Washington with would-be stars and starlets to bowl over a committee of the Congress of the United States who dared to put the spotlight on the Communist foreign agents operating within their very industry."

Thomas reviewed the record thus far:

There can be no doubt in anyone's mind who attended these hearings that Mr. Lawson, Mr. Trumbo, Mr. Bessie, and Mr. Maltz are Communists, that they have been Communists for a long time, and that they will continue to be Communists—serving not the best interests of the United States but the best interests of a foreign government.

And then, at his third direct shot at CFA, he snarled, "Oh, yes, the paid apologists for these people have employed full page ads in an effort to distort and divert the beam of exposure which they saw was descending upon them from this committee."

Thomas concluded with a tribute to his own noble efforts. "This is to state to the American people and to everyone concerned that this beam is not going to be turned off or shut off until all the Communists in Hollywood are exposed."[1]

Samuel Ornitz: "I wish to address this committee as a Jew."

The beam from Thomas's spotlight fell first that morning on screenwriter Samuel Ornitz. For the third day an unfriendly witness went up against an equally unfriendly committee for a bitter exchange. Unlike Lawson, Ornitz was not forcibly ejected, but the rhetoric and passion was just as heated—sometimes at a steady simmer, sometimes boiling over.

If the subpoenaed screenwriters were ranked on a one-to-ten scale for prestige and solvency, Ornitz would have come in last. Alvah Bessie and Ornitz were the only members of the Unfriendly Nineteen who could not pay the up-front fee of four thousand dollars for their high-priced legal representation. Sharing and sharing alike, their more prosperous comrades generously took up the slack.[2]

Ornitz may have looked like a bank clerk—paunchy, jowly, bald, wearing oval spectacles—but he had been toiling in the radical trenches his whole life. Born in 1890 to Eastern European Jews, reared on the Lower East side of New York, and molded by Hebrew School, he embraced and foregrounded his Jewish background. He changed neither his name nor his politics in the interests of assimilation.

Fleeing the family business—a dry goods store—Ornitz became a social worker and never really stopped. In 1923, he wrote a popular novel about New York politics, *Haunch, Punch and Jowl*, which first put him on the Social Realist literary map. In 1928, he moved to Hollywood to work—and agitate. In 1931, as a member of the National Committee for the Defense of Political Prisoners, he joined with Theodore Dreiser, Waldo Frank, John Dos Passos, and other activist writers for a life-threatening expedition into Harlan and Bell Counties, Kentucky, scene of the brutal suppression of a coal miner's strike.[3] He drew on the experience for his agit-prop play, *The New Kentucky*, published in the *New Masses* in 1934.

Though the screenwriters in Los Angeles County worked under conditions less onerous than the coal miners in Harlan and Bell Counties, Ornitz fought as fiercely for unionization in Hollywood as in Appalachia. A founding member of the Screen Writers' Guild, he was dedicated to solidarity across the ranks and joined the picket lines of stagehands who fought for a union more radical than IATSE.

In 1940, Ornitz and his wife Sadie were called before the Communist-hunting grand jury convened by Los Angeles District Attorney Buron Fitts.

Fitts and his "L.A. Red squad" were using the cover of investigating alleged Communist contract murders to break up radical union activity in a city long averse to organized labor. "I murdered people—but only in the movies," Ornitz confessed upon receiving his subpoena.[4] He referred to the Fitts squad as "the Los Angeles Gestapo" and—this being the period during the Hitler-Stalin Pact interregnum—explained the motives behind the investigations in sinister terms: the forces of repression needed "conscription and then war to break the trade union movement."[5]

Lately, Ornitz's Hollywood career had stalled; his last major screen credit was the decidedly B-caliber *Circumstantial Evidence* (1945), a bottom-of-the-bill legal melodrama. Unfazed, he retained his sense of humor and never lost his desire to spit in the eye of capitalist power. Upon receiving his subpoena from HUAC, Ornitz sent a droll telegram to J. Parnell Thomas:

THIS IS TO ACKNOWLEDGE RECEIPT OF YOUR SUBPOENA CALL-ING FOR MY APPEARANCE OCTOBER 23 AND ASSURE YOU OF MY EVERY INTENTION OF BEING THERE AND ADDING TO THE GAIETY OF OUR NATION **STOP** KINDLY FORWARD TO ME AT ONCE PASS FOR TRANSPORTATION AND MAINTAINANCE AS PROVIDED FOR BY LAW TO ENABLE ME TO PURCHASE TICKET WHICH I AM UNABLE TO DO FOR MYSELF BECAUSE AN INVOLUNTARY SEVERANCE OF NEARLY FOUR YEARS FROM THE INDUSTRY YOU ARE SCRUTINIZ-ING LEAVES ME WITHOUT FUNDS. YOURS FOR FREE AMERICA.

SAMUEL ORNITZ[6]

After being sworn in, Ornitz asked to read a statement. Thomas glanced at the prose and testily ruled it "out of order and another case of vilification."

Well he might. Ornitz's statement was not just an assault on the committee but a ploy to raise the issue that Thomas had worked hard to suppress since the hearings began. "I wish to address this committee as a Jew," it began, before launching into an indictment of antisemitism and anti-Catholicism. "Is it mere coincidence that you chose to subpoena and characterize as 'unfriendly' the men who produced, wrote, and directed or acted in" Hollywood films "which attacked antisemitism or treated Jews and Negroes sympathetically?" Certainly it was not coincidental that the committee had singled out for persecution Edward Dmytryk and Adrian Scott, the director and producer of *Crossfire* (1947). "Therefore, I ask, as a Jew, based on the record, is bigotry this committee's yardstick of Americanism, and its definition of subversive?"[7]

The mention of the word "Jew"—and Ornitz's proud admission of embodying same—would have spoken aloud what had been wafting around the testimony for days. "[A] survey of the record of the Hollywood Communist probe shows that the issue of anti-Semitism has been injected on a number of occasions—and always by the group of 19 'unfriendly' witnesses," noted *Variety*, wise to the tactics. "It has not been mentioned once by any member of the House Un-American Activities Committee, and Rep. J. Parnell Thomas, committee chairman, has denounced injection of religious aspects."[8]

Ornitz determined to drag the "religious aspects" of the hearings into the *Congressional Record*. "I accuse!" he shouted, in a grandiose echo of

Screenwriter Samuel Ornitz shouts his defiance from the witness table, October 29, 1947.

Émile Zola's *cri de coeur* against the antisemitism that had railroaded Capt. Alfred Dreyfus in France in 1894, an accusation immortalized in the Warner Bros. biopic *The Life of Emile Zola* (1937).

"You will not accuse anybody!" Thomas shouted back, pounding his gavel as Ornitz matched him decibel for decibel.

Fed up, Thomas ordered Ornitz to "step aside," but a cooler head prevailed. Stripling knew that to nail Ornitz for contempt of Congress the witness had to refuse to answer the $64 question. Thus, Stripling interrupted to halt the ejection. He needed Ornitz's refusal on the record.

Stripling zeroed right in, asking whether Ornitz were a SWG member.

Ornitz paused. "I wish to reply to that by saying that this involves a serious question of conscience for me."

"Conscience?" broke in Thomas, as if he had never heard the word.

"Conscience, sir, conscience," replied Ornitz in a steady voice.

A question of conscience is raised, Ornitz explained, "when you ask me to act in concert with you to override the Constitution."

Asked if he was now or had ever been a member of the Communist party, Ornitz replied that his political, like his religious beliefs, were fully guaranteed by the Constitution, and he had the right to join any party he choose.

"Even if that party is an agent of a foreign power?" pressed Stripling.

Ornitz dug in his heels. "That is a loaded question and I will not reply to it."

With that, Ornitz was dismissed. Stripling had the witness on record refusing to answer. Ornitz's time at the witness table clocked in at less than five minutes.

The usual follow-up act went on next: Louis J. Russell took the stand to produce a photostat copy of Communist Party registration card No. 47181, dated December 2, 1944, made out to "Sam O." A code obtained with the card confirmed that "Sam O." was Samuel Ornitz.

Herbert Biberman: "I would be very suspicious of any answer that would come out of my mouth that pleased this committee."

Herbert Biberman followed Ornitz to the witness table and followed the same script—at a louder register.

Born in Philadelphia in 1900, the son of well-off textile manufacturers, Biberman fled the family business to study drama at Yale and in Berlin, Prague, and Moscow. In 1928, he joined the New York Theater Guild as an assistant stage manager and within two years was directing productions. It was the heyday of the guild and heady times for Social Realist theater. Working in the theater and on radio, he gained a reputation as an artistic innovator who stretched the sonic boundaries of both media.[9] He also stretched the political boundaries. In 1929, Biberman mounted a production of *Red Rust*, the first Soviet play to be produced in the United States. Scoping out the project for Hollywood possibilities, *Variety* voted thumbs down: "Lot of Soviet Russia propaganda unsuitable for either theme or story for the American screen."[10]

In 1935, Biberman was recruited by Columbia Pictures, where, under the stern eyes and impatient ass of Harry Cohn, he helmed an uninspired slate of programmers with marginal Marxist-Leninist content. During the war, Biberman finally got to unsheathe his celluloid weapon, writing and directing *The Master Race* (1944), a daring flash forward set in a postwar Belgian town traumatized by four years of Nazi occupation.

With the exception of Larry Parks, Biberman may have been the most photographed member of the Unfriendly Nineteen—on the arm of his wife, the actress Gale Sondergaard, also his partner in activism, a stunning brunette who had won the first Best Supporting Actress Oscar for *Anthony Adverse* (1936), written by Donald Ogden Stewart, the patrician Communist and cofounder of the Hollywood Anti-Nazi League, who should have been subpoenaed by Thomas to make the count an even Unfriendly Twenty. Besides an aura of glamour-by-association, Biberman also brought a sense of physical prowess to the witness table: at six foot two inches, straight and muscular, with a boxer's fists, he looked like a man who could take care of himself.

Stressing his all-American pedigree, Biberman noted he was "born within a stone's throw of Independence Hall in Philadelphia, on the day when Mr. McKinley was inaugurated as president of the United States, March 4, 1900."* He began good-naturedly enough, saying he would be "as detailed and specific in answers to any questions you direct at me."

---

* A forgivable mistake: William McKinley was inaugurated on March 4, 1901.

First, however, Biberman had a statement to read. Having endured the denunciation from Albert Maltz the day before, Thomas and Stripling balked at giving another unfriendly witness a megaphone to berate HUAC. "It is another case of vilification, and therefore will not be read," decreed Thomas.

"There is no vilification in that statement," Biberman shouted. "I feel your refusal to allow me to read it is a shameful and cowardly act."

Biberman and Thomas yelled at each for the next few minutes, Thomas raising the decibel level with the pounding of his gavel, now virtually a third hand. Stripling somehow managed to get in his two required questions about the SWG and the CPUSA. Biberman was nonresponsive.

"You have only one idea," bellowed Biberman, upping the volume and completing his thought despite the drumbeat from Thomas, "and that is to cause strife in the industry—chaos in the industry—and this I will not permit."

As was his wont whenever an unfriendly witness built up a head of rhetorical steam, Thomas cut Biberman off and told him to stand down.

Biberman angrily spoke over his interrogator, denying that he refused to "answer anything." Finally, as he was escorted from the table by a Capitol policeman, he yelled, "Mr. Stripling, I apologize for one thing and that is raising my voice. I had no intention of doing so."

The Unfriendly claque in the gallery guffawed.

Biberman could not resist a parting shot. "I would be very suspicious of any answer that would come out of my mouth that pleased this committee."

"I would too," fired back Stripling.

"Take him away," ordered Thomas.

Again, Louis B. Russell followed an Unfriendly to the witness table, again he presented a photostat of a Communist Party registration—Card No. 47267—and again Stripling capped the indictment by presenting a lengthy "record of affiliations."

Silenced on the stand, Biberman handed out his prepared statement to reporters. He condemned the "brazen attempt" by the committee to become "the supreme censor and imperial dictatorial wizard of the greatest medium of mass expression in our country." The friendly witnesses from the week before were a "parade of mad hatters forming a smokescreen under which this committee was attempting to proscribe a film diet for the American people."[11]

Ring Lardner Jr. was then called to the witness table, but an abashed Robert Kenny explained that Lardner, unaware that he was going to be called, was not in the hearing room. He promised Lardner would be available later in the day.*

Emmet Lavery: "As a student of Constitutional law, I am not sure the Committee has the right to ask this question."

Screen Writers' Guild president Emmet G. Lavery would not have needed to be subpoenaed. He was eager to defend his profession, his guild, and his character, all of which, he felt, had been smeared by reckless accusations by the MPA-PAI, the Tenney Committee, the *Hollywood Reporter*, and HUAC.

Lavery brought an apt expertise to the matters at hand: a graduate of Fordham Law School in 1924, he was admitted to the New York state bar in 1925 and served as an alderman in his native Poughkeepsie. He understood that a congressional hearing was not a court of law but more like a public grand jury proceeding in which anyone could be subpoenaed, anything could be asked, and anything could be said. He also thought—and in this he was prophetic—that the Unfriendlies were standing on the wrong constitutional amendment: the First rather than the Fifth.

In 1933, Lavery abandoned the certain income from a law firm and a career in New York politics for the precarious vocation of playwriting. In 1935, MGM brought him out to Hollywood, but the first migration didn't take. He returned to New York, only to wind back to Hollywood in 1941, to write the scripts for Edward Dmytryk's low-budget but high-return twinpack *Hitler's Children* (1943) and *Behind the Rising Sun* (1943). A grateful RKO signed him as a writer-producer, but he never forsook the first half of the hyphen. Uniting his love for dramaturgy and the law, he had recently written *The Magnificent Yankee*, a hagiographic piece of Americana about the life of Supreme Court Justice Oliver Wendell Holmes, a play that enjoyed a successful Broadway run in 1946.

---

* Thomas gave Lardner a pass for not being in the hearing room because the chairman had changed the dates of his testimony and sent the notification to the wrong address.

A practical and likeable liberal, acceptable to radicals and centrists alike, Lavery was elected head of the SWG in 1945 and re-elected in 1946 without opposition. He succeeded the doctrinaire Communist Lester Cole and determined to steer the guild toward the mainstream. Upon election, Lavery announced that his first concern would not be cementing inter-union solidarity with the stagehands but finding jobs for the screenwriters returning to Hollywood after military service.[12] As SWG president, he fought a two-front war, beating back anti-Communist malcontents from the defunct Screen Playwrights, Inc. and the Communist zealots on his own executive board.

For Lavery, the imperative was to protect the integrity of the SWG—not defend the unfriendly screenwriters bent on defying the committee. He felt that the guild should take no position on how to respond to HUAC and that individual members were free to follow their own conscience. "[I]n the matter of individual activities of Guild members, either within or outside the industry, the individual defense or individual presentation is a matter for each individual witness," he declared in a memo sent to the SWG membership prior to his testimony.[13] Under no circumstances should the guild *qua* guild be tethered to the dogmatic, defiant position of the Nineteen. Throughout his tenure, he had steadfastly resisted attempts by Lawson, Trumbo, and the other Communist members to turn the guild into a vehicle for whatever political cause, foreign or domestic, animated the CPUSA.[14] The activists on the executive board sometimes overruled him, but the full membership consistently backed his traditional trade union stance. In jousting with critics of the guild, he was not above playing the Irish-Catholic card to deflect charges of fellow traveling. "As an Irishman originally trained in the law at Fordham Law School, I take my social conscience from the Gospels of the Apostles, not from the essays of Karl Marx," he was fond of saying.[15]

Subpoenaed to appear on Monday, October 27, Lavery had waited impatiently to testify. When he was overlooked, he confronted Thomas and demanded his time at the witness table. "I am an eager witness. I am no shy flower," he told newsmen. "If they hadn't subpoenaed me, I'd have been down here knocking on the door."[16] He pledged not to evade, dissemble, or filibuster.

Lavery was as good as his word. When Stripling asked the $64 question, he was prepared with the answer the committee had waited for in vain from six previous witnesses.

"As a student of Constitutional law, I am not sure the Committee has the right to ask this question," Lavery began, reminding the committee of his other vocation. "But let me break your suspense at once. I am not a Communist. I have never been a Communist. I do not intend to become a Communist. I am a Democrat, who in my youth w..s a Republican. Now if the Committee would like to know why I became a Democrat. . . ."

"The committee is not interested," Thomas interrupted, stifling the titters that began to spread through the gallery.

Lavery's admission was cagey: besides avoiding a contempt citation and risking the fortunes of the SWG on the tactics of the Nineteen, he gained a platform denied his fellows. With the exception of Maltz and Bessie, who had been permitted to read brief statements, none of the screenwriters had been allowed to speak his piece. Lavery having accommodated Thomas, Thomas accommodated Lavery.

"I'm here three ways—as a member of the New York Bar, for myself and as counsel for myself, and [as] the only authorized representative of the Screen Writers' Guild," Lavery began.

"You're here because you were subpoenaed," Stripling noted.

"I would have been here anyway," insisted Lavery.

Lavery made his case for the inviolable secrecy of SWG membership and its open-admissions policy on constitutional grounds: it was not up to him or the guild to weed out violent Communists. "If there are any offenders in the Guild, it is for the FBI and the legal processes to act after a complaint is made. Such a function is not up to the Guild." Privately, however, Lavery felt it was silly for the Nineteen not to admit SWG membership: after all, the guild had fought tenaciously for screen bylines that could be read by any moviegoer who cared to pay attention to the title credits.

Lavery vigorously denied the charge that "the Screen Writers' Guild had gotten more crimson" under his regime and argued that the best way to counter the Soviet system was to accentuate the positive elements of the American system. "I think that in our democratic American life the way to meet the challenge of Communism is not repressive legislation or scareheads but to show that we have a better way of life, to dramatize that life."

Stripling asked about the Hollywood Writers Mobilization, which Lavery had spearheaded during the war. The investigator thought it was the successor to the League of Hollywood Writers, a Communist front group, an allegation Lavery denied. As with so many of the witnesses, he was eager to prove his patriotic credentials and brandished a medal given to him by the Treasury Department "in recognition of my services as head of the Mobilization during the war."[17]

Lavery was asked if American citizens should be as militant in expressing their beliefs as the Communists.

Lavery replied patiently and at length:

> I think there is a better way to do it. I think that if we are to keep harping on the note of fear, it is like the old fashioned revival or the old fashioned mission, where you scare the devil out of the parishioners for a week and after that they are rather accustomed to the note of fear. I think these are times when we have to do other things to protect that which we hold dear. I don't think it is enough to make people afraid. It is very easy to make them afraid. I think the problem of all citizens and this Congress is how to make people aware of the love that they have for America. I think that the negative force of fear is distinctly negative, distinctly noncreative. I think the challenge of the theater and the screen is to project an American way of life, particularly in historical drama, that vitalizes the whole tradition of which we are a part. Believe me, I am much more interested as a playwright and a screen writer in trying to show, for instance, what Mr. Justice Holmes was like, rather than showing how bad Mr. Stalin is. It would be very easy to show how bad Mr. Stalin is. But I think that the positive values of our great American leaders are the thing the screen should be showing at this time.

As Lavery spoke, listeners harkened to the dog that did not bark: he was not being interrupted by Thomas. In fact, after giving him the floor, the chairman called Lavery's comments "frank" and "refreshing."

Seizing the platform for some free publicity, Lavery defended his forthcoming stage production *The Gentleman from Athens*, the play that Lela Rogers had labeled a Communist tract during their appearance together on *America's Town Meeting of the Air* in September. He invited "any member of congress" to a performance when it opened. Representative McDowell helpfully asked him to explain the title—a reference to the protagonist, a congressman from the fictional burg of Athens, California. "So great is my love of Congress that I even tried to become a member of its body," said Lavery, referring to his unsuccessful bid in the Democratic primary in 1946. "Since I couldn't become a member of Congress, I decided to write about it."

Screen Writers' Guild president Emmet Lavery tells HUAC he is not and has never been a member of the Communist Party, October 29, 1947.

Impressed by Lavery's forthright responses, McDowell paid him a compliment. "You are a liberal and liberals are a part of the American tradition." Lest he be misunderstood, McDowell hastened to add, "I am not a liberal."

The topic of religion again entered the conversation during Lavery's testimony: not Catholicism, but Judaism, the leitmotif of the day. *Abie's Irish Rose* (1946), a remake of the interethnic romantic comedy about a Jewish man who marries an Irish lass to the consternation of both their ethnically insular families, came up. Written by Anne Nichols, originally produced on

Broadway in 1922, and made into a popular film in 1928, the mixed-marriage romantic comedy was considered in its time a whimsical and progressive tale of how all-American assimilation overcame tribal prejudice. In the post-war atmosphere, however, the once lovable shtick and blarney played as a cringe-inducing throwback. The film had been roundly attacked in liberal circles for its retrograde stereotypes, both Jewish and Irish. Lavery remarked, "You don't have to be a Communist to resent bad taste."

McDowell interjected, "and I think you'll agree that you don't have to be a Fascist to have enjoyed it. I saw it four or five times, and I liked it better each time."

Put in a good mood by a screenwriter who would finally talk to him, Thomas joked, "Come now, if you gentlemen don't stop, you'll have me reading the book."

Lavery's congenial, plain-spoken testimony left everyone on the dais in a good mood. After a succession of obnoxious or recalcitrant screenwriters, Lavery was hailed as a credit to his profession. "Lavery was excellent," commented Red Kann at *Motion Picture Daily*. "Calm and always conveying an impression of a reasoned and reasonable approach."[18] Mary Spargo at the *Washington Post* was also impressed. "There was the usual, yelling screaming fury when the four [Unfriendlies] were ordered from the witness stand, but it was the guild president—no Communist—who stole the show before the House Committee on Un-American Activities."[19]

The well-reviewed SWG president stuck around Washington to lobby Congress to appropriate funds for the Library of Congress to preserve the priceless motion picture heritage held in its collection. However, at the very moment HUAC was insisting on the cultural centrality of Hollywood cinema, the Eightieth Congress doubted that film preservation was a worthwhile expenditure of taxpayer money. The appropriation bill was turned down.[20]

Edward Dmytryk: "I think that what organizations I belong to, what I think, and what I say, cannot be questioned by this committee."

A new species of Unfriendly—a director—was the afternoon's first witness.

Until his subpoena, the thirty-nine-year-old Canadian-born Edward Dmytryk was living the Hollywood-American dream. In the business since

1923, a director since 1939, he proved his bankability at RKO with a back-to-back pair of wartime potboilers and box office hits, *Hitler's Children* and *Behind the Rising Sun*, a twin bill that parceled out the nativist hatred toward two Axis Powers. He moved up to A pictures with *Tender Comrade* (1943), the big-budget, big-star home front melodrama scripted by Dalton Trumbo; *Murder My Sweet* (1944), a stylish film noir that guided musical star Dick Powell into a credible persona shift as a hard-boiled gumshoe; and the timely combat film *Back to Bataan* (1945), in which, he was quite proud to point out, the heroism of John Wayne took a back seat to the courage of the Filipino resistance.

Born in 1904 in Grand Forks, Canada, of Ukrainian-Catholic roots, Dmytryk had come to the Communist party late, in 1944, not through the funnel of the Popular Front of the 1930s, but the Sovietmania of World War II. He was lured by the cloak-and-dagger aspects of a secret society as much as the ideology: the clandestine meetings, the FBI tails, the comradery.

Yet Dmytryk chafed at the party discipline and enforced groupthink. When he casually mentioned to Adrian Scott that he was reading Arthur Koestler's *Darkness at Noon*, a novel on the CPUSA's index of forbidden books, a shocked Scott told him to button his lip. Though troubled, Dmytryk suppressed his doubts.[21]

Dmytryk's latest film—on the nation's marquees at popular prices as the hearings unfolded—was *Crossfire* (1947), produced at RKO with the full support of the most liberal-minded studio head in Hollywood, Dore Schary. It was one of the two social problem films dealing with antisemitism that year, jumping the gate on the more prestigious and ultimately more honored entry, the high-key lit *Gentleman's Agreement* (1947), produced by Darryl F. Zanuck and directed by Elia Kazan from the middlebrow best seller by Laura Z. Hobson. A film noir/social problem film hybrid, adapted from Richard Brooks's novel *The Brick Foxhole*, *Crossfire* was a progressive tract for religious tolerance disguised as a murder mystery.

The slyly titled film was genuinely groundbreaking. For the first time since the enforcement of the Production Code in 1934, blunt ethnic and religious slurs ("Jewboy," "dirty Catholic") were heard on the soundtrack of a Hollywood film: the Breen office granted the project special dispensation in light of its pure intentions. Though preachy and self-satisfied, *Crossfire* gave a good reading of the zeitgeist, which, under the circumstances, must have struck its makers as eerily prescient. "I think maybe it's suddenly not having a lot of enemies to hate anymore," says the soon-to-be-murdered Jewish veteran, pondering the fraught postwar atmosphere. "Now we start looking at each other again. . . . You can *feel* the tension in the air—a whole lot of fighting and hate that doesn't know where to go."

Like most Hollywood social problem films, *Crossfire* was faux-controversial: fearlessly wrestling with an issue most Americans had already pinned to the ground. Yet the fact that the only unfriendly director and producer hauled before HUAC were the pair behind the first feature-length assault on American antisemitism gave credence to the charges that, though John E. Rankin himself was not on the dais, his spirit was.

Keeping to the team script, Dmytryk asked to read an opening statement. He got no further than Ornitz or Biberman. Thomas rejected the request, saying it was "not pertinent to the inquiry."

The players recited their lines. "Mr. Dmytryk, are you a member of the Screen Directors Guild?"

Dmytryk was not going to answer, but he was also not going to make a scene. Feeling that Lawson, Trumbo, and Biberman had miscalculated with their rancorous performances, he was determined to be calm and respectful.

In a subdued voice, Dmytryk challenged the committee's right to ask the question. A brusque Thomas told him to get on with it. "The chief investigator will ask questions, and you will please answer them."

"All right," said Dmytryk politely.

"About how long a time would it require you to answer whether or not you were a member of the Screen Directors Guild?" asked Stripling. "Would five minutes be long enough?"

"A lot less," promised Dmytryk.

"Can't you answer 'yes' or 'no,' are you a member of the Screen Directors Guild?" sighed Thomas.

"There aren't many questions that can be answered 'yes' or 'no,'" Dmytryk ventured, repeating Dalton Trumbo's line but omitting the part about a moron or a slave. The question, said the director, was designed to bring about a split in the talent guilds "when we have just succeeded in getting unity among the guilds."

"Are you now or have you ever been a member of the Communist party?" interrupted Stripling.

"I've been advised that there is a question of Constitutional rights involved here," said Dmytryk, and, after some more parrying back and forth. "I think that what organizations I belong to, what I think, and what I say, cannot be questioned by this committee."

"Then you refuse to answer the question?"

Dmytryk followed the agreed-upon script. "I do not refuse to answer. I answered it in my own way."

Before Dmytryk could continue to answer—or not answer—in his own way, Thomas barked, "Witness excused."

Louis J. Russell was then sworn in to attest to Dmytryk's bona fides as a Communist. He revealed that Dmytryk had joined the CPUSA in Los Angeles in the spring of 1944 after being recruited by Herbert Biberman, who had been a party member for eighteen years. In 1945, Dmytryk had been promoted to a so-called "cultural group," which Russell described as "a special group of the nine most prominent Communists in the industry." A short recitation of Dmytryk's Communist associations was read into the record.

Having heard enough, the committee voted to cite Dmytryk for contempt.

What Russell did not know, and Dmytryk did not reveal, was that the witness was not, Communist party card notwithstanding, a member in good standing of the CPUSA. In 1945, after Dmytryk and Scott had completed *Cornered* (1945), a revenge thriller set in Buenos Aires, he and Scott were called on the party carpet for insufficient anti-Fascist zeal. Living up to his reputation as the Commissar-Gauleiter of the Hollywood cell, John Howard Lawson personally dismissed the pair from the fraternity.[22] In their testimony before HUAC, Dmytryk and Scott were closing ranks with a sect that had excommunicated them.

Though unread before the committee, Dmytryk's statement was released to the press. Like Ornitz, he attributed his appearance before HUAC not to Communism but to *Crossfire*. Undaunted, Dmytryk pledged to continue to devote himself "to a fight against these racial suppressions and prejudices."[23]

Adrian Scott: "I believe that I could not engage in any conspiracy with you to invade the First Amendment."

RKO producer Adrian Scott, Dmytryk's collaborator on *Crossfire*, followed his director to the witness table.

Movie-star handsome, Irish Catholic by heritage but no longer belief, Scott was an Amherst College graduate, former film critic and screenwriter, and current white-hot producer. In 1943, RKO signed him as an associate producer, but despite having moved up the studio food chain, he kept his membership in the SWG.[24] He teamed with Dmytryk on *Murder My Sweet, Cornered, So Well Remembered* (1947), and *Crossfire,* and the two were fated thereafter to be paired as a unit—not just by RKO and HUAC but by the CPUSA. Though also drummed out of the party by John Howard Lawson, Scott, like Dmytryk, refused to break ranks with his officially ex-comrades.

Scott knew what to expect at the witness table. "This fear we've been accustomed to—this adjustment we have made to taboos—are the allies of the Thomas Committee, the Tenney Committee, and their stooges within and without the industry," Scott said at a film panel at the Conference Against Thought Control in the United States held the previous July. "Our Fear makes us beautiful targets—we are in the proper state of mind for the operation of these committees which, in pretending to defend, actually subvert our democratic way."[25]

Naturally, Scott had a statement to read. "It is pertinent," he promised. "It deals with *Crossfire* and antisemitism." The Unfriendlies were determined to drag the issue of antisemitism into the record and Thomas was just as determined to keep it out.

"It is hard to read the statement and listen to you at the same time," Thomas said peevishly. He looked over the statement for a moment. "This may not be the worst statement we have received, but it is almost the worst." It was ruled out of order.

"I would like to speak about the 'cold war' now being waged by the Committee on Un-American Activities against the Jewish and Negro people," the statement read. Speaking of the team behind *Crossfire,* Scott would have said: "We detest anti-Semitism, we detest anti-Catholicism, we detest anti-Protestantism. We detest any practice which degrades any minority or any religion of any people."

Asked about his guild affiliations, Scott replied that the question "invades my rights as a citizen. I do not believe it is proper for the committee to inquire into my personal relationships, my private relationships, my public relationships."

Thomas directed Scott to answer the questions.

"I have answered it in the way I would like to answer it," he replied.

Thomas tried again: was Scott ever a member of the Communist party?

Scott stood firm. "I believe that question also invades my rights as a citizen. I believe it also invades the First Amendment. I believe that I could not engage in any conspiracy with you to invade the First Amendment."

After being dismissed from the witness table, Scott held the distinction of being voted the speediest contempt citation—two seconds.[26]

Louis B. Russell followed with the usual incriminating evidence.

Dore Schary: "Up until the time it is proven that a Communist is dedicated to the overthrow of our government, I cannot determine any grounds for hiring but by the man's competence."

RKO head Dore Schary, the afternoon's second witness, personified a newer generation of motion picture moguls: native born, articulate, urbane, liberal. "A large university casting its faculty roles, could not miss by selecting him as a natural to head up the English Department," observed theater critic Jay Carmody in the *Washington Evening Star*. "Actually, it is hard to write about Mr. Schary without making his opposite numbers in the movie capital sound like Oriental potentates who move through life with intolerable majesty"— which was a polite way of saying you could hardly tell he was Jewish.[27]

Despite the Ivy League demeanor, (Isa)dore Schary was more steeped in Jewish tradition—and more out-front about his heritage—than any of his fellow potentates. Born in 1905 to German-Russian-Jewish stock in Newark, NJ, brought up in the Orthodox faith of the Old World, he was from childhood onward an integral participant in the thriving kosher catering business run by his family. In a tight-knit community that was more *gemeinschaft* than *shtetl*, he got his first taste of show business, acting as master of ceremonies for the "special occasions" the family catered, directing three-act plays for Temple B'nai Abraham in Newark, and putting on shows as a camp counselor in the Catskills. Forever after, he treasured the upbringing and revered his roots.[28]

To his parents' distress, the young man in a hurry dropped out of high school at age fourteen to work as a newspaperman. Realizing his woeful ignorance, he returned to high school at nineteen and graduated.

Already a multi-hyphenate, he worked as a reporter, columnist, actor, and aspiring playwright.

In 1932, Walter Wanger, then an executive at Columbia Pictures, was impressed by an unproduced play Schary had written and offered the unknown playwright a contract at Columbia. "Hire Dore Schary," Wanger wired his New York office. "She writes with a lot of vigor—for a woman." At Columbia, he churned out eleven screenplays before Harry Cohn's tight-fistedness caused a parting of the ways. While freelancing at the studios, he continued to write for the stage, a forum more open to his progressive impulses, or so he thought. In 1937, Schary's *Too Many Heroes* opened on Broadway. An anti-lynching tract in which a mob breaks into a jail and hangs two kidnap-murderers, the play had an interesting twist: the perpetrators have confessed.[29] It closed after sixteen performances.

As an outlet for Schary's social conscience, Hollywood worked out better than Broadway. In 1938, with Eleanore Griffith, he won a Best Screenplay Oscar for *Boys Town* (1938), MGM's paean to democracy and religious tolerance at the orphanage-township in Nebraska founded by Father Flanagan. Even in the Irish-Catholic community of Boy's Town, the Jewish kid is allowed to keep the faith of his fathers, donning a yarmulke at mealtimes to recite grace in Hebrew.

Schary was soon entrusted with MGM's most expensive and prestigious A-pictures—*Young Tom Edison* (1940), *Edison the Man* (1940), and *Married Bachelor* (1941). Hankering to direct, he implored Louis B. Mayer for a chance to helm one of his own scripts, but Mayer counteroffered with a challenge to supervise production on MGM's B unit. Schary was enormously successful, vaulting several B-pictures into A-picture profits, most notably the heart-tugging *Lassie Come Home* (1943). He left MGM not over money but politics: Mayer refused to bankroll an anti-Fascist western Schary had written with Sinclair Lewis entitled *Storm in the West*.

For three years, Schary teamed with David O. Selznick for a string of successes, among them *I'll Be Seeing You* (1944), *The Spiral Staircase* (1945), and, currently in release, *The Farmer's Daughter* (1947). The last was a gentle political satire about a pretty Swedish-American maid (Loretta Young) who runs for Congress against reactionary opposition, a scenario Hedda Hopper deemed subversive. Schary's midas touch—a mix of critical esteem and box office gold—propelled him up the ranks of a studio system that craved both. In 1947, he took over as production chief at RKO, the most unstable of the Big Five, where, over the next eight months, he would oversee one of the studio's most innovative periods. The first project he green-lit was an indication of the temper of the new regime: Adrian Scott and Edward Dmytryk's *Crossfire*.

At the witness table, Schary identified himself as the executive in charge of production at RKO. Stripling asked him to repeat his job title. The chief investigator had had a long day: Schary was the sixth witness, not counting four appearances by the ubiquitous Louis B. Russell.

Composer Hanns Eisler was the first thing on Stripling's mind. Schary admitted that Eisler had been employed by RKO but that he was unaware of Eisler's Communist background until the HUAC hearings in Hollywood in May.

"What is the policy of your company regarding employment of a notorious international Communist?" asked Stripling.

"That will have to be determined by the president, the board of directors, and myself," said Schary. "But my personal view is this: up until the time it is proven that a Communist is dedicated to the overthrow of our government, I cannot determine any grounds for hiring but by the man's competence."

Applause, led by the Unfriendlies, broke out from the gallery. Schary was the first motion picture executive to utter that open-minded sentiment.

"If it was shown by his statement in writing that he was dedicated to the overthrow of the government by force, would you fire him?"

"Yes, sir," responded Schary.

"Then I will give you a copy of the testimony of Hanns Eisler before this committee," said Stripling, handing over a printed pamphlet.

"Will you hire him again?" interjected Thomas.

"I can only judge that in terms of the record. But if the charge is proven, of course I will not hire him. I can only maintain I will hire only those I believe best qualified for their jobs. If it is shown they are dedicated to the overthrow of the government by force, I will not hire them."

Stripling and Thomas persisted: would Schary rehire Eisler knowing what he now knew?

With the best advice of RKO's lawyers in mind, Schary refused to be pinned down. "I don't know if I would hire him. There has been a ruling in the Supreme Court which prohibits me from barring anyone from employment because of his politics. I would not hesitate to rehire him if it is not proven he is a foreign agent."

Thomas tried sarcasm. "Did you ever hear of Rip Van Winkle?"

"Yes, sir, years ago."

"Well, if some people in this country don't wake up out of their long sleep we are going to get what they got in France and Italy."

If that was supposed to be an applause line, the gallery missed its cue.

"I have been opposing Communism a long time," Schary said. "I have fought Communism any time I found it. I fought it in 1940 and I shall continue to fight it, but I do not believe it is as great a danger as some people believe it is today."

Schary's reference to 1940 was not offhand. The date was smack in the middle of the Hitler-Stalin Pact interregnum when the CPUSA had adopted the new Moscow line against a strong national defense policy and American intervention in European affairs. An authentic liberal, Schary had not abandoned his anti-Nazism at the Kremlin's command. That same year, he had also served as chair of the Hollywood for Roosevelt committee. Schary was never a fellow traveler.

"Will you continue to employ Mr. Scott and Mr. Dmytryk?" persisted Stripling.

"They are under contract to RKO," Schary replied matter of factly. "Our associations are very professional. I do not know what these men are pledged to. It would come as a great shock to me to learn they were foreign agents. At no time have I ever heard them say anything subversive, and they have made no attempts to get any Communistic material in their pictures."[30] Referring to the defiant outbursts of the Unfriendlies that morning, Schary said he "disagreed with their methods of answering the committee's question."

"Getting back to Eisler," broke in Stripling, "suppose, as one taking out American citizenship papers, he sent a cable like this: 'It gives us courage in the struggle and binds us to give all our strength in defense of the Soviet Union.'" Eisler's message was from the October 1936 issue of *Soviet Music*. Eisler admitted he had sent the cable during his testimony before HUAC.

A surprised Schary conceded the message would make Eisler less desirable for employment at RKO.

Stripling also held in hand messages from Schary. He produced a letter written by Schary to Emmet Lavery in April 1945 about a memorial tribute to FDR to be held at the Hollywood Bowl. The letter listed the names of several screenwriters—including Alvah Bessie and Dalton Trumbo—who were to ghostwrite remarks for some of the speakers.

"If you had to assign [the task] today, would you call on the same people?"

"If I had to call upon them today, some of my assignments would be different," Schary conceded, "but they wrote very American speeches." He continued: "I think there are Communists in Hollywood, but any time they have attempted to dominate any field or guild, they have been defeated. I don't think they have any weight either in organizations or in what gets on the screen. Most people in Hollywood are middle-of-the-road. I don't know of any subversive films that have been made."

Thomas cut in. "The investigations of this committee are making a very thorough investigation of some of the pictures. Very likely in another phase of the hearings we will devote all of our time to that very thing." The promise of future action was a tacit admission that with the exception of the dissection of *Mission to Moscow* and *Song of Russia* on the first day of the hearings, very little time had been spent on Communist boring-into of actual motion pictures.

Determined not to be goaded, Schary responded courteously to each snide remark and browbeating lecture. "I would only like to make one comment, if I may, sir, that I honestly believe that the people in Hollywood, management, labor groups, guilds themselves, are very, very conscious and very aware of their heritage as Americans." Schary concluded with a remark that was as close as he came to a rebuke: "Our desire to keep all American rights is just as keen as yours."[31]

Thomas then dismissed Schary from the witness table, but not before getting in a final dig. "Don't forget what I said about Rip Van Winkle." The crowd chuckled.

"Thank you, sir," was Schary's lame response.[32]

After the day's testimony, Thomas continued to tease and intimidate in his public pronouncements. He told the press he had a team of investigators scrutinizing a secret list of Hollywood films to determine the degree of Communist infiltration. A new probe, to be held at an as yet unspecified date, would take up the question and deal exclusively with films and scripts.

Thomas also tantalized newsmen with the prospect of a "surprise" and a "new phase" of the hearings the next day when a long-promised "mystery witness" would be called to testify. Speculation about the identity of the "mystery witness" focused on Ayn Rand, who had been in town for a week waiting to be called back, although there was nothing mysterious about her desire to reappear.

Thomas need not have resorted to the hard sell. Despite the lack of famous faces at the witness table or in the back rows, he was again drawing a full house. The high-tension drama of the confrontations between the chairman and the Unfriendlies seemed to compensate for the lack of star power in the hearing room. "Box office at the House Un-American Activities hearings continued to be the best in town today, and might well be the envy of all local exhibitors," reported *Variety*'s Florence Lowe. "Whether ignorant of the fact that Hollywood personalities had already left town, or general white heat of public interest whipped up by proceedings of the past few days was responsible for the long queues is anybody's guess. Whatever the reason, the public got its money's worth at this performance."

Angry face-offs, congenial banter, humorous asides—something for everyone. "It's truly 10 big shows rolled into one," blurbed Lowe.[33]

Chapter 15
THE CURTAIN DROPS

The ninth day was the last day of hearings, something no one that morning knew, except Chairman Thomas, and even he seemed to have rung the gavel down on impulse, or out of petulance. The decision was in keeping with much of his performance during the hearings: abrupt, capricious, out of nowhere.

Two more screenwriters testified, or refused to testify, that morning, rounding out what by day's end would be known forever after as the Hollywood Ten: Ring Lardner Jr. and Lester Cole. Both refused to answer and both were cited for contempt. A possible Eleventh opted to stand apart. Thomas had promised the day would also see a "surprise witness" and dramatic revelations. Neither materialized.

Ring Lardner Jr.: "I could answer, but if I did, I'd hate myself in the morning."

Thirty-two years old, the namesake of the beloved reporter, short story writer, and raconteur, Ring Lardner Jr. seemed to have eased by osmosis into the family business. Chicago born, Long Island reared, and Princeton educated, he was nurtured in an atmosphere that partook in equal measure of the corner saloon and the literary salon. Growing up in fast company, he matched wits with the likes of Dorothy Parker, H. L. Mencken, and Alexander Woollcott. Besides a lifetime of anecdotes to dine out on, the son recalled that his father also bequeathed "intellectual curiosity with a distinctly verbal orientation, taciturnity, a lack of emotional display, an appreciation of the ridiculous"— qualities that would serve him in good stead before J. Parnell Thomas.[1]

Like not a few literateurs born to privilege, Lardner was infatuated with the future that reportedly worked in the Soviet Union. In 1934, he enrolled in the Anglo-American Institute at the University of Moscow, an incubation center for fifth column missionaries to the West. He returned stateside to follow in his father's tabloid footsteps, landing a job as a cub reporter on the *New York Mirror*. In 1935, at just twenty years old, he was lured out to Hollywood by David O. Selznick to do publicity for Selznick-International.

Bored with shilling for the likes of *Little Lord Fauntleroy* (1936) and *The Garden of Allah* (1936), Lardner partnered with Budd Schulberg, another son saddled with a famous name, and broke into his first screen assignment touching up the script to *A Star Is Born* (1937). Moving on to Warner Bros., and out of his father's shadow, he spent eighteen months in the Burbank sweatshop before walking out the door, exhausted, a purgatorial passage that fired his dedication to the Screen Writers' Guild.

In 1941, Lardner and screenwriter Michael Kanin eliminated the studio middleman and wrote an original story for Katharine Hepburn, who in turn pitched the project to MGM, netting the pair one hundred thousand dollars. The result was the first Tracy-Hepburn pairing, *Woman of the Year* (1942).[2] Kanin and Lardner parlayed that success into a lucrative three-picture-a-year deal that granted them control over rewrites and final cut.[3]

When World War II broke out, Lardner enlisted for a trial term of ninety days in the U.S. Army Signal Corps but was rejected from active service due to an asthmatic condition.[4] Back in Hollywood, he scripted war-minded melodramas whose anti-Nazism was so relentless that escape-minded civilians fled: Tay Garnett's *The Cross of Lorraine* (1943), co-written with Michael Kanin, an indictment of Nazi cruelty in Occupied France; and *Tomorrow, the World!* (1944), about the rehabilitation of an eleven-year-old Hitlerjugend twisted by Nazi indoctrination. His current screen credit, *Forever Amber* (1947), was controversial not for politics but sex: though granted a Code seal by the Breen office, the racy costume drama about a saucy wench "who slept her way up and around in seventeenth-century England" (as Lardner described it) had been condemned by the Catholic Legion of Decency.[5]

Though not a founding father, Lardner was an activist member of the SWG, serving on the executive board and as treasurer. He had also fervently embraced the causes of the Popular Front in Hollywood—working for the Hollywood Anti-Nazi League, contributing to the European Film Fund for refugees from Nazi Germany, and standing shoulder to shoulder with the editor-picketers at the *Hollywood Citizen-News* when the ink-stained wretches went on strike. The youngest of the Unfriendly Nineteen called to the witness table, he was relatively unscarred by the Hollywood writers' wars, but not by the era's shooting wars. Lardner had lost two brothers to the anti-Fascist cause: brother James died fighting with the Abraham Lincoln Brigade in Spain and brother David, a war correspondent, died covering the Allied advance against the Nazis.[6]

After Lardner was sworn in and settled at the witness table, Thomas tried a change of tactics: the witness was told that he could read his prepared statement *after* he had testified. Perhaps the prospect of a nationwide soapbox would tempt this Unfriendly to cooperate with the committee.

Lardner wasn't biting, and was therefore denied the floor to read his statement aloud. "I make no claim to the genius of my father or the courage of my bothers, but I do maintain that everything I have done or written has been in keeping with the spirit that governed their work, their lives, and their deaths," he would have said. "My record includes no anti-democratic word or act, no spoken or written expression of anti-Semitism, anti-Negro feeling or opposition to American democratic principles as I understand them." As for un-American activities in Hollywood, a few frightened souls resided there ("men like Adolphe Menjou and John C. Moffitt throw so many furtive glances over their shoulders that they run the risk of serious dislocation"), but compared to what Lardner had seen in Washington over the past few days, "Hollywood is a citadel of freedom."[7]

Stripling asked the first of the two loaded questions: was Lardner a member of the SWG?

"Mr. Stripling, I want to be cooperative about this but there are limits to my cooperation," Lardner replied, and set the limits accordingly: "I don't want to help you divide or smash this particular guild." He then pretended he forgot the deal Thomas proposed, saying that he understood "I would be allowed to read this statement."

Thomas interrupted and demanded a plain answer to a simple question.

"If you can make me answer this question," said Lardner, "tomorrow you could ask somebody whether he believed in spiritualism."

Thomas was not amused by the reference to the supernatural. "That is just plain silly."

The previous eight recalcitrants had taken a toll on Thomas's already thin patience. He instructed the chief counsel to "go on to the $64 question."

"Any *real* American," sneered Thomas, "would be proud to answer that question, 'Are you now or have you ever been a member of the Communist Party?' Any real American."

"It depends on the circumstances," Lardner responded, and then delivered the single most memorable rejoinder of the entire hearings, a laconic comeback that might have been written by Raymond Chandler and rasped by Humphrey Bogart: "I could answer, but if I did, I'd hate myself in the morning."

The line echoed the rueful reflections of a girl, sweet talked by a rogue and plied with champagne, who had agreed to a sexual encounter she regretted in the cold light of morning. Lardner was not about to break ranks with his comrades and prostitute his principles.

However, the riposte was not quite Lardner's curtain line.

"Leave the witness chair!" ordered Thomas.

Lardner tried to break in.

"Leave the witness chair!" Thomas bellowed again, using his gavel as rhythm track.

"I think I am leaving by force," said Lardner good-humoredly, as the Capitol police swooped in. But he was not manhandled and he returned to his seat under this own volition.

Louis J. Russell was then sworn in. He lacked Lardner's quick wit, but not the key document: the screenwriter's Communist party registration card, number 46806.

Lester Cole: "Just let me answer in my own way."

Born in 1904, a Polish Jew who jettisoned the birth name Cohn for a more screen-friendly byline, Lester Cole knew the motion picture business from the ground up. He worked as a theater usher, bit actor in vaudeville, ditch

After delivering the most memorable line of the hearings, Ring Lardner Jr. is escorted from the witness stand, October 30, 1947.

digger at Warner Bros., script reader at MGM, and stage manager at Grauman's Chinese Theatre.

By 1930, Cole was an aspiring playwright trying—and failing—to crash Broadway. Like so many New York scribes, he sought sunnier more solvent horizons and joined the great sound rush to Hollywood. At Paramount, he was teamed with seventeen other screenwriters for the episodic *If I Had a Million* (1932), a resonant wish-fulfillment fantasy for a nation of Hoovervilles. Bouncing back and forth between Fox, Republic, and Universal, he worked on dozens of programmers, writing original stories, polishing, and adapting. His favorite screenwriting assignment was *I Stole a Million* (1939), less because of the end product than the fond memories of collaborating with the great novelist and mediocre screenwriter Nathanael West, a close friend, who wrote the script from Cole's original story.

During the war the only wound Cole received was a broken arm suffered during a baseball game playing for Paramount against MGM, but he made two standout contributions: the one-of-a-kind *None Shall Escape* (1944), a prophetic flash forward to a postwar future in which the victorious Allies prosecute a Nazi for crimes against humanity and the only wartime Hollywood film to depict the slaughter of the European Jews; and the conventional *Objective Burma* (1945), scripted with Alvah Bessie, a popular Errol Flynn combat film that saluted the unsung China-India-Burma theater of operations. His current screen credit was the musical romance *Fiesta* (1947), a piece of Mexican-set fluff that was the price a Communist screenwriter paid for working within the studio system. He was also developing a south-of-the-border project closer to his heart, *Zapata the Unconquerable*, a paean to the Mexican revolutionary.

A proud unionist and founding member of SWG, Cole rivaled John Howard Lawson as a strident, true-believing Communist who looked to the Soviet Union as the sole beacon of light in a cutthroat capitalist world. In 1944–1945, Cole served as SWG vice president and then president, always pushing the guild leftward. He wore his "Hollywood Red" label proudly, which did not mean he was going to reveal his true colors to HUAC.

Cole's appearance was briefer and angrier than Lardner's, but ended the same way. He asked to read a prepared statement that asserted his loyalty as an American citizen, lambasted Roy Brewer and James McGuinness, and assailed the men he was sitting across from:

> From what I have seen and heard at this hearing, the House Committee on Un-American Activities is out to accomplish one thing, and one thing only, as far as the American motion picture industry is concerned; they are either going to rule it, or ruin it.
>
> This Committee is determined to sow fear of blacklists; to intimidate management, to destroy democratic guilds and unions by interference in

their internal affairs, and through their destruction bring chaos and strife to an industry which seeks only democratic methods with which to solve its own problems. This committee is waging a cold war on democracy.[8]

Thomas and Representative Vail took a few minutes looking over Cole's statement. Vail found it insulting; Thomas concluded "it is clearly another case of vilification and not pertinent at all to this inquiry."

Cole objected, but Thomas ignored him and instructed Stripling to ask the first question.

Stripling asked Cole if he belonged to the SWG. Cole began, "I believe the reason the question is asked—"

Losing all composure, Thomas went into full tantrum mode, pounding his gavel furiously and hollering, "No, no, no, no, no, no, no, no, no, no, no, no, no!"

"I hear you, Mr. Chairman," interrupted Cole after the thirteenth "no."

"Yeh, you hear me," agreed Thomas.

Insisting on a binary response, Thomas told Cole to answer yes or no. Sticking to the group strategy, Cole said he was not declining to answer, but "really must answer in my own way."

Asked how long it would take him to so answer, Cole figured "from a minute to twenty." At that, the galley groaned.

Stripling moved on to the second question. "Mr. Cole, are you now or have you ever been a member of the Communist Party?"

Again Cole declined to answer in the prescribed yes-or-no manner. "Can I answer in my own way, please? May, I please? Can I have that right?"

"It would be very simple to answer," Thomas pointed out.

Cole said when he felt it was proper, he would answer, but for now he would stand on his rights of association.

"We'll determine when it's proper," snapped Thomas. "You're excused. Next witness, Mr. Stripling."

By then the Capitol police were approaching Cole to escort him from the witness table. A big round of applause went up from the crowd—most for Thomas's brusque dismissal, some for Cole's stubborn resistance.

The timekeepers among the reporters estimated the exchange lasted no more than six and a half minutes.[9]

Louis Russell took even less time to certify Cole's good standing as a Communist. Not only did he have a CPUSA card, he was a loyal subscriber to the *People's World*, the West Coast edition of the *Daily Worker*.

Bertolt Brecht: "I was not a member or am not a member of any Communist party."

The third witness of the day was a colossus of world theater—the poet, lyricist, and playwright Bertolt Brecht. The Hollywood trade press showed its priorities by identifying Brecht not as the renowned author of the libretto for the Weimar stage sensations *The Threepenny Opera* (1928) and *The Rise and Fall of the City of Mahagonny* (1930), but as the man who pitched the original story for *Hangmen Also Die!* (1943), Fritz Lang's wartime thriller about the assassination of Gestapo chief Reinhold Heydrich by the Czechoslovakian underground. Brecht's most recent play, staged that summer in Los Angeles and soon to open in New York with Charles Laughton in the title role, was *Galileo*, about the medieval astronomer who had recanted his principles rather than be tortured and burned at the stake by the Inquisition. The Brecht name had not yet become an adjective for theatrical wall-breaking and audience distanciation, which may have been just as well for J. Parnell Thomas was not keen on irony.

Before being called to the witness table, Brecht pulled out two cigars and handed them to his lawyer, Robert Kenny. "One is for you, and one is for me," he said. "If you think I am getting excited, please hand me a cigar and we will both light up."[10]

The cigar would be a useful prop. Speaking in a reedy voice, in halting, heavily accented English, the balding, tobacco-addicted forty-nine-year-old displayed none of the nasty temperament he was notorious for during rehearsals. Like many of the stage and screen professionals who came to the table to testify, he seemed uncomfortable with the bank of microphones in his face, which he was politely told to speak into. A translator from the Library of Congress, David Baumgardt, was brought to the witness table to assist him, but the translator's English was no better than Brecht's and his accent worse. "I can't understand the interpreter," Thomas complained, getting one of his few horse laughs of the hearings. Baumgardt and Brecht consulted on a word here and there, but Brecht spoke for himself.*

---

* Thanks to theater critic and blacklist historian Eric Bentley, Brecht's full testimony is readily available for listening. A transcription disk from the radio broadcast was made by a friend of Brecht's. In the 1950s, Brecht played the recording for Bentley during a visit to the playwright's home in Vienna. In 1963, Bentley released *Bertolt Brecht before the House Committee on Un-American Activities*, an album from Folkways Records, with informative liner notes, and Bentley's astute commentary mixed in throughout the recording.

When Stripling asked Brecht if he had ever been a member of the Communist party, Brecht asked first to read a statement. Thomas termed the statement "a very interesting story of German life but not at all pertinent to this inquiry." At that, Brecht gave a philosophical shrug.

The statement traced the all-too-common travails of a German-Jewish artist in the first part of the twentieth century—turmoil, menace, and exile, keeping one step ahead of the Nazis. After service in the Great War and artistic triumph in the Weimar Republic, Brecht had fled Germany in February 1933 for Sweden, where he resided until 1938, and then bolted for Finland. In 1941, in Helsinki, he secured a visa to America and took the Trans-Siberian railroad to Vladivostok. From there, he sailed to the port of San Pedro, California to warmth, safety, and gainful employment.

Brecht knew that ten previous witnesses had refused to answer the $64 question on First Amendment grounds, but the intricacies of American constitutional law were, if not beyond him, then of little concern. Besides, he was a foreigner, subject to deportation or, for all he knew, incarceration. Unburdened by American righteousness, he opted for the sophisticated European solution: he told some of the truth, shaded other parts, and played innocent. In breaking from the unified front agreed to by the Unfriendlies, he assured that the final tally of contempt citations would be an even Ten.

When Stripling repeated his trademark interrogative, Brecht paused a second before answering:

> Mr. Chairman, I have heard my colleagues when they considered this question as not proper, but I am a guest in this country and do not want to enter into any legal arguments, so I will answer your question as fully as I can. I was not a member or am not a member of any Communist party.

For a beat there was only silence, broken when Thomas drily observed, "Well, that's refreshing."[11]

"Is it true that you have written a number of very revolutionary poems, plays, and other writings?" asked Stripling.

"I have written a number of poems, songs, and plays and, of course, they can be considered revolutionary because they called for the overthrow of the German government," Brecht replied.

"We are not interested in any works written for the overthrow of Germany," said Thomas to Stripling.

Asked about Hanns Eisler, the playwright admitted that, yes, Eisler was "an old friend." Brecht could not very well deny knowing the composer; Eisler had just written the score for *Galileo*.

And Hanns's enemy-alien brother Gerhart?

Gerhart had visited Brecht with his brother Hanns and, on occasion, he saw Gerhart alone. "We played chess and we talked about politics."

Stripling pounced. "About politics?"

"Yes, he is a specialist in such. He is a politician, so he knew very much more than I did about the situation in Germany."

"Did you collaborate on a song 'In Praise of Learning' with Hanns Eisler?" asked Stripling.

"Did I collaborate? I wrote it," replied Brecht testily. "He just wrote the music."[12]

Stripling made a desultory attempt to dissect the libretto for *The Three-penny Opera*, the anti-capitalist musical that was too cynical about human nature to be fully embraced by the German Communist party. A convoluted excursion through a sampling of Brecht's writings and lyrics proved that Stripling was no more adept as a critic of Weimar theater than of Hollywood cinema.

On the stand for about an hour, Brecht wound up being complimented by Thomas for his good manners. "Thank you," said Thomas, exonerating a playwright who had composed genuinely Communist-minded theater. "You are a good example to other witnesses of Mr. Kenny and Mr. Crum."

Like Thomas, the press fell for Brecht's act. "The committee's effort to prove that Brecht was a red was futile and backfired to the apparent satisfaction of virtually everyone present," commented Lee Garling, the Washington correspondent for *Box Office*, himself also well satisfied. "Brecht turned out to be a nice guy who was not at all political and just happened to know the Eislers many years ago when they lived in Germany."[13]

Within hours of being dismissed by HUAC, Brecht was at LaGuardia Field boarding an Air France plane to Paris. After so many years on the run, he knew when to get out of town.

Louis J. Russell: "During the summer of 1943, one Mikhail Kalatozov made his appearance in Hollywood."

For days, Thomas had been promising a surprise "mystery" witness whose blockbuster testimony would blow the roof off the caucus room. He had even implied that the most ominous of all Cold War weapons, more powerful than even Hollywood cinema, would make a guest appearance: the atom bomb.

There was nothing surprising or mysterious about the man called to the witness table: the drearily familiar figure of HUAC chief investigator Louis J. Russell, making his twelfth appearance at the witness table. An ex-FBI man of ten years' experience and former director of plant security for the Thomas A. Edison Company in West Orange, New Jersey, Russell had been an investigator for HUAC since May 1945. This was Russell's only appearance as a star witness in his own right, not as a follow-up act to an Unfriendly.

In a tedious afternoon session, Russell tracked the meanderings of Soviet consuls in Hollywood and sifted through a number of back issues of Soviet periodicals that showed a keen interest in Hollywood programming. "In the publication called *International Theater*, which was published in Moscow, Russia, as the official publication of the International Union of the Revolutionary Theater, there is contained a great deal of information concerning the interests of the Communists not only in Moscow but of the Communist International in the motion picture as furthering the class struggle," Russell revealed.

No one, not Thomas, or Stripling, or certainly the disappointed crowd, wanted to listen to Russell drone on and read the articles in question. Stripling suggested that Russell simply cite the reference and the full-length articles would be submitted into the *Congressional Record*. The chairman readily assented.

The presence of Soviet consuls on the ground in Hollywood struck the committee as alarming. "During the summer of 1943, one Mikhail Kalatozov made his appearance in Hollywood," reported Russell. "According to the Soviet Embassy in Washington, D.C., the purpose of Kalatozov's being in Hollywood was to strengthen the artistic and commercial ties with the cinema people of the United States and those of the Soviet Union." Cablegrams revealed that Kalatozov's influence extended no further than a couple of minor distribution deals.

The gallery was already restless and noisy, let down by the head fake from Thomas. The chairman called for quiet. "The testimony is very important to the committee," Thomas told the crowd. "The committee wants to hear every word of it. We will have to maintain the best order possible."

Russell related a number of suspicious meetings between Soviet officials and Hollywood personalities. Just connect the dots and ponder the degrees of separation: Hanns Eisler and his wife socialized with Paul Jarrico, the screenwriter for *Song of Russia*, and all three rubbed shoulders with V. V. Pastoev and Gregor Kherfets, vice consuls at the Soviet embassy, and Joseph North, editor of the *New Masses*. For the prosecution, it was an open and shut case of guilt by association.

Russell also chronicled the animating role of the German Communist agent Otto Katz, alias Rudolph Breda, alias Andrei Simone, in the formation of the Hollywood Anti-Nazi League. Katz boasted that he was the first Communist fundraiser to detect the gold waiting to be mined in the Hollywood hills. "Columbus discovered America and I discovered Hollywood," he quipped.[14]

Russell touched, lightly, on the possible penetration by Soviet agents into radiation labs, but what the tangent into atomic energy had to do with Hollywood was never made clear. The investigator who had dealt out the solid evidence of the CPUSA cards produced no microfilm or secret codes linking the Hollywood Ten, or anyone else, to espionage. Russell's testimony, understated the *New York Post*, "failed to provide the 'sensation' in connection with Soviet espionage concerning the bomb that Chairman Thomas had promised." The *Daily Worker* scoffed: "Atomic Bomb Testimony Fizzles."[15]

After listening to Russell recite an hour's worth of Soviet-Hollywood interpersonal relations, Stripling had heard enough. A future executive session, he declared, was the proper forum to explore the matter before making more names public. Russell, however, was not dismissed from the witness table but told by Thomas to "just sit right there." The chairman had an announcement to make.

J. Parnell Thomas: "We have had before us 11 of these individuals; there are 68 to go."

If Thomas's surprise witness was no surprise, his next move was. Blindsiding the press and the spectators, he announced:

This concludes the first phase of the committee's investigation. While we have heard 39 witnesses, there are many more to be heard. I stated earlier that I would present the records of 79 prominent people associated with the motion picture industry who were members of the Communist party or who had records of Communist affiliation. We have had before us 11 of these individuals; there are 68 to go.

After that bracing threat (who else had dodged the bullet of a HUAC subpoena?) Thomas let the sixty-eight other potential Unfriendlies (or more?) know that the reprieve was only temporary, that they could not for long evade the HUAC net:

This hearing has concerned itself principally with spotlighting Communist personnel. There is an equally dangerous phase of this inquiry which deals with Communist propaganda in various motion pictures and the techniques employed. The Committee has a special staff making an exhaustive study of this phase. Either the full committee or a sub-committee will resume hearings on this matter in the near future either in Washington or Los Angeles, at which time those persons whose Communist records the committee has will be given an opportunity to appear before the committee to confirm or deny those affiliations.

Besides offering a preview of coming attractions, the statement conceded that the committee had engaged in precious little film criticism over the last two weeks: they had the goods on the people—articles in Communist periodicals, activism in Communist and Communist front groups, and, the smoking gun, CPUSA cards—but not on the movies. Thomas felt compelled to emphasize what he said it was not necessary to emphasize:

It is not necessary for the chair to emphasize the harm which the motion picture industry suffers from the presence within its ranks of known Communists who do not have the best interests of the United States at heart.

Thomas closed with a warning: "The industry should set about immediately to clean its own house and not wait for public opinion to force it to do so." He insisted that the committee was not adjourning *sine die* and that the hearings would resume "in the near future."

J. Parnell Thomas (*gesturing*) and Robert Stripling (*behind Thomas*) talk to reporters after the abrupt conclusion to the Hollywood investigation, October 30, 1947.

At 3:00 P.M., Thomas slammed down his much-used, oft-abused gavel for the final time.

Lowell Mellett: "I wish to protest this hit-and-run or smear-and-run action . . . "

The actor Larry Parks and the screenwriter Waldo Salt, who had both been notified they were to testify the next day, must have each breathed a sigh of relief. Also spared were the six other Unfriendlies waiting in the wings, beneficiaries of the luck of Thomas's draw: directors Lewis Milestone and Irving Pichel, and screenwriters Richard Collins, Gordon Kahn, Howard Koch, and Robert Rossen.

However, another potential witness was furious at being overlooked. Lowell Mellett had been fidgeting in his seat in the galley all week, eager to testify and redeem his reputation from the accusation that Robert Taylor had made in Los Angeles in May but retracted the previous week: that the chief of the Motion Picture Bureau of the OWI had dragooned the reluctant actor into starring in *Song of Russia*.

Mellett had been on Thomas's original list of witnesses to be subpoenaed for the October hearings but to Mellett's chagrin he had never been handed his formal pink notification. Once the hearings were underway, Thomas and Stripling had strung Mellett along, assuring him he would be called to deny the two charges that sullied his wartime service: Taylor's claim that Mellett had urged the production of *Song of Russia* at the behest of the White House and Thomas's claim that he had come to Hollywood "specifically on orders of his superior [Elmer Davis, head of the OWI] to see that Mr. Taylor played that leading role."

Immediately after Thomas adjourned the hearings, an indignant Mellett pronounced himself "sore as a pup." As journalists and spectators filed out of the hearing room, a radio reporter from WMAL gave Mellett a microphone and an opportunity to read his prepared statement. Mellett's statement was recorded and broadcast that night over the ABC network.

Mellett denied having anything to do with initiating the production of *Song of Russia*. "As for Mr. Taylor, I did not ask him to appear in the picture, or suggest in any way that he should," he insisted. "The statement that I did so on the order of an unnamed superior could only be to smear Mr. Davis or President Roosevelt." Mellett's role was confined to writing a letter to the Department of the Navy requesting that Taylor's entrance into active service be delayed until he completed the film. Stripling, said Mellett, had asked him to bring a copy of the letter as evidence, which he had.[16]

Mellett said that while in Hollywood in the winter of 1943 he visited Louis B. Mayer, who wanted him "to meet Robert Taylor, saying something to the effect that the latter was unhappy about not being in uniform." Mellett was unaware of what film Taylor was making, only learning about it later when director Gregory Ratoff got in touch by long distance telephone. He told Mellett that *Song of Russia* was in production and the studio needed to hold on to Taylor a while longer.

At first, Mellett misunderstood Ratoff's intentions. "I told Mr. Ratoff he must not ask me to help Mr. Taylor obtain a draft deferment; that our office would not do that for anybody."

Ratoff interrupted to disabuse Mellett of any notion that Taylor was a slacker. On the contrary, the actor was eager to get into the action and begin his commission in the Naval Air Force. Ratoff merely "wanted to know if it was possible for him to work on the picture until it was time to start training." Mellett passed on the request to the Department of the Navy and it was approved.[17]

The next time Mellett thought about the incident was when Thomas named him as having coerced MGM and Robert Taylor into shilling for Joseph Stalin.

Sam Goldwyn: "I had an idea it would be a flop."

Mellett was not the only willing witness left waiting in the wings. Producer Sam Goldwyn, an outspoken critic of the committee, also wanted a public platform to refute Thomas's charges. "The most un-American thing I have observed in connection with the hearings has been the activity of the committee itself," Goldwyn declared.[18]

Subpoenaed on September 25 with the rest of the witnesses, Goldwyn had repeatedly wired Thomas to ask when he would be called—after all, Goldwyn worked for a living. When Goldwyn's informal requests went unheeded, MPAA attorney Paul McNutt sent Thomas a letter making the request formal. Goldwyn, wrote McNutt, "is eminently qualified to testify in these hearings and I respectfully submit that his testimony should be received by the committee in order that it be enabled to accomplish its stated aim to 'give the American people the full facts.'"[19]

A month before Goldwyn was issued his subpoena, HUAC investigators H. A. Smith and A. B. Leckie had a memorable encounter with the famously mercurial and quotable mogul. "Mr. Goldwyn was very eloquent about the fact that he is a great American, that it is impossible for anything to get into any of the pictures that he makes, from a CP standpoint, and that he only makes two pictures a year, approximately," wrote Smith. "Although tending to be cooperative, Mr. Goldwyn's sole desire was to see that he did not testify in Washington, to convince us that he does not know anything, and if he did know anything, he was not going to tell anyway, even as he does not desire to put the finger on anybody. He stated that he does not have any [private] investigators, and does not really know anything."

While emphasizing his profound ignorance about anything ideological or anyone political, Goldwyn also demonstrated his determination to keep his mouth shut:

> He would not even tell us the name of one person with whom he had an argument over liberalism, stating that he offered to send this man to Russia with all expenses paid for six months, and see if he would like to live in Russia rather than America. However, Mr. Goldwyn steadfastly refused to give us the name of this individual.

Smith—knowing when he was outfoxed and not without admiration—concluded, "All in all, Mr. Goldwyn polished us off in pretty good shape without telling us very much."[20]

Testimony from the colorful Goldwyn would have made great theater, especially compared to the performances by the nervous Jack Warner, the meek Louis B. Mayer, and the deferential Dore Schary. "That Cong. Committee ain't heard nuttin' yet," wrote Walter Winchell, relishing the prospect of a good scrap as the second week of hearings commenced. "Wait'll Sam Goldwyn takes the stand."[21]

Alas, Goldwyn was never called. The mogul heard of the sudden adjournment of the hearings while cooling his heels in New York. "I had an idea it would be a flop," he told reporters. "It worked out that way." Having been overlooked, Goldwyn now claimed to have been eager to testify. "There are some views I wanted to express before the committee, but I guess the committee doesn't want to hear from me."[22] Although already famed in anecdotal lore for gruff nostrums ("if you want to send a message, use Western Union") and malapropisms ("an oral contract isn't worth the paper it's printed on"), Goldwyn had been crystal-clear in his denunciations of HUAC—and was poised to come out swinging in defense of *The Best Years of Our Lives*, a film that even Thomas had come to realize was unassailable.

Quentin Reynolds: "No one knows why Chairman Thomas concluded the hearings so abruptly."

Mellett, Goldwyn, and the eight uncalled Unfriendlies did not slip through the cracks. The scattershot nature of who was tagged and who was spared can be attributed to Thomas's work habits—and his expectation that any target missed or overlooked could be called back during the expected sequels.

More puzzling were Thomas's motives for the sudden adjournment. "No one knows why Chairman Thomas concluded the hearings so abruptly," commented Quentin Reynolds at *PM*. "There had been no intimation that they were nearing an end and witnesses who had been subpoenaed had about made up their minds to dig in for the winter."[23]

The next day, Representative McDowell told the International News Service that "some of the biggest Communists in the country were converging on Washington and planning some kind of demonstration," and there was no need to give them "a chance to pursue their usual tactics." Perhaps thinking better of the impression he had given of a committee of the U.S. Congress skedaddling before a band of CPUSA protesters, he further explained that he and his colleagues were flat "worn out" by the last nine days of hearings.[24]

Washington insiders speculated that Speaker of the House Joseph W. Martin was upset by the bad press the hearings were generating. With daily reports of the "circus atmosphere" of Thomas's show trial bringing discredit upon Congress, the speaker was thought to have put the squeeze on the chairman to close down the proceedings. "Reports were current in the capital that the Republican leadership dropped a hint to the Committee to stop the proceedings before they developed into another Howard Hughes fiasco," noted the well-wired trade reporter Manning Claggart in the *Film Daily*.[25]

Robert Stripling later explained that the dignity of Congress was indeed a concern, but insisted that pressure from higher-ups had not dictated the decision. In *The Red Plot Against America*, his 1949 memoir of his ten years as committee counsel, Stripling took full responsibility for the curtain drop. "The entire hearing was taking on the overtones of a broken record," he wrote, forgetting who had switched on the turntable. Like McDowell, he also feared that the CPUSA was going to picket the Old House Office Building and pack the hearing room. "It could have become as ludicrous the Senate's hearing of Howard Hughes," he claimed. Also, Thomas was taken ill soon afterward.[26]

The FBI was as perplexed as anyone about the hasty retreat. No sooner had Thomas whacked his gavel down than agents in the Washington, D.C. headquarters contacted Louis Russell for an explanation. Russell told the FBI that the committee "was running short of funds, and further that the 'friendly press' had advised them that it would be hard to hold the public's interest any further in the hearings if they were drawn out. It was suggested that it might be a good psychological move to discontinue while they were being well received by the public."

Russell confided that Larry Parks and Waldo Salt, the two members of the Unfriendly Nineteen waiting to be called, had indicated a desire to turn Friendly. The committee "felt that by postponing the hearings it would give these two men a chance to prepare material and aid the hearings at a later date."[27] This, of course, was wishful thinking or Russell's attempt to blow smoke in the faces of his former colleagues in the FBI. Parks and Salt had no intention of breaking ranks.

Whatever Thomas's motives, the motion picture industry was thrilled that the ordeal was over and relieved to have emerged, so it thought, unscathed. "The abrupt termination of the Hollywood hearings today is a complete vindication of our position," declared MPAA counsel McNutt. "The Un-American Activities Committee made serious charges against us. It charged that our films contained subversive propaganda. The committee produced no proof whatsoever. It even refused to make public a list of pictures which it said it had in its possession."[28] McNutt savored the irony: in the end, HUAC had refused to name names.

Given the force of Thomas's threat, the motion picture industry fully expected only a brief intermission before a second wave of hearings. "Congressional 'experts,' undesignated, are working now on material promised for unfoldment in a second phase on an undesignated date, in an undesignated city, which might be Washington or Los Angeles," warned Red Kann in *Motion Picture Daily*. "The second chapter in the hippodrome of the last 11 days will be open to the public, of course, so that even now the industry would do well to bolster itself for more sensational headlines provided by witnesses no doubt to be carefully selected by the committee in furtherance of its futile purpose."[29]

To the surprise of everyone, however, no second chapter was forthcoming, not for years, and then featuring a different cast of characters on the dais and at the witness table. Yet even as HUAC turned its attention away from Hollywood to other targets, the motion picture industry, seemingly the victor in a hard-fought battle, was preparing to issue a declaration of surrender.

(*right*): In the wake of the HUAC hearings, a Ring Lardner Jr.-esque screenwriter reacts to Hollywood's new editorial policies, as depicted by *Los Angeles Examiner* cartoonist Burris Jenkins Jr., November 1, 1947.

Part III
BACKFIRE

Chapter 16

THE WALDORF AND OTHER DECLARATIONS

On November 2, 1947, the Sunday after the hearings adjourned, at a dinner given by the Civil Rights Congress to honor Soviet spymaster Gerhart Eisler and seven members of the Hollywood Ten, the screenwriter Dorothy Parker shared a dark epiphany: "Fascism isn't coming—it's here!" Parker, who was not seized by FBI agents and remanded into federal custody, went on to call HUAC "absolutely awful" and "incredibly hideous."[1]

Despite Parker's dire warning, a giddy euphoria gripped the assembled diners. To all appearances, J. Parnell Thomas had scurried away with his tail between his legs. The central charge of his committee—that Communist propaganda infused Hollywood cinema—was risible on its face. "We said: Name the pictures," boasted Eric Johnston. "No corpus delicti was shown, and no crime, therefore, was committed."[2] As for the pro-Soviet films made during wartime, few Americans were afflicted with amnesia. The troika was seen for what it was, a pat on the back for a crucial ally, a form of "intellectual Lend-Lease," as James McGuinness had testified, produced on the theory that the enemy of my enemy is my friend.

"The Hollywood probe fizzled to a sudden end," gloated the *Film Daily*, "leaving a trail of unfounded and undocumented charges against the American motion picture industry."[3] *Daily Variety*'s alliterative headline—"Commie Carnival Closes"—showed its contempt for the wasteful expenditure of congressional time and money. Even if Thomas's pledge to resume the investigation turned out not to be a bluff, the motion picture industry would be primed for the rematch.

Buoyed by the postmortems, Hollywood filmmakers talked tough. Sam Goldwyn issued a statement taking "full responsibility for every word and every bit of action that has appeared in every motion picture I have ever produced" and defied "anyone to point out a single thing in any picture I have ever made which could justifiably be called subversive or un-American." Like director William Wyler, he was outraged that the much-honored *The Best Years of Our Lives* (1946), the film that had tapped into the postwar nervous-out-of-the-service mood and confirmed Hollywood's arrival as a mature art, had been labeled un-American.[4]

More telling than the trade press obituaries and statements from emboldened executives was a directive from the lord protector of the realm. FBI chief J. Edgar Hoover had lent conditional public support to the committee's agenda during his testimony in March, and emphatic confidential support in May, but he disavowed the October hearings once the reviews came in. Always jealous of poachers on his anti-Communist turf, he resented the implication that his agents were at the beck and call of J. Parnell Thomas. Hoover denied FBI involvement and left Thomas dangling. "The Thomas Committee put a couple of ex-FBI agents on the stand and tried to create the impression that John Edgar Hoover and his boys were back of the evidence," reported Broadway impresario and *PM* columnist Billy Rose. "I just got off the telephone with L. B. Nichols, Hoover's assistant at the FBI offices in Washington. He told me the FBI had nothing to do with the Thomas investigation. It was strictly a Congressional show."[5]

Still, for all Thomas's gavel banging and tactical bungling, not all observers felt that Hollywood had come through the crucible unburnt. "Regardless of the merits of [HUAC's] claims, the American public has received from the hearings the impression that there are numerous Communists in Hollywood, and they exercise a great influence on the production of pictures," declared Pete Harrison in *Harrison's Reports*, the trade newsletter that was as critical of Hollywood's Communist-coddling as the Hearst tabloids. As a result of the theatrics of the unfriendly witnesses and the flatfooted response by Johnston and McNutt, Harrison felt "there is hardly a person in the United States that does not believe that pictures are loaded with subtle Communist teachings."[6]

Harrison was only half right. The "subtle Communist teachings" were either too subtle for Thomas to pinpoint—or nonexistent. Except for Ayn Rand's appalled exegesis of MGM's *Song of Russia* (1944), the committee heard minimal textual evidence of Soviet incursions into Hollywood programming—a stray line of dialogue, a portrait of a hard-hearted banker, a communitarian subtext. Yet what the committee had indisputably proven was just as bad: that card-carrying Communists were on the payrolls of the major studios. A cohort of high-priced screenwriters and the occasional director and producer pledged their allegiance to a despised fifth column dedicated to the overthrow of constitutional democracy. The fact that elite artists soaking in the lap of Hollywood luxury were missionaries from Moscow stuck in the craw of millions of moviegoers. How could the moguls so lavishly reward such traitors? The Thomas Committee "has definitely established in the public mind that in Hollywood something is very sick and smelly, decadent and dangerous," wrote Hearst hit man George Sokolsky, warning that Americans "will find means of protecting the United States from Hollywood, perhaps by avoiding Hollywood altogether."[7]

Before the HUAC hearings commenced, a blustery editorial in *Variety* had demanded that Thomas, Rankin, et al. put up or shut up. "They say the picture business is full of Reds on the Hollywood end," the editors demanded. "Well, name 'em."[8]

Name 'em Thomas did, ten in number, with CPUSA cards attached.

Anonymous: "We'll fire them and let 'em sue."

Though the hearings had come to an abrupt halt, HUAC was not finished with the Hollywood Ten. The contempt citations voted on by the subcommittee had to be approved by the full committee (done) and then voted on by the full House (considered a formality). After that, the battle would move from Congress to the courts, with years of judicial hearings and appeals guaranteed to keep the Hollywood Ten—and the link between Communism and Hollywood—boldfaced in the headlines. As the defendants pled their case in federal court and the court of public opinion, the industry would be held hostage to the decrees of unpredictable judges and the loud protestations of employees exposed as known Communists. Only decisive action could fore-stall years of damaging guilt-by-association publicity.

In the weeks after the hearings, in public at least, Eric Johnston posed as a figure of stoic resistance. On November 19, 1947, at the annual Thanksgiving dinner held by the Picture Pioneers, a group of luminaries who had been in the industry twenty-five years or more, the MPAA president took to the podium at the grand ballroom of the Plaza Hotel in New York to once again defend and deflect. "Gentleman," he said, "we've been hexed. We've been excised by the British, excluded from some of the Iron Curtain countries, and X-Rayed for Communism by the House Un-American Activities Com-mittee." He bewailed the irony of it all. "While our industry is being X-Rayed for Communism at home, Russia and some of its satellites are excluding our films as instruments of capitalist propaganda. That is the number one para-dox of a generation."[9]

Behind the scenes, however, Johnston was desperate to stanch the bleed-ing. On the phone and in meetings, he talked with lawyers, moguls, and trusted members of the trade press, groping for a way out of the mess.

When exactly Johnston decided on a course of corrective action is unknown. He had been sending out mixed—actually, contradictory—signals since the crisis swept in with the Eightieth Congress. Sometimes he spoke the rhetoric of free expression, and sometimes the language of conciliation. In private, he was drafting a document of surrender.

Certainly Johnston had contemplated firing known Communists since the previous June when, at the meeting of the Association of Motion Picture Producers in Hollywood, he proposed a preemptive blacklist that would steal Thomas's thunder. Opposition from the lawsuit-wary executives dissuaded him. However, by the time Johnston convened the most famous meeting he would ever preside over, the fix was in. Billy Wilkerson, in New York cov-ering the confab for the *Hollywood Reporter*, published the substance of the statement *before* it was issued.[10] The meeting was less a brainstorming session than a rubber stamp.

On November 24, 1947, Johnston corralled some fifty top motion picture executives, producers, and legal advisors for a closed-door conference in the swank Le Perroquet Suite on the fourth floor of the Waldorf-Astoria Hotel in New York. "The most powerful group of Hollywood brass ever grouped around one conference table," as *PM* put it, had come, as Johnston put it, to "consider problems presented by the alleged subversive and disloyal activities of persons connected with the motion picture industry."[11] Johnston wanted the matter settled once and for all. The conclave was not just closed but unchronicled: no formal minutes were kept because no paper trail was wanted. MPAA bouncers blocked the entryway to the conference room, keeping pushy reporters at bay.*

The press watched as the power brokers from Hollywood and New York walked through the ornate lobby and entered elevators or traipsed up the stairs. Louis B. Mayer and Eddie Mannix from MGM; Jack and Harry Warner; Dore Schary from RKO; the two Cohns from Columbia Pictures, Harry and Jack; and independent producers Walter Wanger and Sam Goldwyn attended. The mogul of moguls, Nicholas M. Schenck, the president of Loew's Inc., the parent company of MGM, lent his august presence, as did his brother Joseph Schenck, representing Fox, with Spyros Skouras, though Darryl F. Zanuck, keeping his hands clean, was a no-show.

The MPAA's two big-name lawyers—behind-the-scenes man James F. Byrnes and HUAC potted plant Paul V. McNutt—were in the room to advise on legal matters, assisted by two legal advisory committees—one from the studios, one from the New York offices—no fewer than seven additional lawyers. The squadron of legal talent was on hand for good reason. The action the MPAA was contemplating placed the association and the member studios in serious legal jeopardy.

The risks were threefold. First, any coordinated action on the part of the producers might be read as a violation of the Sherman Anti-Trust Act—the very law, at that very moment, under which the Department of Justice was prosecuting the industry for monopolistic practices. Maddeningly, just as the

---

* However, the complete roster of the men in the room where it happened was a matter of public record: Eric A. Johnston, Francis S. Harmon, George Borthwick, Sidney Schreiber, Joyce O'Hara, Edward Cheyfitz, Kenneth Clark, and Tom Waller from the MPAA; Harry Cohn, Jack Cohn, and Abe Schneider from Columbia Pictures; Nicholas M. Schenck, Edward J. Mannix, and Louis B. Mayer from Loew's, Inc./MGM; Barney Balaban, Y. Frank Freeman, and Henry Ginsberg from Paramount Pictures; Dore Schary, Ned E. Depinet, and Gordon Youngman from RKO Radio; Jack Warner, Albert Warner, and Robert Perkins from Warner Bros.; Spyros Skouras, Joseph M. Schenck, and Otto Koegel from Twentieth Century-Fox; J. Cheever Cowdin, Nate J. Blumberg, William Goetz, and Charles Prutzman from Universal Pictures; James R. Grainger from Republic Pictures, Walter Wanger from Wanger Productions; William Levy from Walt Disney Productions; Donald M. Nelson for the Society of Independent Motion Picture Producers; Maurice Benjamin, Mendel Silverberg, Herbert Freston, and Alfred Wright from the West Coast Law Committee; Austin C. Keough, J. Robert Rubin, and Nate Spingold from the New York Law Committee; James F. Byrnes, Don Russell, Paul V. McNutt, Earle Hammons, Paul H. Terry, Charles Schlaifer, Samuel Goldwyn, James Mulvey, and Edward A. Golden.

legislative branch of the federal government was pressuring the studios to take collective (political) action against Communists, the executive branch was prosecuting Hollywood for practicing collective (economic) action against the competition. If the producers acted together to dismiss the Hollywood Ten, they were conceding that the studios were in cahoots, conducting a conspiracy in restraint of trade.

Second, the studios had entered into binding contracts with five of the accused screenwriters. Over the years, lawyers for the Screen Writers' Guild had perfected an airtight template for agreements between its members and producers. A major reason the moguls had fought to undermine the guild in the 1930s was because of the expert legal advice it offered members, counsel that kept them from being fleeced in negotiations. Studio writers could be fired for incompetence, disobedience, or moral turpitude, but not for refusing to answer questions before Congress.

Third, the Labor Code of California forbade employers from interfering in the political activities of their employees. The previous June, when Johnston had suggested firing known Communists, the studio heads had rejected the proposal for fear of running afoul of the state statute.[12] Now they were considering action they suspected was unlawful.

For two days, the moguls and the lawyers debated the legally treacherous and culturally sensitive terrain. Memories of the marathon sessions vary; in later years, the participants would give self-serving accounts: that Johnston and Byrnes forced an agreement or that Wall Street bankers threatened to pull the plug unless the poor hapless studio heads swallowed hard and bit the bullet. Up against the men who controlled the cash flow, what else could they do?

Concentrating the minds of the attendees was the disquieting news from Washington. On the first day of deliberations, the producers learned that the House of Representatives had voted overwhelmingly to uphold HUAC's contempt citations. The first to be cited was Albert Maltz by a vote of 346 to 17; next Dalton Trumbo racked up a vote of 240 to 15 (assured of a lopsided victory, many of the affirmatives had left the chamber). Contempt citations for the remaining eight were approved by voice vote, without a floor debate.[13] One of the few negative votes was cast by Helen Gahagan Douglas, who had managed to stop John Rankin in 1945 but was unable to stop J. Parnell Thomas in 1947.[14]

On the first day, the session began at noon. Johnston took charge of the proceedings and moderated throughout. He wanted to fire the Hollywood

Top: Spyros Skouras (*left*), president of Twentieth Century-Fox, and Louis B. Mayer of MGM (*right*) chat between sessions at the Waldorf-Astoria meeting to consider the fate of known Communists on the studio payrolls. *Bottom*: MPAA president Eric Johnston talking to reporters between sessions, November 24, 1947.

Ten outright and blacklist unrepentant Communists and fellow travelers. So lately defiant ("a man has a right to earn a living," he had snapped at John Rankin in March), Johnston had no desire to see his tenure as MPAA president dominated by endless wrangling with HUAC, exhibitors, labor unions, and anti-Communist pressure groups. Before the Thomas Committee, Johnston recited sentiments that might have been written by the Unfriendly Nineteen. Behind the closed doors of Le Perroquet Suite, he was bottom-line minded, risk adverse, and ready to perform triage. Dore Schary recalled that Johnston spoke to the assembly "as if we were members of an industry manufacturing secret deadly weapons by employing Communists."[15]

The MPAA president began with a bracing recitation of the industry's problems: falling revenues from abroad, rebuffs from anti-Communist markets in South America, and the domestic fallout from the hearings. Boycotts were already being planned—an American Legion commander had told him as much. Johnston warned that public opinion was beginning to "snowball" to the point where many Americans believed that "the industry was harboring Communists . . . that it was a feeling that was beginning to permeate the United States."[16]

The group had two options: to continue to employ the men and risk the further alienation of the American public—or flat-out fire the ten liabilities.

Mayer spoke emphatically in favor of the second option. Byrnes concurred; he had some qualms about the legal risks, but felt a strong case for dismissal could be made under the all-purpose "morals clause" inserted into the standard Hollywood contract. Don Russell, another lawyer present, was of the same mind.

By all accounts, a raucous debate ensued. Three liberals (Goldwyn, Schary, and Wanger) and one ornery cuss (MGM plant manager Eddie Mannix) opposed the emerging consensus to fire the ten.

Given the heat of the discussion, Johnston felt a subcommittee should be formed to continue the dialogue after the close of the formal meeting. Nicholas Schenck was appointed to chair the subcommittee made up of Balaban, Harry Cohn, Schary, Joe Schenck, J. Cheever Cowdin, Wanger, Nelson, Goldwyn, and attorneys Mendel Silverberg and Herbert Freson.[17] After the omnibus session was adjourned at 5:00 P.M., the Schenck committee regrouped after dinner to hammer out the details to the agreement.

To insure the opposition viewpoint was represented (or co-opted), Schary was asked to serve on the committee. He balked. "Do it," whispered Goldwyn, "maybe they won't go crazy." That night, as the group drafted its statement, Schary did what he could to dilute the language in the "foggy hope" he "could persuade the guilds to form a defense barrier to prevent wholesale firings and investigations." His editorial input accounts for the inconsistent tone of the end product, whose substance had already been composed and vetted by MPAA lawyers.[18]

The proposal was shared with the full group the next day. Again, memories vary about who said what and how the deal went down, but an inside-man account, related at the time to an official source Americans were unlikely to lie to, has the ring of truth: the FBI had an informant in the room.*

According to the informant, during a recess on that contentious second day, Sam Goldwyn told Johnston that he planned to *hire* some of the Communists who were fired and thus "pick up some good talent" on the cheap "and then watch them closely for possible propaganda."

When the meeting resumed, Johnston "asked permission to address the group," said the FBI's inside man, "and gave a brilliant and bitter speech."

The usually mild-mannered Johnston was furious that the producers refused to commit to decisive remedial action. "Gentleman, I don't know why you hired me. I don't need this job. You won't listen to me. You won't take my advice, you don't mean what you say, and you have no guts."

Goldwyn stood up. "Eric, I feel you are talking to me," he said, preparing to respond.

At that point, Joe Schenck cut him off. "Don't make a speech, Sam," he snapped. "Sit down and shut up or get out."

Goldwyn sat down and the meeting proceeded. "Informant pointed out this incident as one which helped to clarify the air in the New York sessions," was the dry comment from his FBI handler.[19]

At 2:00 P.M., in a tense moment of truth for all, the assembly faced "the fish or cut bait" moment as Johnston called it. The statement was put to a standing vote. Every man rose to affirm his assent.[20]

Thirty minutes later, in time to make the late afternoon editions of the metropolitan dailies, Tom Waller, MPAA publicity man, emerged from the room and handed out mimeographed copies of the statement to newsmen and photographers jamming the corridor. The reporters shouted questions at Waller, a former *Variety* reporter, but he said the MPAA would have no response beyond what was contained in the statement.[21] Johnston did not make an appearance to answer questions, but prior to the statement being released to the press, he filmed a newsreel segment to explain the policy to moviegoers.

Issued jointly by Johnston, on behalf of the MPAA, and Donald M. Nelson, president of the Society of Independent Motion Picture Producers, the statement was a mixture of mealy-mouthed duplicity and steely-eyed calculation. "We do not desire to prejudge their legal rights," Johnston said of the Hollywood Ten,

---

* The name remains redacted in the FBI files.

"but their actions have been a disservice to their employers and have impaired their usefulness to the industry."

Then, the coup de grace:

> We will forthwith discharge or suspend without compensation those in our employ and we will not reemploy any of the 10 until such time as he is acquitted or has purged himself of contempt and declares under oath that he is not a Communist.

However, the vigilance would not cease with the termination of the Ten:

> On the broader issue of alleged subversive and disloyal elements in Hollywood, our members are likewise prepared to take positive action. We will not knowingly employ a Communist or member of any party or group which advocates the overthrow of the government of the United States by force or by any illegal or unconstitutional methods.

Johnston conceded that the policy "involves dangers and risks" and that it had the potential to hurt "innocent persons," but the present emergency demanded stern measures. He invited the talent guilds—actors, writers, and directors—to follow the lead of the producers and purge accordingly. Whether the historical callback was to Hitler purging the Jews from the German film industry or Stalin purging enemies of the state from the Politburo, the word sent back an ugly echo.

What soon become known as the Waldorf Declaration contained no admission of wrongdoing on the part of the studios; the policy was justified as a dose of preventive medicine even though, as Johnston had often said, "nothing subversive or un-American" had ever appeared on the Hollywood screen thanks to the "patriotic services of the 30,000 loyal Americans employed in Hollywood." The declaration also called on Congress to enact legislation to assist the industry in expelling "subversive, disloyal elements." To further protect its flanks, the MPAA maintained that politics per se had nothing to do with the firing of the Ten. "The writers and directors were not dismissed because of their political beliefs," insisted Joyce O'Hara, Johnston's assistant, when letters of protest reached the MPAA office. "The action was taken because, by their refusal to stand up and be counted, these men did a great disservice to the industry and impaired their usefulness to their employers."[22]

Having weighed the legal expenses against the box office grosses, the moguls opted to take a calculated risk. Lawsuits from the five fired men under contract would inevitably follow, but the court judgments against the studios would be less costly than the verdict of moviegoers at the box office window. "We'll fire them and let 'em sue," was the response from a "top executive" quoted in the *Hollywood Reporter*.[23]

On record as an opponent of such actions in public testimony only a month before, an abashed Dore Schary tried to pass the buck upstairs. "The decision was unanimous," he said as he exited the conference room. "What I told the committee was my own personal view. However, I stated that the ultimate policy would have to be made by the president of RKO. That policy has now been established. As an employee of the company, I will abide by the decision." How would the studios actually carry out the policy? reporters asked another producer—Sam Goldwyn?—as he rushed from the room. "I'll be damned if I know," he snapped.[24]

The response from the Hollywood Ten was swift: see you in court. "As citizens and workers in the motion picture industry, we will avail ourselves of the fullest possible legal action," they promised. "Loyalty and disloyalty are being posed as loyalty and disloyalty to the corrupt practices of the Thomas-Rankin Committee rather than to the principles, practices, and traditions of the American people."

That same night came the first break in the (American) ranks of the original Unfriendly Nineteen. Howard Koch, who had won an Oscar with the Epstein twins for writing *Casablanca* (1942), and whose most seditious screen credit was the counter-factual *Mission to Moscow* (1943), signed an affidavit and released an open "Letter to My Fellow Workers in the Motion Picture Industry" declaring his non-Communist credentials. Koch had not been called before HUAC "to face my accusers," but he had been "libeled many times" during the testimony. For the record, he wanted it known:

I am not and have never been a member of the Communist Party. I state this unequivocally as a fact. In making this statement, which I do under oath, I reserve the right to refuse to make it, if I so chose, at any future hearing of the House Committee on Un-American Activities.

Published in a full-page ad in the *Hollywood Reporter*, the letter was an act of dignified self-preservation: Koch answered the $64 question but not at the witness table in reply to Chairman Thomas.[25]

In and beyond Hollywood, reactions to the Waldorf Declaration traced an arc of relief, resignation, and rage.

Billy Wilkerson took the edict as a personal vindication—though firing was too good for men who had betrayed their industry and nation. "If an authorized agency of our government, as is the un-American Activities Committee, asks the question 'Are you or are you not a Communist?' and receives no answer, those refusing should be jailed or taken to the Russian border and dumped there, never to return to disturb our peace and happiness."[26]

The nation's exhibitors, the branch of the motion picture business closest to the moviegoing public, were grateful to be let off the hook. Speaking for small-town theater owners, *Harrison's Reports* congratulated Johnston and the studio chieftains "for this forthright declaration of policy" and praised the decision to toss the Communists out on their collective ear.[27] No longer need a theater manager fear being accosted by angry patrons in the lobby or—worst of all—confronted with platoons of pickets in military uniform marching under his marquee.

From the ranks of anti-Communist liberals—an increasingly isolated breed—the response to the turnabout was stunned disbelief. "Rep. Thomas and his cohorts must be in ecstasy," wrote a disgusted Max Lerner at *PM*. "William Randolph Hearst must be giddy with the afflatus of one his biggest personal victories."[28] Lerner was right on both counts. From Washington, Thomas called the Waldorf Declaration "a constructive step and a body blow to the Communists. I am gratified."[29] The Hearst press salivated at the news that "not only the deep-dyed Reds but all the rest, all the way out to the palest pink fringe, were in for it."[30]

Only a few weeks before, HUAC seemed routed, discredited. With the Waldorf Declaration, the studios had sent up a white flag just as the enemy had left the field in disarray. Why, Lerner wondered, had "Hollywood surrendered without making a fight"?

At the time and ever since, historians have asked the same question. What had compelled the MPAA and the studios to cave in "so soon and so abjectly," as Otto Friedrich wondered in *City of Nets*, his 1986 guidebook to Hollywood life in the 1940s.[31]

The obvious culprits were the big money boys in New York. "It should be fully realized that this action was engineered by the major New York executives, the industry's overlords, and not by the 'Hollywood producers,' who form a different and subordinate group," explained Bosley Crowther at the *New York Times*. "It is doubtful whether they favored such a positive and drastic step."[32] The following year, testifying in a federal suit brought by Lester Cole to reinstate his studio contract, Louis B. Mayer said he was only following orders from MGM's parent company, Loew's, Inc. The executive ranks "felt something should be done about the men who wouldn't answer," Mayer testified. "They ordered us to do it."[33] That is, the great Louis B. Mayer was just a messenger boy for Nicholas Schenck, higher in the MGM hierarchy than even Mayer.

Yet not everyone was ready to give the studio heads such convenient fall guys. Johnston always insisted the decision was consensual and not coerced. "I presented the producers with two alternatives," he said in 1948 after a federal judge had ordered Lester Cole reinstated by MGM, "either they could employ persons thought by the public to be Communists and defend their employment or they could dismiss them. The choice was up to the producers and I told them it was up to them to fish or cut bait. The decision was entirely theirs. They made it unanimously."[34]

Unanimously, perhaps, but under duress. Johnston and the moguls were being squeezed from all sides: from the banks in New York; from trade journalists with their fingers on the pulse of the public; from powerful patriotic groups, none more feared than the American Legion, its ranks swollen by World War II veterans; and from the Hearst press, which was calling for federal censorship to "prevent further privileged indoctrination by the high-salaried camp followers of revolutionary Stalinism."[35] The ever vigilant Hedda Hopper published a letter from a housewife whose response to the hearings must have made the blood run cold in studio boardrooms. "We hung a huge sheet of paper on our kitchen wall," the woman said. "Each time new names were made public anent the un-American activities investigation, we wrote those names in with red crayon. Before attending any movie, we check cast, writers, directors against those names and, unless the picture had a clean bill of health, we cancel out."[36] If Hollywood refused to blacklist the Communists, moviegoers would blacklist Hollywood.

As if to confirm Hopper's prediction, unsettling news about the damage the HUAC hearings had done to Hollywood's box office revenues trickled back to the front offices. By one account, attendance at movies declined 20 per cent after the hearings. Reports from the hinterlands—anecdotal and unscientific but unnerving—told of an alienated vox populi. "The paying customers will gladly sacrifice an evening's movie entertainment rather than support what they consider the Commie menace," needled Hopper.[37] In Norfolk, VA, theatergoers were heard hissing during a trailer for Katharine Hepburn's current film *Song of Love* (1947).

The post-hearings consensus around Hollywood was that the tide had turned against the industry in the second half, when the unfriendly witnesses testified, or refused to testify, and Lawson and Trumbo were evicted from the witness table. "Editorial and critical comment, while not entirely uniform, was preponderantly adverse to the positions taken by Dalton Trumbo and the other witnesses," Johnston recalled under oath in 1948. "The volume and sharpness of this comment increased substantially after these witnesses had appeared."[38] To a generation taught public decorum and deference to lawful authority, the raucous disrespect of the unfriendly witnesses was a repellent blend of bad manners and bad politics. Hollywood's "product depends on the public's good will," wrote Victor Riesel, the labor columnist for the Hearst syndicate. "And that's what the Commie screaming in Washington was threatening to kill deader than a Pearl White serial."[39]

Along with the antics of the unfriendly witnesses, the wild rhetoric about the cloud of Fascism descending upon America galled the moderate center, which, after all, had fresh memories of the real thing. The *Washington Evening Star* was no friend of the "clumsy, flat-footed" hearings, but the Nazi-baiting from the Hollywood Ten was really a bit much. "They are not yet in concentration camps. The Capitol is not yet going up in the smoke of a Reichstag fire," it pointed out. "And Chairman Thomas, even if he be the sinister character that some seem to believe, has not yet reached the point where he can single out citizens for annihilation."[40]

Not annihilation, just dismissal and ostracism. In short order, all of the Hollywood Ten under contract with a studio received termination notices similar to the letters RKO sent to Adrian Scott and Edward Dmytryk, so lately the fair-haired boys behind *Crossfire*:

> By your conduct (in refusing to answer questions) and by your actions, attitudes, and public statements and general conduct before, at, and since that time, you have brought yourself into disrepute with large sections of

the public, have offended the community, have prejudiced this corporation as your employer and the motion picture industry in general, have lessened your capacity fully to comply with your employment agreement and have otherwise violated your employment agreement with us.

Scott and Dmytryk vowed to fight the dismissal. "As a footnote to the perversion of justice," they said, "history will record the temporary triumph of John Rankin of Mississippi, who in the halls of Congress brought the citation debate to an end with a calculated antisemitic reference." (During the floor debate, Rankin gave a mock-Yiddish inflection to the surnames of the men cited for contempt.) "We, the producer and director of *Crossfire*, a picture which opposes the degrading practice of antisemitism, feel that the film will stand as testament of our Americanism long after Rankin and Thomas are dead."[41]

In the long run, Scott and Dmytryk proved right. In the short run, they were the first official causalities of the battle plan laid out by the Waldorf Declaration. Neither savored the irony when, the week after they got their walking papers from RKO, Eric Johnston went to Philadelphia to accept the year's "Golden Slipper Humanitarian Award" on behalf of Dore Schary. The award was for *Crossfire*. [42]

Pete Harrison: "Gag the Prima Donnas!"

As Johnston and the moguls weighed their options and the contempt citations for the Hollywood Ten wound their way to the House floor, the members of the Committee for the First Amendment—founded in passionate idealism and flooded with artists eager to defend a precious constitutional right— fretted, panicked, and, in the end, bailed. Within weeks of deplaning in Los Angeles, Hollywood's liberal alternative to the extremes of HUAC and the Unfriendly Nineteen imploded. The middle ground, which Huston, Wyler, and Dunne had struggled to stand on, had fallen out from under their feet.

On the morning of October 29, 1947, when the Hollywood contingent departed Washington for the long trip back home, via Philadelphia, New York, Cincinnati, Indianapolis, and Chicago, the passengers had reason to feel satisfied with a job well done.

The broadcast media was still friendly, waiting at every tarmac. At the first stop in Philadelphia, a radio interviewer for the Mutual Broadcasting System cornered Bogart and asked whether he thought the Unfriendlies would be convicted of contempt of Congress. "I don't think I'd be able to answer that question because I am not educated enough in law," he replied. "I'm an actor, not a lawyer." The interviewer turned to Bogart's wife.

> *Interviewer:* I see Miss Bacall here. I wonder if she'd care to come to the microphone for just a moment. Miss Bacall, now that you've absorbed some of the Washington atmosphere and discussed the matter with many officials, what's your viewpoint at this time?
>
> *Bacall:* Well, I officially would like to say that I'm not in sympathy with Communism and I don't like it. But after witnessing the conduct of the hearing, I was really amazed and a little bit frightened by it, and I felt all through both hearings that I witnessed, that every American man, woman, and child should be there to see what was going on and see the way it was being conducted and the way I felt the Bill of Rights was being abused.
>
> *Interviewer:* Thank you very much for your opinion. Mr. Bogart, do you have something else to say?
>
> *Bogart:* No, I'm just obliging a photographer at the moment.
>
> *Interviewer:* Danny Kaye is in the room. I wonder if I could talk to him for just a moment. Danny, we're very happy to welcome you here to Philadelphia. You know your charming female lead in *The Secret Life of Walter Mitty*—plug—Virginia Mayo was in town last week.
>
> *Kaye:* Oh, fine! Does that have anything to do with constitutional rights?
>
> *Interviewer:* No, I'm afraid it doesn't. We just wanted to welcome you to Philadelphia.

Kaye managed to turn the conversation away from *The Secret Life of Walter Mitty* to the issue at hand.

> Actually I would like to talk to you people in the radio audience for just a minute. I was a member of a group that was present at the hearings one morning, and the industry, of which I am very proud to be a member, was constantly smeared and attacked as Communist-led, Communist-dominated, Communist-infested, which in turn makes us

seem like complete fools. So I would like to put the question to you ladies and gentlemen listening right this moment: Have you seen and enjoyed any of the pictures we have made? Have you ever read a line or heard a line or seen any overt act? Have you ever left the theater thinking that perhaps you might like the form of government being portrayed on the screen better than the American form of government?[43]

Back in Hollywood, the reception from the hometown crowd certainly lifted the spirits of the stars. On October 31, at Los Angeles airport, they were welcomed as conquering heroes by eight hundred jubilant supporters. "We knew we were sticking our necks out when we flew East, but I am certain that each one of us is deeply glad we went," Marsha Hunt told reporters. "We believe in the American tradition of one is innocent until proven guilty and the hearings were not conducted in that tradition." John Huston beamed. "I think this has been something of a victory for Hollywood."[44]

On November 2, Sunday afternoon, ABC radio broadcast the second episode of *Hollywood Fights Back!* The follow-up echoed the polemics and structure of the first, but the mood was audibly more self-satisfied. Myrna Loy opened the broadcast by claiming that "a rising tide of anger and public indignation" had forced the hearings to end early. Loy was followed by forty-two stars, writers, and politicians, many of whom spoke firsthand about what they had seen from the back rows of the caucus room: witnesses yelled at, gaveled down, and bum-rushed from the witness table.

The victory lap was premature. The second *Hollywood Fights Back!* show was the last time that CFA felt it was sailing with the cultural wind at its back. Henceforth, the group would be fighting back not only against HUAC but Hollywood.

The glare of publicity, as the passengers well knew, cut both ways, and the publicity blowback from the flight was turning harsh—remarkably so. Even before touchdown in Los Angeles, the scent of trouble was in the air. The TWA Constellation that picked up the delegation in Washington was named *The Star of the Red Sea*. Clearly visible on the fuselage in wire photos, the label seemed to mock the anti-Communist protestations of the passengers.[45] Had their would-be patron Howard Hughes tried to sabotage the trip with a sly setup?

Radio interviewers, eager to have the stars talk into their microphones, cozied up to delegation from Hollywood, but in the trades, the tabloids, and the mainstream press, the criticism of the trip to Washington was withering. *Life* magazine featured CFA in a three-page spread portraying the actors as credulous naïfs just this side of useful idiots.[46] Hedda Hopper's correspondents pledged punitive action. "Our clubwomen are going to boycott each one of the clique that went to Washington to protest against sincere Americans," wrote an angry matron.[47] More ominous than a boycott by Hopper's readership was the opprobrium of a patriotic organization Hollywood never wanted to be on the wrong side of. "The spectacle of a caravan of actors going to Washington to ridicule the hearings is an indictment of these individuals," declared James F. O. Neil, National Commander of the American Legion.[48]

Of all the scathing reviews of the trip to Washington none was more venomous than the screed penned by Pete Harrison, the exhibitor's guardian. Under the headline "Gag the Prima Donnas," he railed at the stars for their arrogant presumptions. "[D]id they stop and think of the harm they were doing to the entire industry, particularly to the exhibitors, by misleading the American public into believing that the entire motion picture industry approved of the attitude of the Ten 'hostile' witnesses, who defied the Congressional committee and accused it of Fascist tendencies?" he demanded. "Who gave them the right to speak for the rest of us?"[49]

The stars who flew to Washington had sought to present themselves as average American citizens who happened to be well-known Hollywood artists, men and women exercising their constitutional right to protest and petition their government. The popular impression was of pampered celebrities, alighting from the clouds like celestial beings to dispense their wisdom to the yokels before cheering on known Communists. For all the media savvy at the disposal of the stars, the flight to Washington had been a public relations disaster. How should they have played it? Traveled by train? Flown commercial?

Always too, despite the best efforts of the leadership, the residue from the Unfriendly Nineteen clung to the group. Encouraging the confusion, the Nineteen embraced the better-known stars and directors at every turn. "No nineteen men alone could have accomplished what has been done here in Washington," the Unfriendlies stated, after Thomas adjourned the hearings, ceding "the greater part of this first round victory" to "the Committee of [sic] the First Amendment for its principled stand."[50] In the public mind, the two groups were joined at the hip.

Tied to the Unfriendly Nineteen, castigated by influential voices in the trades, and importuned by panicked agents, CFA's membership began to peel away and run for cover. A pair of fundraisers—one held before the hearings, the other after—showed how deep the chill had settled in. Before CFA flew to Washington, Ira Gershwin had hosted its inaugural soiree at his home—a well-attended affair that raised thousands of dollars. When the delegation returned, Gershwin held another fundraiser—with only half the attendance of the first. A furious Danny Kaye shouted, "Here I am all the way out on a limb. I'm out there and I can see you guys jumping off right now."[51]

In the midst of the incoming fire, William Wyler wrote Billy Wilkerson at the *Hollywood Reporter* to plead his case. "Dear Billy," he began familiarly. "As one of the founders of the Committee for the First Amendment, I should like to have the opportunity to set the record straight on a few important items" in justice to "the actors and actresses who depend on public favor for their livelihoods and who exhibited great moral courage in publicly taking the stand they did."

Among the misrepresentations Wyler wanted corrected:

In the first place, no member of our group is a Communist, or in any way sympathetic to Communist doctrine.

In the second place, we have continuously emphasized that we did not, nor do we now, defend or attack any individual or group within the motion picture industry.

We spoke up and will continue to speak up in defense of our industry as a whole, and in defense of the basic civil rights of all American citizens.

Our organization is non-partisan, including both Democrats and Republicans. It is anti-totalitarian and pro-democratic. We welcome the support and participation of anyone in the motion [picture] industry who believes with us that the motion picture screen should remain free of intimidation, coercion or censorship by any agency of the government.

Wyler closed with a plea to Wilkerson that "you, personally, will feel able to support our stand."[52]

Not likely. Wilkerson answered Wyler on the front page of the *Hollywood Reporter* the next day. Well-meaning doe-eyed liberals like Wyler and the other members of the Committee for the First Amendment were blind to how cynically the Communists had played them. "All you liberals who have been liberal in your thinking and, innocently, have lent your names, your voices, and some of your money to causes you felt were in need of support, only to find out, if you have but a slight ability to analyze, that you were supporting a COMMUNISTIC cause, why not change your sights and plot a new course for liberalism?" he jeered. "True, most of the causes and issues that our suckers here go for, lend their names and donate money to support, are not immediately recognized by the suckers," but it was time for Wyler and his ilk to wake up and admit they'd been hoodwinked.[53]

Writing in support of the Waldorf Declaration a few weeks after receiving Wyler's letter, Wilkerson used numerology to link CFA with the men who had just been sacked from the studios. Johnston's timely action "will immediately take the sting off motion pictures that was triggered by the 'unfriendly 19' and the 'airborne 22' who flew to Washington to support those who refused to answer that $64 question."[54]

Soon enough, the airborne 22, and their allies on the ground, would have more to answer for than the $64 question.

Humphrey Bogart: "I ended up with my picture on the front page of the *Daily Worker*."

Unlike the expendable Hollywood Ten, the cargo aboard *The Star of the Red Sea* was too valuable to toss overboard. Still, it was tainted and needed to be cleansed before being fit again for the screen.

After the Waldorf Declaration, Louis B. Mayer returned to Hollywood to begin what he called "backyard cleaning."[55] "I am going to start in when I go to my office Friday and other film leaders are going to do likewise," Mayer promised. "The people who are wrong are going to be out. The people who are right will be protected."[56] A committee made up of Mayer, Joe Schenck, Dore Schary, Henry Ginsberg, head of Paramount Pictures, and Harry Cohn was tasked with making the guilds toe the MPAA line. In a series of hastily scheduled meetings arranged for a "full discussion of the industry's purge" (as *Variety* frankly called the policy), the producers explained to the guilds the need for drastic action and tried to persuade them to vote their support.

Of special concern were the dozens of prominent actors—representing a huge capital investment—who had signed up with CFA. "Problem of removing any stigma from the First Amendment Committee made up of Hollywoodites who are above suspicion but whose patriotic and emotional actions perhaps may handicap their professional status and box office value, will be among the things discussed," reported a tactfully phrased report in *Daily Variety*. "In regards to the First Amendment group, executives take [the] attitude that it would be [un]fortunate if [the] committee's zeal should harm [the] professional standing [of the stars]."[57]

More than any member of CFA, Bogart stood squarely in the crosshairs. In Chicago, on the trip back to Hollywood, while still raising money and fronting for the group, he received a "frantic telephone call" from producer Mark Hellinger, his partner in an independent film venture. Hellinger informed Bogart that the Wall Street banks had refused further financing unless Bogart disassociated himself from CFA.[58] Sniping from the sidelines, Hedda Hopper reprinted letters from readers whose sentiments echoed her own. "These gee-gaws, led by hero Humphrey Bogart into Washington, are not for me," wrote a woman from Iowa City. "I wouldn't see one of Bogie's pictures if he stuck his smoking rod into my ribs."[59] The Hearst press matched Hopper's Bogart fixation and did not forget his wife. "The Thomas Committee is investigating America's foremost enemy, the hater of our people, the foe of our way of life, the poisoner of the minds of our children—Communism!" bellowed the *New York Mirror*. "Speak Bogart and Bacall! Is that your grievance?"[60]

Bogart was not the only passenger feeling the heat. "Remaining members of the Committee claim they have been under great pressure to disavow the organization," *Variety* reported. "They fear that if they take any stand against the Thomas Committee, they risk being branded as Commies."[61]

When the Waldorf Declaration put the full weight of the motion picture industry behind a blacklist, Bogart and his co-stars were up against Hollywood as well as Washington. "We don't intend to stand still in the future for those people who continue to shoot off their mouths on all issues and on many and various subjects contrary to our good American democracy," an unnamed motion picture executive told Billy Wilkerson. "We won't permit them to place our industry in jeopardy any longer through their private opinions that become public because of the value of their names and the prominence the motion picture has given them through their employment."[62] Bogart could choose his principles or his profession.

The decision was never in doubt. On December 2, while in Chicago doing publicity for *Dark Passage* (1947), Bogart and Bacall made a very public, very humiliating recantation. "The purpose of our trip was to go to defend the First Amendment of the Constitution, but in the shuffle we became adopted by the Communists," Bogart said. "And I ended up with my picture on the front page of the *Daily Worker*." He wasn't exaggerating: the week he flew to Washington, Bogart's picture was on the front page of the *Daily Worker*—twice.

Bogart expanded on his comments in a formal statement of apology. "My recent trip to Washington, where I appeared with a group of motion picture people, has become the subject of such confused and erroneous interpretations that I feel the situation should be clarified," he began. For the record:

> I am not a communist.
>
> I am not a Communist sympathizer.
>
> I detest Communism just as any other decent American does.
>
> I have never in my life been identified with any group which was even sympathetic to Communism.
>
> My name will not be found on any Communist front organization nor as a sponsor of anything Communistic.

Then, in person, facing the press, Bogart ate his diet of crow. "I went to Washington because I thought fellow Americans were being deprived of their Constitutional Rights, and for that reason alone," he declared. "I am an American. And very likely, like a good many of the rest of you, sometimes a foolish and impetuous American." He paused. "I see now that my trip was ill-advised, foolish, and impetuous, but at the time it seemed the thing to do."

As Bogart read the statement, he stumbled slightly over the word "impetuous." "That word never came out of me," he muttered, indicating that the press-agent-written apology was something of a forced confession. "We went in green and they beat our brains out," he said after reading the formal statement, which sounded more like him. Bogart was asked if the statement also represented his wife's views. "I am making the statement, but it includes her," he replied. "I still believe the man wears the pants in the family and what I say goes for the whole family." Having surrendered his masculinity in one realm, Bogart may have felt compelled to overcompensate in another. "I agree 100 percent," said Bacall loyally.[63] Bogart's act of contrition was capped with an article published under his byline in *Photoplay* in May 1948: "I'm No Communist."[64]

Also under siege, Katharine Hepburn followed Bogart to the confessional. Though not a member of the Washington delegation, she had been a prominent critic of the Thomas Committee and a signatory to the CFA advertisements. In May, she had assailed the HUAC hearings in Los Angeles and lent her support to the far-left Progressive Party and its soon-to-be fellow traveling candidate for president, Henry A. Wallace.

On December 9, 1947, Fulton Lewis Jr., the popular conservative radio commentator, announced on his broadcast:

> Miss Hepburn has followed the lead of moving picture actor Humphrey Bogart in disavowing any further connection with the so-called Hollywood Committee for the First Amendment—the group that published that advertisement against the House Un-American Activities investigation and which sponsored the protest to Washington which was led in person by Mr. Bogart and his wife, Lauren Bacall.

Like the famously hard-boiled Bogart, the famously sharp-minded Hepburn posed as a ditzy thespian mouthing lines she was too dim to understand:

> A spokesman for Miss Hepburn told me today she has withdrawn from the Committee and that she never made any contribution to it. He said that Miss Hepburn was dragged unwittingly into making the speech for the Henry Wallace rally—someone else was supposed to make it and could not appear so she stepped in at the last moment not knowing just what she was getting into.[65]

For CFA, the recantations of Bogart and Hepburn were the final nails in the coffin. On February 24, 1948, the group formally disbanded. The obituary in *Variety* was terse. "Under present conditions in the film industry, members of the Committee for the First Amendment have found it virtually impossible to keep the group functioning," read the death notice. "Any attempt for fund raising for such a cause is hopeless. This has been particularly true since Humphrey Bogart issued his retraction, after accompanying the other Committee members to Washington."[66]

"Bogart was a frightened man," recalled his agent Sam Jaffe. "He talked big but he didn't take any risks. He wanted to play it safe. He was frightened by [his business agent] Morgan [Maree]. Morgan said, 'you better get out, withdraw,' and he did." More kindly, Jaffe reflected, "I mean, you know, let's face it, when your career is at stake, what else have you got in life?"*

The pressure Bogart was under—and a sense of the toxic atmosphere and rattle-brained nature of the times—is captured in a story Ring Lardner Jr. told about two women who attended the HUAC hearings. Outside the caucus room, Lardner eavesdropped on the pair as they discussed Bogart's involvement in the Committee for the First Amendment.

"He's a Communist," said one of the women. "I won't be going to any more of his movies."

"No, he isn't," her friend corrected her. "He's an *anti*-Communist."

"I don't care what kind of Communist he is," responded the first woman. "I'm still not going to go to any more of his movies."

---

* Barbara Hall, *An Oral History with Sam Jaffe*, Margaret Herrick Library, Academy of Motion Picture Arts and Sciences, 1992: 257; 270.

Chapter 17

BLACKLISTS AND CASUALTY LISTS

hen J. Parnell Thomas banged his battered gavel down on Hollywood for the last time, he vowed that the hearings he had presided over for the past nine days would be but the first round in an ongoing congressional grudge match. It was the final unfulfilled promise of his meandering show trial.

For Hollywood, 1947 had been a bad year. For Thomas, 1948 would be worse. In January, while on a trip to investigate Communist activity in the Panama Canal Zone, he was stricken with internal hemorrhaging. Evacuated to Walter Reed Hospital, he contracted jaundice from a blood plasma transfusion and spent much of the first half of the year recuperating. In June, George Dixon, the Hearst columnist who wanted to see unfriendly lawyer Charles Katz throttled by Capitol police, visited the convalescing congressman. "I wished to consult him about the Red menace, not the yellow," Dixon couldn't resist joking. "The usually red-faced Commie-curber was a dull saffron."

Keeping to the color scheme, Thomas spoke with enthusiasm about his future plans. "The Hollywood hearing last October will seem like pink tea compared to the one coming up," he promised. "Our investigators have uncovered sensational evidence. We are going to expose 26 members of the industry as Communist party cardholders! Among them are some of the most celebrated names in filmdom!"[1]

Thomas's hospital-bed declaration confirmed a tactical shift in HUAC strategy. Nothing could shake Thomas's conviction that Hollywood was "an important vineyard for the Communists to cultivate," but, in a recantation almost as stunning as Humphrey Bogart's, he had come to see the error of one of his ways. Examining Hollywood pictures for Communist subtexts was no job for politicians. "I have since realized," he told *Liberty* magazine in June 1948, "that my idea was both overambitious and dangerous." Overambitious because HUAC investigators simply didn't possess the film smarts to undertake a close textual analysis of American cinema, dangerous because congressional pressure jeopardized the rights of "a free screen." Henceforth, "the Committee feels that it is sufficient to point out Communists in Hollywood jobs."[2]

However, a more pressing threat, an actual one, soon forced HUAC to turn attention away from the studio system to an institution closer to home, across town in fact, the U.S. Department of State. On August 3, 1948, a frumpy, obese, manic-depressive editor from *Time* magazine named Whittaker Chambers testified, first in executive session and later that day in a public hearing, that an urbane, trim, and seemingly well-adjusted cynosure of the Washington-New York establishment named Alger Hiss had been a Communist agent in the 1930s.[3]

Over the dog days of August 1948, the Hiss-Chambers case mesmerized the nation with a crossfire of charges and countercharges, a he-said/he-said political thriller not about subliminal boring-from-within but flat-out espionage. Not only were the stakes higher—the trading of top-secret material and the penetration of Soviet agents into the highest levels of the American government—but a clear narrative line shot through the inquiry: which man was telling the truth. Also, in a harbinger of a media revolution in the making, the Hiss-Chambers face-off was televised to a small but influential demographic in Washington, D.C. and New York.[4]

The Hiss-Chambers case was a mystery story from out of the past with shadowy characters, taut suspense, surprise revelations, and even a romantic undercurrent of the kind the Production Code would never have permitted: did the ugly duckling Chambers harbor a grudge against the swan-like Hiss for spurning his homosexual overtures? Sharpening an eye for the jugular that would serve him well, Richard Nixon, who had wisely stood down in the Hollywood hearings, led the charge against Hiss, an unctuous patrician ripe for the takedown by a poor Quaker-bred nobody.

On August 26, 1948, with the sensational Hiss-Chambers hearings off the plate for the time being and thrown into the courts, Thomas tried to make good on his promise with the announcement that a new round of hearings into Hollywood and Communism was to begin on September 7. The targeted twenty-six Hollywood figures whose "Communist records" were in the committee files would be subpoenaed.[5]

Communists, former Communists, and standard-issue liberals braced for a second raft of summonses. Yet in time-honored end-reel fashion a last-minute reprieve arrived from an unlikely quarter. On November 8, 1948, after being on the receiving end of a subpoena of his own, Thomas was indicted by a federal grand jury for padding his congressional payroll and taking kickbacks. A long-time Thomas nemesis, Washington columnist Drew Pearson, broke the story, possessed the incriminating documents, and instigated the prosecution. Busy fighting a federal indictment, Thomas announced he was unable to "devote full time" to HUAC.

In Hollywood, the air was thick with schadenfreude. Thomas's plans to resume his probe of the motion picture industry, gloated *Variety*, "may now be filed and forgotten."[6]

The news from the 1948 elections was even better: HUAC committee members Richard B. Vail and John McDowell were defeated at the polls; Thomas barely survived. "Let Us Give Thanks," declared the Hollywood Ten, who held a holiday-themed "Thanksgiving meeting" to celebrate "the downfall of the inquisitors."[7]

Of course, the inquisitors without portfolio were still operating in Hollywood. After the Waldorf Declaration, the blacklist was official policy throughout the motion picture industry. Eric Johnston, the great hope of enlightened postwar business practices, oversaw a regime more intolerant and destructive than the moral policing put in place by Will Hays. Johnston earned a derisive moniker: "Eric the Red-hunter."[8]

An array of anti-Communist sentinels inspected, condemned, cleared, and booted from employment suspected Communists and fellow travelers: Roy Brewer at IATSE, Ronald Reagan at SAG, and a battery of self-styled security experts and legal fixers hired by the studios, the radio and television networks, and the advertising agencies awarded their version of a Code purity seal to aspiring workers. Set up in 1948, a group with a euphemistic name, the Motion Picture Industry Council (MPIC), coordinated the implementation of the blacklist across the studios and throughout the guilds and unions. In 1951, the council commandeered the newsreels to assure moviegoers that "Hollywood is 100 percent anti-Communist and bears no sympathy for individuals who have taken refuge behind the First and Fifth

Amendments to refuse to answer the questions of the House Un-American Activities Committee."[9]

From a hard-nosed business perspective, the blacklist was a splendid success. By purging card-carrying CPUSA members and sundry fellow travelers, the motion picture industry assured politicians and the public that Hollywood was no more tolerant of Communists than the rest of the country. "The issuance of [the Waldorf Declaration] and its contents received extensive and wide notice and publicity in newspapers and over radio throughout the United States," stated Johnston, under oath in 1948, testifying in Dalton Trumbo's breach of contract suit against MGM. "Almost immediately, I noted a sharp change in public attitude toward the motion picture industry in respect of the matters as to which the public, until then, had been sharply critical." Threats of boycotts evaporated, calls for federal censorship were suspended, and congressmen expressed condign approval.[10]

Meanwhile, the Hollywood Ten had taken the studios up on their so-sue-us taunt. In the next years, even as the case against the Ten for contempt of Congress wound its way to the Supreme Court, five of the ten under contract with the studios sued in civil court for breach of contract. The plaintiffs had the satisfaction of forcing Waldorf conspirators Eric Johnston, Louis B. Mayer, Eddie Mannix, Jack L. Warner, and Sam Goldwyn to endure a grilling, under oath, from unfriendly lawyers. Ultimately, the screenwriters won financial settlements from the studios, who wrote off the payments as the cost of doing the blacklist business.

The Hollywood Ten were less fortunate in their case against HUAC. On April 10, 1950, the U.S. Supreme Court upheld the contempt of Congress citations and, after sentencing in June, the Ten went off to jail. Bessie, Cole, Lardner, Lawson, Maltz, Ornitz, Scott, and Trumbo each received a fine of one thousand dollars and a one-year sentence; Biberman and Dmytryk, lucky enough to stand before a more lenient judge, received a fine of one thousand dollars and a six-month sentence.

Ring Lardner Jr. and Lester Cole served their time at the Federal Correctional Institution in Danbury, CT. "It was just a little tougher than being in the Army," recalled Lardner, true to character.[11] While in stir, in a moment of poetic justice neither would have dared insert into a screenplay, the pair happened upon a fellow inmate with a familiar beet-red hue. Serving out a nine-month sentence for payroll padding and fraud, J. Parnell Thomas was now presiding over the prison's chicken coops. Cole also worked outside, cutting hay with

Screenwriters John Howard Lawson (*left*) and Dalton Trumbo board a van to be taken to a Washington, D.C. jail after being sentenced June 9, 1950.

a scythe. One day, he spied Thomas with hoe, not gavel, in hand, atop the roof of a coop, cleaning out chicken droppings. Their eyes locked.

"Hey, Bolshie," yelled Thomas, "I see you still got your sickle. Where's your hammer?"

Cole shouted back: "And I see, just like in Congress, you're still picking up chickenshit!"[12]

Larry Parks: "Don't present me with the choice of either being in contempt of this Committee and going to jail or forcing me to crawl through the mud and be an informer."

By the time Lester Cole let fly his wisecrack for the ages, a lot besides Thomas's legal status had changed. China had fallen under the red tide.

The Soviet Union had acquired nuclear weapons, a technological leap forward—so felt many Americans—that could only have come from the spoils of espionage, incubated in the CPUSA. On July 17, 1950, confirming suspicions, atomic spies Julius and Ethel Rosenberg were arrested, giving two forlorn faces to the Communist fifth column. Just a few weeks earlier, under the euphemism of a police action, the nation had entered into a hot war on the Korean peninsula.

The man who would give his name to the era had also stepped on to the national stage, dominating the postwar anti-Communist crusade with a charisma that J. Parnell Thomas, for all his gavel-banging, neck-bulging fury, could not match. But while always ready for a close-up, Sen. Joseph R. McCarthy (R-WI) tended to stay clear of Hollywood, preferring to concentrate his firepower on the U.S. Army and the Department of State. Watching from the sidelines, Thomas saw an opening. In 1954, seeking to hitch his wagon to the new star, the ex-con tried for a political comeback, running for his old House seat on a pro-McCarthy platform. He was roundly trounced in the Republican primary.

On March 21, 1951, with the Democrats now holding the gavel, the long dormant—that is, in Hollywood terms—HUAC bestirred itself for a new round of media-centric hearings. Energized by an appreciation of the career opportunities offered by a high anti-Communist profile in postwar America, HUAC chairman John S. Wood fulfilled Thomas's promise to reopen the inquiry into alleged subversion in Hollywood. Held in Washington and featuring a trio of suspect actors (the distressed Larry Parks, the sneeringly defiant Howard Da Silva, and the politely defiant Gale Sondergaard), the initial salvo lasted just one day. Wood resumed his investigations in April and May in Washington and, in September, convened hearings in Los Angeles.

Harkening to the ominous rumblings on Capitol Hill, MPAA vice president Joyce O'Hara, serving as temporary head of the MPAA while Eric Johnston was on leave of absence, called together a meeting of studio representatives in New York to lay down the law, or reiterate it: film people who did not deny their association with Communism or Communist front outfits (the latter a designation that had become increasingly elastic) would be barred from the studio grounds.

Having learned the hard lessons of 1947, the moguls did not need reminding. O'Hara pledged that the studio heads "would not repeat the mistakes they had made" in the 1947 HUAC hearings. They would not oppose the investigation and, by way of exchange, HUAC would not paint the entire industry with the red brush. "For sensational and sweeping charges against the industry, the Hollywood red hearings of 1951 will not compare with those of 1947 when sessions were interrupted with uproars and the entire film industry was accused of Communist coddling," predicted a relieved *Variety*.[13]

Even the next generation of Unfriendlies cooperated by claiming their Fifth, not First, Amendment rights, refusing to answer the $64 question on grounds of self-incrimination and clamming up at the microphone. In doing so, they fully understood that the constitutionally protected silence that shielded them from criminal prosecution was the kiss of death for a screen career. The high decibel shouting matches and hands-on ejections from the witness table were replaced by a lawyerly dialogue that was almost sedate. "Industry has an advantage this time over 1947 in being able to figuratively separate the sheep from the goats, since the probe is taking a different turn," *Variety* explained. "In 1947 the entire industry was being tarred as Communist. [The Wood] Committee now has its guns trained on only a relatively small and specific group." Rather than play good shepherd, the studio heads would help the wolves thin out the herd. "We must recognize that this is a period of strong anti-Communism in this country and live with that," shrugged O'Hara, yielding to the inevitable.[14]

As HUAC refocused its eyes on Hollywood, the trauma of 1947 was ever in the background. At his confidential meeting with the moguls in New York, O'Hara confided that the MPAA now believed that Paul McNutt had blundered in defying the Thomas Committee. O'Hara felt the error in strategy was the result of Hollywood's victorious encounter with the Senate War Propaganda Hearings in 1941, when the aggressive pushback by Wendell Willkie and the moguls had sent the senators reeling. The lessons of 1941 having proven inapplicable in 1947, the lessons of 1947 would serve as a better guide on how to handle HUAC in 1951–1952. The MPAA took the same approach in 1953–1954, when control of HUAC returned to the Republicans under the chairmanship of Harold V. Velde (R-IL).

With Hollywood and Washington in harmony, the cementing of the blacklist regime proceeded apace, albeit with fewer histrionics. The political purge of the entertainment industry—radio and television had joined the motion picture industry—settled into a routine business practice. Neither Chairman Wood nor Chairman Velde was as floridly red-faced as Thomas or as prone to break gavels. Each just went calmly about the work of forcing confessions, pulling out names, and evil-eying witnesses who took the Fifth. "It was a dull, droning session punctuated by exchanges on legal technicalities and by open evidence of frayed tempers," wrote a bored *Variety* reporter of a typical episode of the Wood show.[15]

A few obstreperous rebels refused to submit quietly. Testifying on May 6, 1953 before the Velde Committee in New York, the gruff, chain-smoking Lionel Stander (who in 1940 may have been the first actor to lose a job to what was not then a systemic anti-Communist blacklist) was abrasive and loud. "I don't want to be responsible for what a stableful of stool pigeons, psychopaths, and informers have testified about me," he growled. "I may be here as a witness but I am not charged with anything. I am not here as a dupe, a dope, a mope, a mole, or a schmoe." After eighty minutes of furious back and forth, Stander left the witness table to a round of applause.[16] He was blacklisted from Hollywood for fourteen years.

If the witnesses had learned which constitutional amendment to depend upon, Washington had also taken away a lesson from 1947. The newsreel cameras—and the television cameras—were barred from covering the Wood Committee hearings in Washington.* No blinding Klieg lights, no banks of 35mm Mitchells, no scrum of camera-and-sound men, no circus atmosphere, just a slow and steady parade of witnesses—some naming names, some taking the Fifth, some trying to walk the tightrope between informing on friends and ruining their own careers.

Being out of camera range, the HUAC hearings of the 1950s lacked the high-tension drama of the original attraction. "In general, the atmosphere is less frightening than in the fall of 1947 when Representative Thomas called in the Klieg lights and the newsreels and put himself and his heavy gavel in the starring role," observed the *Los Angeles Daily News*. Moreover, "although there are plenty of taxpayers who want to see the show, the committee has

---

* In 1951, Speaker of the House Sam Rayburn (D-TX) banned newsreel and television camera from the House of Representatives. However, from September 17–26, 1951, in Los Angeles, away from Rayburn's territory, HUAC agreed to allow local television stations to broadcast its hearings live, in the mornings, with witnesses having the right to nix the coverage. In January 1953, Speaker of the House Joseph W. Martin (R-MA), reversed Rayburn's decree and left the decision to admit newsreel and television cameras up to the discretion of individual chairman. During seven days of HUAC hearings in Los Angeles beginning on March 23, 1953, subcommittee chairman Donald L. Jackson (R-CA) permitted live television coverage. No kinescopes of either session seem to have survived. ("5 LA Stations Televise H'wood Red Hearings," *Variety*, September 26, 1951, 2; "L.A. Red Probe on Air," *Broadcasting/Telecasting*, March 2, 1953, 48.)

so far refused to move into the auditorium-like House caucus room where the 1947 sessions were conducted. . . . The refusal to move to larger quarters cuts the audience down to a couple of dozen or so."[17,*] The new crop of HUAC congressmen pledged that *their* hearings would be no "publicity seeking circus."[18] Lawyerly exchanges, not shouting matches, would be the operative mode.

Even without newsreel or television cameras and a cavernous room packed with spectators, the next rounds of HUAC hearings were show trials—perhaps, in the sinister Stalinist sense, even more so than the original. The hearings of the 1950s were less concerned with flushing out Communists in Hollywood than in providing a stage for the heretics to confess and repent. In the 1947 hearings, friendly witnesses needed little coaxing to name names. They sought not to exculpate themselves but to raise the alarm, Paul Revere-style, against the enemy inside the studio gates. In subsequent hearings, many of the penitent witnesses named names reluctantly, under pressure, not wanting to play Benedict Arnold.

As a second and third generation of defendants from Hollywood were hauled before HUAC, no witness was more anguished than Larry Parks, the only actor among the Unfriendly Nineteen. Though not called before the Thomas Committee, he had been a self-effacing, even-tempered spokesman for the group. While admitting membership in "a profession more concerned with endorsing soda pop than democracy," he still felt entitled to protest Thomas's attempts to "make traitors out of patriots" whose "only loyalty is to the American tradition."[19]

On March 21, 1951, Parks kept his long-delayed appointment with HUAC. He testified frankly about his membership in the Communist party from 1941 to 1945, chalking it up to youthful idealism and an affinity for the underdog. Pressed for the names of associates, he pleaded with the committee to allow him a dignified silence. "Don't present me with the choice of either being in contempt of this Committee and going to jail or forcing me to crawl through the mud and be an informer," he begged. "I don't think it is fair for you people to do this. I have come at your request. I would prefer not to be questioned

---

* Circumventing the media blackout decreed by Speaker Rayburn, HUAC chairman John Wood and his colleagues out-showboated the Thomas Committee in one way: by being featured in the first reel of the anti-Communist film *Big Jim McLain* (1952), where they appear as themselves asking Hollywood actors (playing Communist professors not Hollywood screenwriters) the $64 question.

about names. I will answer any questions about myself." Desperate not to incriminate his friends, Parks was reduced to tears, almost whimpering, "They were small type people, no different than you or I."

In a closed executive session later that day, however, Parks did name names, ten of them, men and women who were then duly subpoenaed. "I am probably the completest ruined man that you have seen," Parks told HUAC counsel Frank S. Tavenner Jr.[20] Satisfied with Parks's self-abasement, Representative Velde praised him as a "loyal true American" for making a clean breast of things and for being "the first member of his profession whom I have felt told the truth about the treacherous techniques that are used by the enemies of Constitutional government."[21]

Parks's tormented testimony did him no good. Not being a marquee name like Bogart or Hepburn, he was shunned by producers who saw no percentage in forgiving and forgetting a confessed Communist. Contemplating the fallout, *Variety* offered a clinical analysis of how Hollywood performed triage under the blacklist:

Parks is one of those in-between names whose billing on a marquee has perhaps been helpful to a picture but who is in no sense a sock b.o. draw. Thus, there's no urge to hire him as long as there's any sort of taint attached to his name. As a result, it can be expected that a producer given a choice of names for casting will prefer to skip Parks in favor of a number of other male leads with equal marquee power. Action may be practically subconscious, but practical filmmakers are certain Parks is going to be hurt.[22]

He was. MGM shelved Parks's current film, *Love Is Better Than Ever* (1951), and Columbia recast the role he was to play in *Small Wonder* (1951). The breakout screen sensation of 1946 was forced to seek a new career in the construction business.

The Wood Committee also played host to another ideological defection from Thomas's original lineup. Never a blindly loyal party member, director Edward Dmytryk had plenty of time to reassess his life priorities while serving out his sentence at the Mill Point Federal Prison in West Virginia. "I am not a Communist sympathizer and I recognize the United States of America as the only country to which I owe allegiance and loyalty," Dmytryk declared in an affidavit from prison issued on September 9, 1950, explaining that "the troubled state of world affairs" had compelled him "to declare without equivocation where I stand toward my country."[23]

On April 25, 1951, Dmytryk appeared before HUAC to reaffirm his break with Communism and his nine comrades. "I had no lawyer by my side and I was no longer held captive by false group loyalty," Dmytryk recalled. His testimony, he insisted, came not from coercion or careerism, but "from a free man, following his own conscience guided by his own ideals."[24] He named six fellow directors and sixteen others as Communists.[25]

John Garfield: "I think they got me for a sucker."

Unlike Larry Parks, John Garfield was not an in-between name—or an in-between liberal. A fellow traveler since the 1930s, generous in lending his name and pocketbook to left-wing causes supported by the CPUSA, he was considered a comrade in all but formal membership. During the storm of 1947, Garfield had not kept any distance between himself and the Unfriendly Nineteen. In the rallies he attended and the statements he made, he muddled distinctions the leadership of the Committee for the First Amendment wanted kept clear.

The actor had escaped a subpoena in 1947 but not in 1951. He had been named too many times by too many people in too many places.

Besides HUAC, an anti-Communist journalist was on Garfield's trail, not Billy Wilkerson or Hedda Hopper but Victor Riesel, the Hearst columnist based at the *New York Mirror*, who covered the labor beat. In a speech before the MPA-PAI, Riesel charged Garfield with having always been a faithful and quite witting tool of the CPUSA—indeed, during the Hitler-Stalin Pact interregnum, he remembered "Julie" Garfield coming out "for the Soviet invasion of Finland just like his comrades are now condoning the death of American boys" in Korea.[26]

Garfield read Riesel's charges with "stunned consternation" and refuted them point by point.[27] "I have always hated Communism. It is a tyranny which threatens our country and the peace of the world," the actor insisted when he received his summons from HUAC. "I will be pleased to cooperate with the Committee." Stung at the defection, Garfield's former soulmates at the *Daily Worker* howled at his betrayal of "everything that's decent and honorable in our land" in order to endear himself "to the fat pigs of Wall Street who are wallowing in their blood-soaked profits."[28]

On April 9, 1951, Garfield testified before HUAC in executive session. Asked about his role in the Committee for the First Amendment, he said that either John Huston or Billy Wilder had telephoned him in New York and asked him to go down to Washington to protest the Thomas Committee hearings. "I was never in on the organization of the Committee," he said. "We were not interested in protecting anybody that was a Communist or subversive. That was absolutely and positively out."

What about his feelings toward CFA now? asked Louis J. Russell, still head investigator for HUAC.

"There is no such thing," Garfield replied, trying to dodge.

Do you think it was legitimate? Russell pressed.

"I think they got me for a sucker," replied Garfield, figuring it was better to play the sap than the subversive. "If it did exist today, I wouldn't be a member of it."[29]

On April 23, 1951, this time in public testimony, Garfield—pale, tense, speaking haltingly at times—endured three hours of grilling by interrogators who did not bother to conceal their skepticism at his professed obliviousness to all things Communist. "I am no Red," he insisted. "I am no Pinko. I am no fellow traveler." He had never been approached by anyone to join the Communist Party and, if he ever had been, "I would have run like hell." He said he had never even met a single Communist.[30]

Garfield, who had certainly met all the members of the Hollywood Ten, not to mention his wife, Roberta Seidman, a former CPUSA cardholder, was lying, unconvincingly, and the committee was not buying his act: even unwitting dupes could not be that witless. "I am not convinced of the entire accuracy and cooperation you are giving this committee," Rep. Donald L. Jackson (R-CA) told him straight out. "It shows a naïve or unintelligent approach to live with this problem for 11 years and not know anything about it." Velde threatened to investigate Garfield for perjury.[31]

Nothing ever came of Velde's threat, but Garfield's acting prospects on screen dried up. After wrapping *He Ran All the Way* (1951), he returned to the place—and the very same play—that had launched his career, playing the title role in a Broadway revival of *Golden Boy*, the Group Theatre production by Clifford Odets where, in a minor part, he had first been pegged

Edward G. Robinson tells the Wood Committee he was "duped and used" by the Hollywood Communists, April 30, 1952.

for stardom in 1937. On April 27, 1952, after a six-week run, the show closed, in the red. The best offer currently on the table was to appear at the Cameo Playhouse in Miami in a summer stock version of his noir hit *The Postman Always Rings Twice* (1946).[32]

By then, for the Communist-accused or tainted, two approved paths to rehabilitation had been marked out: cooperative name-naming before HUAC or public recantation. Bogart and Hepburn had weathered their career crises with just the latter. Garfield, a more extreme case, might need to do both to regain his footing in Hollywood.

Edward G. Robinson, another New York Jew of liberal bent who made good in Hollywood under a WASP name, showed how to wash away the stigma of an activist past. Like Garfield, Robinson had lent his star power to the Popular Front in the 1930s. However, during the Hitler-Stalin Pact interregnum, he was no obedient fellow traveler, standing up for causes anathema to CPUSA orthodoxy: FDR, a strong national defense, and refugee relief. He maintained his liberal-to-left orientation during and after World War II. A vocal member of the CFA, he was too busy to join the delegation in Washington, but his was the first voice heard in its two radio broadcasts, bellowing out the titular battle cry *"Hollywood Fights Back!"*

The postwar era found Robinson's name being mentioned in all the wrong places. During the Thomas Committee hearings, he had been tagged by Howard Rushmore as a designated "sacred cow" of the CPUSA. In 1949, at the espionage trial of the Soviet spy Judith Coplon, Robinson had been named as a member of the CPUSA. "I am not now, nor have I ever been a member of the Communist party," he responded, using the correct wording. "Nor have I ever been remotely connected to the party."[33] He had also acquired ten black marks from *Red Channels: The Report of Communist Influence in Radio and Television*, the blacklister's index, published in June 1950.[34]

To clear his name, Robinson, at his own insistence, underwent an intense grilling—more like a slow roast. He testified first in an executive session with the HUAC staff on October 27, 1950; then, on December 21, 1950, in an executive session with a HUAC subcommittee; and finally, on April 30, 1952, in public testimony before HUAC. "I have always been a liberal Democrat," he said, reading from a prepared statement in which he denied any tinge of Communist coloring. "The revelation that persons who I thought were sincere liberals were, in fact, Communists, has shocked me more than I can tell you." Robinson reminded the Wood Committee that he had just finished appearing in close to 250 performances of *Darkness at Noon* all over the country. "It is perhaps the strongest indictment of Communism ever presented," he said of Arthur Koestler's tale of forced confession and Stalinist mind games. "I am sure it had a lasting effect on all who saw it."

Rep. Francis E. Walter (D-PA) bestowed a pardon on Robinson that under other circumstances might have been deemed an insult. The committee, Walter told Robinson, "has never had any evidence to indicate that you were any more than a very choice sucker."[35] Robinson borrowed Jackson's appellation for the confession he published in *American Legion Magazine* in 1952: "How the Reds Made a Sucker Out of Me."[36] First in person, then in print, Robinson had performed the rites required for absolution.

To revive his knocked-out screen career, Garfield had no option but to do what he refused to do as the boxer in *Body and Soul*: take a fall. Like Robinson,

John Garfield (*left*), accompanied by attorney Louis Nizer (*right*), tells the Wood Committee he was never a member of the Communist party and had never even met a Communist, April 23, 1951.

he penned a mea culpa portraying himself as a well-meaning dupe. It was entitled "I Was a Sucker for a Left Hook" and slated for publication in *Look* magazine. The author hoped he might avoid the ordeal of a public, and this time frank, exculpatory, and perhaps name-naming appearance before HUAC.

Unlike Bogart and Robinson, Garfield was not to accrue the career benefits from a written apology. On May 21, 1952, the thirty-nine-year-old actor was found dead of a heart attack in the Gramercy Park apartment of a paramour, across the river, and light years away, from the slum-pent neighborhood in Brooklyn where he was born Jacob Julius Garfinkle.[37]

Victor Riesel, Garfield's accuser turned confessor, had spoken with the actor just hours before he died. Riesel ran with his scoop—the near deathbed confession of a penitent ex-fellow traveler, the inside story "by an eyewitness of the invasion of Hollywood by an enemy force, the exposure (by a man it victimized) of a vast conspiracy to capture the power and impact of the motion picture industry." Garfield, said Riesel, was ready to tell all, to expose what the Hollywood Communists did "to the decent instincts of sentimental and emotional actors who wanted to be honest crusaders, but whose endless movie work kept them from knowing the weird international Communist plots into which camouflaged comrades hurtled them."[38]

Three days after the shocking news of Garfield's death, ten thousand people lined the streets outside the Riverside Memorial Chapel at Amsterdam and 66th Street to pay their last respects to the native son. Though the actor had experienced pulmonary problems since at least 1949, when he collapsed on a tennis court ("heat prostration," lied the studio publicists), his death soon settled into the realm of myth, with Garfield cast as a martyr hounded to death by HUAC.[39] Garfield's friend, the heartbroken Clifford Odets, blamed "the witch-hunters searching his closets" as much as bad health, and eulogized his beloved Julie as a true American patriot. "Despite any and all gossip to the contrary, I, who was in a position to know, state without equivocation that of all his possessions, Garfield was proudest of his American heritage, even rudely so."[40]

The experience of Lionel Stander, Larry Parks, Edward Dmytryk, Edward G. Robinson, John Garfield—and the hundreds of others who ran into the buzz saw of the blacklist in the 1950s—proved that the machinery J. Parnell Thomas had put into motion in 1947 was chugging along just fine without him. Thomas's name appeared on no piece of congressional legislation, but the work of his committee and its Hollywood auxiliaries had the force of law in the motion picture industry. Bolstered by HUAC, a network of interlocking organizations with dire acronyms (MPA-PAI, MPIC, IATSE) sifted the names of suspects from their lists of forbidden artists, purging the guilty and allowing the penitent, suitably chastened, to be admitted back into Hollywood's good graces. In June 1952, well pleased with the work of punishment and rehabilitation, a spokesman for the American Legion boasted, "If John Garfield were alive today, he'd be working."[41]

Chapter 18
NOT ONLY VICTIMS

"The Ten is always with us," reflected Alvah Bessie in a letter to Ring Lardner Jr. in 1977, mulling over the scars, the backfire, and the bad feelings from the long strange trip he, Lardner, and their eight fellow passengers had traveled over the past thirty years.

Bessie was still annoyed that Lardner had fessed up to Communist party membership in a 1961 article in the *Saturday Evening Post*.[1] He also took a swipe at their old comrade and co-defendant Albert Maltz ("Who Has No Faltz") for not liking either *Inquisition in Eden*, Bessie's 1965 memoir of Hollywood and HUAC, or Lardner's just-published *The Lardners: My Family Remembered*, an affectionate look back at his literary gene pool.

Lardner responded in good grace, reminding Bessie that "I didn't consider my political beliefs anything to hide; that I objected only to being made to reveal them under threat of compulsion." He then voiced a criticism of his own, chiding Bessie for an editorial blurb on the back jacket of *The Heart of Spain*, Bessie's memoir of his proud service with the Abraham Lincoln Brigade during the Spanish Civil War, published in 1952. The blurb lauded Bessie as having been "investigated, together with eight other writers, producers, and directors [and] these nine men served prison sentences" for heeding the call of conscience.

Lardner pointed out that the number count was "either bad arithmetic or the unpleasant practice of creating nonpersons."[2] The erasure of director Edward Dmytryk, who had stood loyally with his fellow Unfriendlies during the hearings and trials and served four and a half months in federal prison only to recant and name names before HUAC in 1951, was a Stalinist rewriting of the past. The point of correction was a measure both of how far Lardner had veered from the party line and how tight were the old ties. Like siblings bound by blood whether they liked it or not, the veterans of 1947 were yoked together by history. They might snipe at each other or even leave the fold, but in the end they were kindred. It was, after all, "always" the Hollywood Ten.

Dalton Trumbo: "There's no problem in *proving* authorship. The problem in Hollywood is to *admit* authorship."

After the hearings in Washington closed, only a privileged few of the witnesses could be said to have gone back about their business. Of course, the Hollywood Ten were persona non grata, exiled from the studio system and in some cases from America itself, fleeing to Mexico or England to sit out what Dalton Trumbo called "the time of the toad" and Lillian Hellman called "scoundrel time." Scarlet-lettered by HUAC, they eked out a living with pseudonymous scripts and uncredited touch-ups and turned to novels, plays, and piece work. Some also had to resort to non-literary toil.

After serving nine months in federal prison, Samuel Ornitz went back to his original vocation, writing novels, including the highly successful *Bride of the Sabbath* in 1951, an insider's portrait of Jewish life on the Lower East Side at the turn of the twentieth century. Already sickly at the time of his sentencing, he was the first of the Hollywood Ten to die, in 1957, never experiencing the lionization his fellows would know once the worm turned.

Against long odds, industry resistance, and government harassment, Herbert J. Biberman completed a promethean task, the independent film *Salt of the Earth* (1954), produced by fellow blacklistee Paul Jarrico and written by fellow blacklistee Michael Wilson, a pro-labor, pro-Communist, multi-cultural, and feminist tract, made on location in the heart of New Mexico in the belly of Cold War America. It received scant stateside exhibition: Roy Brewer's IATSE projectionists refused to handle such combustible celluloid. (The few playdates the film secured made for a risky night out. Knowing that FBI agents wrote down the license plates of cars near theaters daring to book the film, radical cinephiles parked blocks away from the ticket window.)

Not until 1969 did Biberman manage to finish another film, writing and directing *Slaves*, a revisionist plantation melodrama about a heroic slave who trades Christian salvation for Marxist revolution. "I think that in the '40s I had a deep social conscience toward my fellow man," he said at the time. "If I was a subversive then, I am a subversive now."[3] He died in 1971.

After serving ten months in federal prison, Lester Cole made ends meet working as a short order cook, waiter, manual laborer, and, when he was lucky, screenwriter, though not bylined as Lester Cole. Under a pseudonym, he wrote *Operation Eichmann!* (1961) before coming out of the shadows with the screenplay for *Born Free* (1965), about a pride of lion cubs not workers of the world. Even at that late date, however, Cole hid his screen credit under the Brahmin handle Gerald L. Copley. "I did it for 15 percent of what my salary was before I was blacklisted," he said in 1967. "People still come under a lot of harassment."[4] He remained an unrepentant Communist all his life, never doubting or rethinking, still parroting the Soviet line on the Hitler-Stalin Pact and the invasion of Finland. He put his colors up front in the title of his 1981 memoir, *Hollywood Red*.[5] He died in 1985.

Alvah Bessie suffered a hard fate, never working again as a screenwriter either under his own name or that of others. He took a job for seventy dollars per week as a stage manager at the hungry i nightclub in San Francisco, where he worked for seven and a half years for a boss, who "while totally unpredictable and erratic in most areas, is basically a kind man and doesn't give a hoot in hell, what I've done in the past."[6] The night job gave him time to write novels: *The Un-Americans* (1957), based on his experience with the title characters, and, after being bounced from the hungry i, *The Symbol* (1967), a *roman à clef* about Marilyn Monroe. He was also the first of the Ten to publish a HUAC-themed memoir, *Inquisition in Eden* (1965). In later years, he wrote, lectured, and maintained a voluminous correspondence on blacklist matters, but the good fight he treasured most was the one he fought for the Abraham Lincoln Brigade. He died in 1985.

Edward Dmytryk and Adrian Scott, paired together by HUAC and fired together by RKO, went separate ways. In ill health at the time of sentencing, Scott had delayed serving his time until a court-appointed physician decreed that "he did not feel Scott's health would suffer in a federal penitentiary." Upon release, he moved to London, worked in film production, and ghosted episodes of *The Adventures of Robin Hood*, a British series telecast on CBS from 1955–1958, with a merry-men-as-revolutionaries subtext. Under an obliging front, his wife Joan LaCour, he also wrote for American television. In 1963, *Variety* quietly announced that MGM had appointed Scott as a production executive tasked with script supervision at its British branch.[7] Asked if he was bitter about the blacklist, he replied, "Only for sixteen years."[8] Back in Hollywood, Scott struggled to mount a television version of his Popular Front-dated play, *The Great Man's Whiskers*, about the little girl who wrote Abraham Lincoln about his lack of facial hair. Shot in 1969, it was shelved until February 13, 1973, when on NBC's small screen the credit "Produced by Adrian Scott" unspooled for the first time since *Crossfire* (1947). Scott had died six weeks earlier.

Having performed the requisite penance before HUAC, Dmytryk faced a bumpy road back to studio good graces until producer Stanley Kramer gambled on him for the all-star big budget version of Herman Wouk's best-selling military courtroom drama, *The Caine Mutiny* (1954). The film was a huge commercial and critical hit. Hollywood being Hollywood, the pariah was back on the A-list. A reliable, no-nonsense filmmaker, he directed twenty feature films in the next twenty years, sailing smoothly across genres: westerns (*Broken Lance*, 1954), melodramas (*Raintree Country*, 1957), combat films (*Anzio*, 1968), and trash (*The Carpetbaggers*, 1964). In one of his best-reviewed films, *The Young Lions* (1958), a sprawling World War II drama from the Irwin Shaw novel, he returned to the theme of antisemitism, following a secular Jewish GI across Europe as he confronts the Nazis, the Holocaust, and his own identity. Dmytryk ended his career teaching film at the University of Southern California, where some of the left-wing undergraduates refused to enroll in his courses. He died in 1999.

After years in the wilderness, Ring Lardner Jr. returned to the Hollywood screen with *The Cincinnati Kid* (1965), strolling again through the gates of MGM, now a toothless version of its once-roaring self. He revamped Richard Hooker's Korean War-set service comedy into an anti-Vietnam War allegory, Robert Altman's *M*A*S*H* (1970), for which he won an Oscar for Best Adapted Screenplay. In 1971, at the Academy Awards ceremony, Lardner heard in the rising applause that greeted his walk to the podium the sound of tectonic plates shifting. In accepting his trophy, he made no mention of the blacklist, but he did refer to his long hiatus, saying that he seemed to win an Oscar every twenty-eight years—the last time was for *Woman of the Year* (1942)—and that he planned to repeat the trick in 1998.[9] Though the last of the Hollywood Ten to die, in 2000, he failed to make good on the promise.

John Howard Lawson, the "cultural Commissar of Hollywood" who enforced party discipline on unruly CPUSA screenwriters, never again saw his name on the Hollywood screen. Though he exerted influence on generations of socially conscious screenwriters with his guidebooks *Theory and Technique of Playwriting* (1936) and *Film: The Creative Process* (1964), he died, an industry outcast, in 1977.[10] "I'm much more completely blacklisted than the others," Lawson explained. "I'm much more notorious and I'm very proud of that."[11] Also—more to the point—he never wrote a hit.

Among the purged, Dalton Trumbo fared best and, in time, emerged most triumphant. Even during the darkest days of the blacklist, he was in demand, albeit underpaid and uncredited. Too prolific, too talented, and too deft at screenplay scaffolding and dialogue punch-up to be shunned by bargain-hungry producers, Trumbo worked under the table and off the books. He—or rather his front, Ian McLellan Hunter—won an Oscar for Best Screenplay for *Roman Holiday* (1953) and, under the name of Robert Rich, for *The Brave One* (1956), by which time his covert authorship was an open secret around Hollywood. On January 16, 1959, in a television interview with newsman Bill Stout on KNXT-CBS, he blew the whistle on the racket. "There's no problem in *proving* authorship," Trumbo said, brandishing his original script for *The Brave One*. "The problem in Hollywood is to *admit* authorship."[12]

While the above-the-line Ten hustled for work, the rout of the below-the-line stage hands was even more complete. After representing the sturdy, made-in-USA brand of Hollywood labor at HUAC, Roy Brewer ruled over IATSE for the next six years. As the sternest of judges on the Motion Picture Industry Council, the clearance tribunal that passed judgment on Hollywood employees, he earned his moniker as "the straw boss of the Hollywood political purge."[13] He always insisted that "the Waldorf Declaration did not create a blacklist," but was merely "an open declaration of policy that persons whose Communist party loyalties were stronger than their obligation to tell the truth to the House Committee or other appropriate governmental committee would not be employed."[14] Brewer never expressed second thoughts about the role he played as enforcer. "We insisted that you had to come clean," he told an interviewer in 1995. "Name names? Absolutely!"[15]

Brewer's defeated rival Herbert K. Sorrell died forgotten in 1973, after a long illness, at age seventy-three. Stripped of his leadership position in the Painters Brotherhood under the anti-Communist provisions of the Taft-Hartley

Act, he become a painting contractor, no longer on the front lines but still a union man until the day he died.[16]

The other colorful personality from Hollywood's bygone labor wars, the mobster Willie Bioff, succumbed to an occupational hazard. On November 4, 1955, while living under an assumed name in Phoenix, AZ, he hit the ignition of his pickup truck and was blown to bits in a dynamite explosion. "He didn't have an enemy in the world," insisted his wife afterward.[17]

Ring Lardner Jr.: "The choice we faced was between being 'heroes' and being complete shits."

As if the changeover to a new decade required a flip of the cultural as well as the calendar page, 1960 marked a new frontier for the original names on the Hollywood blacklist.

Promising omens, presaging more open skies, could already be discerned. On January 12, 1959, the Board of Governors of the Academy of Motion Picture Arts and Sciences voted to junk an amendment, adopted on February 6, 1957, that barred Communists and Fifth Amendment witnesses from receiving Oscars. "I'm opposed violently to these Fifth Amendmenters, but I do think it's not the function of the Academy to adjudicate in the matter of credits," said board member Samuel Engel. "We honor solely for merit."[18] Former president Harry Truman agreed. "I don't believe in a blacklist of any kind," he told newsman Lew Irwin on KABC-TV in a report telecast on April 8, 1959. Irwin asked specifically about the Hollywood version. "If they're not efficient, they ought to be fired," Truman replied. "If they are, they ought to have a chance at a job."[19]

Six months later, Lew Irwin broached the topic of the blacklist again in an interview with producer Stanley Kramer. It was a bedrock American value "that a man has a right to work . . . on his merit irrespective of an association of the past," Kramer stated.[20] As good as his rhetoric, Kramer had already hired blacklisted screenwriter Nedrick Young, who had taken the Fifth Amendment before HUAC in 1953, for *The Defiant Ones* (1958). Young wrote under the name Nathan E. Douglas purely as a conceit not a disguise: he told anyone who asked who was who.

By early January 1960, Hollywood was rife with rumors that producer-director Otto Preminger and actor-producer Kirk Douglas were going to defy the blacklist by hiring, under his own name, Dalton Trumbo to write the screenplays for *Exodus* (1960) and *Spartacus* (1960), respectively. It would not be an official defiance of the Waldorf Declaration—both men oversaw independent productions and were not signatories to the statement—but the personnel decision would certainly break the back of the MPAA edict.

Preminger went public first. On January 20, 1960, in a front-page story in the *New York Times*, he bragged that he had retained Trumbo to write the script for *Exodus*. "As long as there is no legal reason not to employ a writer or an actor, I don't think it is my job to inquire into the politics of the persons I sign," Preminger explained.[21] Miffed that Preminger had given the scoop to a civilian paper, *Variety* speculated that the director had announced the hiring of Trumbo only *after* the screenwriter had delivered a satisfactory script. The trade paper also picked up on the not-always-subsurface hum beneath the politics of the blacklist. "Since *Exodus*, based on the bestseller by Leon Uris, deals with the establishment of Israel, a number of people of the Jewish faith expressed disappointment that Preminger chose this particular project to upset the blacklist."[22]

Also spilling to the *New York Times*, Stanley Kramer followed up on Preminger's push. He would hire whomever he pleased regardless of the person's "past affiliations or suspected affiliations," he declared. The methods of the American Legion were "reprehensible" and (repurposing the trigger word) "un-American." He planned to re-hire Nedrick Young—Nathan E. Douglas—for his next film, *Inherit the Wind* (1960), about the Scopes Monkey Trial of 1925. Kramer referred to the blacklisted as "people who blundered into the Communist party in the Thirties and Forties," as if they were confused students who had walked into the wrong classroom during freshman year.[23]

Preminger's grand gesture and Kramer's tough talk did not immediately break the hiring freeze on verboten talent. On March 28, 1960, an emboldened Frank Sinatra announced that he had hired Albert Maltz to adapt *The Execution of Private Slovik*, the book by William Bradford Huie about the only American soldier executed for desertion during World War II. Maltz had spent most of his post-prison exile in Mexico, where for ten years he wrote under fronts and pseudonyms, or anonymously and uncredited (only lately has his contribution to the biblical epic *The Robe* [1953] been recognized and only with the Sofia Coppola remake of *The Beguiled* [2017] has he been given screen credit under his own name for a screenplay he cowrote in 1971 as John B. Sherry).

Sinatra sensed the time was right to bring Maltz in from the cold. He was "the best man to do the job," said Sinatra of the screenwriter who had written his lines for the Oscar-winning short *The House I Live In* (1945). In a statement published in *Daily Variety*, the singer explained:

> I spoke to many screenwriters but it was not until I talked to Albert Maltz that I found a writer who saw the screenplay in exactly the terms I wanted. This is, the Army was right [to execute Slovik].

To back up his decision, Sinatra cited a familiar authority, Justice Robert T. Jackson, the favorite jurist of the Unfriendly Nineteen:

> Under our Bill of Rights, I was taught that no one may prescribe what shall be orthodox in politics, religion, or other matters of opinion.[24]

The singer was not prepared for the chorus of catcalls the greeted his declaration. "If Sinatra loves his country, he won't do this," hissed Hedda Hopper, who also warned of the collateral fallout to the presidential candidate Sinatra was backing. "Frank's done himself a great deal of harm, not to mention the harm he'll do Sen. Jack Kennedy if he goes out campaigning for him, as he declares he will."[25] Fearing electoral blowback from the American Legion, JFK told Sinatra to scotch the deal.[26]

An abashed Sinatra did as instructed. In a second open letter to his colleagues, he explained:

> In view of the reaction of my family, my friends, and the American public, I have instructed my attorneys to make a settlement with Albert Maltz and to inform him that he will not write the screenplay for *The Execution of Private Slovik*.
>
> I had thought the major consideration was whether or not the resulting script would be in the best interests of the United States. Since my conversations with Mr. Maltz had indicated that he had an affirmative, pro-American approach to the story, and since I felt fully capable as producer of enforcing such standards, I have defended my hiring of Mr. Maltz.

But the American public has indicated it feels the morality of hiring Albert
Maltz is the more crucial matter, and I will accept this majority opinion.[27]

Unlike Trumbo, Maltz was denied a high-profile return to the screen.
He waited another decade before securing a major screen credit on a minor
diversion, Don Siegel's *Two Mules for Sister Sara* (1970), a western with
Clint Eastwood as a gunfighter and Shirley MacLaine as a bogus nun. In the
interim, Maltz had assumed the role of unofficial custodian of the legacy of
the Hollywood Ten. He picked the brains of his comrades for memories of
1947, spoke to college students, journalists, and documentarians, and corrected the record when a revisionist article got the past, as he saw it, wrong.
He died in 1985.

As the blacklist breaker of record, Preminger had beaten Kirk Douglas into
print, but not into theaters. On October 19, 1960, at the standing-room-only
premiere of *Spartacus* at the RKO Pantages Theater in Hollywood, Dalton
Trumbo saw his name on screen for the first time in fifteen years. Bleacher
seats erected on either side of a red carpeted entryway were packed with
fans who squealed and applauded as the stars strolled by, a reminder that
Hollywood could always stage a Klieg-lit spectacle better than Washington.[28]
On December 21, 1960, *Exodus* premiered amid similar hoopla at the Fox
Wilshire Theater.[29]

Reading the name named in the credits to *Spartacus* and *Exodus*, the
forces that created and enforced the blacklist saw it fading before their eyes.
The American Legion warned that if the Trumbo double bill succeeded at the
box office, the studios would scrap the Waldorf Declaration and Hollywood
would again "be open to the horrible nightmare of Communist infiltration
of the 1930s and 1940s."[30] Legion-backed pickets went up at screenings of
both films at scattered locations around the country, but with no deterrent
effect on the box office.[31] American moviegoers, so discombobulated by the
infiltration of Communism in Hollywood in 1947, were nonchalant about its
re-infiltration in 1960.[32]

In fact, *Spartacus* was a must-see film in the city, now under new management, that had for so long been the bane of Hollywood's existence. Among
its legion of fans was the Attorney General of the United States, who recommended the film to his brother. On February 3, 1961, John F. Kennedy, newly
inaugurated President of the United States, Roman Catholic naval veteran,
and second-generation film aficionado, took an unannounced excursion from

the White House to the Warner Theatre three blocks away to see what everyone was talking about (the White House screening room was not equipped with the 70mm projection facilities to screen the film in its proper format). Veterans groups had been picketing the theater, but JFK—no longer skittish about being linked to a member of the Hollywood Ten—paid no heed. "An extraordinary angle to the President's choice of *Spartacus*," reported the breathless account in *Variety*, "is that the picture has been attacked by the American Legion because the screenplay was written by Dalton Trumbo, a member of the so-called Hollywood 10."[33]

JFK's executive action quickened the death of the blacklist. In 1961, responding to accusations by the American Legion that Hollywood was "surreptitiously employing known Communists," Eric Johnston restated the MPAA's support for the Waldorf Declaration. "The policy of the Motion Picture Association is not to employ known Communists," he said in a formal statement. "The policy has not changed." But the game was up.[34] By then, there was nothing surreptitious about the employment of known Communists. The enabling document of the Hollywood blacklist was never publicly revoked or repudiated by the MPAA; it was just ignored.[35]

The man who had invested so much of his political and moral capital in the Waldorf Declaration was soon to follow its demise. In 1963, the dynamic, articulate Eric Johnston began to suffer memory lapses and hesitation of speech. On June 17, after checking himself into Doctor's Hospital in Washington D.C., he suffered a stroke, slipped into a coma, and died two months later.[36] Over five hundred mourners, an elite congregation more parts Washington than Hollywood, attended the funeral rites at St. John's Episcopal Church; former presidents Dwight Eisenhower, Harry Truman, and Hebert Hoover served as honorary pallbearers. None of the eulogies mentioned the Waldorf Declaration or the blacklist.[37]

Other remnants of the era—organizations and personalities that had so lately instilled fear and decided fates—were also passing from the scene. After the release of *Spartacus* and *Exodus*, the MPA-PAI was unable to preserve itself. In 1965, *Variety* pronounced HUAC's civilian support group "moribund" and functionally dead.[38]

The legislative body that had lent the coercive power of the state to the Hollywood blacklist also suffered a swift decline in public esteem. By the late 1950s, HUAC could no longer meet without squadrons of angry picketers decrying its very existence, protesters whose ranks grew as the anti-Communist heat of the 1950s cooled. In 1969, the house committee that Martin Dies built was rechristened the House Internal Security Committee before being abolished for good, so far, in 1975. Though "un-American" remains an oft-uttered epithet in American political discourse, the label is no longer worn by an official arm of the U.S. government.

As the blacklist faded, the men who had inspired it were transformed into honored veterans of a noble fight against Cold War repression. By the late 1960s, the pariahs of 1947 were being hailed as models and martyrs; the men and women who cozied up to HUAC and named names, scorned as weasels and stool pigeons. "I never thought the day would come when the Hollywood Ten were the only ones working," semi-joked Writers Guild president Mel Shavelson in 1970.[39]

Dalton Trumbo tried to put the cultural turnabout in perspective with an odd and out of character comment. On March 13, 1970, while accepting the Laurel Award for achievement in screenwriting from the Writers Guild, he looked back at the blacklist era and told his fellow screenwriters:

> There was bad faith and good, honesty and dishonesty, courage and cowardice, selfishness and stupidity, good and bad on both sides. . . . When you who are in your forties or younger look back with curiosity on that dark time, as I think occasionally you should, it will do no good to search for villains or heroes or saints or devils because there were none; there were only victims.
>
> Some suffered less than others, some grew and some diminished, but in the final tally we were *all* victims because almost without exception each of us felt compelled to say things he did not want to say, to do things he did not want to do, to deliver and receive wounds he did not want to exchange.
>
> That is why none of us—right, left, or center—emerged from that long nightmare without sin.

Trumbo's fellow Unfriendlies were stunned. His "only victims" line scrambled stark distinctions into a mushy moral equivalence. Albert Maltz considered Trumbo's formulation "an appalling distortion of the period" and a misguided attempt at reconciliation.[40] An incensed Lester Cole derided Trumbo's "lofty benediction upon all (no heroes, no villains, only victims)" and thoughtless "blessing and forgiveness of the 'villains' " of 1947.[41] In 1977, reflecting on the phrase in a letter to Lardner and Maltz, Alvah Bessie wrote, "I have never QUITE recovered from Dalton's Olympian judgment on us all at the Laurel Award ceremony, because I DO feel there were villains and we know their names, and I do think we behaved very well indeed and we were the ONLY victims of what the industry did to us at the time, as well as the newspapers, etc."[42] Though impatient with the "nostalgic image of us as heroes," Ring Lardner Jr. was no less emphatic about the only solution to the moral dilemma. "The choice we faced was between being 'heroes' and being complete shits."[43]

True to type, Hollywood commemorated the new order of things with a self-caressing motion picture, *The Way We Were* (1973). Directed by Sidney Pollack and written by former member of the Committee for the First Amendment and blacklistee Arthur Laurents, the soft-focus love story traced the timeline from the Popular Front to the Hollywood blacklist, with a star-crossed romance between a vapid WASP and a socially conscious Jew set against a more passionate romance with American Communism. The syrupy theme song warbled by Barbra Streisand ("mem-o-ries/ in the corners of my mind/misty water colored memories/of the way we were") went to number 1 on the *Billboard* pop charts. "That wasn't the way we were at all," groused Alvah Bessie, refusing to fall under the spell.[44]

By mid-decade, *The Front* (1976), a dramedy about a schlemiel cashing in on the television blacklist, directed by blacklistee Martin Ritt and written by blacklistee Walter Bernstein, and *Hollywood on Trial* (1976), the most complete archival record of the 1947 hearings and their aftermath, directed by David Helpern Jr. and written by Arnie Reisman, spearheaded a full-on blacklist-themed pop-cult wave. Surveying the proliferation of feature films, documentaries, plays, books, and memoirs that flashed back to the era, the critic Hilton Kramer wondered how long it would be "before some jolly spirit mounts a Broadway musical about J. Parnell Thomas and the Hollywood Ten," a project as yet unrealized.[45]

Albert Maltz was also looking around and marveling at the zeitgeist shift. "Today [1975], in a manner of speaking, the Hollywood Ten have been reha-bilitated. Once mercilessly excoriated, we get honored nowadays for having stood up for what we believed while so many others sat by."[46] The full story of what they believed—the party discipline they accepted, the ideological somersaults they performed in 1939, and 1941, and again in 1945—was shaded over and covered up. What they resisted—J. Parnell Thomas and HUAC—was more important than what they had once embraced—Joseph Stalin and the CPUSA.

Screenwriter Dalton Trumbo recalls the blacklist era in *Hollywood on Trial* (1976).

In deference to a narrative of heroes and villains, noble resisters and complete shits, graduations of placement along the left-to-right grid, crucial at the time, disappeared, with no middle ground marked out between defiance and complicity. Watching *Hollywood on Trial*, screenwriter Philip Dunne was "amazed to hear John Huston, who was my partner in the Committee for the First Amendment, saying 'We went to Washington to back up the Hollywood Ten.'" Dunne was having none of it:

> Well, somebody had written his copy for him, that's *not* why we went. And he *knew* better than that. But there he was saying it! So, here we are together, who are you going to believe? Well, you can believe me in this case, because I knew what we were doing! We went over to back up Eric Johnston. We timed our arrival to back up Eric Johnston who, like Byron's nymph, having sworn he would ne'er consent to a blacklist, *consented*.[47]

Screen Writers' Guild president Emmet Lavery, who in 1947 had piloted his union through dangerous shoals, also tried to set the record straight, or at least complicate the morality play. Lavery had always believed that "life in America was not necessarily a choice between two reactionary extremes: between the shouting Congressman J. Parnell Thomas on the one hand, and the shouting non-responsive witnesses from Hollywood on the other."[48] Under Lavery, the guild would not do HUAC's bidding and toss out the Communists, but neither would it risk its future by embracing them. "I think that the achievement of that era is that under extraordinary and difficult circumstances we preserved the Guild," Lavery recalled in 1977. "Let's face it, the group that liked Jack Lawson and Dalton Trumbo and preferred their leadership wanted the Guild to be a political action forum." Lavery prevailed because the majority of the guild "believed you could be a liberal and a non-Communist liberal. Now I don't think Jack and Dalton believed that at all. And I think that's really the line of cleavage that isn't stressed very much in the memoirs and recollections of the Guild."[49]

However, not all liberals, name-namers or not, felt they had emerged from the HUAC wringer with a clean smell. Dore Schary always regretted his role in writing—and enforcing—the Waldorf Declaration. As was so often the case in 1947, the liberal's good-faith attempt to nudge an extreme position toward a middle ground brought him only grief. Schary became "a target for the right and the left," he recalled ruefully. "I should never have listened to Goldwyn" about working on the Waldorf Declaration.[50] In 1948, Schary left RKO to return to MGM as vice president in charge of production, saying he hoped "to maintain a balance between being a picture maker, a citizen, and a creative artist," a credo that he strived to live up to until his death in 1980.[51]

On the other side of the ledger book, the second-billed Friendlies, nominally in the fold, paid their own price in lost friendships and career opportunities. The big stars who testified in 1947 were shielded by their close-mouthed dignity—or bankability—but the expendable supporting players found their prospects drying up in the industry they had bad-mouthed. Though not to be equated with the state-coerced, institutionally enforced blacklist of Communists, fellow travelers, and stubborn liberals, the cooperative witnesses discovered that friendly testimony exacted its own penalties from producers who didn't need a Waldorf Declaration to stay clear of men who so readily blurted out the names of vulnerable coworkers to a congressional committee. Even for those spared a sojourn at a federal penitentiary, the repercussions from the HUAC hearings could be a life sentence.

Adolphe Menjou struggled to regain his career momentum. Forced into an unfashionable comedown in syndicated television, he attributed the slump to his elegant anti-Communist profile, claiming he did not work in Hollywood for years. He returned to style, however, with a magnificent performance as a suavely cynical French Army officer in *Paths of Glory* (1957), and ended his career with an against-type role as an ill-dressed codger in Walt Disney's *Pollyanna* (1960). At the time of his death in 1963, he was an ardent member of the John Birch Society.

Ayn Rand finally scored a name-above-the-title credit on a major motion picture, collaborating with director King Vidor, a fellow member of the MPA-PAI, on a right-wing dream project, *The Fountainhead* (1949). A big-budget mounting of Rand's opus maximus produced by Warner Bros. and starring the sort-of friendly Gary Cooper as the author's masculine ideal, an inner-directed architect-ubermensch, the film lived up to the source material: turgid, didactic, ridden with hectoring speeches spouting the Objectivist philosophy that would be Rand's permanent legacy to American thought. Thanks to Cooper's star appeal, the film did okay at the box office.[52]

Director Sam Wood's antipathy to Communism was so fierce it reached out from beyond the grave. On September 22, 1949, shortly after giving a speech to the MPA-PAI, he was felled by a heart attack. Wood's last will and testament specified that his heirs, before receiving their inheritance, would need to file an affidavit in court affirming they had no Communist affiliations. He exempted only his wife.[53]

Leo McCarey's anti-Communist zeal did not extend beyond the grave, but it warped his next project. After testifying before HUAC, the director returned to Hollywood to finish work on *Good Sam* (1948), a critical and commercial failure not even Gary Cooper could salvage. McCarey then embarked on his most controversial and bizarre film, *My Son John* (1952), an anti-Communist sermon disguised as a familial melodrama, or vice versa. "The idea came to me when I was in the middle of a show business story, *Born in a Trunk*. The new story was so imperative that I dropped everything else to get to it," McCarey said in 1951. His entry would be different from the rest of what was already a discredited cycle, the spate of heavy-handed thrillers made to placate HUAC, protection payments in 35mm like *The Iron Curtain* (1948), *The Red Menace* (1949), and *The Red Danube* (1949).[54]

My Son John tells the tale of an Alger Hiss-like espionage agent, the son of patriotic Irish-Catholic parents. The mother is going through menopause and a crisis of conscience: she suspects that her beloved son John has betrayed both his faith and his country. A box office and critical bomb, the film poisoned McCarey's once blue-chip stock in Hollywood. Better had he never abandoned *Born in a Trunk*.

Howard Rushmore, the former film critic for the *Daily Worker*, moved further away from his journalistic roots. In 1955, after being let go from the *New York Journal America* and working briefly on the staff of Sen. Joseph McCarthy, he took the editorial reins at *Confidential* magazine, the scandal sheet that peeked into windows and opened closets that Hedda Hopper and Louella Parsons kept shut. Besides his politics, he had jettisoned his dowdy Communist spouse to marry a sleek blond fashion editor and former model, Francis Everett McCoy. Her career soared while his bottomed out. On January 3, 1958, the couple had a nasty fight at a New York restaurant. McCoy fled into a taxicab. Rushmore followed her into the back seat, took out a pistol, and fatally shot her before turning the gun on himself.[55]

MGM story editor James K. McGuinness had caused Louis B. Mayer too much trouble to remain for long under the Lion's paw. (Asked about MGM's anti-Communist vigilance during the HUAC hearings, McGuinness was unwisely honest. "I don't think it is the whitest condition in the industry. I think we have our share of Communists in our employ.")[56] In 1949, after eighteen years with the studio, the company man was pushed out. He went into independent production and still worked at his first trade, earning his most notable screenwriting credit in 1950, the year he died of a heart attack, with the second of John Ford's magisterial cavalry trilogy, *Rio Grande*. His friend Hedda Hopper believed McGuinness "literally worked himself to death" in the fight against Communism.[57]

The venerable libertarian and polymath Rupert Hughes continued to write and lecture on Communism while also busying himself with a dizzying array of assignments for music encyclopedias, popular magazines, and radio. When he died in 1956, he was still working on the fourth volume of his omnibus biography of George Washington.[58]

After obliging HUAC by naming and spelling names, Jack Moffitt found his worst fears realized. Two days after testifying, he was fired from his post as film critic for *Esquire*.[59] Save for an adaption credit on *The Story of Will Rogers* (1952), screen work dried up; he hustled as a freelance writer.[60] In 1955, Billy Wilkerson hired him as a film reviewer for the *Hollywood Reporter*, a position he held for the next eight years. He died in 1969.

The Hollywood career of Fred Niblo Jr. also saw a fast fade to black. *Convicted* (1950) was his last major screen credit, and that was an adaptation of his screenplay for *The Criminal Code* (1930). Cold-shouldered by the studios, he turned to writing religious films for Father Patrick Peyton's television series *Family Theater* (1951–1953) before finding permanent employment making documentaries for the State Department.

Morrie Ryskind, the friendly screenwriter with the most impressive list of screen credits, returned to Hollywood and a telephone that no longer rang. "In the twelve years prior to my testimony at the 1947 HUAC hearings in Washington, I was consistently one of the ten highest paid writers in Hollywood," he recalled in 1983. "I turned down, on the average, at least three assignments for every one that I accepted, and I feel safe in saying that I was welcome at every studio in town. After I testified against the Hollywood Ten, I was never again to receive one single offer from any studio, and the same fate befell McGuinness, Niblo, and Moffitt, all of whom had credentials that matched mine."[61]

Nonetheless, tallying up what his testimony had cost him in friendships and career opportunities, Ryskind had no regrets. "Had the Hollywood Ten been advocating voodoism, blank verse, or a return to the silver standard, I would have defended their right to privacy of association," he wrote. "But when it came to their support—their very active support—of a political party which had, as its stated objective, the overthrow of the American constitutional form of government, I couldn't help but look at them as agents of a foreign power, nor could I keep myself from thinking they got off rather lightly by just being blacklisted."[62]

Most of Ryskind's former colleagues in Hollywood—and their descendants—felt otherwise. Looking back with shame and righteousness, they felt an abiding need to make amends for the sins of their fathers and sometimes their own. Not a congressional hearing but the Academy Awards ceremony became the favored forum for rituals of forgiveness and reparation, with the blacklisted and the exiled welcome back as honored guests. The cascading applause that greeted the blacklisted screenwriters Waldo Salt for *Midnight Cowboy* (1969) and Ring Lardner Jr. for *M*A*S*H* became rapturous standing ovations for Charles Chaplin, who in 1972, returned to Hollywood after a twenty-year absence to receive an honorary Oscar, and for Lillian Hellman, invited to present the Academy Award for best short and feature length documentary in 1977. In introducing Hellman, kindred spirit Jane Fonda called

HUAC "a travesty of human rights," but Hellman, "her conscience intact," was back. No one mentioned Finland.

Unlike Chaplin and Hellman, Elia Kazan was not greeted with unanimous applause. In 1999, the director of *Gentleman's Agreement* (1947), *On the Waterfront* (1954), *East of Eden* (1955), and a dozen or more other certifiable motion picture classics, stood on the stage of the Dorothy Chandler Pavilion with a nervous Martin Scorsese and Robert De Niro to accept an honorary Oscar for Lifetime Achievement. The rub was that Kazan had named names during a closed session of HUAC in 1952. Outside, protesters waved pickets signs reading "Don't Whitewash the Blacklist." Inside, many in the crowd sat on their hands.[63]

With a vengeance Sam Wood might have appreciated, the payback was sometimes posthumous. In 1989, the name of Robert Taylor was stripped from the Robert Taylor Building at Lorimar Studios, formerly the MGM lot in Culver City. A group of producers, screenwriters, and tenants were aggrieved that the Navy veteran and MGM superstar, who had given the names of two actors and one screenwriter to HUAC, was being honored in architecture. Overnight the edifice became the George Cukor Building, after the MGM director who had played no part in the show trial of 1947, either as Friendly, Unfriendly, or member of the Committee for the First Amendment. "The 'man with the perfect profile' has a lower one now," joked *Variety*.[64]

As ever, the clash between Hollywood and HUAC was still all about names.

A BIBLIOGRAPHICAL NOTE

The scholarship generated by the decision of the House Committee on Un-American Activities to go Hollywood is voluminous—academic studies, edited volumes, memoirs, oral histories, documentaries, and, lately, blogs and websites.[1] With the exception of the storied alliance between the motion picture industry and the U.S. government during World War II, it is probably the most chronicled slice of history from the golden age of the studio system, not to say a raw wound that, even into the twenty-first century, rips open whenever a ghost from the past is resurrected or a blacklist-themed melodrama enters the pop-cult bloodstream. Anyone presuming to add another entry to the bookshelf should offer a few words of justification.

I have focused on the first of HUAC's postwar Hollywood hearings in 1947 because it set the pattern for the congressional-media confrontations that followed; because it launched the blacklist era; and because it was a distinctly cinema-centric event (not only were the Thomas Committee hearings focused on the motion picture industry but the motion picture medium, via the newsreels, assumed proprietary rights to the archival record). I sought also to explore the overlooked backstories and to expand the cast of characters caught in the crossfire. Though the Hollywood Ten will always get top billing, thirty-one other witnesses—and myriad players in the gallery and commentators on the sidelines—have tales worth telling. Finally, no single study has been devoted exclusively to HUAC's Hollywood year.[2]

True to its source, the library devoted to Hollywood and HUAC grinds a sharpened selection of ideological axes. To understate the case, the confrontation has attracted parades of passionate stakeholders with vested interests—scholarly, political, and personal. Most stand on the ideological left, in spirit with the gallery that hissed at Chairman Thomas and cheered on the Unfriendly Nineteen. They conjure an American inquisition, a Red scare, a time of great fear and grand inquests.[3] Against that tidal wave of indictment, a ripple of scholarship from the other side has sought to correct the balance. Politically conservative and revisionist in outlook, it challenges the notion that the Unfriendly Nineteen were heroic defenders of the First Amendment and argues that HUAC got things pretty much right—and that the Hollywood Communists and fellow travelers, whether jailed or blacklisted, got what was coming to them.[4]

A third strand of HUAC-Hollywood historiography might be called neo-revisionist in temper. It shares the contempt for HUAC on the left but agrees with the right that the committee was following a hot trail. "They can't put their ideas into Hollywood pictures," cracked a studio factotum, scoffing at the notion that Communists had infiltrated the air-headed chambers of Hollywood entertainment. "Nobody can."[5] Nonsense, say the neo-revisionists. Communist artists in Hollywood worked tenaciously, and with some success, to inject a pro-civil rights and anti-capitalist agenda into Hollywood cinema. Had the moguls and the congressmen the wit to see it, the evidence was right before their eyes. Look not to the pro-Soviet troika of World War II or the preachy social problem films of the postwar era, but to the shadowy netherworld of film noir, where brutalist melodramas like *Body and Soul* (1947), *Brute Force* (1947), and *Force of Evil* (1948) whispered that something really was rotten in the heart of America. The Hollywood left did indeed bore into the architecture of Hollywood cinema—and a good thing too.[6]

For myself, I wanted to avoid the lenses of left and right—and, frankly, stay clear of a partisan narrative of stand-up guys on the one hand and craven finks on the other. To capture a sense of the 1947 hearings as they unfolded, I've gone back to the original sources. The baseline archival resource for all things congressional is the *Congressional Record*, in this case the ominously titled *Hearings Regarding the Communist Infiltration of the Motion Picture Industry. Hearings Before the Committee on Un-American Activities, House of Representatives, Eightieth Congress. First Session*, pursuant to Public Law 601, published in 1947. Unless otherwise noted, and unless an audio record was available, the testimony quoted throughout is derived from this source. However, the official account as taken down by civil service stenographers and distributed by the U.S. Government Printing Office is a dry and sometimes inaccurate rendering of what was said and what went on in the hearing room. The official transcript corrects grammar, elides asides, and ignores atmospherics. If Chairman Thomas called for a remark to be stricken from the record—such as Rupert Hughes's accusation that the University of California at Los Angeles was a hotbed of Communism—it was duly stricken, leaving no federal record of a charge that went out in the press and over the radio. Eric Bentley, whose Folkways Record LP of Bertolt Brecht's appearance before the committee offers a complete recording of the actual testimony, reprinted the *Congressional Record* transcript of Brecht's remarks as part of the liner notes for the album. "It is not wholly accurate as anyone who compares [the official transcript] with the dialogue of the disk will discover," Bentley pointed out.[7] In his 1990 memoir *Being Red*, the Communist novelist Howard Fast, who was hauled before HUAC on October 23, 1946 for his work on the Joint Anti-Fascist Refugee Committee, noted that "the record differed considerably from what went on in that room" and complained about the bowdlerization, both of his own vulgarities and that of the committee chairman. "Wood reacted with rage and did some name calling of his own, using four-letter Anglo-Saxon words with a facility that matched my own gutter training," Fast recalled. "The record printed none of that."[8] In his 1965 memoir *Hollywood on Trial*, screenwriter Alvah Bessie was still annoyed that the official record did not acknowledge the gales of laughter he got from the gallery, but was sure to harken to the chuckling whenever Thomas lanced Bessie with a caustic remark—"which does not jibe with my total recollection," he commented sourly. Bessie was also perturbed that the committee members could not seem to pronounce the word "Communist" correctly. "They invariably said 'Commonist.'"[9] The stenographer invariably wrote "Communist."

Except for the occasional prim notation of [laughter] or [applause], the *Congressional Record* conjures little of the passion of the performances or the buzz from the crowd. To call up the drama and din of the spectacle, the electric tension of being in the room where it happened, I have turned to the trade press, letters, telegrams, studio memos, legislative archives, and, when they existed, the radio recordings and newsreels of the actual hearings. Throughout, I have privileged contemporary over retrospective sources. Hollywood memoirs were used sparingly: the genre is notoriously unreliable and never more so than when recounting a passage that was so painful, so bitter, and, for many, so humiliating. Also, people just forget. In Paul Henreid's chapter on his experience as a member of the Committee for the First Amendment in *Ladies Man: An Autobiography*, the actor gets almost everything wrong except the mode of transportation the group took to Washington.[10] I have applied the standard scholarly tests in gauging the reliability of an autobiography—reality testing the narrator's memory against verifiable history and awarding points for credibility to writers who refused to spare themselves. Philip Dunne and Lauren Bacall score well; John Huston and Lester Cole, not so much.

Since 1967, another record has opened a window into Hollywood and HUAC: the files of the FBI made available under the Freedom of Information Act, particularly the copious and regularly updated Communist Infiltration-Motion Picture Industry (COMPIC) files on Communist activity in the motion picture industry. In addition to the blunt if often ill-informed observations of FBI men, the inside dope from informants in the CPUSA, SAG, CFA, and most every guild and union laboring in the studio system, sometimes on the record, sometimes with names redacted, offers a clandestine insight into the backbiting and score-settling of the era. But while the surveillance was extensive, it is also marked by suspicious omissions in the official record: W. R. "Billy" Wilkerson, a friend of J. Edgar Hoover and a front-line warrior in Hollywood's Cold War, has no extant FBI file. Neither does the thorny MGM executive Eddie Mannix. Nor does the most ideologically influential player in all of Hollywood, Joseph I. Breen, head of the Production Code Administration. Perhaps the gaps are merely the result of bad record keeping.

Whatever political wing produces the scholarship on Hollywood and HUAC, the prose tends to be polemical in cast and intemperate in tone. I've tried to turn down the rhetorical heat and avoid the language of psychosis and pathology that colors so many cultural histories of the period—the metaphors of fevers and hysteria, plagues and infections, where anti-Communists are rabid, Communists are termites, and liberals are unwitting dupes. The stories are more complicated and the questions, however phrased, are not easily answered by the simple yes or no demanded by the members of the House Committee on Un-American Activities.

NOTES

Abbreviations

AMPAS   Margaret Herrick Library of the Academy of Motion Picture Arts and Sciences in Beverly Hills, CA

HUAC-NARA   Records of the House Un-American Activities records at the Center for Legislative Archives at the National Archives and Records Administration in Washington, D.C.

COM PIC   FBI files on Communist Infiltration of the Motion Picture Industry

NIXON   The Richard Nixon Presidential Library in Yorba Linda, CA

UWISC   Wisconsin Center for Film and Theater Research at the University of Wisconsin-Madison, WI

Program Notes

1. "Red Quiz Barnum Show," *Daily Variety*, October 20, 1947, 1.
2. Lillian Hellman, "The Judas Goats," *Screen Writer*, December 1947, 7.
3. Fred Othman, "I'll Tell the Truth If It Kills Me," *Washington News*, October 28, 1947, 27.
4. Eric Bentley, liner notes to *Bertolt Brecht before the Committee on Un-American Activities Committee*, Folkways Records, 1963.
5. "Public Hearings on Studio Red Probe," *Motion Picture Daily*, April 30, 1947, 2.
6. "Red Probe on Today; 50 Called," *Hollywood Reporter*, October 20, 1947, 1, 11.
7. Florence S. Lowe, "Hearing Opens with Pomp of Big Show Debut," *Daily Variety*, October 21, 1947, 9.
8. "Film Industry to Fire Reds; Votes to Suspend Cited Ten," *Box Office*, November 29, 1947, 8–9.

9.   W. R. Wilkerson, "Tradeviews," *Hollywood Reporter*, October 20, 1947, 1–2.

10. Terry Ramsaye, "On the Potomac," *Motion Picture Herald*, October 25, 1947, 7.

1. How the Popular Front Became Unpopular

1.   Raymond Moley, *The Hays Office* (New York: Bobbs-Merrill, 1945), 122.

2.   Douglas Bell, *An Oral History with Philip Dunne* (Academy Foundation Oral History Program, 1991), 64.

3.   Harvey Klehr, *The Heyday of American Communism: The Depression Decade* (New York: Basic Books, 1984), 365–367. Accurate numbers for CPUSA membership are hard to come by: party leaders and FBI agents alike inflated the numbers and not everyone attended meetings or paid their dues. Klehr bases his figures on CPUSA recruitment reports to the Poltiburo and statements by Earl Browder, who after leaving the party admitted that membership in the 1930s never rose above one hundred thousand. "Irish Groups Hail Pope," *New York Times*, March 5, 1939, 40.

4.   "Chicago Throng Fills Hall to Honor Lenin," *Daily Worker*, Janaury 25, 1937, 2.

5.   Robert Osborne Baker, *The International Alliance of Theatrical Stage Employes and Moving Picture Machine Operators of the United States and Canada* (Lawrence, Kansas, 1933), 66–73. The original title of the union contained only one "e" in "Employes."

6.   Murray Ross, *Stars and Strikes: Unionization of Hollywood* (New York: Columbia University Press, 1941), 14, and 3–22 passim.

7.   "Studios Go Closed Shop Jan. 2," *Daily Variety*, December 16, 1935, 1, 4; "Full Text of Producer and Union Agreement Pledging Closed Shop," *Daily Variety*, December 20, 1935, 4.

8.   Charles Higham, *Hollywood at Sunset* (New York: Saturday Review Press, 1972), 33.

9.   Florabel Muir, " 'All Right, Gentlemen, Do We Get All the Money?,' " *Saturday Evening Post*, January 27, 1940, 9–11, 81–82, 84.

10. Otto Friedrich, *City of Nets: A Portrait of Hollywood in the 1940s* (New York: Harper and Row, 1986), 247.

11. "Actor's Chief on Stand in Labor Inquiry," *Hollywood Citizen-News*, November 17, 1937, 1, 5.

12. Muir, " 'All Right, Gentlemen, Do We Get All the Money?,' " 82.

13. Arthur Ungar, "Willie, the 'Keedle,' " *Daily Variety*, November 22, 1939, 1, 3.

14. Oliver Pilat, *Pegler: Angry Man of the Press* (Boston: Beacon Press, 1963), 166–171.

15. "Hollywood Inside," *Daily Variety*, December 1, 1939, 2; Westbrook Pegler, "Fair Enough," *Los Angeles Times*, December 8, 1941, 7.

16. Arthur Ungar, "Thugs and Pictures," *Daily Variety*, December 1, 1939, 1, 3.

17. Ralph Roddy, "Studio Labor Rides Gravy Train," *Daily Variety*, October 29, 1941, 12.

18. "Independent Studio Locals Federating," *Motion Picture Herald*, November 8, 1941, 34.

19. F. Scott Fitzgerald, *The Pat Hobby Stories* (New York: Scribner, 1962), xi; S. J. Perelman, *The Best of S. J. Perelman* (New York: Random House, 1962), 79.

20. Lester Cole, *Hollywood Red: The Autobiography of Lester Cole.* (Palo Alto: Ramparts Press, 1981), 123–127.

21. "Reorganized Screen Writers' Guild Pledges Members to Closed Shop," *Variety*, April 11, 1933, 4.

22. "Mayer Swats Writers," *Daily Variety*, September 20, 1933, 1.

23. Morrie Ryskind with John H. Roberts, *I Shot an Elephant in My Pajamas: The Morrie Ryskind Story* (Lafayette, LA: Huntington House, 1994), 155–156.

24. "New Writers Group Votes Constitution," *Motion Picture Daily*, May 23, 1936, 1, 4.

25. "Hughes Won't Quit," *Daily Variety*, August 4, 1937, 13.

26. "Writers' Guild Is Dissolved on Coast," *Motion Picture Daily*, March 3, 1937, 7.

27. "Writers to Revive Guild on the Coast," *Motion Picture Daily*, June 2, 1947, 1, 8; "SWG Seeks Position as Labor Bargainer," *Motion Picture Daily*, June 15, 1937, 1, 9.

28. "NLRB Rules Out Coercion Instances," *Motion Picture Daily*, October 17, 1937, 9; "Pioneer Testifies," *Motion Picture Daily*, October 7, 1937, 4; "Jones Resumes Testimony," *Motion Picture Daily*, October 20, 1937, 11.

29. "Writers' Guild Sweeps Studios in Collective Bargaining Voting," *Motion Picture Herald*, July 2, 1938, 17.

30. Theodore Draper, "The Man Who Wanted to Hang," *The Reporter*, January 6, 1953, 26–30.

31. "In 19 Months League Has Grown to Organization of Nearly 5,000 Members," *Hollywood Now*, January 26, 1938, 5.

32. "Film Artists Rally in Support of Labor," *Hollywood Now*, April 23, 1938, 1.

33. Melvyn Douglas, "Voice of Hollywood," *Hollywood Now*, May 28, 1938, 1, 3.

34. "7,000 Roar OK to Collective Action Against War-Makers," *Hollywood Now*, February 4, 1938, 1; "Highlights from Shrine Messages," *Hollywood Now*, February 4, 1938, 2.

35. August Raymond Ogden, *The Dies Committee: A Study of the Special House Committee for the Investigation of Un-American Activities* (Washington, DC: Catholic University of America Press, 1945), 47.

36. Martin Dies, *Martin Dies' Story* (New York: Bookmailer, 1963), 30–31.

37. Douglas Warrenfels, "House Probers Ask Red Curb, Uphold Butler," *Washington Post*, February 16, 1935, 1; Robert K. Carr, *The House Committee on Un-American Activities, 1945–1950* (Ithaca: Cornell University Press, 1952), 13–14.

38. Howard Lancaster, "Martin Dies Grows in U.S. Esteem as 'Ism' Investigation Bears Fruit," *Lima (NY) Recorder*, January 11, 1940, 2.

39. Francis L. Burt, "Charges Arouse Little Interest in Washington," *Motion Picture Herald*, August 20, 1938, 28; Vance King, "Hollywood's Anti-Nazis Repudiate U.S. Agents Charge of 'Communist,'" *Motion Picture Herald*, August 20, 1938, 20; "Federal Official Protects Bridges, Dies Aide Charges," *New York Times*, August 15, 1938, 1, 6.

40. J. B. Matthews, *Odyssey of a Fellow Traveler* (New York: Mount Vernon, Inc., 1938), 269.

41. Robert E. Stripling, *The Red Plot Against America*, ed. Bob Considine (Drexel, PA: Bell Publishing Company, 1949) 29.

42. "'Reds' Run WPA Theater; Film Players, Dies Group Hears," *Motion Picture Herald*, August 27, 1938, 29–30.

43. Stripling, *The Red Plot Against America*, 30.

44. "'I'll Bare Everything,' Tease Girl Declares," *Albany Times-Union*, November 26, 1938, 4.

45. The extent of antisemitic activity and fifth column Nazism in Hollywood in the 1930s is chronicled in Steven J. Ross, *Hitler in Los Angeles: How Jews Foiled Nazi Plots Against Hollywood and America* (New York: Bloomsbury, 2017), and Laura Rosenzweig, *Hollywood's Spies: The Undercover Surveillance of Nazis in Los Angeles* (New York: New York University Press, 2017).

46. Ring Lardner Jr., "Confessions of a Coughlin Reader," *Hollywood Now*, June 23, 1939, 3. See also Alan Brinkley, *Voices of Protest: Huey Long, Father Coughlin, and the Great Depression* (New York: Vintage, 1982), 269–273.

47. Representative Martin Dies, "The Reds in Hollywood," *Liberty*, February 17, 1940, 47–50; Representative Martin Dies, "Is Communism Invading the Movies?," *Liberty*, February 24, 1940, 57–60. Dies and *Liberty* give the date of Dies's visit with Harry Warner as 1938, impossible given the screening of *Confessions of a Nazi Spy*. He actually visited the Warner lot on May 2, 1939. See "Dies Guest at Warner," *Daily Variety*, May 3, 1939, 4.

48. "Bogart Carries 'Red' Denial Before Dies," *Hollywood Citizen-News*, August 16, 1940, 1, 3.

49. "Dies Clears March, Cagney, Bogart of Red Charges," *Los Angeles Times*, August 21, 1940, 1, 3.

50. "'Communists' in Hollywood," *Variety*, August 21, 1940, 3; "Films Fight Red Charges," *Variety*, August 21, 1940, 3.

51. Martin Dies, *The Trojan Horse in America* (New York: Dodd, Mead, 1940).

52. "Fitts Gives Actors Clean Bill of Health," *Daily Variety*, August 12, 1940, 6.

53. Charles Glenn, "The Cameras Shoot for War," *New Masses*, June 11, 1940, 31.

54. "The Writers Don't Want War," *New Masses*, June 25, 1940, 21.

55. William Wright, *Lillian Hellman: The Image, the Woman* (New York: Simon and Schuster, 1986), 161–162; "Sees Finnish Aid Imperiling Peace," *New York Times*, January 21, 1940, 27; "Actors Widen Split on Finn Benefits," *New York Times*, January 20, 1940, 11.

56. Dunne, quoted in Bell, *An Oral History with Philip Dunne*, 64.

57. "The Soviet-Nazi War," *New Masses*, July 1, 1941, 3, 8.

58. Walter Winchell, "In New York," *New York Mirror*, November 6, 1947, 11.

2. Hollywood's War Record

1. James Dugan, "The First War Film," *New Masses*, February 13, 1940, 29; Alvah Bessie, "Out of Hollywood," *New Masses*, August 20, 1940, 22; Joy Davidman, "Rover Boys on Wings," *New Masses*, April 8, 1941, 28–29.

2. A. U., "Always the 'Patsy,' " *Daily Variety*, August 4, 1941, 1, 3.

3. "U.S. Probe of Films War Stand Asked," *Motion Picture Daily*, August 4, 1941, 2.

4. "The Washington Idea on Hollywood," *Variety*, August 27, 1941, 4.

5. "Film Blasting Starts Today," *Daily Variety*, September 9, 1941, 1, 7.

6. Bertram F. Linz, "Public Influences Pictures: Schenck," *Motion Picture Daily*, September 25, 1941, 4.

7. "Willkie Tells Sen. Clark Off," *Daily Variety*, September 26, 1941, 9; "Warner Defends Picture Policy," *Motion Picture Daily*, September 26, 1941, 1, 6.

8. "Zanuck Attacks Censor Attempt," *Motion Picture Daily*, September 29, 1941, 5.

9. Bureau of Motion Pictures, *The Government Information Manual for the Motion Picture Industry* (Washington, DC: Office of War Information, 1942), Section III, 1, 5.

10. "World Premiere of 'North Star' Set," *Motion Picture Herald*, October 16, 1943, 40.

11. "Hollywood in Wartime," *Yank*, September 24, 1943, 21.

12. Phil M. Daily, "Along the Rialto," *Film Daily*, April 29, 1943, 5.

13. Martin Dies, *The Martin Dies Story* (New York: Bookmailer, 1963).

14. Robert K. Carr, *The House Committee on Un-American Activities 1945–1950* (New York: Cornell University Press, 1952), 19–22. Carr calls Rankin's gambit to make HUAC a standing committee "one of the most remarkable procedural coups in modern Congressional history."

15. "We Agree with You, Walter Winchell," *Pittsburgh Courier*, February 5, 1944, 1; "Winchell Defended Against Rankin," *Jamestown Post-Journal*, February 22, 1944, 5; "Rankin Silenced in Winchell Attack," *Philadelphia Inquirer*, February 13, 1946, 10; Neal Gabler, *Winchell: Gossip, Power, and the Culture of Celebrity* (New York: Alfred A. Knopf, 1994), 332–333.

16. Carr, *The House Committee on Un-American Activities 1945–1950*, 19.

17. Milton Murray, "House Liberals Seek Caucus to Fight Rankin Coalition," *PM Daily*, January 8, 1945, 8.

18. "Offer Jackson Film Probe Group Chairmanship," *Motion Picture Daily*, July 3, 1945, 5.

19. "'Witch Hunt' Bar May K.O. Rankin's Hollywood Probe; Cal Dems Oppose," *Variety*, July 8, 1945, 2.

20. Ibid.

21. Ralph A. Edgerton, "The Eric Johnston Story," *Pacific Northwesterner*, Fall 1989, 55–62.

22. "Eric Johnston Dies; Aided Three Presidents," *New York Times*, August 23, 1963, 1, 3.

23. "Johnston Takes Over Next Week," *Daily Variety*, September 15, 1945, 1, 14.

24. "Eric Johnston Studies Film Job Offer," *Daily Variety*, July 13, 1945, 9.

25. Terry Ramsaye, "Johnston New President of MPPDA; Directors Name Hays as Consultant," *Motion Picture Herald*, September 22, 1945, 12–13.

3. The Preservation of American Ideals

1. "H'wood Alliance Formed to Combat Alien Isms in Pix; Sam Wood Prexy," *Variety*, February 9, 1944, 8.

2. "Motion Picture Alliance States Its Principles," *Daily Variety*, February 7, 1944, 5; "Wood Outlines Aims of New Alliance," *Motion Picture Daily*, February 8, 1944, 4.

3. David Platt, "Robert Taylor Struts His Stuff for House Un-Americans," *Daily Worker*, May 19, 1947, 11.

4. W. R. Wilkerson, "Another Vote for Stalin!," *Hollywood Reporter*, August 14, 1946, 1, 4, 14.

5. W. R. Wilkerson, "Tradeviews," *Hollywood Reporter*, August 19, 1946, 1, 2.

6. W. R. Wilkerson, "Red Beach-Head!," *Hollywood Reporter*, August 20, 1947, 1, 4; W. R. Wilkerson, "More Red Commissars!," *Hollywood Reporter*, August 22, 1947, 1, 2.

7. Ezra Goldman, *The Fifty-Year Decline and Fall of Hollywood* (New York: Simon and Schuster, 1961), 63.

8. For a complete account of Hopper's political career, see Jennifer Frost, *Hedda Hopper's Hollywood: Celebrity Gossip and American Conservativism* (New York: New York University Press, 2011).

9. Hedda Hopper, "Looking at Hollywood," *Los Angeles Times*, May 7, 1947, 9; Hedda Hopper, "Looking at Hollywood," *Los Angeles Times*, May 5, 1947, A3.

10. Hedda Hopper, "Looking at Hollywood," *Los Angeles Times*, October 4, 1946, 9.

11. Hedda Hopper, "Looking at Hollywood," *Los Angeles Times*, August 24, 1946, A5.

12. Burton Crane, "Hearst Built Corporate Empires in Newspaper, Magazines, Radio, and Real Estate," *New York Times*, August 15, 1951, 21.

13. Kenneth MacGowan, "Keep the Lines Open," *Screen Writer*, February 1946, 22.

14. Milt Watt, "Meet Today to Settle Coast Union Problem," *Motion Picture Daily*, April 27, 1947, 1, 6.

15. "Who Is Roy Brewer?," *North American Labor*, September 1948, 2.

16. Victor Riesel and Murray Kempton, "Labor's Antidote for Communism," *North American Labor*, September 1948, 22.

17. "Threat to Shut Theaters," *Daily Variety*, March 14, 1945, 6.

18. For the official Warner Bros. version, see "The Facts About Violence at Warner Bros. Studios!" *Daily Variety*, October 12, 1945, 12–13.

19. "Pickets Seek to Close Warner Bros. Studio," *Motion Picture Daily*, October 8, 1945, 3.

20. "35 More Injured at Studio Picket Line," *Motion Picture Daily*, October 9, 1945, 1, 10.

21. Griffin Fariello, *Red Scare: Memories of the American Inquisition, An Oral History* (New York: Norton, 1995), 115.

22. "Coast Hails AFL's Directive, Era of Labor Peace Seen," *Motion Picture Daily*, January 4, 1946, 1, 11.

23. "Police Hunt Two Men in Sorrell Shooting," *Daily Variety*, October 31, 1945, 10.

24. Sherwin Kane, "Tradewise," *Motion Picture Daily*, October 29, 1945, 2.

25. "Coast Hails AFL's Directive, Era of Labor Peace Seen," *Motion Picture Daily*, January 4, 1946, 1, 11.

26. "6-Man Union Committee to Pick Labor Arbitrator Points the Way to Strike Settlement This Week," *Variety*, October 30, 1946, 10.

27. "IBEW Charter Threat Told," *Daily Variety*, October 21, 1946, 1, 10. On July 1, 1946, there had earlier been a brief two-day work stoppage by the painters and carpenters unions.

28. "CSU Calls Strike," *Daily Variety*, July 1, 1946, 1, 20.

29. Robert J. Landry, "Pat Casey: The Man Behind the Scenes," *Variety*, February 14, 1962, 4.

30. Pat Casey, "The Truth About the Strike!," *Daily Variety*, November 18, 1946, 8–9.

31. "MPA Starts Work on Editorials," *Motion Picture Herald*, May 3, 1947, 24.

32. Details vary in accounts of Sorrell's abduction. "Brass Knucks of Chi Mobsters Seen in Kidnap-Beating of CSU's Sorrell," *Variety*, March 5, 1947, 9, 18; "CSU Head Shot and Beaten in Calif.," *Motion Picture Daily*, March 4, 1947, 2; "Need Mediator on Coast: Johnston," *Motion Picture Herald*, March 8, 1947, 25.

33. "Need Mediator on Coast," *Motion Picture Herald*, March 8, 1947, 25.

34. "Labor," *Motion Picture Herald*, June 28, 1947, 13.

35. "Congressmen Get Story of Strike," *Motion Picture Herald*, August 16, 1947, 22.

36. "Hope Grows for Coast Settlement," *Motion Picture Herald*, August 30, 1947, 16.

37. "Labor Tops Talk Good Fight as House Group Tours Lots; Not a Blow Tossed," *Daily Variety*, August 22, 1947, 3.

4. The Magic of a Hollywood Dateline

1. "Federal Theater Project Dies at Congress' Hands," *Film Daily*, July 3, 1939, 1, 7.

2. J. A. Otten, "Screen Sets Careful Stage for Red Inquiry Hearings," *Motion Picture Herald*, October 4, 1947, 25–26.

3. Crosswell Bowen, "The 'Americanization' of J. Parnell Thomas," *PM Daily*, November 30, 1947, 8.

4. Robert E. Stripling, *The Red Plot Against America*, ed. Bob Considine (Drexell Hill, PA: Bell Publishing, 1949), 13, 14, 22.

5. "'Thought Control' Fight," *Daily People's World*, October 28, 1947, 3.

6. "Hollywood Communist Probe to Be 'Sensational,' Prober Says," *Washington Evening Star*, July 30, 1947, A-3.

7. J. Parnell Thomas, "The Price of Vigilance" (unpublished manuscript, 1957), 3-C-2, 107, 5-C-2, J. Parnell Thomas file, Richard Nixon Presidential Library.

8. Willard Edwards, "One Man's War on Communism," *Chicago Tribune*, April 27, 1947, G5, G32.

9. "Californians Ask Probe of Communism in Hollywood," *Motion Picture Herald*, February 1, 1947, 27.

10. "'Good Airing' for Hollywood Reds, Says Rep. Thomas," *Hollywood Reporter*, January 23, 1947, 1.

11. "Activities of Reds Effective Here, Says FBI Chief," *Hollywood Reporter*, March 27, 1947, 1, 2.

12. "FBI Head Warns of Reds' Aim to Destroy U.S.," *New York Times*, March 27, 1947, 1.

13. "FBI Hits H'd Red Menace," *Daily Variety*, March 27, 1947, 1, 10.

14. "Johnston Defends H'd," *Daily Variety*, March 28, 1947, 1, 8.

15. Manning Clagett, "Reds Fear American Films," *Film Daily*, March 28, 1947, 1, 6.

16. "Statement by Eric Johnston, President, Motion Picture Association of American Before the House Committee on Un-American Activities," March 27, 1947, Eric Johnston FBI file.

17. "Johnston Scoffs at Red Danger," *Hollywood Reporter*, March 28, 1947, 1, 6.

18. "Reds Failed in Effort to Take Studios: Johnston," *Motion Picture Herald*, April 5, 1947, 21.

19. "Hollywood Probe Urged by Head of Un-American Committee," *Film Daily*, March 31, 1947, 2.

20. "Red Quiz Goes on Despite Johnston," *Hollywood Reporter*, March 31, 1947, 1, 3.

21. W. R. Wilkerson, "Tradeviews," *Hollywood Reporter*, May 12, 1947, 1, 2; W. R. Wilkerson, "Tradeviews," *Hollywood Reporter*, March 31, 1947, 1, 2.

22. "Red Menace Very Real in Hollywood Declares IA Exec," *Hollywood Reporter*, April 3, 1947, 1, 14.

23. Hoover's handwritten responses in Memo from D. M. Ladd to J. Edgar Hoover, April 21, 1947; Memo from D. M. Ladd to J. Edgar Hoover, April 20, 1947, Eric Johnston FBI file.

24. "Nixon Lauds 20th Anti-Red Feature," *Hollywood Reporter*, April 11, 1947, 2.

25. "Just for Variety," *Daily Variety*, April 4, 1947, 4.

26. Clyde Tolson to L. B. Nichols, May 13, 1947, 2, HUAC FBI files. See also Seth Rosenfeld, *Subversives: The FBI's War on Student Radicals and Reagan's Rise to Power* (New York: Farrar, Straus and Giroux, 2012), 128–129; Athan G. Theoharis and John Stuart Cox, *The Boss: J. Edgar Hoover and the Great American Inquisition* (Philadelphia: Temple University Press, 1988), 254–256.

27. J. Edgar Hoover to SAC [Special Agent in Charge], Los Angeles, May 13, 1947, 2, HUAC FBI file.

28. "House Group Starts Red Probe," *Hollywood Reporter*, May 9, 1947, 1, 3.

29. "Red Probers Quiz Three," *Hollywood Reporter*, May 12, 1947, 1, 4.

30. "Congress Red Hunters to Quiz Hanns Eisler," *Daily Variety*, May 12, 1947, 14.

31. "House to Probe Hollywood Reds," *Motion Picture Herald*, May 3, 1947, 34.

32. "Sumner Welles to Be Called in Film Probe," *Film Daily*, August 27, 1947, 1, 3.

33. Tony Sharp, *Stalin's American Spy: Noel Field, Allen Dulles, and the East European Show Trials* (London: Hurt & Company, 2014), 35–36, 94–96, 143–145.

34. Stripling, *The Red Plot Against America*, 63.

35. "U.S. Officials to Figure in Hollywood Red Inquiry," *Los Angeles Times*, May 10, 1947, A1, A8.

36. Alvah Bessie, "Meet Hanns Eisler," *New Masses*, May 13, 1947, 8–10.

37. "Hanns Eisler Hearing Halts," *Los Angeles Times*, May 13, 1947, 1, 2; "Hanns Eisler Answers Un-American Witch-Hunters," *Daily Worker*, May 17, 1947, 11; " 'Publish Text of Hanns Eisler's Testimony,' Un-Americans Told," *People's Daily World*, May 14, 1947, 4.

38. "Quiz H'wood Tunesmith on Commie Activities," *Variety*, May 14, 1947, 22.

39. "Eisler Evasive at Grilling: Will Be Quized at Capital," *Hollywood Reporter*, May 13, 1947, 4.

40. "New Dealer Forced Taylor to Enact Red Roles, He Says," *Los Angeles Times*, May 15, 1947, 5.

41. Ibid., 1.

42. "Pressured Into 'Song of Russia,' Role, Says Taylor," *Hollywood Reporter*, May 15, 1947, 1, 2.

43. "Mellett Denies Actor's Claim That He Forced Role in Film," *Motion Picture Herald*, May 16, 1947, 3.

44. Red Kann, "On the March," *Motion Picture Herald*, May 24, 1947, 18.

45. "Mayer Invites Red Probers to 'Song,' " *Hollywood Reporter*, May 19, 1947, 17.

46. "Coast Red Probe Draws Headlines," *Motion Picture Herald*, May 24, 1947, 51.

47. "Menjou Wants Role of 'Modern Paul Revere,' " *People's Daily World*, May 16, 1947, 1; "Probers Learn 'Hundreds' in Films Pro-Red," *Hollywood Citizen News*, May 15, 1947, 1.

48. "Warner, Menjou at Coast 'Red' Inquiry," *Motion Picture Daily*, May 16, 1947, 3.

49. "Former Russian Office Surprise Inquiry Witness," *Los Angeles Times*, May 16, 1947, 1, 2.

50. Ibid.

51. "Red Probers Pledge Wide Film Inquiry," *Hollywood Citizen-News*, May 16, 1947, 1.

52. "'Red Herring' Just Another Fish Story, Major H'Wood Opinion Feels of Baiting," *Variety*, May 21, 1947, 2.

53. Terry Ramsaye, "Those Un-Americans," *Motion Picture Herald*, May 31, 1947, 7.

54. "Katharine Hepburn Explains Why Artists Are Targets of Witch-Hunts," *Daily Worker*, May 24, 1947, 11.

5. Smearing Hollywood with the Brush of Communism

1. "Byrnes Joins Industry As Special Legal Advisor," *Motion Picture Herald*, June 7, 1947, 15.

2. "Mr. Byrnes' Assignment," *Motion Picture Herald*, June 7, 1947, 7.

3. "McNutt Named to Speak for Industry," *Motion Picture Daily*, September 17, 1947, 1, 7.

4. Hearings Before the Committee on Un-American Activities (Eightieth Congress), 312.

5. Eddie Mannix testimony, *Loew's Inc. v. Lester Cole*, December 8, 1948, 277–281.

6. Communist Infiltration-Motion Picture Industry (COMPIC) Excerpts, File Number 100–138754, Part 6 of 15, 193.

7. Communist Infiltration-Motion Picture Industry (COMPIC) Excerpts, File Number 100–138754, Part 6 of 15, 184.

8. Eddie Mannix testimony, *Loew's Inc. v. Lester Cole*, December 8, 1948, 287–291.

9. Mary Spargo, "Meyer Flees and Hughes Chuckles at Irate Senator," *Washington Post*, August 9, 1947, 1, 2.

10. William S. White, "Senators Suspend Inquiry on Hughes; Cowardly, He Says," *New York Times*, August 12, 1947, 1.

11. Mary Spargo, "Meyer Flees and Hughes Chuckles at Irate Senator," *Washington Post*, August 9, 1947, 1, 2.

12. Florabel Muir, "Just for Variety," *Daily Variety*, August 7, 1947, 4.

13. Russell Birdwell, "You Don't Have to Take It," *Daily Variety*, August 4, 1947, 9.

14. J. A. Otten, "Screen Sets Careful Stage for Red Inquiry Hearings," *Motion Picture Herald*, October 4, 1947, 24.

15. "Coast Commie Probe May Be Postponed," *Film Daily*, August 1, 1947, 3.

16. "Rankin Will Miss Red Probe Hearings," *Motion Picture Daily*, September 23, 1947, 7.

17. "Wall Street Rules H'd Production, Graham Charges," *Daily Variety*, July 7, 1947, 4.

18. "McManus' Pix Forum of the Air," *Variety*, September 3, 1947, 6.

19. George V. Denny, "Forum," *Daily Variety*, September 3, 1947, 9.

20. "Lavery Admits SWG Coin Goes to Kenny Group," *Daily Variety*, October 8, 1946, 4.

21. "A Disgraceful Debate on Communism and Hollywood," *Harrison's Reports*, September 20, 1947, 152; "Town Hall 'Red' Debate Offers Sound and Fury, Few New Facts," *Daily Variety*, September 3, 1947, 3; Red Kann, "Insider's Outlook," *Motion Picture Daily*, September 4, 1947, 2.

22. Hobe, "Public Dis-service," *Variety*, September 10, 1947, 6.

23. "Unique Angle of Radio Delivery in Libel Suit vs Mrs. Lela Rogers," *Variety*, September 10, 1947, 6, 22; "Lela Rogers, Co-Defendants Pay Lavery in Full for Rap on 'Gentleman,'" *Daily Variety*, September 28, 1951, 1, 13.

24. "43 Called to House 'Red' Probe on Oct. 20," *Motion Picture Daily*, September 22, 1947, 1, 5.

25. Albert Maltz, who kept track of such things, affirmed with certainty that "the nineteen divided into nine Christian, nine Jews, and one of mixed parentage." I rounded up. "Interview of Albert Maltz," November 21, 1978. UCLA Oral History Project, http://oralhistory .library.ucla.edu/viewFile.do?itemId=30065&fileSeq=3&xsl=http://oralhistory.library .ucla.edu/xslt/local/tei/xml/tei/stylesheet/xhtml2/tei.xsl#session16a.

26. "Chaplin Denies Communism, Says He Will Testify," *Motion Picture Herald*, July 26, 1947, 32.

27. "Can't Scare Me," *Motion Picture Herald*, September 20, 1947, 9; "Chaplin Would Play Host to Probers," *Motion Picture Daily*, September 19, 1947, 3; "Chaplin Comedy 'Verdoux' With Kick Off of H'd Red Inquiry," *Daily Variety*, September 15, 1947, 3.

28. "Chaplin On Deck for Un-American Hearing," *Film Daily*, July 11, 1947, 1, 6.

29. Letter from Eric Johnston to J. Parnell Thomas, September 29, 1947, Eric Johnston HUAC-NARA file.

30. "MPA-Sponsored Short Stresses Nation's Power," *Motion Picture Herald*, September 20, 1947, 14.

31. Sherwin Kane, "Tradewise," *Motion Picture Daily*, September 25, 1947, 2.

32. "Note From Mrs. Roosevelt in Eisler Red Hearing," *Daily Variety*, September 25, 1947, 1, 10.

33. "Statement Made by Hanns Eisler to the House Committee on Un-American Activities," September 24, 1947, Hanns Eisler HUAC-NARA file.

34. Fred Vast, "Un-Americans Tough on Diplomat at Eisler Hearings," *Daily Worker*, September 26, 1947, 12.

35. Hedda Hopper, "Looking at Hollywood," *Los Angeles Times*, September 27, 1947, A5.

36. Rob F. Hall, "Hanns Eisler, Rankin Duel," *Daily Worker*, September 25, 1947, 1, 2.

37. "House Group Opens Hanns Eisler Probe," *Motion Picture Daily*, September 25, 1947, 4.

38. William S. White, "Eisler Plea Made by Mrs. Roosevelt to Sumner Welles," *New York Times*, September 25, 1947, 1, 19.

39. Fred Vast, "Un-Americans Demand, S. D. Deport Hanns Eisler," *Daily Worker*, September 27, 1947, 3.

40. "Hanns Eisler Released on Bail," *Daily Worker*, October 7, 1947, 3.

41. "Hanns Eisler Flies For London; Lays Exile to Truman," *Washington Post*, March 27, 1948, M8; "Hanns Eisler Calls Hollywood 'City in State of Hysteria,' " *Washington Post*, March 30, 1948, 6.

42. Westbrook Pegler, "Westbrook Pegler Says," *Jamestown (N.Y.) Post-Journal*, November 5, 1947, 7.

43. Philip Dunne, who offers the most reliable take on CFA's origin and strategies, says Huston, Wyler, and he were the founders, not mentioning Wilder. *Take Two: A Life in the Movies and Politics* (New York: Limelight Editions, 1992 [1980]), 190–208.

44. Gordon Kahn, *Hollywood on Trial: The Story of the Ten Who Were Indicted* (New York: Boni & Gaer, 1948), 135.

45. John Huston to Harry L. Kingman, April 23, 1948, John Huston papers, Margaret Herrick Library, Academy of Motion Picture Arts and Sciences.

46. According to blacklist historians Larry Ceplair and Steven Englund, "Dunne, Wyler, and Huston *were* the Committee for the First Amendment." Ceplair and Englund, *The Inquisition in Hollywood: Politics and the Film Community, 1930–1960* (Chicago: University of Illinois Press, 2003 [1979]), 275.
47. "Protest Group to Fly to Capital," *Los Angeles Times*, October 25, 1947, 3.
48. Sam Jaffe was a prominent Hollywood agent who should not be confused with the popular character actor of the same name.
49. "'The 19' Back to Coast; B'Way Legit Alerted," *Daily Variety*, November 5, 1947, 4.
50. John Huston to Harry L. Kingman, April 23, 1948, John Huston Papers, File 1138, AMPAS.
51. Hedda Hopper, "Looking at Hollywood," *Chicago Daily Tribune*, November 3, 1947, 29.
52. Chris Mathisen, "Hollywood Red Probe Becomes One of Capitol's Biggest Shows," *Washington Star*, October 26, 1947, A-6.

6. Showtime

1. Herbert Golden, "School Kids Jam Hearing and 2 Film Openings," *Daily Variety*, October 24, 1947, 11.
2. Gordon Kahn, *Hollywood on Trial* (New York: Boni & Gaer, 1948), 4.
3. "Hollywood, D.C.," *New York Times*, October 26, 1947, E2.
4. Florence S. Lowe, "Washington Hullabaloo," *Daily Variety*, October 21, 1947, 10.
5. I. F. Stone, "The Grand Inquisition," *Nation*, November 8, 1947, 492–493.
6. George Dixon, "Washington Scene," *New York Mirror*, October 23, 1947, 4.
7. "Radio's Big Coverage," *Variety*, October 29, 1947, 4.
8. Manning Clagett, "Ready to Smash Smear Attack on Films," *Film Daily*, October 20, 1947, 4; "Tele Abandons Show on Red Hearings," *Daily Variety*, October 21, 1947, 9.
9. Martin Codel, "Every Home a Newsreel Theater," *Television Digest*, November 1, 1947, 1.
10. Attorneys Kenny, Crum, Katz, Margolis, and McTernan to J. Parnell Thomas, October 10, 1947, WISC.
11. "Fight Moves to the Advertising Columns," *Motion Picture Herald*, November 1, 1947, 15.
12. Virginia Gardner, "So Long, Washington," *New Masses*, September 23, 1947, 5; Virginia Gardner, "J. Parnell Thomas: Headsman," *New Masses*, March 18, 1947, 11.
13. J. Parnell Thomas, "The Price of Vigilance" (unpublished manuscript, 1957), 104, J. Parnell Thomas file, Richard Nixon Presidential Library.
14. Stanley R. Brav, "Mississippi Incident," *American Jewish Archives* (June 1952), 59–65.
15. "Call 43 Industry Figures for Red Inquiry," *Motion Picture Herald*, September 27, 1947, 23.
16. Walter Winchell, "In New York," *New York Mirror*, October 22, 1947, 10.
17. Kahn, *Hollywood on Trial*, 4.
18. *News of the Day*, MGM, vol. 19, Issue 214, October 20, 1947.

19. Ibid.

20. Quentin Reynolds, "Film Magnates, on Stand, Play Roles as Though Coached," *PM Daily*, October 21, 1947, 2.

21. "U.S. Honors Jack Warner," *Motion Picture Herald*, March 15, 1947, 33.

22. Thomas, "The Price of Vigilance," 251, J. Parnell Thomas file, Richard Nixon Presidential Library.

23. In 1964, in his highly embroidered autobiography, Warner told a different story: that he had made the film at the personal request of FDR. "This picture *must* be made, and I am asking you to do it," FDR said during a dinner at the White House in 1942, according to Warner. Presumably, Warner kept quiet so as not to aid HUAC in discrediting the late president. "I kept silent for twenty years because I had no choice, but the principals are all dead now, and I can tell the facts for the first time." He makes no mention of either his May or October testimonies before HUAC in 1947 in the entire memoir. Jack L. Warner with Dean Jennings, *My First Hundred Years in Hollywood* (New York: Random House, 1964), 290.

24. Manning Clagett, "Ship 'Ideological Termites' to Russia—Warner," *Film Daily*, October 21, 1947, 1, 6.

25. Florence S. Lowe, "Washington Hullabaloo," *Daily Variety*, October 21, 1947, 10.

26. "Sam Wood Says Reds Seek Control of Hollywood Guilds and Unions," *New York Sun*, October 20, 1947, 12.

27. Morrie Ryskind with John H. M. Roberts, *I Shot an Elephant in My Pajamas: The Morrie Ryskind Story* (Lafayette, LA: Huntington House Publishers, 1994), 115.

28. H. A. Smith, September 2, 1947. Sam Wood HUAC-NARA file.

29. Fred Niblo Jr., "Correspondence," *The Screen Writer*, November 1945, 43.

30. Dalton Trumbo, "Samuel Grosvenor Wood: A Footnote," *The Screen Writer*, June 1945, 30.

31. Telegram to Lewis Milestone from the Screen Directors Guild, October 20, 1947, WISC.

32. Kahn, *Hollywood on Trial*, 27–28.

33. Neal Gabler: *An Empire of Their Own: How the Jews Invented Hollywood* (New York: Crown Publishers, 1988).

34. "Rites Tomorrow for L. B. Mayer," *Daily Variety*, October 30, 1957, 1, 12; James M. Jerauld, "L. B. Mayer Career a Record of Many Ambitions Realized," *Motion Picture Daily*, October 30, 1957, 3.

35. Memo from A. B. Leckie, August 28, 1947, Louis B. Mayer HUAC-NARA file.

36. "Regulate Reds Employ—Mayer," *Film Daily*, October 21, 1947, 1, 4.

37. Herman Lowe, "Hollywood Red blues Sung by Congressional Probe Witnesses," *Variety*, October 22, 1947, 24.

38. Robert Mayhew, *Ayn Rand and* Song of Russia: *Communism and Anti-Communism in 1940s Hollywood* (Maryland: The Scarecrow Press, 2005), 71–82.

39. "From Dresses to Scripts," *Variety*, July 25, 1933, 7; "Ayn Rand," *Daily Variety*, March 8, 1982, 6.

40. H. A. Smith, September 2, 1947, Ayn Rand HUAC NARA file.

41. Bob Considine, "Film Group Fighting for Americanism," *Philadelphia Inquirer*, September 27, 1947, 10.

42. Joseph North, "Torquemada in Technicolor," *New Masses*, November 4, 1947, 6.

43. Herman Lowe, "Hollywood Red Blues Sung by Congressional Probe Witness," *Variety*, October 22, 1947, 24.

44. "Filmites Named as Reds," *Daily Variety*, October 21, 1947, 1, 7, 8.

45. Quentin Reynolds, "Film Magnates, on Stand, Play Roles as Though Coached," *PM Daily*, October 21, 1947, 2.

46. Ibid, 3.

47. "McNutt Offers to Screen Films for Probers to Decide First Hand," *Variety*, October 22, 1947, 4; Ralph Izard, "Probers Call for Pro-War Films," *Daily Worker*, October 21, 1947, 3.

48. "McNutt Offers to Screen Films for Provers to Decide First Hand," *Variety*, Octover 22, 1947, 4.

49. Guy Hottell to Director, FBI, "Communist Infiltration of the Motion Picture Industry," October 21, 1947, 2.

7. Lovefest

1. "Menjou's Debut," *Variety*, October 22, 1947, 24.

2. Walter Winchell, "In New York," *New York Mirror*, October 26, 1947, 10.

3. Adolphe Menjou and M. M. Musselman, *It Took Nine Tailors* (New York: McGraw-Hill, 1948), 179. Written several months before his HUAC testimony, Menjou's charming, sartorially titled memoir is chock full of amusing Hollywood anecdotes, but it contains not a hint of political commentary, either about Communism or his membership in the MPA-PAI.

4. Memo from H. A. Smith, September 2, 1947, Adophe Menjou HUAC NARA file.

5. Quentin Reynolds, "House Movie Probers Carry On Almost the Way Hitler Did," *PM Daily*, October 22, 1947, 3.

6. Hedda Hopper, "Looking at Hollywood," *Los Angeles Times*, November 14, 1947, A10.

7. "Menjou's Debut," *Variety*, October 22, 1947, 24.

8. Herman Lowe, "Hollywood Red Blues Sung by Congressional Probe Witnesses," *Variety*, October 22, 1947, 4.

9. Ibid., 24.

10. John Mason Brown, " 'It Can't Happen Here' Staged at the Adelphi," *New York Post*, October 28, 1936, 26.

11. Archer Winsten, "Washington Film Tempest Judged from the Record," *New York Post*, October 27, 1947, 30.

12. Jack Moffitt to Rep. Norris Poulson, April 7, 1947; Jack Moffitt, "Communism in Hollywood" (unpublished manuscript, 1947), 5; Jack Moffitt to Rep. Norris Poulson, April 11, 1947. Moffitt wrote his local congressman, who passed his letters on to Thomas.

13. Memo from H. A. Smith, September 2, 1947, James C. Moffitt HUAC NARA file.

14. Herman A. Lowe, "Hughes Tells Red Threats," *Daily Variety*, October 22, 1947, 8.

15. Quentin Reynolds, "House Movie Probers Carry On Almost the Way Hitler Did," *PM Daily*, October 22, 1947, 3.

16. "Ejected from the Show," *New York Post*, October 21, 1947, 29.

17. Earl Wilson, "It Happened Last Night," *New York Post*, October 24, 1947, 67.

18. Joseph Kahn and Robert C. Williams, "Broadway Producers Deny Red Tinge," *New York Post*, October 22, 1947, 5.

19. James O. Kemm, *Rupert Hughes: A Hollywood Legend* (Beverly Hills: Pomegranate Press, 1997).

20. "Against Censorship," *Variety*, April 9, 1920, 1.

21. "Women Reformers 'Told Off' in Rupert Hughes Speech," *Variety*, June 18, 1924, 1, 33.

22. Rupert Hughes, "Hughes Wired Howard This—," *Daily Variety*, May 12, 1936, 5.

23. Herbert Lowe, "Hollywood Red Blues Sung by Congressional Probe Witnesses," *Variety*, October 22, 1947, 4.

24. Red Kann, "Washington Ringside," *Motion Picture Daily*, October 22, 1947, 6.

25. "Newsmen Shout Down Morris Ryskind at McNutt's Press Parlay," *Variety*, October 22, 1947, 4.

26. Telegram from Chalmers H. Goodlin to J. Parnell Thomas, October 28, 1947, HUAC NARA.

8. Friendlies, Cooperative and Uncooperative

1. Paul Trivers, "Town Meeting Comes to Hollywood," *Screen Writer*, October 1945, 9; "McGuinness Resigns," *Screen Writer*, November 1945, 42.

2. Memo from H. A. Smith, September 2, 1947, James McGuinness HUAC NARA file.

3. Lee Garling, "Industry Points for a Fight on Freedom of the Screen," *Box Office*, October 25, 1947, 10.

4. J. A. Otten, "Trying to Dictate and Control,' Says McNutt," *Motion Picture Herald*, October 25, 1947, 13–14, 16.

5. Ibid.

6. "Links Hollywood Reds to Espionage," *New York Sun*, October 22, 1, 2.

7. "McNutt Reneges on Talk About McGuinness," *Daily Variety*, October 24, 1947, 10.

8. "Thomas Hints at 'Sensation,' " *New York Sun*, October 22, 1947, 1; "Links Hollywood Reds to Espionage," *New York Sun*, October 22, 1, 2.

9. Letter from Robert Taylor to H. A. Smith, September 23, 1947, Robert Taylor HUAC NARA file. See also Linda Alexander, *Reluctant Witness: Robert Taylor, Hollywood, and Communism* (Swansboro, N.C.: Tease Publishing, 2008), 213. Alexander's sympathetic account of the actor's brush with HUAC argues that he was a reluctant, not friendly, witness.

10. H. A. Smith to Robert Taylor, September 24, 1947, Robert Taylor HUAC NARA file.

11. Florence S. Lowe, "Taylor Steps Hearing Out of Bush League," *Daily Variety*, October 23, 1947, 9.

12. Ralph Izard, "Taylor Plays Hero of 'Un-American' Script," *Daily Worker*, October 23, 1947, 2, 10.
13. George Dixon, "Washington Scene," *New York Mirror*, October 27, 1947, 4.
14. Samuel A. Towers, "79 In Hollywood Found Subversive, Inquiry Head Says," *New York Times*, October 23, 1947, 1, 15.
15. Mary Spargo, "Women Cheer Robert Taylor as He Urges Ban on Reds," *Washington Post*, October 23, 1947, 1, 2.
16. George E. Sokolsky, "Difficult Life," *The Leader Herald*, January 9, 1958, 4.
17. Howard Rushmore, "Life on the Daily Worker," *American Mercury*, June 1940, 215–221.
18. James Dugan, "G'wan with the Wind," *New Masses*, January 2, 1940, 28–30.
19. Herb Golden, "Press 'Wolves' Yap at Chaplin's Politics, But Get Little of His Hide," *Variety*, April 16, 1947, 4, 20.
20. George Dixon, "Washington Scene," *New York Mirror*, October 27, 1947, 4.
21. Herman A. Lowe, "Reds Have Hollywood Inside," *Daily Variety*, October 23, 1947, 1, 8.
22. Irving Hoffman, "Tales of Hoffman," *Hollywood Reporter*, October 27, 1947, 3.
23. "Repudiation of a Smear, Affirmation of a Purpose," *Daily Variety*, March 17, 1944, 14–15.
24. H. A. Smith, September 2, 1947, Morrie Ryskind HUAC NARA file.

9. Hollywood's Finest

1. "Montgomery and 2 Other Stars Call Reds Active in Actors Guild," *New York Sun*, October 23, 1947, 11.
2. Herbert Golden, "Barricades Bar Gate Crashers as Stars Testify," *Daily Variety*, October 23, 1947, 11.
3. Archer Winsten, "Washington Film Tempest Judged from the Record," *New York Post*, October 27, 1947, 30.
4. Memorandum from A. B. Leckie, September 13, 1947, Richard Macaulay HUAC NARA file.
5. Richard Macaulay, "A Little of This and That," *Daily Variety*, October 20, 1947, 10.
6. Telegram from Ranald MacDougall, October 25, 1947, HUAC NARA.
7. Keith Love, "Robert Montgomery, Film and TV Star, Dies at 77," *Los Angeles Times*, September 28, 1981, A9, 26.
8. David Bird, "Robert Montgomery, Actor, Dies at 77," *New York Times*, September 28, 1981, B6.
9. George Murphy, *Say . . . Didn't You Used to Be George Murphy?* (Bartholomew House, LTD, 1970), 220–224.
10. Louella Parsons, "Hollywood," *Albany (NY) Times Union*, November 7, 1947, 14.
11. Murphy, *Say . . . Didn't You Used to Be George Murphy?*, 5–44.
12. Kathleen O'Steen, "Actor, SAG Prexy, Senator George Murphy Dies at 89," *Daily Variety*, May 5, 1992, 3.

13. A Wounded Marine, "Open Forum," *Hollywood Reporter*, August 20, 1946, 13; Edith Gwynn, "Rambling Reporter," *Hollywood Reporter*, August 21, 1946, 2; Audie Murphy, et al., "A Letter to the *Hollywood Reporter*," *Hollywood Reporter*, August 22, 1947, 13. The exchange was precipitated by a letter Reagan wrote to the *Hollywood Reporter*, defending the American Veterans Committee, of which he was a member, from charges of being a Communist front.

14. Memo from H. A. Smith, September 2, 1947, Ronald Reagan HUAC NARA file.

15. Communist Infiltration-Motion Picture Industry (COMPIC) Excerpts, File Number 100-15732. Part 6 of 15: 24. Reagan is identified by his code designation, T-10.

16. Carl Levin, "Inquiry Takes New Turn With Insistence on Retaining Civil Rights," *New York Herald Tribune*, October 24, 1947, 1, 2; Quentin Reynolds, "Ronald Reagan, Foe of Both 'Isms,' Faces Film Probers Today," *PM Daily*, October 23, 1947, 3.

17. Samuel A. Tower, "Hollywood Communists 'Militant,' But Small in Number Stars Testify," *New York Times*, October 24, 1947, 1, 12.

18. "Montgomery and 2 Other Stars Call Reds Active," *New York Sun*, October 23, 1947, 1.

19. Quentin Reynolds, "Movie Probers Let Down by Stars But Customers Love the Show," *PM Daily*, October 24, 1947, 3.

20. Telegram from Loyd Wright to J. Parnell Thomas, October 14, 1947, Gary Cooper HUAC NARA file.

21. J. Parnell Thomas to Loyd Wright, October 15, 1947, Gary Cooper HUAC NARA file.

22. Memo from H. A. Smith, September 2, 1947, Gary Cooper HUAC NARA file.

23. George Dixon, "Washington Scene," *New York Mirror*, October 27, 1947, 4.

24. Peter Bogdanovich, *Who the Devil Made It* (New York: Alfred A. Knopf, 1997), 388.

25. Mark Kelly, "At $2.48 a Bushel, Corn Ain't Hay," *Daily Variety*, October 20, 1947, 20.

26. Bob Thomas, "'Bells' Termed Christmas Gift to the Nation," *Binghamton Press*, November 28, 1945, 27.

27. "Herald-Tribune Blasts Quiz Again," *Daily Varity*, October 27, 1947, 6.

28. Mona Z. Smith, *Becoming Something: The Story of Canada Lee* (New York; Farber and Farber, 2004), 241–249. Like the Los Angeles branch, the New York branch of CFA had been infiltrated by an informant who kept tabs on the group for the FBI.

29. "Running Memorandum on Communist Infiltration into the Motion Picture Industry," January 3, 1956, 3–4 (*Communist Activity in the Entertainment Industry: FBI Surveillance Files on Hollywood 1942–1958*, edited by Daniel J. Leab, a microfilm project of University Publication of America, 1991).

30. Oliver Pilat, "Film Probers Told Odets Is Communist," *New York Post*, October 24, 1947, 4.

31. Earl Wilson, "It Happened Last Night," *New York Post*, October 24, 1947, 67.

10. Doldrums

1. "Moment of Reality," *New York Herald Tribune*, October 25, 1947, 10.

2. Florence S. Lowe, "Washington Hullabaloo," *Daily Variety*, October 29, 1947, 6; "Johnston Faces Probers Today," *Hollywood Reporter*, October 27, 1947, 4.

3. "Committee for the First Amendment," *Daily Variety*, October 24, 1947, 9.

4. "Hollywood Is Angered at Hearings," *People's Daily World*, October 22, 1947, 1; "Broadway Stars Joining in 'Thought Control' Fight," *People's Daily World*, October 25, 1947, 3.

5. Lauren Bacall, *By Myself* (New York: Alfred A. Knopf, 1978), 174.

6. "New Dealer Forced Taylor to Enact Red Role, He Says," *Los Angeles Times*, May 15, 1947, 5.

7. Memo from H. A. Smith, September 2, 1947, Lela Rogers HUAC NARA file.

8. Carl Levin, "Disney Testifies Reds Took Over Studios," *New York Herald Tribune*, October 25, 1947, 1, 9.

9. Oliver Carlson, *Red Star Over Hollywood* (New York: Catholic Information Society, 1947), 3.

10. Mary Spargo, "Reds Tried to Ruin Him, Disney Says," *Washington Post*, October 25, 1947, 1, 2.

11. See either Richard Schickel, *The Disney Version: The Life, Times, Art, and Commerce of Walt Disney* (New York: Simon and Schuster, 1968) or Neal Gabler, *Walt Disney: The Triumph of the American Imagination* (New York: Knopf Doubleday, 2006).

12. "Mickey Mouse Guild," *Daily Variety*, December 17, 1937, 13.

13. Walt Disney, "To My Employees On Strike," *Daily Variety*, July 2, 1941, 5.

14. Memo from H. A. Smith, September 8, 1947, Walt Disney HUAC NARA file.

11. Crashing Page 1

1. Abel Green, "That Commie 'Probe,'" *Variety*, October 22, 1947, 3.

2. Quoted in "As the Press Views the Inquiry," *Film Daily*, October 30, 1947, 6.

3. Joseph North, "Nuremberg in Technicolor," *New Masses*, November 4, 1947, 3.

4. Eleanor Roosevelt, "No Art Flourishes on Censorship and Repression," *Washington News*, October 29, 1947, 35.

5. Herb Golden, "Tactics of '41 'Warmongering' Probe and Now Put Pix Biz in Eclipse in '47," *Variety*, October 29, 1947, 4, 18.

6. "Communism in Hollywood," *Los Angeles Examiner*, October 31, 1947, 18.

7. Quoted in "As the Press Views the Inquiry," *Film Daily*, October 29, 1947, 6.

8. George E. Sokolsky, "These Days," *New York Sun*, October 24, 1947, 21; George E. Sokolsky, "These Days," *New York Sun*, October 31, 1947, 31.

9. "Hollywood in Washington," *New York Herald Tribune*, October 22, 1947, reprinted in the *Hollywood Reporter*, October 23, 1947, 5. See "Hollywood in Washington," *Daily Variety*, October 23, 1947, 12.

10. Walter Winchell, "In New York," *New York Mirror*, November 28, 1947, 10.

11. Walter Winchell, "In New York," *New York Mirror*, October 26, 1947, 10.

12. Press release, "The Citizen Before Congress," October 25, 1947. Eric Johnston HUAC NARA file.

13. A complete program for the Conference on Cultural Freedom and Civil Liberties is in the Herbert Biberman HUAC NARA file.

14. "Two Sessions Here Score Film Inquiry," *New York Times*, October 26, 1947, 53.

15. "Quiz Witnesses Blast Inquiry at NY Meets," *Daily Variety*, October 27, 1947, 7.

16. Lillian Hellman, "The Judas Goat," from "House Un-American Activities" file, William Wyler papers, AMPAS.

17. Samuel Sillen and Louise Mitchell, "Film Snoopers Front for War Planners, Pepper Tells PCA," *Daily Worker*, October 27, 1947, 2, 10.

18. R. P. Hood to Director, FBI, COMPIC, October 25, 1947, 1.

19. R. B. Hood to Director, FBI, COMPIC, October 28, 1947, 1–4. The name of the Warner Bros. official supervising the license plate surveillance is redacted in the FBI report but he could only have been Blayney Matthews, head of security on the Warner Bros. lot.

20. Telemeter from Los Angeles to Director, FBI, October 21, 1947, COMPIC.

21. Bryson Rash, "Heard and Seen on the Air," *Washington Evening Star*, October 26, 1947, C-8.

22. Gladwin Hall, "Stars Fly to Fight Inquiry into Films," *New York Times*, October 27, 1947, 1.

23. Norman Corwin, "On a Note of Warning," *Screen Writer*, December 1947, 6.

24. "Actor Charles Boyer Becomes U.S. Citizen," *Atlanta Constitution*, February 14, 1942, 6.

25. "On the Air," *Hollywood Reporter*, October 29, 1947, 12.

26. Telegram from Stan Anderson to Norman Corwin, care of Ethel Kirshner at CBS, October 27, 1947, Norman Corwin Papers, Thousand Oaks Library, Thousand Oaks, CA.

27. Hedda Hopper, "Looking at Hollywood," *Chicago Daily Tribune*, October 29, 1947, 30.

28. "Movie Protest Group Flies to Inquire on Reds," *New York Herald Tribune*, October 27, 1947, 1, 7.

29. Wyler quoted in Paul Jacobs "Fund for the Republic" (unpublished manuscript, March 9, 1956), File 596, William Wyler Papers, AMPAS.

30. "30 Filmites Leave on Protest Dash to Washington," *Daily Variety*, October 27, 1947, 6.

31. Lauren Bacall, *By Myself* (New York: Alfred A Knopf, 1978), 175.

32. "Movie Protest Group Flies to Inquire on Reds," *New York Herald Tribune*, October 27, 1947, 7.

33. Philip Dunne, *Take Two: A Life in the Movies* (New York: Limelight Editions, 1992 [1980]): 194, 198. In 1951, before HUAC, Hayden admitted Communist Party membership. Kober, a loyal contributor to the *New Masses*, never veered from the CPUSA line.

34. "Stars Fly East to Fight Film Probe," *Daily Worker*, October 27, 1947, 1, 16.

35. "Protesting Stars Attending Film Inquiry Today," *Washington Evening Star*, October 27, 1947, 5.

36. "Lawson Is Cited for Contempt After Refusing to Tell Probers Whether He Is a Film Communist," *Washington Evening Star*, October 27, 1947, A6.

37. Florence S. Lowe, "Washington Hullabaloo," *Daily Variety*, October 29, 1947, 6.

12. Contempt

1. "Johnston Faces Probers Today," *Hollywood Reporter*, October 27, 1947, 1.

2. "Speech by Robert W. Kenny," November 9, 1947, WISC.

3. Robert W. Kenny to Albert Maltz, March 22, 1973, WISC.

4. Charles J. Katz to Albert Maltz, April 2, 1973, WISC.

5. Interview with Dalton Trumbo in the documentary *Hollywood on Trial* (1976).

6. Ben Margolis to Albert Maltz, April 6, 1973, WISC.

7. News of the meeting leaked a couple of days later. Jim Brady, "Split Injures Movies' Case," *Hollywood Citizen-News*, October 21, 1947, 2.

8. In 1949, his testimony in *Loew's, Inc. v. Lester Cole*, Johnston recalled his reassurance to Kenny less emphatically. "Of course I have made no deal with the House Un-American Activities Committee to blacklist these men." United States Court of Appeals, *Loew's, Inc. v. Lester Cole*, (1949), 771. Bartley Crum's recollection, recounted in his daughter's biography, accords with Kenny's. Patricia Bosworth, *Anything Your Little Heart Desires: An American Family Story* (New York; Simon and Schuster, 1997), 233–234.

9. Herman A. Lowe, "Johnston Fights Gov't Pix Rule," *Daily Variety*, October 28, 1947, 1, 10.

10. For a comprehensive and largely laudatory account of Lawson's career, pre- and post-hearings, see Gerald Horne, *The Final Victim of the Blacklist: John Howard Lawson, Dean of the Hollywood Ten* (Berkeley: University of California Press), 2006.

11. John Howard Lawson, "Notes from an Exile," *Screen Guilds' Magazine*, July 1934, 5, 22.

12. Advertisement for *The International, Daily Worker*, January 14, 1928, 6.

13. "Inside Stuff—Pictures," *Variety*, March 4, 1931, 56.

14. "Double Cross Charged to SWG," *Daily Variety*, October 20, 1937, 15.

15. Griffin Fariello, *Red Scare: Memories of the Inquisition, An Oral History* (New York: Norton, 1995), 297.

16. Virginia Waner, "Hollywood Writers Rise to Defense of 'Mission,' " *Daily Worker*, July 6, 1943, 7.

17. Herbert Cohn, "Picture Parade," *Brooklyn Daily Eagle*, July 25, 1938, 5.

18. Carl Levin, "Johnston Rejects Any Dictate to Hollywood by Government," *New York Herald Tribune*, October 28, 1947, 1, 14.

19. Willard Shelton, "Row at Movie Probe Opening Gun in Court Test," *PM Daily*, October 28, 1947, 3.

20. Earl Wilson, "Reputations Are the Stakes in Capital's Commie Card Game," *New York Post*, October 29, 1947, 34.

21. "Lawson Brings Near Riot to His Brief Act," *Daily Variety*, October 28, 1947, 11, 12.

22. Gordon Kahn, *Hollywood on Trial* (New York: Boni and Gaer, 1948): 77.

23. "Lawson's Statement 'Silence,' " *Variety*, October 29, 1947, 4. This is the truncated version of Lawson's statement printed in the trade press and elsewhere, which he handed out to reporters. A longer version appears in Kahn's *Hollywood on Trial*, 72–77.

24. "Lawson Is Cited for Contempt After Refusing to Tell Probers Whether He Is a Film Communist," *Washington Evening Star*, October 27, 1947, A6.

25. "Johnston Says Movies Will Insist on Rights," *New York Sun*, October 22, 1947, 2.

26. "H'd Group Holds Press Sessions in Washington," *Daily Variety*, October 28, 1947, 12.

27. "Glamour Takes a Back Seat," *Washington Post*, October 31, 1947, B10.

28. "Prober Nixon Flees Bogart and Bacall," *Daily Worker*, October 29, 1947, 3.

29. Tom Donnelly, "The Hearing Needs a Hero," *Washington Daily News*, October 28, 1947, 5.

30. Cecelia Agar, "How Free Speech Committee Practices It," *PM Daily*, October 28, 1947, 3.

31. "Johnston Faces Probers Today," *Hollywood Reporter*, October 27, 1947, 1.

32. Cecelia Agar, "How Free Speech Committee Practices It," *PM Daily*, October 28, 1947, 3.

33. Manny Claggart, "Weary of Whipping Boy Role–Johnston," *Film Daily*, October 28, 1947, 1, 5; "Johnston Asks Three Corrections," *Film Daily*, October 28, 1947, 1, 3.

34. Kahn, *Hollywood on Trial*, 77.

35. Samuel Sillen, "Prober Nixon Flees Bogart and Bacall," *Daily Worker*, October 28, 1947, 3.

36. Florence S. Lowe, "Probe Sidelights," *Variety*, October 29, 1947, 4.

37. Florabel Muir, "Just for Variety," *Variety*, November 5, 1947, 4.

38. Lowe, "Probe Sidelights," *Variety*, October 29, 1947, 4.

39. "2 More Screen Writers Ejected by Red Inquiry," *Washington Evening Star*, October 28, 1947, A6.

40. Lauren Bacall, "Exclusive: By Lauren Bacall, Why I Came to Washington," *Washington Daily News*, October 29, 1947, 1.

13. $64 Questions and No Answers

1. Dalton Trumbo, "Dalton Trumbo's Own Story," *Daily Worker*, March 13, 1940, 7. Trumbo's story is sympathetically and comprehensively told in Larry Ceplair and Christopher Trumbo, *Trumbo: Blacklisted Hollywood Radical* (Lexington: University Press of Kentucky), 2014.

2. Dalton Trumbo, "Trumbo Hits War Makers," *Hollywood Now*, January 19, 1940, 1, 3.

3. Eileen Creelman, "Thirty Seconds over Tokyo," *New York Sun*, November 16, 1944, 23.

4. Frank Scully, "Scully's Scrapbook," *Variety*, October 25, 1944, 2.

5. Dalton Trumbo, "Dalton Trumbo's Own Story," *Daily Worker*, March 13, 1940, 7.

6. Alvah Bessie, *Inquisition in Eden* (New York: Macmillan, 1965), 184–185.

7. Dalton Trumbo, WQQW radio address, October 19, 1947, WISC.

8. Gordon Kahn, *Hollywood on Trial* (New York: Boni and Gaer, 1948), 78.

9. As usual, the crowd reaction is in the ear of the beholder. The *Congressional Record* notes applause *after* Chairman Thomas's line, as if it might have been for him. The *New York Sun* reported "loud applause" for Trumbo as he was excused from the witness table.

10. "2 More Writers Ejected by Red Inquiry," *Washington Evening Star*, October 28, 1947, A1, A6.

11. Red Kann, "Washington Ringside," *Motion Picture Daily*, October 29, 2947, 6.

12. "Writers Statements Admitted to Record," *Daily Variety*, October 29, 1947, 9.

13. "Sorrell Asks Chance to Tell His Side," *Daily Variety*, October 29, 1947, 8.

14. Herschel Brickell, "Books of Our Times," *New York Post*, July 20, 1938, 11.

15. "Interview of Albert Maltz," August 26, 1976, by Joel Gardner, UCLA Oral History Project. http://oralhistory.library.ucla.edu/viewFile.do?itemId=30065&fileSeq=3&xsl=http://oralhistory.library.ucla.edu/xslt/local/tei/xml/tei/stylesheet/xhtml2/tei.xsl#session1a.

16. Albert Maltz, "Should Ezra Pound Be Shot?," *New Masses*, December 25, 1946, 4.

17. Kahn, *Hollywood on Trial*, 90. The moment is confirmed in the HRCIMPI, *Congressional Record*, 366.

18. Earl Wilson, "Reputations Are at Stake in Commie Card Game," *New York Post*, October 29, 1947, 34.

19. Albert Maltz, "What Shall We Ask of Writers?," *New Masses*, February 12, 1946, 19–22.

20. Howard Fast, "Art and Politics," *New Masses*, February 26, 1947, 6–8; Joseph North, "No Retreat for the Writer," *New Masses*, February 26, 1946, 8–10.

21. Alvah Bessie, "What Is Freedom for Writers?," *New Masses*, March 12, 1946, 8–10.

22. John Howard Lawson, "Art Is a Weapon," *New Masses*, March 19, 1946, 18–20.

23. Albert Maltz, "Moving Forward," *New Masses*, April 9, 1946, 8–10, 21–22.

24. Earl Wilson, "19 Ready to Stick to 'Rights' If It Means Jail for Contempt," *New York Post*, October 22, 1947, 5.

25. Crosswell Bowen, "Congress' Bouting Thomas," *PM Daily*, December 7, 1946, M7.

26. HRCIMPI, *Congressional Record*, 367.

27. Red Kann, "Washington Ringside," *Motion Picture Daily*, October 29, 2947, 6.

28. "Four Are Cited for Contempt," *Washington Evening Star*, October 29, 1947, A3.

29. Alvah Bessie, "Letters to the Eagle," *Brooklyn Daily Eagle*, September 2, 1939, 8.

30. Bessie, *Inquisition in Eden*, 26.

31. Bessie, *Inquisition in Eden*, 210.

32. Herman A. Lowe, "MPA Challenges Committee," *Daily Variety*, October 29, 1947, 8.

33. "Cheyfitz with MPA Two Years," *Motion Picture Herald*, November 1, 1947, 15.

34. Ibid.

35. "Effects of the Hearings on the MPAA," COMPIC, LA 100-15732, 12–13.

36. "Glamour Strikes Back," *Variety*, October 29, 1947, 5.

37. Manning Clagett, "MPAA to Fight Charges of Probe 'Fix' Try," *Film Daily*, October 29, 1947, 5.

38. Quentin Reynolds, "Hollywood Probe Unmasks Itself as Political Trial," *PM Daily*, October 29, 1947, 3. Reynolds pretended to be more starstruck than he really was: he and his wife were close friends of the Bogarts.

39. "H'Wood Tourists Will Start on New Junket," *Daily Variety*, October 29, 1947, 8.

40. Garfield was a signatory to "The Moscow Trials: A Statement by American Progressives," *New Masses*, May 3, 1938, 19.

41. Joseph North, "Crossfire," *New Masses*, November 11, 1947, 9.

14. Jewish Questions

1. "Thomas Charges Move to Stop H'D Inquiry," *Daily Variety*, October 30, 1947, 15.

2. Alvah Bessie, *Inquisition in Eden* (New York: Macmillan, 1965), 188.

3. "Dreiser Group of Ten Indicted," *Los Angeles Times*, November 17, 1931, 5.

4. Quoted in Charles Higham, *Hollywood at Sunset* (New York: Saturday Review Press, 1972), 36.

5. Samuel Ornitz, "Hollywood Blitsmear," *New Masses*, April 27, 1940, 12.

6. Telegram from Samuel Ornitz to J. Parnell Thomas, October 2, 1947, Samuel Ornitz HUAC NARA file.

7. "A Jew Before the Un-American Committee," HUAC NARA, also reprinted in *Jewish Life* (December 1947). As with several of the statements by the Unfriendlies, the wording of Ornitz's statement varies depending on the draft. Two versions appear in his HUAC file, an early handwritten version that begins "In speaking as Jew" and the version cited here. The version Ornitz provided Gordon Kahn in *Hollywood on Trial* also varies from the other two. Samuel Ornitz HUAC NARA file.

8. "Racial Issue Is Raised by 'Unfriendly' Witnesses," *Daily Variety*, October 30, 1947, 17.

9. "$22,000 for Sound in Guild's Stage 'Verdun': Projectors Employed," *Variety*, March 18, 1931, 5; "Legends of America," *Variety*, October 10, 1933, 34.

10. "Picture Possibilities," *Variety*, December 25, 1929, 32.

11. "Two More Movie Figures Cited for Contempt," *New York Sun*, October 29, 1947, 2.

12. "Lavery's First Concern Is Jobs for SWG War Vets," *Daily Variety*, November 9, 1944, 3.

13. Emmet Lavery to SWG Members, "Washington Hearings," October 20, 1947, WISC.

14. On February 22, 1979, Lavery recollected his political agenda in October 1947 as part of the History Project of the Writers Guild of America, Writers Guild of America West, on file at the Writers Guild of America.

15. Emmet Lavery, "You Never Can Tell," *Screen Writer*, August 1946, 35.

16. "Contempt," *Daily Sentinel, Rome, New York*, October 28, 1947, 9; "Lavery Wants to Tell Probers How Motion Pictures Are Made," *Washington Evening Star*, October 28, 1947, A6.

17. "Four Are Cited for Contempt Probe Today," *Washington Evening Star*, October 29, 1947, A3.

18. Red Kann, "Washington Ringside," *Motion Picture Daily*, October 30, 1947, 5.

19. Mary Spargo, "Four More Hollywood Figures Cited in Contempt," *Washington Post*, October 30, 1947, 1, 2.

20. Florence S. Lowe, "Washington Hullabaloo," *Daily Variety*, May 26, 1948, 6.

21. Edward Dmytryk, *Odd Man Out: A Memoir of the Hollywood Ten* (Carbondale: Southern Illinois University Press, 1996), 14–15.

22. Dmytryk, *Odd Man Out*, 20–21.

23. "Racial Issues Raised by 'Unfriendly' Witnesses," *Daily Variety*, October 20, 1947, 17.

24. Jennifer E. Langdon, *Caught in the Crossfire: Adrian Scott and the Politics of Americanism in 1940s Hollywood* (New York: Columbia University Press, 2008), 301–353.

25. Adrian Scott, "You Can't Do That!," *Screen Writer*, August 1947, 7.

26. "Ornitz, Biberman, Scott, Dmytryk, Draw Citations," *Daily Variety*, October 30, 1947, 15.

27. Jay Carmody, "RKO's Schary, Not the Tycoon Type, Talks as Practical Idealist," *Washington Evening Star*, October 29, 1947, B14.

28. Schary fondly recalled his kosher childhood in *For Special Occasions* (New York: Random House, 1961).

29. "Too Many Heroes," *Daily Variety*, November 16, 1937, 1, 4.

30. Jennifer E. Langdon expresses skepticism about Schary's professed obliviousness to the political leanings of Scott and Dmytryk in *Caught in the Crossfire*, 348.

31. Herbert A. Lowe, "Schary, Lavery Talk Frankly," *Daily Variety*, October 30, 1947, 1, 14.

32. Schary always regretted he didn't have the presence of mind to tell Thomas, re Rip Van Winkle, "Yes, Mr. Chairman, I've read that story. I am quite familiar with the art of fiction and the many uses of it." Dore Schary, *Heyday: An Autobiography* (Boston: Little, Brown and Company, 1979), 163.

33. Florence S. Lowe, "Inquiry Big Show in Wash.—Really 10 Shows in One," *Daily Variety*, October 30, 1947, 17.

15. The Curtain Drops

1. Ring Lardner Jr., *The Lardners: My Family Remembered* (New York: Harper and Row, 1976), 124.

2. "Hollywood Inside," *Daily Variety*, August 25, 1941, 2.

3. "Inside Stuff—Pictures," *Variety*, April 8, 1942, 26.

4. Ring Lardner Jr., *I'd Hate Myself in the Morning: A Memoir* (New York: Nation Books, 2000), 105, 107.

5. Lardner, *I'd Hate Myself in the Morning: A Memoir*, 5.

6. "David Lardner Killed," *Daily Variety*, October 23, 1944, 1.

7. "Statement of Ring Lardner Jr.," Ring Lardner Jr. HUAC NARA file.

8. "Statement by Lester Cole," Lester Cole file, WISC.

9. A recording of Lester Cole's testimony is available at the WISC.

10. Doyce B. Nunis Jr., "*Robert W. Kenny: My First Forty Years in California Politics, 1922–1962*" (Oral History Program: University of California, Los Angeles, 1964): Oral History 349.

11. Herman A. Lowe, "Commie Carnival Closes," *Daily Variety*, October 31, 1947, 1, 12–13.

12. "Witness Called to Tell Inquiry of Red 'Spying,' " *Washington Evening Star*, October 20, 1947, A1, A4.

13. Lee Garling, "Probe Falls of Own Weight As Industry Chiefs Predicted," *Box Office*, November 1, 1947, 8–9.

14. Jonathan Miles, *The Dangerous Otto Katz: The Many Lives of a Soviet Spy* (New York: Bloomsbury, 2010), 164.

15. Oliver Pilat, "Soviet Agents Pumped Oppenheimer for Radiation Data, Film Probe Told," *New York Post*, October 30, 1947, 3.

16. "Mellett Broadcasts Statement Planned at Hollywood Probe," *Washington Evening Star*, October 31, 1947, 14.

17. "Mellett Offers Subversive Test," *Daily Variety*, October 31, 1947, 13.

18. "Goldwyn Says Movie Hearings Were a 'Flop'," *New York Herald Tribune*, October 31, 1947, 7.

19. "Lawson Is Cited in Contempt After Refusing to Tell Probers Whether He Is a Film Communist," *Washington Evening Star*, October 27, 1947, A6.

20. Memo from H. A. Smith, August 8, 1947, Sam Goldwyn HUAC NARA file.

21. Walter Winchell, "In New York," *New York Mirror*, October 26, 1947, 10.

22. "Goldwyn Says Movie Hearings Were a 'Flop,'" *New York Herald Tribune*, October 31, 1947, 7.

23. Quentin Reynolds, "A Bomb 'Plot' Fizzles, Thomas Calls Halt to Movie Probe," *PM Daily*, October 31, 1947, 3.

24. "Hearing Halt Laid to Move By Reds," *Washington Post*, November 1, 1947, 3.

25. Manning Claggart, "Film Probe Fizzles Out with Suddenness," *Film Daily*, October 31, 1947, 3.

26. Robert E. Stripling, *The Red Plot Against America*, ed. Bob Considine (Drexel, PA: Bell, 1949), 75.

27. Guy Hottel to Director, FBI, "COMPIC-International Security," October 30, 1947, 1–2.

28. "Film Business Vindicated Says MPA Statement," *Daily Variety*, October 31, 1947, 1, 12.

29. Red Kann, "Washington Ringside," *Motion Picture Daily*, October 31, 1947, 1.

16. The Waldorf and Other Declarations

1. "Eisler Is Among 8 Honored Guests at Civil Rights Dinner," *New York Mirror*, November 3, 1947, 10.

2. "Johnston Hits Cited Ten," *Daily Variety*, November 19, 1947, 14.

3. Manning Clagett, "Film Probe Fizzles Out with Suddenness," *Film Daily*, October 31, 1947, 1, 3, 6.

4. "Goldwyn Brands Com. Activity 'Un-American,' " *Film Daily*, October 31, 1947, 1, 6.

5. Billy Rose, "Pitching Horseshoes," *PM Daily*, November 11, 1947, 2.

6. "Eric Johnston and Paul McNutt Are 'Kidding' Themselves," *Harrison's Reports*, November 8, 1947, 177.

7. George E. Sokolsky, "These Days," *Kingston Daily Freeman*, November 3, 1947, 4.

8. "The Un-American Way," *Variety*, June 4, 1947, 3.

9. "Johnston Hits Cited Ten," *Daily Variety*, November 19, 1947, 14.

10. "Film Industry to Ban all Reds," *Hollywood Reporter*, November 26, 1947, 1, 4.

11. "Film Bigwigs Confer on Purge," *PM Daily*, November 25, 1947, 2.

12. "50 Meet Today to Map Policy on Reds," *Film Daily*, November 24, 1947, 4; "May Announce Policy on Pix Reds Today," *Film Daily*, November 25, 1947, 1, 7.

13. "Congress Votes 10 in Contempt," *Motion Picture Herald*, November 29, 1947, 13, 14.

14. "Statement by Helen Gahagan Douglas on the Un-American Activities Committee," November 24, 1947, 1, 3.

15. Dore Schary, *Heyday: An Autobiography* (Boston: Little, Brown and Company, 1979), 164–167.

16. Johnston's version of the Waldorf discussion was put on the record, under oath, in *Loew's Inc. v. Lester Cole*, United States Court of Appeals, 1949, 785–799.

17. "Recalls Waldorf Creed of 1947," *Variety*, November 18, 1964, 11.

18. Schary, *Heyday*, 165–166.

19. "Effects of the Hearings on the MPAA," no date, COMPIC, 11–12.

20. "Studios Vote to Ban Red Employment," *Film Daily*, November 28, 1947, 1, 8. Although no reporters were in the room where it happened, the New York–based *Film Daily* seems to have had the best sources and most precise chronology. I have relied on its contemporaneous account for the timeline of the decision making. In his memoir, Dore Schary insisted, "No vote was ever taken."

21. "Industry Drives on Reds As House Cites Ten," *Motion Picture Herald*, November 29, 1947, 13.

22. Joyce O'Hara to Helen Clare Nelson, December 9, 1947, WISC.

23. "Film Industry to Ban All Reds," *Hollywood Reporter*, November 25, 1947, 1.

24. "Film '10' Plan Court Fight on Moguls' Edict," *Daily Worker*, November 25, 1947, 3, 7.

25. Howard Koch, "Letter to My Fellow Workers in the Motion Picture Industry," *Hollywood Reporter*, November 26, 1947, 14.

26. W. R. Wilkerson, "Tradeviews," *Hollywood Reporter*, November 27, 1947, 1, 2.

27. "The Industry Takes Positive Action," *Harrison's Reports*, November 29, 1947, 189, 192.

28. Max Lerner, "The Surrender of Hollywood," *PM Daily*, November 26, 1947, 10.

29. "Film Chiefs Vote Purge, Cited 10 Go First," *PM Daily*, November 26, 1947, 2.

30. John Maynard, "Film Chiefs Meet to Map Red Drive," *New York Journal American*, November 24, 1947, 10.

31. Otto Friedrich, *City of Nets: A Portrait of Hollywood in the 1940's* (New York: Harper and Row, 1986), 335.

32. Bosley Crowther, "A Business Matter," *New York Times*, December 7, 1947, 85.

33. "Mayer Tells Cole Firing," *Daily Variety*, December 9, 1948, 1, 11.

34. "Johnston Denies He Pressured Films on Red Issue," *New York Star*, December 22, 1948, 25.

35. "The Federal Government Must Censor Motion Pictures," *Los Angeles Examiner*, November 3, 1947, 1.

36. Hedda Hopper, "Looking at Hollywood," *Los Angeles Times*, November 7, 1947, 10.

37. Hedda Hopper, "Looking at Hollywood," *Los Angeles Times*, November 18, 1947, 8.

38. Affidavit of Eric Johnston, *Dalton Trumbo v. Loew's Inc.*, April 22, 1948, 11.

39. Victor Riesel, "Ranting Could Hurt Filmland," *Hollywood Citizen-News*, November 1, 1947, 10.

40. "Who Is Hysterical?," *Washington Evening Star*, October 30, 1947, A16.

41. "'Crossfire' Pair Fired as Movies Launch Purge," *PM Daily*, November 27, 1947, 4.

42. "Thomas Group Seeks Propaganda in Films," *PM Daily*, December 7, 1947, 14.

43. Transcription of MBS radio show, October 29, 1947, Danny Kaye FBI FOIA file.

44. "Hollywood Hails Return on the 22," *New York Sun*, October 31, 1947, 1.

45. Ed Sullivan, "Behind the Big-City Scenes at Broadway and 42nd Street," *Hollywood Citizen-News*, October 30, 1947, 22; "Going Home," *Philadelphia Inquirer*, October 30, 1947, 20. Above the doorway, the "red sea" part of the logo was hastily painted out.

46. Sidney Olsen, "The Movie Hearings," *Life*, November 24, 1947.

47. Hedda Hopper, "Looking at Hollywood," *Los Angeles Times*, November 7, 1947, 10.

48. "Indianapolis," *New York Mirror*, October 31, 1947, 26.

49. "Gag the Prima Donnas," *Harrison's Reports*, December 6, 1947, 193, 196.

50. " 'The Unfriendly Nineteen,' " *Daily Variety*, October 31, 1947, 15. See also N. A. Daniels, "Hollywood After the Hearings," *New Masses*, November 25, 1947, 4.

51. "Committee for the First Amendment," E. P. Kirby Papers, File 24, no date.

52. William Wyler to Billy Wilkerson, November 6, 1947, William Wyler Papers, Committee for the First Amendment, File 596, AMPAS. The letter was printed as an "Open Forum" submission in the *Hollywood Reporter*, November 7, 1947, 11. Wyler always insisted that the group was not in league with the Hollywood Ten. CFA "was *not* a Communist front organization. There may have been some Communists in the group, but there are probably Communists in any organization. The point is, they did not run the Committee and a Communist-front organization is one that is run by Communists. *We* ran the Committee and we were not Communists."

53. W. R. Wilkerson, "Tradeviews," *Hollywood Reporter*, November 7, 1947, 1.

54. W. R. Wilkerson, "Tradeviews," *Hollywood Reporter*, November 25, 1947, 1.

55. "Rankin's Needle Caught in Groove," *PM Daily*, November 28, 1947, 4.

56. "RKO Fires Scott, Dmytryk In Studio Red 'Cleanup,' " *Hollywood Citizen-News*, November 27, 1947, 2.

57. "Guild Execs, Film Toppers Meet Today on Ousted 10," *Daily Variety*, November 28, 1947, 1, 9.

58. " '1st Amendment' Group Folds; Urges Members to Join Committee of 1,000," *Variety*, February 25, 1948, 16.

59. Hedda Hopper, "Looking at Hollywood," *Chicago Daily Tribune*, November 1, 1947, 14.

60. "Exhibitionism," *New York Mirror*, October 29, 1947, 26.

61. " '1st Amendment' Group Folds; Urges Members to Join Committee of 1,000," *Variety*, February 25, 1948, 4, 16.

62. W. R. Wilkerson, "Tradeviews," *Hollywood Reporter*, November 25, 1947, 1, 2.

63. "Bogart Admits Red Defense Was 'Mistake,' " *Los Angeles Times*, December 3, 1947, 2; "Bogart Flays Reds, Regrets D.C. Visit," *Washington Times Herald*, December 3, 1947, 1. *By Myself*, Lauren Bacall's otherwise detailed and reliable memoir, elides this episode from her adoring portrait of her life with Bogart.

64. Humphrey Bogart, "I'm No Communist," *Photoplay*, May 1948, 53.

65. "Katherine Hepburn," Katherine [*sic*] Hepburn HUAC NARA file.

66. " '1st Amendment' Group Folds; Urges Members to Join Committee of 1,000," *Variety*, February 25, 1947, 4, 16.

17. Blacklists and Casualty Lists

1. George Dixon, "Washington Scene," *Washington Times-Herald*, June 10, 1948, 17.

2. J. Parnell Thomas as told to Stacy V. Jones, "What I Really Think of Hollywood," *Liberty*, June 1948, 18–19, 75–76.

3. Allen Weinstein, *Perjury: The Hiss-Chambers Case* (New York: Vintage, 1979), 5. Chambers initially charged Hiss merely with being a Communist, and thus a foreign

agent by implication. In a subsequent affidavit on November 4, 1948, he ratcheted up the accusation to espionage.

4. "Hill Coverage," *Broadcasting/Telecasting*, June 2, 1952, 30. Ultimately, twenty-one days of the Hiss-Chamber hearings were televised.

5. "Film 'Red' Hearings to Be Resumed in Sept: Thomas," *Motion Picture Daily*, August 27, 1948, 1.

6. "Few D.C. Changes for Pix Biz," *Variety*, November 10, 1948, 11.

7. "Let Us Give Thanks," *Daily Variety*, November 24, 1948, 9.

8. N. A. Daniels, "Hollywood Letter," *New Masses*, July 1, 1947, 16.

9. "Newsreels Back Anti-Red Stance," *Variety*, September 26, 1951, 20.

10. Eric Johnston affidavit, *Dalton Trumbo v. Loews Inc.*, April 22, 1948, 16–17.

11. Lardner Jr. quoted in Griffin Fariello, *Red Scare: Memories of the American Inquisition.* (New York: Norton, 1995), 263.

12. Lester Cole, *Hollywood Red: The Autobiography of Lester Cole* (Palo Alto, CA: Ramparts, 1981), 320. Cole's memoir is fraught with mistakes and misrememberings—and he always seems to get the best lines—but Ring Lardner Jr. tells the same story in Fariello, *Red Scare*: 263.

13. "Congress' New Pic Probe Seen Calmer Than '47's," *Variety*, March 14, 1951, 55.

14. Herb Golden, "Job Blues for Hollywood Reds," *Variety*, March 14, 1951, 1, 55.

15. Mike Kaplan, "Hollywood Red Probe at Close, Report to Congress by End of Year," *Variety*, September 26, 1951, 20.

16. "Stander Taunts Red Probe; Gorney Sings—Only a Song; Mrs. Abe Burrows Names 24," *Daily Variety*, May 7, 1953, 3.

17. *Los Angeles Daily News*, April 24, 1951, 10.

18. "TV Turndown on Red Hearing," *Hollywood Reporter*, March 21, 1951, 1, 2.

19. Larry Parks, WQQW broadcast, October 19, 1947, WISC. Parks made the same statement on WWBC on October 22, 1947.

20. Sworn testimony of Larry Parks, Executive Session testimony, March 21, 1951, 7. Larry Parks HUAC NARA file.

21. "What's the Risk of Opening Up," *Variety*, March 28, 1951, 5, 55.

22. "Jury Still Out on Parks' Future," *Variety*, March 28, 1951, 5, 16.

23. "One of Hollywood Ten Denies Red Ties," *Los Angeles Times*, September 11, 1950, 30.

24. Edward Dmytryk, *Odd Man Out: A Memoir of the Hollywood Ten* (Carbondale: Southern Illinois University Press, 1996), 156.

25. C. P. Trussell, "Once a Communist, Dmytryk Reveals," *New York Times*, April 26, 1951, 17.

26. "Riesel Warns That Pix Face 'Worst Black Eye,' " *Variety*, March 28, 1951, 16.

27. "Will Co-op Fully With Red Probers, Say Garfield, Ferrer, Denying Charges," *Variety*, March 28, 1951, 5, 16.

28. David Platt, "Sorry Spectacle of Garfield, Ferrer," *Daily Worker*, March 20, 19051, 11.

29. Sworn testimony of John Garfield, April 9, 1951, 89. John Garfield HUAC NARA file. On the front page of the printed transcript, someone on the HUAC staff wrote the word: "*Deceased.*"

30. "Never Was a 'Red': Garfield," *Motion Picture Daily*, April 24, 1951, 1, 10.

31. Herman Lowe, "Garfield Does a Solo in Taking Mon. Stand," *Variety*, April 25, 18, 20; "'Red' Probe," *Motion Picture Daily*, May 21, 1951, 6. Jackson and Velde had reason to be skeptical: Garfield also lied about speaking at the "Keep America Free" rally for the Unfriendly Nineteen on October 25, 1947.

32. "Name Policy Mapped for Summer Stock," *Variety*, May 21, 1952, 57.

33. "Film Figures Deny Being Members of the Communist Party," *Daily Variety*, June 10, 1949, 9.

34. *Red Channels: The Report of Communist Influence in Radio and Television* (New York: American Business Consultants, 1950), 122–123.

35. "E. G. Robinson No Commy, At Worse 'Choice Sucker' Say D.C. Red Probers," *Daily Variety*, May 1, 1952, 1, 11.

36. Edward G. Robinson, "How the Reds Made a Sucker Out of Me," *American Legion Magazine*, October 1952, 11, 62, 64–65, 66–67, 68, 70.

37. "John Garfield of Films Dead of Heart Attack," *Washington Post*, May 22, 1952, B2.

38. Victor Riesel, "Red Pressure Revealed by Actor on Day of Death," *Philadelphia Inquirer*, May 25, 1952, B19.

39. "Heat Floors Garfield," *Variety*, September 28, 1949, 2.

40. "Tribute by Clifford Odets to the Late John Garfield," *New York Times*, May 25, 1952, X3.

41. "Legion 'Clearing' Most Filmites," *Daily Variety*, July 30, 1952, 1, 7.

18. Not Only Victims

1. Ring Lardner Jr., "My Life on the Blacklist," *Saturday Evening Post*, October 14, 1961, 38–40, 42–44.

2. Alvah Bessie to Ring Lardner Jr., February 2, 1977. Ring Lardner Jr. to Alvah Bessie, February 8, 1977, Ring Lardner Jr. papers, AMPAS.

3. Leonard J. Berry, "Herbert Biberman at 69; Still Not Beaten, Afraid or Tired," *Albany Times-Union*, July 6, 1969, H-2.

4. "Lester Cole Dies; In 'Hollywood 10,' " *New York Times*, August 18, 1985, 36.

5. Lester Cole, *Hollywood Red: The Autobiography of Lester Cole* (Palo Alto, CA: Ramparts Press, 1981), 171–172.

6. Alvah Bessie, *Inquisition in Eden* (New York: Macmillan, 1965), 268.

7. Harold Myers, "In London," *Daily Variety*, July 30, 1963, 11.

8. Jennifer E. Landgon, *Caught in the Crossfire: Adrian Scott and the Politics of Americanism in 1940s Hollywood* (New York: Columbia University Press, 2009), 377–382.

9. A. D. Murphy, "20th Wins 9 Oscars," *Variety*, April 17, 1971, 6.

10. Gerald Horne, *The Final Victim of the Blacklist: John Howard Lawson, Dean of the Hollywood Ten* (Berkeley: University of California Press, 2006), xxii.

11. G. Gerald Fraser, "John Howard Lawson, 82, Writer Blacklisted by Hollywood in '47," *New York Times*, August 14, 1977, 46.

12. "Dalton Trumbo Admits Identity as 'Robert Rich,' Oscar Winner," *Daily Variety*, January 19, 1959, 1, 4.

13. "Heated Denial by Brewer to Charge of Bossing H'wood Purge," and "Brewer Gives Views," *Variety*, May 12, 1954, 5.

14. Roy M. Brewer, "Waldorf Declaration: A Perspective," *Variety*, March 21, 1962, 15.

15. Griffin Fariello, *Red Scare: Memories of the American Inquisition, An Oral History* (New York: Norton), 1995, 117.

16. "Herb Sorrell, Firebrand of H'wood Labor Front in '40s, Dies at 76," *Daily Variety*, May 10, 1973, 7.

17. "Racketeer Willie Bioff Blown to Bits by Bomb," *Los Angeles Times*, November 4, 1955, 1, 3.

18. "Academy Repeals 'Blacklist' Ruling," *Daily Variety*, January 14, 1959, 1, 4.

19. "Harry Truman Blasts Hollywood Blacklist," *Daily Variety*, April 9, 1959, 1, 14.

20. "Blacklist Scribes Work Upheld by Kramer," *Daily Variety*, October 15, 1959, 1, 5.

21. A. H. Weiler, "Movie Maker Hires Blacklisted Writer," *New York Times*, January 20, 1960, 1, 8.

22. Robert Landry, "Licensed to Handle Dynamite," *Variety*, January 27, 1960, 5; Hy Hollinger, "Preminger's Private Hornet: Trumbo," *Variety*, January 27, 1960. The previous October, Preminger had denied to *Variety* that he had hired Trumbo.

23. Murray Schumach, "Kramer Defies American Legion Over Hiring of Movie Writers," *New York Times*, February 8, 1960, 1, 35.

24. "A Statement from Frank Sinatra," *Daily Variety*, March 28, 1960, 7.

25. Hedda Hopper, "Wagner Signed for Olympic Film," *Los Angeles Times*, April 8, 1960, A9; Hedda Hopper, "Columnist Tells of Her Travels," *Los Angeles Times*, April 1, 1960, A8.

26. Tom Santopietro, *Sinatra in Hollywood* (New York: Thomas Dunne, 2008), 300–301.

27. Frank Sinatra, "Statement," *Daily Variety*, April 4, 1960, 7.

28. "Spartacus LA Bow Nets Cedars $100G," *Daily Variety*, October 20, 1960, 4.

29. "'Exodus' Is Picked by American Legion," *New York Times*, December 22, 1960, 16.

30. "Am. Legion Halts School Bus' Use to See Spartacus," *Daily Variety*, December 12, 1960, 4.

31. "Hearst Keeps Up Drumfire on Writers Cited for Past Ties to Communism," *Variety*, April 6, 1960, 15.

32. "Trumbo B.O. OK; Raps Vs 'Exodus, Spartacus' Fail," *Variety*, March 7, 1962, 12.

33. "Kennedy as Fan," *Variety*, February 15, 1961, 15.

34. "Film Hiring Defended," *New York Times*, July 3, 1961, 9.

35. Asked if the MPAA had ever voted to officially revoke or repudiate the Waldorf Declaration, the association responded: "Unfortunately, at this time the information you are seeking is not available to the public. A vote, such as the one you are inquiring about, would be recorded in meeting minutes of the MPAA's Board of Directors and/or Members and as such, such information is confidential and solely intended for the MPAA Board and its Members." From the MPAA in an email to the author, August 25, 2017.

36. "Eric Johnston, MPAA Prez Who Sold Hollywood Around Globe, Dies at 66," *Variety*, August 28, 1963, 4, 22.

37. "Ike, Top-Tier D.C. Officialdom at Johnston Rites," *Daily Variety*, August 27, 1963, 1, 11.

38. "Gunther R. Lessing," *Variety*, October 6, 1965, 67.

39. "Standing Ovation for Trumbo," *Daily Variety*, March 16, 1970, 32. In 1954, the SWG divided into two geographical entities, Writers Guild of America, West, and Writers Guild of America, East.

40. Albert Maltz, "A Command Performance," *Los Angeles Times*, April 3, 1977, T2.

41. Lester Cole to Alvah Bessie, November 29, 1947; Lester Cole to Albert Maltz, November 15, 1947, WISC

42. Alvah Bessie to Albert Maltz and Ring Lardner Jr., December 8, 1977, WISC

43. Ring Lardner Jr. to Albert Maltz, October 29, 1977, WISC.

44. Alvah Bessie to Emmet Lavery Jr., October 7, 1975, WISC

45. Hilton Kramer, "The Blacklist and the Cold War," *New York Times*, October 3, 1976, 63.

46. "Albert Maltz," *Variety*, April 29, 1985, 11.

47. "An Oral History with Philip Dunne," interviewed by Douglass Bell, 1991, Academy Foundation Oral History Program, Margaret Herrick Library, Beverly Hills, CA, AMPAS.

48. Emmet Lavery to SWG Membership, "Re: Dalton Trumbo Pamphlet [The Time of the Toad]," November 1, 1949, 3, WGA.

49. Interview with Emmet Lavery by Steve Cohen, February 29, 1969, 6, WGA.

50. Dore Schary, *Heyday: An Autobiography* (Boston: Little Brown, 1979), 165–166.

51. Todd McCarthy, "Dore Schary, Studio Prod'n Chief, Producer, Director, 74, Dies of Cancer," *Daily Variety*, July 8, 1980, 1, 12.

52. Nat Kahn, "Performers as Top Salesman," *Variety*, January 25, 1950, 71.

53. "Sam Wood Will Bars Reds from Estate Share," *Daily Variety*, September 29, 1949, 10.

54. Bob Thomas, "Red Peril Shown Up in Film," *Binghamton News*, April 18, 1951, 38.

55. Army Archerd, "Just for Variety," *Daily Variety*, January 6, 1958, 2.

56. *Congressional Record*, 141.

57. Hedda Hopper, *The Whole Truth and Nothing But* (New York: Doubleday, 1963), 273.

58. James O. Kemm, *Rupert Hughes: A Hollywood Legend* (Beverly Hills: Pomegranate Press, 1997), 292–296.

59. Earl Wilson, "It Happened Last Night," *New York Post*, October 24, 1947, 67.

60. "Rep. Dempsey Cites Pix As Democracy's Best Salesman," *Daily Variety*, April 14, 1953, 3.

61. Morrie Ryskind, with John H. M. Roberts, *I Shot an Elephant in My Pajamas: The Morrie Ryskind Story* (Lafayette, LA: Huntington House, 1994), 166.

62. Ryskind, *I Shot an Elephant in My Pajamas*, 164.

63. Leonard Klady, "Kazan: No Apology," *Variety*, March 22, 1999, 1, 67.

64. Will Tusher, "Taylor Building Renamed for Cukor," *Daily Variety*, December 26, 1989, 6; Hy Hollinger, "The 'Man With the Perfect Profile' Has a Lower One Now," *Variety*, January 3, 1993, 6.

A Bibliographical Note

1. A small sampling of the worthwhile reading: Otto Friedrich's *City of Nets: A Portrait of Hollywood in the 1940s* (New York: Harper and Row, 1986); William Goodman, *The Committee: The Extraordinary Career of the House Committee on Un-American Activities* (New York: Farrar, Straus, and Giroux, 1968); Larry Ceplair and Steven

Englund's *The Inquisition in Hollywood: Politics in the Film Community, 1930–1960.* (Urbana: University of Illinois Press, 1979); Robert Vaughn's *Only Victims: A Study of Show Business Blacklisting* (New York: Limelight Editions, 1996 [1972]); Griffin Fariello, *Red Scare: Memoirs of the American Inquisition, An Oral History* (New York: Norton, 1995); Patrick McGilligan and Paul Buhle, *Tender Comrades: A Backstory to the Hollywood Blacklist* (New York: St. Martin's, 1997); John J. Gladchuk, *Hollywood and Anticommunism: HUAC and the Evolution of the Red Menace, 1935–1950* (New York: Routledge, 2007); and Steven J. Ross, *Hollywood Left and Right: How the Movies Shaped American Politics* (New York: Oxford University Press, 2011).

2. An unpublished MA thesis is, however, devoted exclusively to the 1947 hearings: Howard Suber, "The 1947 Hearings of the House Committee on Un-American Activities into Communism in the Motion Picture Industry," University of California at Los Angeles, 1966.

3. Early exemplars include Telford Taylor: *Grand Inquest: The Story of Congressional Investigations* (New York: Simon and Schuster, 1955); John Cogley, *Report on Blacklisting I: The Movies* (New York: The Fund for the Republic, 1956); and Frank J. Donner, *The Un-Americans* (New York: Ballantine, 1961). David Chute, *The Great Fear: The Anti-Communist Purge Under Truman and Eisenhower* (New York: Simon and Schuster, 1978).

4. The titles give a sense of the outlook: Kenneth Lloyd Billingsley, *Hollywood Party: How Communism Seduced the American Film Industry in the 1930s and 1940s* (New York: Prima Publishing, 1998); Ronald Radosh and Allis Radosh, *Red Star Over Hollywood: The Film Colony's Long Romance with the Left* (San Francisco: Encounter Books, 2005); Paul Kenger, *Dupes: How America's Adversaries Have Manipulated Progressives for a Century* (Wilmington, DE: ISU Books, 2010), 182–230; Alan J. Ryskind, *Hollywood Traitors: Blacklisted Screenwriters—Agents of Stalin, Allies of Hitler* (Washington, DC: Regnery History, 2015).

5. Lillian Ross, "Onward and Upward with the Arts," *New Yorker*, February 21, 1948, 32.

6. Thom Andersen's 1985 essay "Red Hollywood" and his 1996 documentary with Noël Burch, *Red Hollywood* (1996) make the case for a thoroughgoing boring from within by Communist artists in Hollywood. Andersen's seminal essay is reprinted in Frank Krutnik, Steve Neale, Brian Neve, and Peter Stanfield, eds., *"Un-American" Hollywood: Politics and Film in the Blacklist Era* (New Brunswick, N.J.: Rutgers University Press, 2007), 225–263.

7. Eric Bentley, liner notes to *Bertolt Brecht before the Committee on Un-American Activities*, Folkways Records, 1963.

8. Howard Fast, *Being Red* (Boston: Houghton Mifflin, 1990), 153–154.

9. Alvah Bessie, *Inquisition in Eden* (New York: Macmillan), 1965, 213; 216.

10. Paul Henreid with Julius Fast, *Ladies Man: An Autobiography* (New York: St. Martin's, 1984), 180–188.

INDEX

FILM AND CULTURE A SERIES OF COLUMBIA UNIVERSITY PRESS EDITED BY JOHN BELTON